ARCHER'S DIGEST

6th Edition

by
Roger Combs

DBI BOOKS, INC.

Staff

Senior Staff Editors
Harold A. Murtz
Ray Ordorica

Production Manager
John L. Duoba

Editorial/Production Associate
Jamie L. Puffpaff

Editorial/Production Assistant
Holly J. Porter

Editorial Assistant
Laura M. Mielzynski

Electronic Publishing Manager
Nancy J. Mellem

Electronic Publishing Associate
Robert M. Fuentes

Managing Editor
Pamela J. Johnson

Publisher
Sheldon Factor

About Our Covers

Browning understands the passion an archer feels every time full draw is reached. Our covers show a selection of equipment that should make any archer's pulse quicken, whether hunter, 3-D competitor or target shooter.

At far right is the new Mantis Hunter Brown Camo bow, Model 5-9028, with the Whisper Cam System and Y-Bar carbon bow stabilizer. It's also equipped with Browning's Optima sight, Ballistic Arrow Rest, quick-detachable Stabi-Lock Stabilizer, Dual Mount quiver in matching brown camo and a leather bowsling. With the forged, machined aluminum riser, the Mantis is a high-performance bow for discriminating hunters.

At center is Browning's Pro 600 6T6L Custom Target bow, all ready for the range with the Browning 3000 Target Sight and Radial Cam System. The Pro 600 riser is made from a single billet of machined aluminum and custom anodized in a blue/black color.

The distinctive red bow at left is the Browning 3-D Mantis Model 5-9228 with black riser and the Whisper Cam system. Made of multi-layered, laminated fiberglass/high-modulus graphite/Kevlar, the limbs of this bow are sure to last several lifetimes.

Photo by John Hanusin.

The views and opinions of the authors expressed herein are not necessarily those of the publisher, and no responsibility for such views will be assumed.

Arms and Armour Press, London, G.B., exclusive licensees and distributor in Britain and Europe, India and Pakistan. Media House Publications, Sandton, Transvaal, exclusive distributor in South Africa and Zimbabwe. Forrester Books N.Z. Limited, Auckland, exclusive distributor in New Zealand.

ISBN 0-87349-167-X

Library of Congress Catalog Card 77-148722

Contents

Contents

Introduction

AS THE SPORT of archery approaches the end of the 20th century, it continues to grow. The fastest growing segment of archery is 3-D target shooting. Only a few years ago, the animal targets were homemade. The professionally produced, lifelike foam targets available today offer tournament target shooters and practicing bowhunters plenty of challenge.

Both bowhunters and non-hunters have embraced 3-D target shooting with enthusiasm and excitement. The number and size of the tournaments are expanding, and already, several professional archery shooters are earning tens of thousands of dollars a year shooting arrows. One aspect complements the other and helps new archers become interested in the sport. Hopefully, this book will do the same.

Make no mistake about it: Bowhunting and bowhunters are still the driving force behind modern archery. Most archers are bowhunters, and most of the available equipment developments are designed for bowhunters. Most of the money spent by archers in North America is for bowhunting.

This all-new Sixth Edition of ARCHER'S DIGEST will take the reader into the 21st century with the knowledge of the latest available equipment and shooting techniques. New materials, new production methods and different approaches to traditional hurdles put a new spin on an ancient sport. While most new bowhunters learn the sport with the latest compound bows, there has developed a strong movement to return to the simpler days of traditional archery. Technological developments seem to take place almost daily in the world of bows and arrows. Some of these developments are beneficial and some are not. New materials are being invented, and new uses for old commodities are announced every season. Some will be around for decades ahead, but many will disappear as easily as a deer through heavy timber.

This book is an attempt to guide the reader toward some of the better equipment and ideas, leading to more and better archery, higher scores and more bowhunting success, all the while avoiding some of the technical and economic pitfalls along the way. The author's objective is to assist the new archer in choosing the correct equipment, learning and perfecting the basics of archery, and moving smoothly into target shooting or bowhunting, or both, all the while enjoying the journey.

1 Archery Today

In The Beginning, Bows And Arrows Were Tools Of Survival—Today, They're Mostly For Fun

THE SPORT of archery has enjoyed a steady growth during the past couple of decades, with bowhunting experiencing a genuine advance in popularity in recent years. Traditional target archery has gained recognition and participants, probably stemming from the many gold, silver and bronze medals won by U.S. archers in Olympic and World competitions.

The latest area of growth with respect to archery has been, and continues to be, in three-dimensional target shooting. What started as practice during the summer for bowhunters getting ready for the fall hunting season has become a multi-million-dollar series of competitions conducted throughout most areas of North America. Many of the competitors do not and will not bow hunt. They enjoy the competition for itself. Others have become professional archers, able to bring in as much as $50,000 a year in prize money.

As with most other things, interest in archery has moved in several cycles. If one looks back in time far enough, one may presume that the first archers were hunters. We do not know exactly where and when bows and arrows were invented. From an historical perspective, the development of archery probably took place in several geographical areas at about the same time. However it came about, there would seem little doubt that the device was invented with the purpose of killing animals and people. Bows and arrows will still do that.

To defeat enemies or to eat better, the early archer had to practice with the weapons. Some sort of target was devised—dead stumps, clumps of grass, leaves on the ground, perhaps small game—at which to shoot. One may surmise that, at some point, friendly competition broke out among the warriors and hunters. Who could place the most arrows nearest the center of the chosen target? As the correlation between practice and actual combat and hunting became apparent, more emphasis might have been placed on target shooting.

The importance of practice and competition was recognized

Field archery, shooting at lifelike targets in natural settings, has gained considerable popularity in recent years.

Target competition at fixed, known distances is an ancient sport, dating back at least to the Middle Ages when English bowmen were required to be proficient with their famous longbows.

long before the discovery or invention of gunpowder, but when firearms became readily available to soldiers and hunters, the military use of bows and arrows began to fade. The first efforts at firing cannons loaded with rocks and stones against enemy soldiers was less than successful. Well-trained longbowmen could aim and shoot their missiles several times faster than primitive artillerymen. It was several hundred years after the introduction of gunpowder that bows and arrows were outclassed by muzzleloaders.

As early as the 14th century, the English were required to carry and become proficient with the longbow. An early statute insisted that every Englishman age sixteen to sixty should have a bow "of his own length." Henry VIII let his subjects know that archery practice must be from 220 yards. A good archer could put twelve arrows per minute into a man-size target. The longbow changed military tactics forever.

Hunting had to wait until firearms became more accurate, cheaper to shoot and considerably more portable. When that happened, given some exceptions, most hunters embraced guns as the primary tool for killing wild game. Interest in archery faded among the majority of Europeans and even Americans. It did not fade among the Native Americans until modern firearms became available to them.

As the modern Olympic Games were revived, there were few countries able to field a competitive archery team. The sport of archery, as we know it, was practiced by only a few hundred hardy souls. Technological developments with applications for archery were few. Archery was dropped from the list of official Olympic sports for several decades in the early part of this century, but was returned to favor at the Munich Games in 1972.

Bullseye target shooting is a challenge for young and old, for men, women and children. Compound bows have opened the sport to all. This tournament was held in Tucson, Arizona.

The National Archery Association (NAA) is the governing body for the sport in the United States.

Archery in the Olympics now has a huge following throughout much of the world. Many of the former Communist countries, Iron Curtain countries and republics reformed after the fall of the Soviet Union have been able to field teams of expert archers who are able to rack up their share of medals. The Koreans, Chinese and Japanese have introduced plenty of champion athletes in international competition—and archery is no exception.

As new or additional sports are added to the Olympic list every four years, some of the older sports, such as archery, are

High schools, colleges and clubs compete in Olympic-style competition at outdoor and indoor ranges. Amateurs shoot only for trophies and points.

Northern Quebec caribou have become favorite game for international bowhunters. The terrain is rugged, isolated and sometimes teems with game.

forced to re-justify their presence in the Games. Because of the nature of shooting arrows at far targets with complete concentration and silence, archery has a limited spectator appeal. The sport gets little coverage by television. Sports such as beach volleyball and women's softball were threatening to displace archery at the 1996 Olympic Games, but the position of archery seems safe, at least through the Atlanta Games.

The Olympic Games are not the only tournaments open to bullseye target shooting. Competition may be found on high school and college campuses, in public parks, indoor tennis courts and exhibit centers. Most beginning archers learn and practice first with basic recurve bows shooting arrows at the familiar round bullseye targets. The NAA administers the Junior Olympic Archery Development (JOAD) program to develop future world-class competitors. The program is open to boys and girls under the age of eighteen, and has helped develop several champions through the years.

In these days of limited public funds available to two-year and four-year colleges, several of the former powerhouses in collegiate archery competition have been forced to drop their programs. The argument is made that the sport does not appeal to a wide enough group of students to justify the expenditures. On the other hand, recent gender-equal-opportunity legislation has forced a reevaluation of the value of archery on public campuses. Women archers can compete on many levels for a minimal cost compared to some other college sports.

Field archery became an important component of the archery sports several decades ago, as bowhunters looked for more realistic practice for the coming hunting seasons. Early on, potential bowhunters might have roamed the woods shooting at targets such as leaves on the ground, clumps of grass, tree stumps and anything that might not damage the arrows.

From this roving, it was an easy move to shooting various cardboard targets placed against hay and straw bales. The targets might have had bullseyes of various sizes, but these soon became drawings and paintings of game animals. Competition and interest in the activity led to more formalized rules as field archery grew. Soon, archers who might never have considered shooting at live animals became involved for the thrill of competition and the social aspects of most tournaments.

The plastic foam three-dimensional targets appear almost alive in realistic settings. Northern Arizona was the setting for this tournament.

Field archery remains popular in many parts of North America, but the fastest growing part of the sport is three-dimensional target shooting, known as 3-D. These targets are moulded of special foam materials into accurate depictions of game animals. They resemble live animals in size, shape and color.

The foam is of a consistency that will stop arrow penetration within a few inches of depth, rather than permit it to pass through, as with a live animal. The targets are placed in realistic locations, distances and poses, adding to the challenge of scoring well during tournaments. The 3-D foam targets also have found favor with bowhunters tuning up their shooting abilities for the next deer season.

Three-D target archery will be explored more fully in later chapters, but it should be noted that the growth and popularity of the sport has been dramatic during the past few years. The cleverly built foam targets have been around for at least three decades, but the increase in the number of participants became highly noticeable in about 1990.

Today, during the spring and summer months, there are sure to be at least two or three tournaments every weekend, each within a day's drive of nearly every archer in the U.S. and in many parts of Canada. As it is with field archery, many, if not most, of the 3-D target shooters do not and will not hunt. They participate for the competition, the camaraderie and, in some cases, the money.

The use of bow and arrow to hunt wild game must date from the invention of the devices, but the beginnings of modern bowhunting extend back about eighty years. In 1911, a man named Dr. Saxton Pope became acquainted with Ishi, the last living member of California's Yana Indian tribe. Before Ishi

Three-dimensional animal target shooting has been the driving force in archery for the past decade. Large tournaments draw thousands of shooters competing for large prizes.

died in 1916, he taught Pope a great deal about making bows and arrows and hunting game with these seemingly primitive tools.

Pope went on to teach the skills to another man named Arthur Young. Together they hunted big and dangerous game throughout North America and Africa. They helped prove to skeptics that arrows, properly placed, could dispatch any big game efficiently and humanely.

Pope published two books describing his and his friends' exploits while bowhunting in various parts of the world. Those who read of these adventures wanted to try archery hunting.

Charles Markwood traveled from central Texas to the high prairies of northeastern New Mexico to arrow this antelope. Markwood also enjoys field archery tournaments.

Bowhunter Mickey Pope downed this whitetail deer in his home state of Tennessee. Shooting does its part of the state game department's herd management process.

Archery lobbyists in Wisconsin convinced lawmakers to open the first separate deer season for bowhunters in 1934. Other states followed, but the real growth of bowhunting came some time after World War II.

The tremendous growth and popularity of bowhunting may be attributed directly to the invention and development of the compound bow. A large majority of field archers and 3-D shooters use compound bows. It would be difficult to picture the wide acceptance of archery today without considering their importance.

The development of the compound bow, with its relaxation—let-off—of holding percentage at full draw, is less than three decades old. H.W. Allen applied for a U.S. patent in 1966 and was granted it December 30, 1969. He called it an Archery Bow With Draw Force Multiplying Attachments. The two-wheel bow—the eccentrics looked more like today's radical cams—changed everything.

At the time, there were several others working on the principle, but Allen held the patent. One of the earliest manufacturers and promoters of the compound bow was Tom Jennings. His was not an easy task. Many individuals and some of the largest archery organizations were opposed to the concept.

But within a few years, the public embraced compound bows and their popularity cannot be denied or ignored. Only a small percentage of all bows manufactured and sold in North America are other than compounds. In countries of Europe or Asia where bowhunting is prohibited, most field archers and 3-D target shooters use compound bows.

There are still some traditionalists who claim compound bows are too complicated, too high-tech, too heavy or awkward to carry, too easy to shoot and too difficult to keep tuned. There are some elitists claiming that the invention of the compound bow brought too many bowhunters into the woods.

The development and refinement of compound bows continues unbridled. Lighter-weight and stronger materials, new synthetic ingredients, modernized production techniques, the use of CAD-CAM and production efficiencies borrowed from other industries have helped manufacturers turn out better, more efficient products, accepted in the marketplace. Many of these developments will be discussed in detail in later chapters.

Perhaps the greatest danger to expanding bowhunting opportunities is the threat and influence of anti-hunting groups masquerading as animal-rights organizations.

Small in number, these groups have influence and control far beyond their membership size. Through the skillful use of words and pictures, and seemingly huge sums of money, they threaten to sway the majority of non-hunting citizens to oppose hunting in general and bowhunting in particular.

Bowhunters are, by their nature, solitary individualists. They seem not as well organized to counter the threat to their sport and the anti-hunting groups seem to sense this. Archers of all types must be aware of the threat and remain ready to act positively to preserve an honorable outdoor activity.

In the meantime, archery equipment manufacturers continue to produce wonderful and amazing products to help us improve accuracy, efficiency and success. The pages that follow will help the archer select and utilize the best of them.

2 Learning To Shoot

The Basic Techniques Of Putting Arrows In The Target Must Be Practiced, Practiced, Practiced!

ARCHERY IS A simple activity. It relies on a stick with a string tied to each end, some other slightly smaller, shorter sticks that fly through the air and a modest amount of muscle power.

That statement is an oversimplification and does not calculate the amount of diligent, determined practice necessary for a beginner to become a good archer and for a good archer to become highly accurate. Nor does it take into consideration the mechanical engineering and production steps necessary to produce a modern bow.

The novice archer will appreciate the necessity for archery practice using acceptable physical and mental procedures from the first day. As with any sport, it is much more difficult to retrain the muscles after poor habits have become standard than to learn and use the best methods from the beginning.

More advanced students often practice archery each day, perhaps as much as an hour at a time. The beginner would do well to limit his practice sessions to fifteen to thirty minutes at a time, at least once a week, but more often for faster progress. The beginning archer must be patient. It may take several weeks or months to condition the muscles and become proficient at the sport. But progress will be evident with each practice session. It is largely a mental game!

Locate a practice area with a safe background. If any arrows should miss the target—and some will from time to time—there cannot be any sort of building, animal or person behind or around the target that would be damaged or injured by the arrow. The student archer will be using target or field-tipped arrows not intended for hunting, but even the cheapest arrow shot from a low-draw-weight school bow can do injury or cause death to humans and animals. Always think safety when shooting arrows, no matter what the target.

Most formal archery classes or lessons are conducted on large athletic fields when other sports are not in session. The targets are set up with wide, open spaces behind them and with warning flags or ribbons to indicate the danger areas. Arrows that miss a target will fly harmlessly past and land in the grass at a distance. A hill of soft sand, rock-free dirt or grass, or several straw bales stacked up will serve the purpose of catching

Good, appropriate equipment, knowledgeable instruction and plenty of practice can ensure there will be enough new archers in the future.

errant arrows. Each archer is responsible for watching where each arrow hits and tracking down those that miss. In some fields, locating the passed arrows can be difficult and time-consuming.

The beginning archer—especially the youngster—should determine which eye is dominant. A right-handed person may be "left-eyed" or "right-eyed." There is no correlation between hand domination and eye domination. To make the determination, one of the simplest methods is to point at a distant vertical object, such as a telephone pole. Keep both eyes open and point with the index finger. Then close the right eye. If the telephone pole seems to remain in place, the archer is left-eye dominant. If the object seems to jump to the right, leaving the finger pointing to the right of the pole, the right eye is the stronger eye.

The beginning archer should learn to shoot with a left- or right-handed bow according to which eye is stronger, regardless of which is the dominant hand. Many first-time archers are surprised to learn which eye is dominant. Shooting left-handed may seem awkward at first for the right-hander, but a couple of practice sessions will usually smooth things out.

One of the most important elements of good shooting is stance. The feet should be planted firmly and evenly on the ground about a shoulder-width apart. The knees should not be locked, creating too much tension, but flexed slightly and comfortably. Keep equal weight on each foot and avoid cocking either hip toward or away from the target. The upper torso must be kept as erect as possible. It is not unusual to see advanced longbow and recurve bow shooters bent considerably at the waist while aiming. The late Fred Bear, one of the most famous advocates of modern archery, would bend forward considerably at the waist when shooting. However, that is for more experienced archers. The beginner must practice standing as straight as possible, holding the bow vertically. Imagine a string tied to the top of the head, pulling the back, neck and head upward.

Most instructors recommend some sort of mental checklist before shooting each and every arrow. Begin with the feet.

They should be on either side of the real or imaginary shooting line. The toe nearest the target may be pointed slightly toward the target. The feet and body should begin at a 90-degree angle to the shooting line. Later, with more experience, the archer may wish to use a more open or more closed stance. Each archer will develop a stance best suited to him. It may take several months to determine; nothing is absolute in archery.

After the feet are firmly planted, look at the target over the bow-hand shoulder. That will be the left shoulder for the right-handed shooter. The torso should be natural and relaxed, not twisted. It should feel comfortable throughout the shot. Keep the shoulders level. There may be a tendency for the archer to raise the bow-hand shoulder, which should be avoided. The coach should spot this error and correct it immediately.

Without nocking an arrow, a good step is to raise the bow up as if shooting to get a feel for the way the target will look through the bow sight, if such an aid is being used. The bow arm elbow should be locked out, but not so rigidly as to cause undue tension. Some archers will find that the position feels more comfortable with the elbow slightly bent.

Avoid the tendency by many beginners to roll the lower, inward part of the elbow toward the bowstring. That position will put the inside of the forearm and elbow in line for a smart slap from the bowstring as the arrow is released. Most archers only do that once. Not only will it hurt, but will result in an errant, inaccurate arrow.

Lower the bow to a relaxed position and prepare to nock an arrow. An examination of the nock will reveal an indexing feature in the form of a protrusion on one side of the nock. That side should face away from the bow riser. Nock the arrow beneath the nock indicator on the string. Double-check the body's position and grasp the string with the fingers. Some beginners will feel more comfortable with all three fingers under the arrow. A more common mode is to have two fingers below and one above the nock. The fingers should not actually contact the arrow nock. Touching the nock can result in the

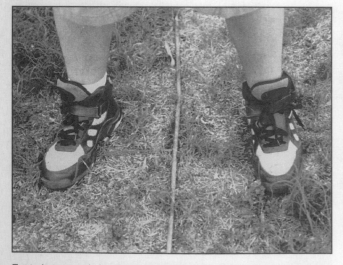
Foot placement is important. As a starting point, both feet should be evenly placed and square along the shooting line.

The archery student may wish to experiment with a more open stance. The target is to the archer's left, to the right of the page.

(Right) A good learning technique is to visualize the bow and the arrow. Picture the arrow flying to the middle of the target.

(Below) After the arrow is nocked, the shaft is placed on the arrow rest.

(Right) The most common finger placement is two fingers below and one above the nocking point on the string.

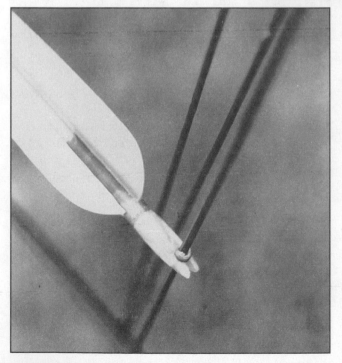

When the nock indicator is correctly placed on the string, the arrow nocks below. It should be snug up against the indicator.

arrow falling off the arrow rest and a poor arrow flight. The fingers should grip the string just ahead of the first joints. Later, when muscle strength is built up, the string may ride farther toward the finger tips.

The bow hand should grip the bow only tight enough so that the bow does not fall out of the hand. A bow sling is an excellent aid to maintaining the hold on the bow throughout the shot while letting the bow hand relax as much as possible. Experienced archers will flex and relax the bow hand fingers consciously so as to not grip too tightly.

With an arrow nocked and placed on the arrow rest, push the bow out toward the target; then look at the target. Look at the spot where you wish the arrow to strike. Some archers will concentrate on the target and let the bow sight pin find its way to the bullseye. Others will focus on the sight pin, letting it move into the target. Try both methods to determine which works the best for you.

Keep the bow arm shoulder down and draw the string back toward the face. The draw should be straight back, smooth and even. The muscles of both arms should be as relaxed as possible. Most of the draw should be done by the back and shoulder muscles. If the draw seems too difficult or jerky, perhaps a bow with less draw weight should be substituted. If shooting a compound bow, the draw weight is usually easy to raise or lower.

Good form is indicated by the high right elbow and straight, upright head and neck. The back and hips are solid and straight.

In this case, the archer is showing the effects of trying to bring the head and face down to the string. The elbow is a bit too high and the bow is not perfectly vertical.

(See Chapter 4 or the bow instruction booklet for details of such changes.)

The string-hand arm should remain as high as possible, never dropping below shoulder level. The drawing elbow should move directly to the rear. Imagine the bow arm and the drawing arm forming the top of the letter T with the rest of the body. Use the back muscles more than the arm muscles as the bow is drawn. Think about pulling the shoulder blades together behind your back as the bow comes to full draw. The chest should open up as the back muscles are contracted. However, do not let the bowstring touch any part of the body or clothing. The slightest contact will affect arrow flight adversely.

The natural anchor point on the face must be determined by experience. Some archers like to draw the string hand to the cheekbone so they can sight directly down the shaft. Others prefer the corner of the mouth, while some anchor under the jaw. Anchoring under the jaw is typical for those who prefer to use a mechanical release aid. There is no rule about where the anchor point is, as long as it is in the exact same spot for

each arrow. The slightest variance will send the arrow flying off the target.

Some target archers use what is called a kisser button. The kisser button is a small disc attached to the bowstring a few inches above the nocking point. The archer draws the string back until the kisser button touches his or her lips. It acts as an index to ensure the anchor point is exactly the same for each shot.

Another of the mental checklist items is to make certain the string is drawn back to the face and head, rather than moving the head down or to the side to meet the string. Moving the head at this time will put tension on neck and shoulder muscles, causing inconsistent arrows. Head movement will not be exactly the same each time, throwing the arrow flight off the target.

With the arrow drawn, aim at the target. Keep the bow absolutely vertical and focus the mind and eye on the target. Think of where the arrow will go. Archery is as much about the mind as it is about the physical body.

As the draw begins, the left (bow) hand should push the bow toward the target. The string hand must draw back smoothly, bringing the shoulder blades together in the back.

Release the arrow by relaxing the hand. Gradually and smoothly relax the fingers until the string is pulled from them, sending the arrow on its flight. As the bowstring leaves the fingers, the drawing hand should continue rearward past the face and neck until it stops behind the head. It should not fly to the side or upward. A coach, instructor or fellow archer is in a better position to detect draw, hold, release and follow-through errors than the shooter. Another self-coaching device is the video camera. Have someone tape the shooting process and review it yourself. You should be able to detect any errors immediately.

The bow should be held in a relaxed manner so it begins to rotate downward in the bow hand. Do not attempt to watch the arrow as it flies. If you lift your head or try to look around the string at the arrow, the arrow flight will be affected. Concentrate on the bullseye until you hear the arrow hit the target. Correct draw and hold—using mostly back and shoulder muscles—will usually result in a good release and follow-through.

Most advanced archers will tell beginners they should not worry about where the arrow lands. Concentrate on form and do not attempt to "steer" the arrow to the target. It won't work. Think only about the correct form; the arrow's flight will take care of itself. Mentally review each shot and run through the positioning checklist before beginning the next shot process. Then forget about the last arrow. It is gone and cannot be changed.

After some shooting, the archer may wish to assume a more open stance. Move the back foot a bit forward so the body faces slightly toward the target. It is easy to experiment with various stances while running through the mental checklist. Different body types will be more comfortable with different stances. The best stance for the individual will be determined by the archer's

These lads must use care when pulling arrows from the targets. Only one archer should be pulling arrows at once, and the shaft must be grasped close to the target face.

size, weight, arm length, torso girth, strength, muscle tone, type of bow and dozens of other variables. Only plenty of practice will bring it about.

Most beginning archers seem to prefer holding the bow in a low-wrist grip, with the palm of the hand firmly in contact with the bow handle. Those using a bow sling will find it easier to use the high-wrist grip and have less contact with the bow handle. Try both ways to determine which works best for you. Again, there is no substitute for plenty of practice.

Make sure the bow-hand elbow is straight as the bow is raised for the shot. Slightly bending the elbow may cause torque on the bow, resulting in too-large shot groups at the target. Think about pushing the bow toward the target, rather than swinging the straight arm up from a vertical position by the body.

Keep the string-hand elbow up and pulling to the rear as the string is drawn. Relax the muscles of both arms as much as possible. The beginner may experience some muscle soreness at first after using this draw technique. These are muscles not often stressed during most other activities. A few days of practice with a light-draw-weight bow will build up the muscle tone so the draw will become smoother and easier. This is an added argument in favor of starting out with low draw weights. Learning bad habits on a bow that is too heavy will lead to nothing but frustration.

Remember to bring the string hand back to the same anchor point for each shot. It must become part of the mental checklist before releasing an arrow. An eighth of an inch difference in anchor point will mean a miss of several inches at the target. Both the archer and the instructor must remind each other of this importance from time to time. After enough practice, reaching the same anchor point will become easier and natural.

This youngster has first checked to his rear to make sure no others are nearby in case the arrow is pulled too far and fast from the target.

As with any sport, there is no substitute for practice. But practice without good technique is frustrating and counterproductive. As suggested early in this chapter, 15 to 30 minutes a day is ideal as a practice session for the beginning archer. More than that may cause undue muscle fatigue, followed by development of bad habits and improper shooting techniques. Get plenty of practice time, but do not overdo it. Rest is as important as muscle build-up.

Every arrow must land somewhere—hopefully in the center of the intended target. If more than one student is shooting, safety procedures require every archer to place his or her bow on the ground before moving forward to score and pull arrows. Each archer should pull all his own arrows from the target before another shooter begins. Beginners should ignore scores. The mission at first is to learn good shooting techniques only; score count will come later.

Almost any target strong enough to stop an arrow will grip it firmly. Before pulling any arrows, look to the rear to ensure that no one is within four or five feet of the target. To remove an arrow, place one hand against the target with the shaft between spread fingers. Grab the shaft with the other hand, also against the target. Pull straight to the rear, firmly and steadily until the arrow is free. A slight clockwise twist will often help break the friction. Pull each arrow and move to the rear several feet so that other archers, if any, may retrieve their arrows safely.

Do not pick up your bow from the ground until every archer has returned to the shooting line. The coach will remind each student of this safety rule. When your coach—or your body—tells you that you have shot enough arrows for one day, put your gear away and look forward to another day of archery enjoyment. You will shoot better tomorrow than you did today.

When a group of students is shooting, each archer should retrieve his own arrows. All bows must be grounded before archers move forward to pull arrows.

3 Equipment, Accessory Selection

There Are Thousands Of Choices For The Archer— The Best Will Make You Better!

The simplest form of archery is a smooth recurve bow with the arrow resting on the bow shelf. The arrangement is lightweight and uncomplicated.

THE SPORT OF ARCHERY can be as simple or as complicated as you wish it to be. In its simplest form, the whole thing consists of a bent stick with a string tied to each end, plus some smaller, straighter sticks that fly through the air after they have been launched by the flexing of the larger stick with the string.

This is an oversimplification of the process. There are all sorts of natural laws at work as the bow is drawn back by the archer's muscles, imparting the muscle energy to the bow limbs, then transferring that energy to the arrows as the string is released.

Even with the action described, it immediately becomes somewhat more complicated. Arrows are not simply straight sticks; they are specially built, absolutely straight sticks, metal tubes or modern carbon-fiber rods. In a single set of arrows, all should weigh the same and bend or resist bending alike. Each should be exactly the same length and diameter.

The arrows should have matched, precision-shaped and weighed points on one end. The other end should have carefully matched plastic nocks that fit tightly into or onto the arrow's shafts; the nock gaps are aligned with the feathers or plastic vanes glued just ahead of the nocks. The nocks must all be the same weight and size, and the string gap must grip the string serving uniformly for each shot. The arrows must resist damage when shot into a target and should be able to be removed easily from the target material. They should also resist the effects of gusty winds as much as possible.

The above constitutes but a brief overview of arrows. Each of the components mentioned is subject to interpretation and selection by the archer. Several options are available within each of the components. Color and finish were not mentioned, but they must be selected, along with a variety of other items. Elsewhere in this book, the choice and care of the correct arrow for a bow are discussed.

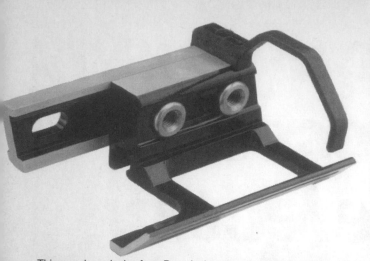

This overdraw device from Bear Archery is adjustable for the amount of shaft shortening desired.

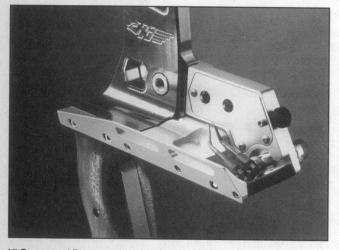

Xi Compound Bows combine the Quantum overdraw device with a built-in arrow rest. There are plenty of adjustments on this accessory.

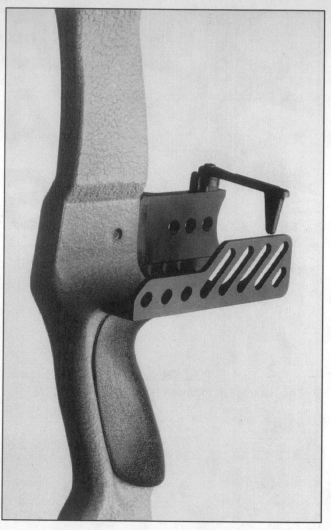

Browning's Optima FPS overdraw attachment has lightening slots as well as a top gate to help protect the shooter's hand.

An arrow is perhaps the simplest of all the gear needed by the successful archer. The range of options for bows and dozens of other pieces of equipment may number in the hundreds, if not the thousands. Such an array can be bewildering and confusing at times. Just when we think we have all the right gear, a dozen new products or new colors or new sizes of an old product are introduced, each with the promise of more accurate, easier shooting and better hunting. Choosing what is best for each is difficult and, if we are not wary and informed, can be expensive.

Be aware that new products are introduced to the marketplace all the time. Dozens of new bows are offered by the major manufacturers every year, and some old models are dropped from production. New materials, new production techniques and additional research leads to annual modifications and radical changes. New strings, cams, cables, adjustment techniques, carbon/fiber combinations, materials and dozens of other creations are commonplace almost every day. Some become absolutely essential for every archer, and some are worthless at best. What follows is a primer on some of the available equipment, how to choose, what to choose and, hopefully, how to save money in the process.

A bow and some arrows—what more do you need? In its simplest form, archery requires nothing else. A bow is drawn back, energy is stored, and the energy is released to propel the missile—an arrow—toward its target.

There are those individuals shooting in the traditional manner who require almost nothing else to enjoy the sport. It is possible to carry extra arrows in the bow hand, without a quiver, as seen in some illustrations of early warriors, hunters and Native American Indians. If that is your kind of shooting, read no more. You have everything necessary to shoot at targets or wild game and have fun while doing it.

On the other hand, most of us need more help to enjoy the sport to its fullest. In fact, it might seem that there is almost no limit to the type and number of added accessories to hang on the bow or carry along on belts and in pouches. The experienced target shooter or bowhunter will know which of these choices will help raise scores or success rates and which will not. Some items are simply a waste of money for some archers; other gadgets can raise scores by a significant amount.

At the outset, let it be said that the single most important ingredient to good archery scores, successful hunting seasons

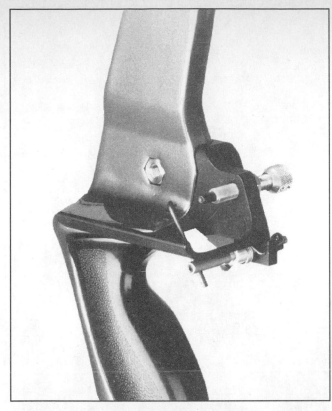

The Hoyt Hunt Master 2000 Speed Tune overdraw is available in two lengths, designed to be used with Hoyt bows.

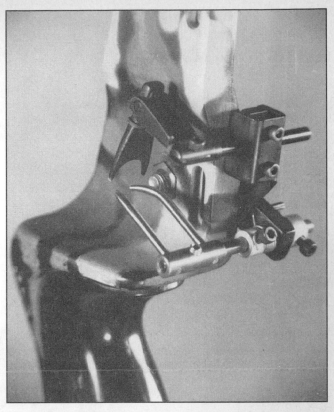

The Golden Key-Futura arrow holder is placed nearer the shooter, permitting a shorter overdraw arrow without an overdraw device.

or any other improvement is practice. There is no substitute for proficiency with the gear we use. Proficiency can come only from diligent and careful practice.

Overdraw Devices

So, we have just purchased a new colorful target bow or camouflaged hunting bow with smooth-drawing cams, 65-percent let-off and an overdraw device already attached. We have some super arrows of just the right weight and spine to shoot from the new bow. They are known to fly smooth and fast. What more do we need?

Actually, the overdraw device is the first accessory to think about. Many modern bows have the accessory built in or built on, but other bows will accept the optional overdraw shelf. Overdraws permit the use of a shorter, lighter-weight, lighter-spine arrow. A shorter arrow has the same effect on flight as a stiffer spine. The archer saves the few grams of arrow weight by using a shorter, lighter-spined shaft. The overdraw shelf permits a shorter arrow to be drawn back past the shooter's hand. It must also have provisions in its design to protect the hand, should the arrow slip off the shelf or arrow rest, especially when using broadheads.

Not everybody shooting arrows uses this aid, but a great many of the top shooters and bowhunters seem to find it helpful. The shorter arrow does not need to be so stiff or heavy-walled to provide an appropriate spine for the bow. An overdraw-equipped bow will usually result in a faster, flatter-trajectory arrow flying at the target.

Some archers find that tuning a bow with shorter, lighter overdraw arrows is more difficult than with standard-draw-length arrows. Most experts agree that an arrow can be too short, no matter the spine or how much shaft shortening the overdraw device will permit. The rule of thumb seems to be to use an arrow no more than five inches less than a standard-draw-length shaft. A shaft cut shorter than that, no matter the spine reading, will prove to be too erratic in flight, and repeated shooting could damage equipment. The best compromise seems to be to shorten the shaft two to three inches at most. Consult the arrow manufacturer's arrow-selection charts to determine the arrow's best weight, spine and length for the particular type of bow involved. Tune the equipment carefully and check the tune before each tournament and hunting season.

Arrow Quivers

The next most important item is probably an arrow quiver. Those shooting traditional bows, recurves or longbows may prefer a back quiver. Some old-timers could carry almost two dozen arrows in a traditional back quiver, nocking arrow after arrow with amazing speed. The typical back quiver is made of thick, heavy leather, with a foam- or cotton-lined bottom to protect the broadheads, as well as the life of the quiver.

In some hunting situations, however, a back quiver is not an asset, as arrows can spill out or rattle if the hunter leans too far forward when passing under low-hanging brush. The arrows protruding out of the quiver may also catch on overhanging branches when moving through thick growth.

But shooters are not faced with this sort of problem on most archery tournament trails. If the arrows rattle in a back quiver, the foam 3-D animals will not spook to the sound. Most back

Beman offers three arrow rests specifically for its carbon arrows to suit different shooter requirements.

quivers will carry plenty of arrows. Even if the archer should lose a number of them, he should have enough to complete a long tournament.

Those archers shooting in the bowhunter classes may want to utilize their regular hunting bow quivers over the entire course. If the only reason for competing in target tournaments is pre-season hunting practice, select a tournament and class that permit a quiver on the bow. Not every class or tournament will allow it. And not every bowhunter or target shooter is happy with the few ounces of weight the average bow quiver will add to the mass of the bow.

There are dozens, if not hundreds, of bow quiver styles and models from which to choose. Basically, what the archer needs is a quiver that will mount solidly on the bow without rattles or changes in position. It must be quick and easy to mount and dismount. Most bow manufacturers offer a specific quiver made especially for their bow. On some bows, the only quivers that can be attached are those made to match the mounting design of that specific bow.

On the other hand, there are several brands of universal bow quivers manufactured to fit most bows. All are lightweight and rugged, with foam rubber or plastic pockets to keep the arrows from rattling.

Most quivers mount near the sight location on the bow window, opposite the arrow rest. A quiet, plastic quick-detach system lets the quiver be mounted or removed in an instant, requiring only a simple twist. Incidentally, the quiver may be mounted with or without arrows in it.

A couple of manufacturers include mounting provisions near the limb bolts, rather than at the bow window. The quivers are produced to match the mounts and usually are not interchangeable from one bow brand to another. The wider mounting provisions provide a rigid, lightweight system that many bowhunters prefer. Any bow company catalog or archery shop will offer several quiver choices for each bow, with sizes and colors to match.

The archer will want a quiver that holds at least ten and preferably more arrows. Theoretically, most target tournaments could be completed with only two arrows, and it only takes one well placed arrow to down even the largest big-game animal. If the target archer never missed and never hit the backstop, the ground or another arrow already in the tar-

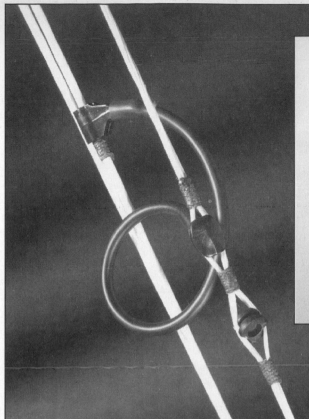

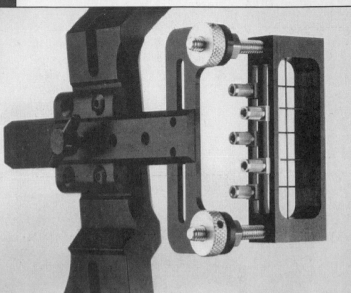

Fine-Line's crosshair bow sight is a popular adjustable model to fit most compound bows.

The AIM-140e peep sight from Arrowzona Archery uses rubber tubing to align the aperture on the string.

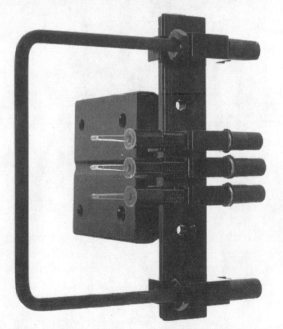

Timberline's three-pin sight features light-gathering fiber-optic pins.

get, two would be enough. The same would be true if the bowhunter never missed a deer. However, realism dictates plenty of extra matched arrows in the quiver for a full day of shooting.

With the growing popularity of the thinner carbon/fiber arrow shafts, most quivers are now available with either alter-

nating grippers to fit carbon or aluminum arrows, or with special optional-size gripper slots that accept the appropriate arrow shafts.

Most bow quivers are adaptable to handle any arrow length. Make sure the one you choose will accommodate shorter shafts, if you are shooting the shorter overdraw-length arrows. For most bows, the quiver should be as light as possible. A couple dozen arrows and a heavy quiver may add up to discomfort after two or three days of shooting fifty, sixty or seventy targets across all sorts of terrain, or after a week climbing up and down steep canyons and ridges after elk or bear.

The choice of most target shooters and a few bowhunters is a belt quiver. In some tournaments, belt quivers are required. Most serious target shooters do not want the added weight and balance problems a bow quiver might yield for their highly tuned bows.

Belt quivers are made of leather, vinyl, plastic or a combination of all three. Most are equipped with internal plastic tubes to separate groups of arrows within the quiver. Through experience, most archers realize that not every arrow in their supply flies exactly the same. That would be ideal but is not practical. There may be four or five that are matched closely and others that seem to perform differently. These should be marked and carried separately in the quiver. A supply of spare nocks and arrowheads should be kept in a quiver side pocket, along with the necessary glue. Another shorter cylinder on the quiver is ideal for a scoring pencil and scorecard.

Most experienced archers will attach or carry a small cloth towel on the outside of the quiver to wipe off their hands and/or clean shafts. A silicone or Teflon dressing and an applicator to clean and shine arrow shafts may be seen hanging from most belt quivers. The quiver is also a good place for your sunglasses case, in case you need them.

A belt quiver may be carried and used by bowhunters, but as a practical matter, few bowhunters use them. In heavy undergrowth or tightly growing timber, or when traveling to the base camp on horseback, a belt quiver could be a hindrance. In the wide open spaces of the desert Southwest or across the Far North tundra, a belt quiver is no problem. It may have an additional advantage because it can carry more arrows than a typical bow quiver.

Identifying badges, buttons, club affiliations, names or initials are also seen on many belt quivers. Some even have side pockets roomy enough for a couple cans of cold refreshments. It can be a long way between water stops.

Belt quivers should be adjusted to present the arrows to the hand, with minimum effort by the archer. The angle of the arrows should be about halfway between vertical and horizontal. The arrows should not slip out of the quiver when the archer bends over to pick up something off the ground, and the fletch-

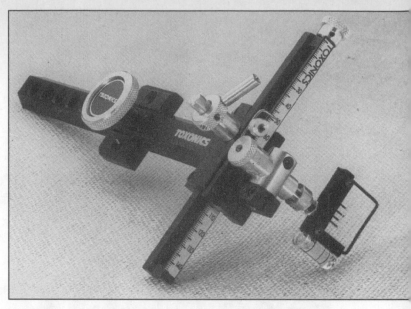

Toxonics sights have been popular with target shooters for many years.

The Browning Tri-Select peep sight features interchangeable apertures to satisfy hunters and target shooters.

ing and nocks must not interfere with the string hand and arm. A variation of belt quivers, hip quivers are almost always strapped on with their own belts and are not held on by the trouser belt.

Binoculars

Another item carried by many target archers is a lightweight pair of binoculars or a monocular to check arrow location on far-away targets. It helps to know just where that first arrow went, in case adjustments are needed for the second. Most hang their optics on their quiver, but some use a neck strap.

No bowhunter will—or should—venture out from the lodge without a pair of the best binoculars he can afford. The ability to gather in light and help identify animals or other objects under shadows or in shady canyons is essential to any bowhunter. Sheer magnification power by itself is not necessarily the only criterion the bowhunter should use when choosing a pair of binoculars. The best optics are lightweight enough to be carried all day without too much discomfort; are armored against knocks on rocks, trees and archery gear; and have excellent light-gathering properties.

Binoculars will save countless miles of walking, even in the heavy undergrowth areas of the East and Midwest. Use them to

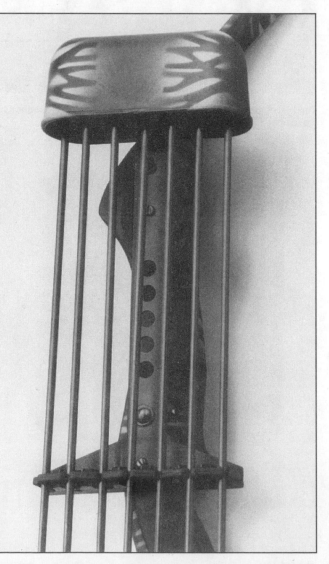

The Browning Twist-Lock bow quiver is designed specifically for carbon-arrow shafts.

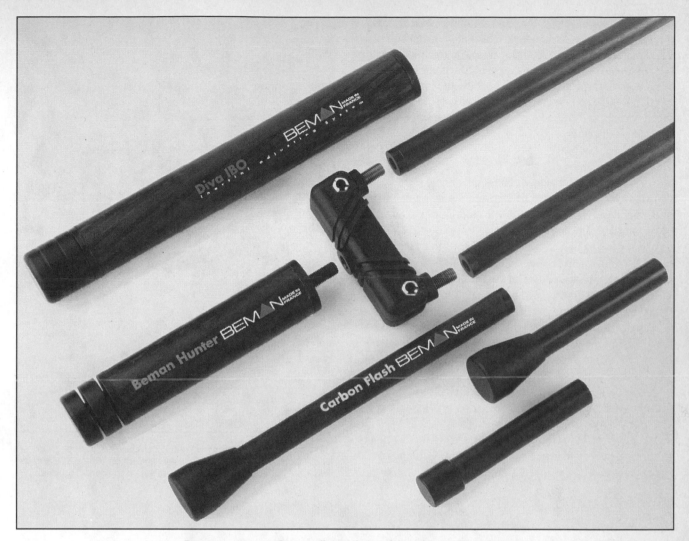

For target shooters, Beman offers a choice of one of several possible stabilizers to balance and help dampen bow vibration. Several weight and length options may be selected.

judge antlers, even as close as thirty or forty yards in whitetail country. Replace the narrow strap or cord that comes with most binoculars with a wide padded or elastic neck strap. It is surprising how heavy even a few ounces around the neck can seem after a couple of hours. When you want to move quickly or quietly, simply tuck the glasses inside your jacket or sweater to keep them from bouncing around.

Mechanical Release Aids

A two-day tournament with sixty or more targets—two arrows at each target—plus several novelty shoots, adds up to a lot of shooting. Most tournament shooters opt for a mechanical release aid, although there are those bowhunters and traditionalists who rely on a finger tab or leather glove. Some state laws prohibit mechanical releases for bowhunters, and most tournaments have special classifications for those who use fingers only and those who prefer the release.

There are dozens of brands and perhaps hundreds of models of releases from which to choose. All are intended to provide a smooth, consistent string release, performing exactly the same for each shot. The minimum string drag or friction should be built in

One of the long-time favorites is Colby's Own quiver from Bohning.

to give a consistent release, as well as keep wear on the serving to a minimum. The device should fit the hand of the archer and match his shooting style.

There are all styles and types of release aids. Some are set off by pressing with the thumb, others by the trigger finger. Some release by a pull of the trigger; others are held down during the draw and are released by relaxing the pressure. These are called relax releases. Many archers find them a challenge to get used to, but when the technique is mastered, a desirable surprise release of the string is the result.

Some models wrap around the wrist so the fingers and hand are relaxed throughout the draw. There are concho styles, pistol-grip styles, finger styles and some that automatically release when the draw reaches a certain point. Some are held with the palm down; others with the palm in, palm out or palm up. Some have adjustable release pressure and sensitivity. Most of the top target archers use some type of mechanical release whenever the rules of the class permit.

Arrow Rests

Most overdraw devices include an arrow rest or arrow launcher as an integral part. If an overdraw is not on the bow, most tournament shooters will add a shoot-through, rather than a shoot-around type rest.

The shoot-through arrow rest is designed to take advantage of a mechanical release. The adjustments to the rest should be quick and easy to make, even in the field, and with a minimum of tools. The rest must be rugged enough to stand up to hundreds of arrows during practice sessions and tournaments. No bowhunter wants problems with an arrow rest just as that trophy of a lifetime walks past the tree stand. Absolute silence as the arrow is drawn back and released is the minimum requirement.

As the lighter, stiffer, thinner carbon shafts have gained popularity, manufacturers have introduced several models of rests that are designed especially for those arrows.

With the trend toward lighter-weight arrows for fast, flat trajectories, correctly matched equipment and fine tuning of components become more critical. Combine that with a heavy-draw

The typical target shooter will wear a belt quiver with enough arrows for the tournament. Belt quivers may be worn on either side, and can hold extra gear such as binoculars, towels and scoring pencils.

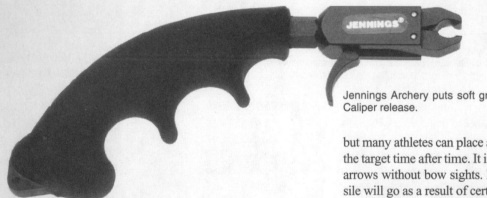

Jennings Archery puts soft grip material on its Pro Caliper release.

bow and the requirement for the best arrow rest possible becomes evident. The selection is large.

Perhaps the best rest is one recommended by the bow manufacturer, but there are dozens of other types and brands available. Check with other archers who may be using the same brand of bow and arrows as your own. Use the rest that works best for you.

Sight Systems

Another obvious accessory for target shooters is a sight system. As mentioned, some traditional archers use bows with no sights. They aim "instinctively." They may sight down the arrow shaft and know where the arrow will strike—based upon plenty of practice. There are no sights on a baseball or football, but many athletes can place a ball within fractions of an inch of the target time after time. It is the same principle when shooting arrows without bow sights. Experience tells us where the missile will go as a result of certain muscle actions.

Most target archers use a bow sight and a complementary string peep. These two accessories work together much the same as front and rear sights on a rifle. The longer the distance between the front and rear sights, the more accurate will be the sight alignment.

There are about a dozen brands of string peeps on the market, with several models available from each manufacturer. Essentially, the string peep acts as the rear sight aperture through which the eye peers at the front bow-mounted sight. It must be placed on the string in a location that the archer naturally finds when at full draw.

Experienced archers will have the distance between the arrow nocking point and the aiming eye measured and recorded. First-time peep sight users will need some help in finding the correct location.

A rope release may be popular with target shooters because it does not cause so much wear on the string serving. This model is from Winn Archery.

The Tru-Fire Custom Concho is well made and has finger grooves formed in the handle for shooting comfort.

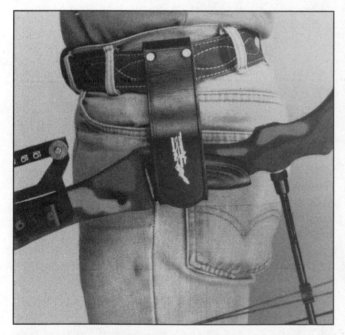

Another archery accessory might be a bow cradle, such as this one from High Country; it frees the shooter's hands.

The most popular method to find that location is to first draw the bow with eyes closed. Bring the string hand to the anchor point. Draw back several times to make sure the spot is firm. Have an assistant mark the location of the aiming eye on the string, using a felt marking pen or perhaps a short piece of tape. That will be the location of the peep sight aperture.

The peep may be installed on the string as it is, but the easiest method is to place the bow in a press to relieve pressure on the bow string. Use a pencil or other blunt instrument to part the strands of the string in the center. For optimum arrow flight each time, count the strands to ensure the peep is exactly centered in the string. The aperture opening must be placed so it turns with the peep open to the eye at full draw.

Most peeps will have some sort of arrangement to ensure the aperture turns the same for each draw. It may be a short length of rubber tubing that attaches to a cable or to the bow limb. The

bowhunter must be concerned with a wide-angle view of his game target, but the target shooter may use the smallest aperture opening in the string peep. Some brands feature adjustable apertures, especially helpful when using a hunting bow for a target match.

The string peep may be held in place by a pair of nock indicators locked above and below the peep. Or, neatly tied serving string may be used to lock in the peep at just the right height. Experiment with the aperture several times to ensure it opens fully for the best archer view each time it comes back. If the string twists the peep out of line each draw, try putting the bow in a press and untwisting the string a half turn at a time before replacing the loop over the tear drop.

There are hundreds of bow sights available. Some rely on pins; others have crosshair sights. The sight pin tips and crosshairs have become smaller in diameter in recent years because of flatter arrow trajectories.

For the fastest arrows, one pin will often take care of multiple distances, such as everything between twenty and twenty-five yards. Plenty of whitetail deer hunters who place their treestands in the same location every year mount only one pin on the bow to avoid possible confusion in the heat of the hunt. Some manufacturers mount the pins on two slots. The pin points are almost touching one another from the archer's viewpoint. Some designs slant the pins inward so the points almost merge in the center. Several models, designed for target shooting, include a built-in spirit level. Some have light-gathering fiber optic sight pins for dim-light shooting.

Most such sights trace their heritage back to those used on hunting bows, but a number have their origins in target archery. These models may have front and rear sights mounted on a single unit at the bow window. In that case, the string peep is optional and would result in three points of sight alignment.

Some target competitors prefer a scope sight mounted on the bow. The scope is the same type as used for pistol shooting and is of low or no magnification. Typically, the scope will be of 1-2x. The mount must have provisions for quick range adjustments and some models appear to have a "floating" dot in the center of the optics.

Stabilizers

Most serious 3-D target shooters will mount one or more stabilizers on their bows. Those competing in the bowhunter classes or who are out for pre-season hunting practice will use the short, camouflaged stabilizer for hunting use. But those with target bows may have one, two, three or more stabilizers, three or more feet long. The number, length, placement and configuration of stabilizers is a matter of individual preference and must be arrived at through considerable experimentation.

Stabilizers may be of aluminum or steel tubing or of carbon fiber, solid or hollow, and of almost any length. They may point forward or backward, up or down. Some have hydraulic-dampened or spring-loaded pistons inside to help absorb the shock of the arrow release. Others have internal weight adjusters for the archer's experimentation. The weights may be moved forward or back inside the stabilizer tube to determine the best balance in the hand as well as the least shock upon release. At rest, held lightly, the bow should tend to tip forward, the upper limb swiveling away from the shooter, but not too top-heavy.

Bow Straps

Another accessory many target shooters and bowhunters use is a bow strap. This simple device attaches to the bow handle, often at the threaded hole that also accepts the stabilizer bar. Some are elastic, some are leather, others are padded fabric. Some adjust by way of a standard buckle and others use a hook and loop closure.

Properly adjusted, a bow strap can ease much of the strain on the bow hand when carrying and shooting a bow for several hours a day over forty to sixty targets or miles of canyon climbing. The strap should let the hunter get the bow into action fast and quietly when game is spotted. The strap also lets the archer grip the bow handle more loosely without fear of dropping the bow after the shot, as it pivots forward. The bow strap is more practical where the growth is open and distances are long. In heavy woods when walking only from camp to a tree stand, it might be more trouble than it's worth. Shooters who also might not benefit from a bow strap are those with traditional bows—longbows or recurves.

Bow Cases

Most of us must travel some distance to any tournament, so some sort of bow case is a necessity. Usually, a hard case is called for—one large enough to accommodate all the gear. The case may be of polypropylene, some other hard plastic or aluminum.

A hard case is an absolute must if travel is done by airplane. Some equipment is delicate and easily damaged or loosened. The case has to be tough enough to withstand considerable bumps and bounces. The bow, arrows and other accessories should all be strapped down inside the case and/or protected by foam padding. The best bow cases have provisions for this protection, as well as a solid locking mechanism.

For the serious archer, the case may hold two bows, in addition to arrows and accessories. Most bow cases cradle the arrows in padded foam grippers and have enough slots for at least two dozen arrows. The wise shooter will include a set of Allen wrenches, nock pliers, an adjustable wrench, glue, tape and an extra bowstring, as well as plenty of spare parts.

It would be a tragedy to get as far as halfway through the second day of a major tournament with a good score or on the

The large Doskocil bow case has room for two compound bows, a couple dozen arrows and accessories. A good case is essential when traveling.

MTM Case Gard offers a roomy arrow case with space for repair parts, broadheads, hunting stabilizers, releases and other equipment.

Bear Archery offers several types of mechanical releases, including a wrist release (left), a thumb release and a typical concho type.

approach for a record-book caribou, only to end the game prematurely with a broken part and no way to repair it. It might require days of travel to reach the nearest archery shop. The bow and accessories must be well protected whenever they are not in your hands.

Special Accessories

There are several special accessories archers might carry or attach during a target tournament. Some gadgets are prohibited by the various governing bodies. Always check with the local club or consult an organizational rule book for your shooting class before adding accessories.

The bowhunter will want to have the quietest bow in the field. Some bows simply make more noise than others when the

arrow is released. If the string is setting up vibration harmonics, causing too much noise, the addition of string silencers is needed. These may be as simple as a dozen cut pieces of rubberband tied to each section of the string near the wheels, or they may be made of wool or artificial yarn. The silencers break the harmonics as well as change the sound of the string moving through the air.

In the time it takes the average reader to get from the beginning to the end of this chapter, inventors, researchers and manufacturers will have developed several more accessories and improvements on equipment to tempt archers. Some of the devices will become standard, and others will not be heard of again after the initial announcement. Stay tuned for the latest!

3

The Hand-Laid Flemish Bowstring

The Butler kit arrived with an instruction video, already-made jig (the board with pegs) snap knife, Dacron B-50 string, Tex-Tite wax and nylon-filled string server.

THERE ARE some things we just don't try, because we feel they might be too hard to do. The Flemish hand-laid string is one of those subjects bowhunters shy away from, since it looks complicated.

This is not really true, and if you get the courage to make a few of these strings, you will find they are not only fun, but simple in execution.

Before you can make a Flemish string, you need to find the materials to make it with and have a constant source for those materials.

Butler's Traditional Bowhunting Supplies offers kits for making Flemish strings. They also include a good wrinkle in that kit, as you soon will see. Butler's is run by Vern and Claris Butler. Vern Butler is a bowhunter, so he knows our problems. We assigned Bob Learn, self-styled king of the do-it-yourself cadre, to handle this project.

The Butler kit was ordered and it arrived in a small box. The kit includes a video tape that demonstrates how to make the Flemish string jig and the string itself. Also included are a 1/4-pound spool of Dacron B-50 string, a server loaded with #4 nylon, a small snap knife and the already-assembled string jig. The snap knife is one of those little razor types in which the dull blade is snapped off and replaced with a new, sharper blade—slick and simple.

The video is in standard VHS format. Butler shows how to make the string jig that comes already assembled, but it doesn't hurt to know how to make one, if you want another for camp.

Learn first viewed the video to pick up pointers on how to lay out the jig, set up for the string and lay the strands and make the string.

"A good idea is to watch the video first, then make notes for measurements you will need later. With stop framing on the VCR, you can get these easily if you miss them on the first go 'round.

"You can make the string in your lap if you like—I did so as a challenge—or you can position the jig on a table and make it that way. The jig is only 28 inches long, so it takes up little room."

To make the string, you need to know the actual length of your recurve or longbow. That is the measurement used for making these strings.

If you want to make a 62-inch string, set the center pin at that mark. Tie off one end of the spool of Dacron to the right side of the number one pin at the top of the jig. Move across the top from right to left and down the outside to the bottom pin on the left. The jig should be facing away from you with the ten pins at the top.

After getting to the left bottom pin, go up to the center pin set on the 62 spacing, down the outside of the center pin to the bottom right pin, then around and up the outside to the number two pin and across, as you did with the string on the number one pin. Continue this around, down and up method of laying the string until you have the required number of strands.

To determine how many strands you need to lay up and how many units you need, it is necessary to know how many strands your bow weight requires. A 16-strand string is strong enough for bows drawing from 55 to about 80 pounds. This is far more than most of us need, so for this project let's make the string at 16 strands with two sections of eight strands each in the string.

Continue to wrap the strands around the jig until you have moved to the number eight pins. Move across the pins to the left and tie off the string on the left side of the number eight

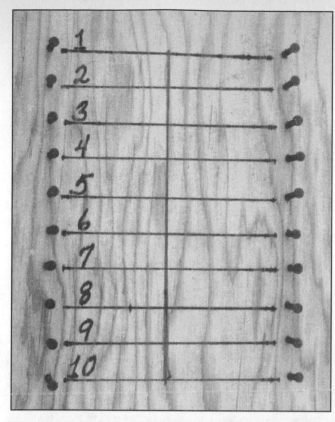

The upper section with the numbered pegs is the area on which the string is laid to end up with a tapered, hand-laid string. The center mark was added for cosmetics.

The bottom section of the jig has two pegs shown at the far right for the string length used in conjunction with the center-numbered pegs used according to bow length.

pin. You have just laid up one strand of a two-strand, eight-section Flemish string.

Place your left hand on the left side strands to keep them from moving. With a knife, cut the strands between the pins at the top down the center. Some string makers mark a center line for ease of cutting, but the cut isn't critical. Retain the tension on the strands and lift the section from the board.

Move your hand to the jig and hold the strands with a length equal to half the board length. Using some of the Tex-Tite wax supplied with the kit, heavily wax the strands about twelve inches from your hand to the end. This helps hold the strands together when working them.

Clamp the loose, waxed strands to prevent them from separating as you move to the other end of the eight-strand section and repeat the waxing process. Clamp the bottom strands and move back to the jig for your second lay-up.

Repeat your previous work to make a second identical set of strands and finish by cutting, waxing and clamping them to prevent separation.

With the two eight-strand sections completed, you are ready to make the Flemish splice string for the bow by twisting these sections to form the finished string. This is the part that spooks many bowhunters, but it is relatively simple.

Make a mark on the side of the jig that is $7^1/_2$ inches long using the Butler measure. This is the length you need from the tips of the strands in order to form the loops for the bow limbs' tips.

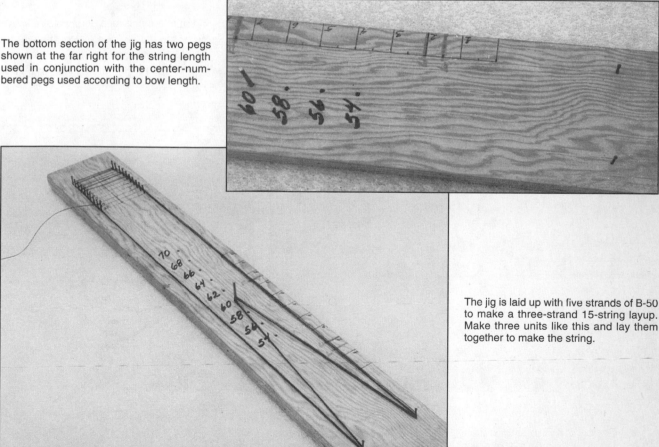

The jig is laid up with five strands of B-50 to make a three-strand 15-string layup. Make three units like this and lay them together to make the string.

We made one set of strands from white Dacron and another set from black Dacron so the twisting and forming of the string might be easier to see in the photos. You can obtain various string colors from your dealer or by ordering from Butler.

Hold both strands in your left hand with the seven-plus inches extending from your thumb and first finger grip. Take the most distant strand and use your right hand to twist that section of string away from you until it is twisted together snugly.

When snug, bring that section over the top of the forward strand and lay it against your left hand to keep it from untwisting. Move to the second strand and twist away until snug; then bring the top of the forward strand over and continue this twist-away, bring-over procedure until you have about 1½ inches twisted up. Get these measurements during the second or third viewing of the video and write them down on your notepad for reference while working your string. Take your time; there's no hurry.

When you have the required inch or two twisted, it is time to mate the two strands from the short section with matching strands from the main body of the string. The wax helps hold these sections together as you twist them. Hold the two eight-strand sections in your left hand as you did before. Twist away, bring over and down until you have about an inch or more twisted below the tapered end pieces of the string.

When you reach that approximate length, clamp off the string at that point using a paperclip, paper clamp or even a clothespin. Then move to the other end.

Measure that 7½ inches from the end as you did before and repeat the twist, bring over the top and down procedure just as you did for the other loop. The first loop formed was basically for the upper section of the bow limbs. This upper loop should be larger than the lower loop, since it lays on the bow limb

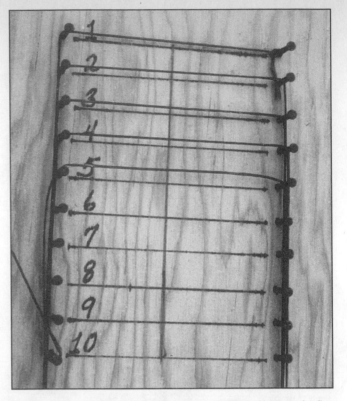

The string is turned around the pegs, top, middle and bottom, for five turns, until all have crossed the number five set pins at the top. Make three like this.

when the bow isn't braced, and the loop needs to be wide enough to slip over the wide recurve limb.

When you have a loop of about one-inch diameter formed on the lower string section, mate the stranded sections with the formed loop. Twist away, bring over and continue working the strands until you again have the twisted area about an inch or more from the end of the loose strand section.

Before cutting strands at the top of the jig, get a solid hold on them along the side of the jig.

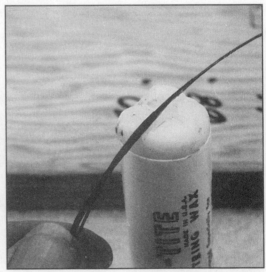

Hold the strands about 12 inches from the end and wax them heavily to keep them together. This works best by applying pressure on the string at both ends and pulling it through the wax.

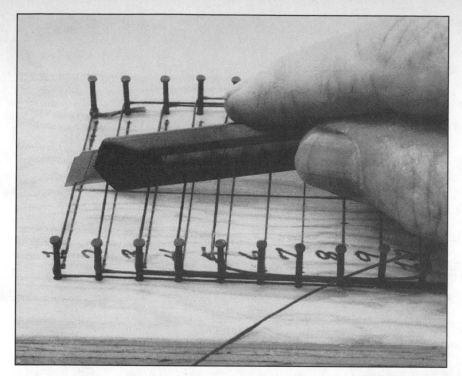

After tying off the last strand on the number five pin, hold the string along one side about halfway down and, using the snap knife, cut the strands between the pegs. The center line will help keep the cut centered, but it isn't important.

You have just made the basic section of a Flemish hand-laid string. You have a wide upper loop, a narrower lower loop and the string for a 62-inch bow. Now all you need to do is install it on the bow.

Use your bow stringer to brace the bow with the narrow loop on the bottom limb and the wider loop on the upper limb. Brace the bow and check the brace height. Oops!

When all else fails, read the directions and figure out what you think you should be doing. We just *knew* that our bow was 62 inches long, the length of the string we made. Actually, our bow was 60 inches long, which meant the brace height dropped from eight to six-plus inches. Not good!

What to do? Well, the simple thing is to hang up that string and make another one of the correct length.

Another alternative is to remove one end loop and make the string shorter by taking it up and retwisting it, but one gets into complicated nonsense here. It is simpler to make a new string of the right length.

The second string went more rapidly, since we knew what to do. We were certain to change the center pin from the 62-inch mark to the 60 so as not to repeat that mistake.

After making the new, shorter string, we again placed it on our bow and checked the brace height. This time it was a tad too long at about 8¼ inches. We removed the string from the

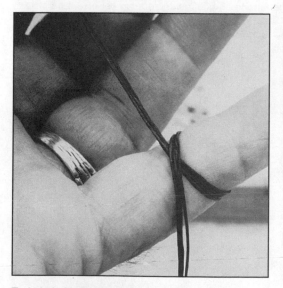

To help hold tension on the strands as you wax and work them, make a loop on your little finger with all the strands. It is easier to keep them even this way.

When you have three strands of five strings each laid and waxed, tie them off with clamps to prevent them from coming undone. Then you are ready to mate the three together.

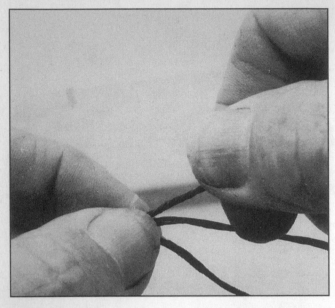

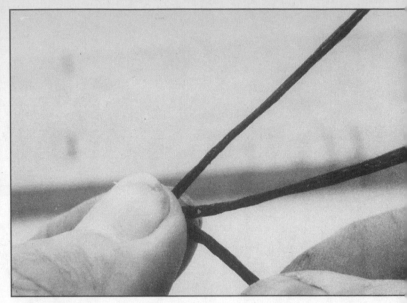

Hold all three strands with the thumb and first finger of the left hand, if you happen to be right-handed, use the loop over your little finger and twist the strand farthest from your fingers away from you. You can see the twist forming here.

After the strand is twisted to your satisfaction, bring it over the top of the other two, go up to the new upper strand, twist it and bring it over and so on.

upper loop and twisted it tighter to get the brace height shorter. Butler recommends about fifteen or so twists on the string. It is important to twist the string to tighten it, not loosen it, or the string will separate.

Again checking the brace height, we found it measured just under $7^1/_2$ inches. These hand-laid strings will stretch when they are new. There is no way to hold them tight as they are twisted up, so the strands need to stretch to equalize length, and this takes a bit of time.

(Left) Serve the center section on the string while it is braced on the bow. Serve about eight inches or so until it looks as this does. By adjusting the tension on the server, you can get nice, clean, close strands like this. At this point, you are ready to tie off the serving.

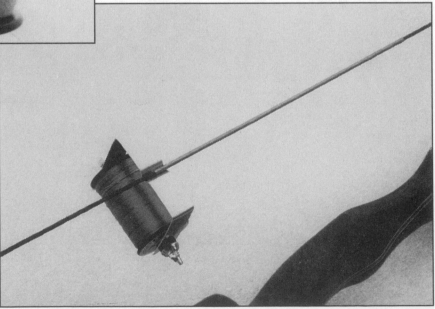

When both loops, upper and lower, are twisted you are ready to mount the string on the bow. Make about 15 or more twists to tighten it; if you go the wrong way with the twist the string will loosen and become shorter. When satisfied with the brace height, you are ready for the center serving shown here. Lay the loose end of the nylon thread along the center of the string and twist some strands like this to get started.

Twist and turn the strand until you have about an inch or more that looks like this. This will form either the upper or lower loop, depending on how long the center twisted section is. This one could be tighter.

Take the three strands with the open end, mate them with the three long strands and continue to twist away and bring them over until the loop end looks like this. This has some bumps in it that will smooth out under tension, but don't expect perfection on your first try.

The stretching can be sped up by running a section of light leather up and down the string with applied pressure. This heats up the string through friction, causing it to stretch quickly and evenly.

If your string is too long, remove the upper loop and twist some more; if it is too short let out a few twists to lengthen it.

When you feel your string is the correct length and has stretched to fit properly, you are ready to serve the center section. Leave the string braced on the bow. Place a bow square on the string with the bottom of the square on the arrow rest or bow shelf. Make a mark on the upper section of the square. Measure down 8 inches and make another mark. This will be the length of your center serving for the string.

Using the nylon thread in the string server supplied with the kit, lay a section one-inch or so in length on the string, starting at the lower mark. With the server, hand-lay some turns on the bowstring to get it started. The turns will hold the end in place as you serve over it; continue to turn and serve until you have the center section served from mark to mark.

To tie off the upper section, pull out about twelve inches of nylon from the spool. Cut it off at this length and place the loose end to the right of the string. Note the direction the serving is moving and place a loop on the string in the opposite direction. Bring the loose end through the loop and loop it around the string about ten times.

Turn the loop onto the string by hand. As you lay on the

Pull off about a foot or more of thread from the server and cut it. Make a loop similar to that shown and take the loose end and back serve it in between the two strands. If you do it right, the loop end on the left will move off the string as you turn the right end onto the string by hand. If the loop and strands are wrong, they will tighten up. Merely remove the section and do it over the right way.

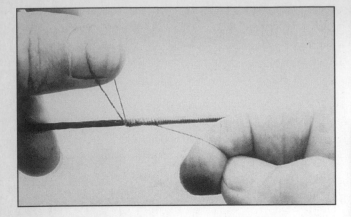

When you have a single loop like this, grab the long, loose end on the right and pull the loop tighter to bring the loop onto the string. You should have run about twelve or so backwraps.

string from the formed loop, you will be serving from the end at which you stopped. The string will be unraveling from the upper section until you have only one loop left. Merely pull that through until you have a fine, tight end on the string. You also will have about twelve inches of serving string; use scissors to cut it flush with the string.

Your string is now completed. You might want to let it set to get the final stretch, or you can go ahead and place a nocking point on the string and shoot it to loosen it up.

You will have those little ends of string from the tapered end lay-up sticking out like twigs from the upper and lower string where they came out of the twist. This is normal and you can leave them to act as a partial silencer or trim them off for a neater look.

One point to check when making your center serving: If you are right-handed and serve the string so the twist will tighten on the string as you draw the bow, it will work better. If you serve from the wrong direction, your serving will loosen, causing problems in the field. To avoid problems, check this as you set up and make the center serving.

We took our string, now on our 60-inch bow, to the butt to shoot-in. This recurve had been noisy when first received. Noisy strings can be silenced easily and a hand-laid string is supposed to be quieter. This bow proved to be much quieter than with the original string. We had removed most of the noise, but some silencers on the string would still help.

While you have the Flemish hand-laid string system fresh in mind, it might not be a bad idea to go back to the string jig and make one or two more strings. They become faster and easier to make with experience. This simple system works well, and the strings are stronger than needed for most bows.

The normal number of strands for a 55-pound bow is 16. You can make this as two sections of 8 strands, twisted style, four sections of four strands or a lighter string of three strands of five each to give 15 strands. Some archers prefer the 15-strand three twister. It is easy to make and is a bit smaller in diameter to fit the bowstring nocks better.

By dropping a line to Butler Traditional Bowhunting Supplies, you can get their latest catalog. One good thing about their jig is that it is small, portable and can go into hunting camp with you. A good hand-laid string is hard to come by when you're fifty miles from town. Take the kit with you and be prepared for any string emergency.

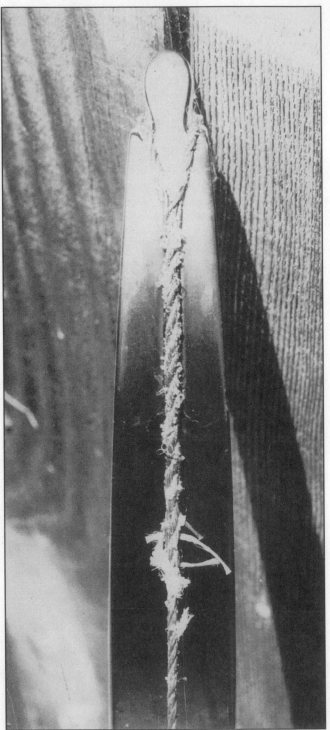

The finished string will fit the upper and lower string grooves on the bow and will come down past the notch in the center of the limbs. This string hasn't been trimmed so the loose ends are still showing. You can trim them off for a neater appearance or leave them as mini silencers.

4 Matching, Tuning Equipment

Obtaining The Right Gear Is Only Half The Battle

Plus Experts Discuss:

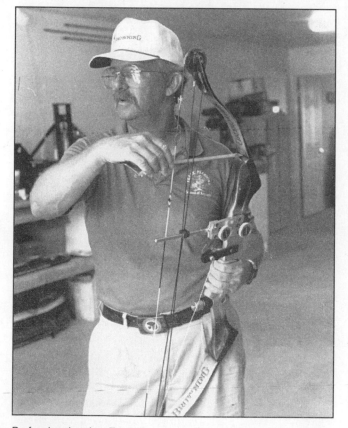

Professional archer Frank Pearson believes in thoroughly checking and tuning every aspect of his bows for better scores. He uses a tape measure to check the tiller, the distance from the limb base to bowstring, top and bottom.

GETTING THE RIGHT GEAR is important. But simply visiting a professional archery shop or looking through a catalog, then ordering one each of everything that looks good is not the answer. It has to be the right gear for you and each component must match or be compatible with all the others.

With that task accomplished, each bit of equipment must be mounted and tuned carefully to be compatible with everything else. Most importantly, everything must be matched for you, the individual archer.

In this chapter, the selection and tuning of compound bows will be discussed, although the concepts—and most of the procedures—are similar for all bows. However, modern compound bows are the most difficult to tune properly. Once a longbow or recurve has been matched to the shooter, there is not much more for the archer to do, except practice.

The first consideration for any archer is draw length. Most longbows and recurves are designed to produce their listed draw weight at 28 inches of draw. There is nothing magic about that figure, it is simply the length with which most people will be comfortable. Such bows may be designed and built to any optimum draw length, but that is usually a function of a custom bowyer. Any such traditional bow may be pulled past its listed draw length, of course, if the archer has the strength to do so. However, most people will find an additional inch of draw length considerably more difficult to achieve than the previous 28 inches. The procedure is not recommended.

Compound bows may be built to almost any listed draw length—within certain limitations. For adults, draw lengths of 25 or 26 are considered minimum. Maximums of around 32 or 33 inches are the most common. Custom builders can go beyond those limitations, especially on shorter-draw bows built for youngsters and smaller women, but the most commonly found draw lengths are from 28 to 30 inches.

Most modern compound bows have provisions for easily changing the draw length within a two- or three-inch range. Most beginners will find that, as they gain strength and experi-

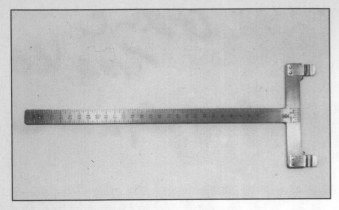

An archer's bow square serves many purposes.

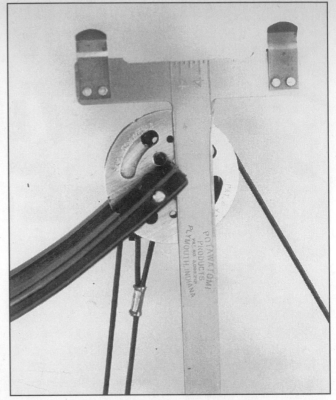

A bow square has been attached to the eccentric wheel of a compound bow with two-sided tape to check the synchronization of the wheel turn-over. Another square is on the opposite end; they should come to the same angle at the same time. Some new compound bows now have index marks on the wheels to aid tuning.

ence, their comfortable draw length will increase by an inch or more. As the back muscles strengthen and the chest expands, longer draws become easier. Each bow brand has its own draw-length adjustment procedures, but most rely on a change of the cable ends in the slots or holes found in the eccentric wheels or cams.

Before determining draw length, every new archer must learn if he is right- or left-eye dominant. The stronger or dominant eye has nothing to do with right- or left-handedness. It is not uncommon for an archer to be right-handed, but left-eyed. One simple method of determining the dominant eye is to point at a distant, small object with both eyes open; then close each eye while still pointing. If the object remains in focus when the left eye is closed, you are right-eye dominant, and vice versa. Learning to shoot a bow that is matched to the dominant eye from the start will be more satisfactory than simply picking a bow that matches the dominant hand. Same-side hand and eye dominance does not necessarily match in all individuals.

After determining which eye is dominant, measure your natural draw length. If a bow is available—as several would be at an archery shop—simply draw a full-length arrow all the way back to your natural anchor point—most use the corner of the mouth or the jaw bone—then have an assistant mark the arrow at the point that it touches the arrow rest. A dab of paper correction fluid or a bit of fingernail polish will mark the arrow. The bow arm must be fully extended for an accurate measurement. Then measure the length from the mark to the inside of the arrow nock. That is the draw length to be remembered.

A second method may be used when a bow is not available in advance. Stand near a wall or doorway in a good shooting stance. Extend the bow hand forward, the hand in a fist, until it touches the wall. The assistant should use a tape measure to determine the distance from the wall to the corner of the archer's mouth. That, again, will be your draw length.

Once the draw length has been determined, a comfortable draw weight is selected for the bow. Every archer is different. Younger shooters, some women and some men will be comfortable with draw weights of no more than, say 45 pounds. Many states and provinces have minimum draw weights for hunting bows, so if you are to become a bowhunter some day, the bow should be within those requirements of where you live or will hunt.

Today's modern compounds have adjustable weight ranges of 15 or 20 pounds, so it is not a problem to start out with a draw weight of 45 pounds to learn the correct shooting techniques, and later boost the bow up to its maximum of 60 pounds, still well within hunting parameters. Most archery coaches recommend learning the basics on a low-draw-weight bow to avoid possibly developing bad habits from a bow too strong to easily draw.

Knowing draw length and weight restrictions, you must select a bow. As outlined elsewhere, the selection of available bows can be almost overwhelming. There are hundreds of models and types on the market. Talk over the problem with other archers and bowhunters, study books and magazines, pour over catalogs and talk to the local professional archery shop operator. There will be a dozen or more bows that will fit your needs. The choice may come down to a specific color or price. Whichever bow you select, make sure it has the capability of growing and changing with you as you grow in experience and strength.

After a bow is purchased, arrows are the next consideration. The pros and cons of most types of arrows are discussed elsewhere in this book. Study the arrow selection charts offered by the major shaft manufacturers: Easton, AFC and Beman. The arrow spine selected will have a wide range of draw adjustments to grow with the archer.

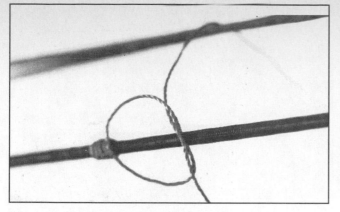

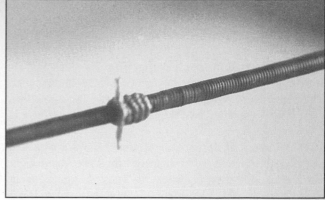

Frank Pearson and others prefer to use braided nylon line tied to the bowstring in place of metal nock sets.

After about seven knots over the serving, the nylon is cut and later burned on the end to prevent unraveling.

Tiller is a measurement that should be checked on any new bow or any bow that has not been shot for some time. Essentially, this is a measurement that is taken from the base of the bow limbs to the bowstring. Any simple marked ruler or metal tape measure may be used, although the archery shop will have a bow square that serves the purpose. Lacking anything else, an arrow shaft may be used, holding the thumbnail at the first distance and testing to see if the second distance matches.

Upper and lower measurements should be the same for most bows and most shooters. More sophisticated archers may want to alter this, but most shooters want the distance to be equal. This measurement is especially important if the draw weight of a compound has been changed or if the bow has been shot by someone else. If there is a discrepancy, turn in the limb adjustment bolt at the base of the limb. Turn the bolt slowly and carefully, measuring after each slight turn, checking each distance. If in doubt about the process, tighten down both limb bolts as far as they will go and re-measure the tiller. If upper and lower limbs are equal, loosen the limb bolts the same number of turns until a comfortable draw weight is again established.

A problem found on many compound bows is a lack of exact synchronization of each of the eccentric wheels. This means that both wheels (or cams) do not roll over and reach their maximum rotation at precisely the same moment. The process may be detected by pulling a bow all the way back to its listed draw length. If the final stopping point seems sharp and clean, the wheels are probably in synch. If the stop feels spongy or soft, that indicates the two wheels are not turning exactly together and an adjustment should be done. The problem is not uncommon and may be found on bows fresh from the factory, as well as those in use for years. If the bow in hand is one of the newer single-cam designs, the question is moot.

A simple method of synchronization is to first mark each eccentric wheel with correcting fluid or felt-tip pen at some easily identified spot such as the area where the wheel crosses the limb tip before it is drawn. As the bow is drawn back, ask someone to observe the two marks to determine if they turn the same amount and come to rest together at full draw. Professional archer Frank Pearson uses a trick to make this easier to determine. He uses two-sided tape and attaches 6-inch straight edges on the wheels. This makes it easy to observe the turning of the wheels as the bow string is pulled back. Once the two straight edges reach the same angle at the same time, the wheels are in synch.

An arrow rest should be the next accessory attached. The type of rest used is determined by whether the archer will be

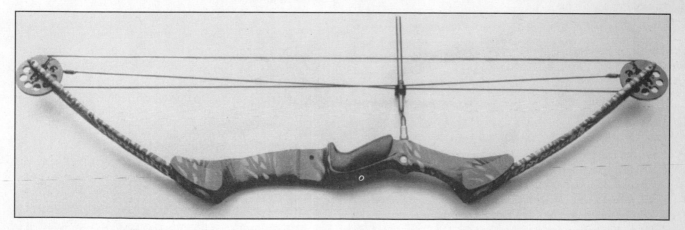

Browning's modern compound bows are among the easiest on which to change draw lengths. Two Allen bolts are removed at each end and placed in the same relative holes. Holes are marked and the adjustment is made without added tools or equipment.

shooting with a mechanical release or with fingers only. A finger shooter will want to attach a shoot-around rest. The arrow bends or curves around the bow handle as it is released by the fingers.

Those shooting with a mechanical release will prefer a shoot-through rest. The arrow certainly bends a slight amount upon release, but does not bend around the handle. The arrow flies straight from the string past the bow as the release trigger is pulled or pushed.

Today, many, if not most, compound bows are packed with an appropriate arrow rest, arrow quiver, perhaps a sight and, in many cases, a cable guard. The cable guard is an integral part of about 95 percent of compounds today. It is a simple bent rod with a cable slider or a set of wheels running on the rod adjusted to keep the cables away from the bowstring. The space between the cables and the bowstring must be far enough so the flying arrow does not come in contact with the cables as it is released. The wider the fletching vanes, the more space is required. The amount of space can be adjusted on most bows by turning the dog-leg cable guard rod, moving the cables in or out and re-tightening the rod in place. It is not necessary to adjust the cables away from the string more than the necessary vane or fletching clearance requires.

Pick up the bow square again and snap it onto the bowstring, with the arm portion across the arrow rest. There are measuring marks on the bow square where it meets the string. A nock indicator may be placed on the string about 3/8-inch above the horizontal line of the bow square. This allows an adequate amount of space to accommodate the diameter of the arrow shaft and nock while allowing the shaft to remain at 90 degrees to the string.

Special nock pliers are available from many suppliers that allow the nock set to clamp on the string without cutting the

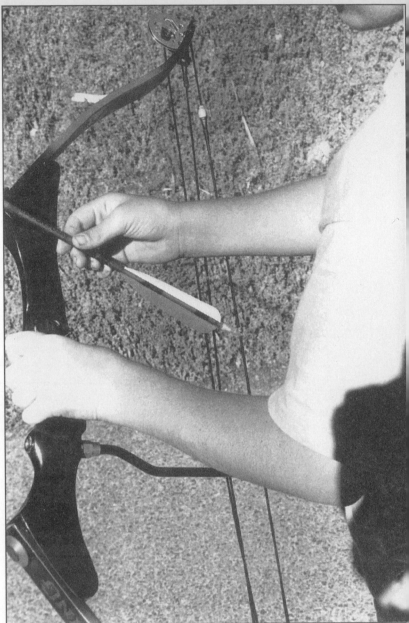

Most younger shooters prefer to learn by shooting with their fingers and a simple arrow rest.

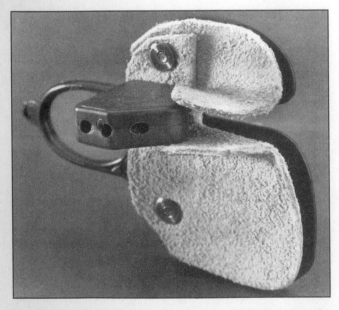

The Saunders finger tab features a spacer on the inside to keep the first and second fingers from touching the arrow shaft.

string or crushing the nock set. At first, the nock set should be clamped only enough to hold it gently in place until some initial tuning shooting has been done with the bow. If it has not been tightened down, the nock set can be turned up and down on the bowstring serving to find the correct location before it is finally clamped in place. In many situations, the 3/8-inch setting may be the best and final location, although those shooting thin carbon arrows will want less space. Most archers prefer to lock on a second nock set above the first after the final location has been determined. The second nock set locks the first in place.

If a string peep is to be used with the bow sight, its location must be determined. An assistant is needed for this procedure, too. Draw the string back to the anchor point with your eyes closed. Your assistant should then mark the string at your eye

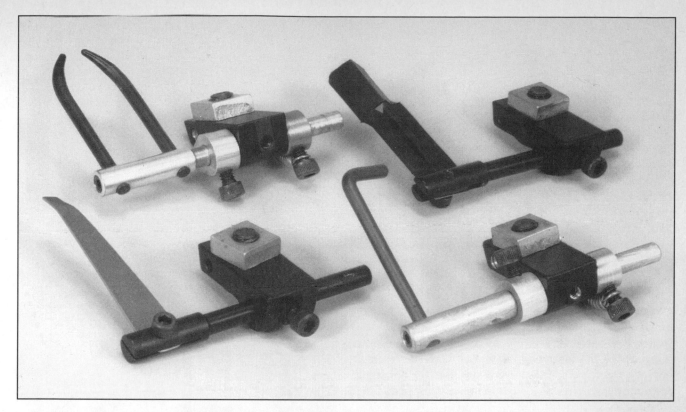

Bear Archery and others offer a wide variety of shoot-through arrow rests for those using mechanical releases.

location with a soft felt-tip pen or with a tiny piece of tape or string. That will be the location of the string peep aperture. Simply part the strands of the bowstring equally and insert the aperture of choice. Follow the directions for the peep sight to lock it in place on the string. Some brands require only that two bolts be tightened.

Most peeps have some sort of rubber tubing attached to ensure that as the aperture turns as the bow is drawn, it will remain open to the shooter's eye. Every bowstring rotates somewhat as the bow is drawn. The target shooter has plenty of time to readjust the string peep, so some target archers do not use the tubing. The bowhunter, however, wants the aperture to rotate the same for every shot. There would be nothing more frustrating than to draw down on a giant deer or elk only to find you could see nothing through the peep sight. The string peep could be thought of as the rear sight on a rifle.

The bow sight would play the part of the front sight if this were a rifle. The dozens of types of bow sights available are discussed elsewhere. A target shooter will have more sight adjustments than a bowhunter. Many bowhunters prefer a bow sight with but one pin or crosshair, set for about twenty-five yards. They do not want to worry about making a mistake and picking the wrong sight pin. Plenty of whitetail deer hunters in the East and Midwest never take shots longer than twenty-five yards and can easily hold slightly under the pin location for shorter shots. Target shooters may shoot from fifteen to sixty or more yards and will want more pins and adjustments.

Before shooting the bow, there are a couple more adjustments to make.

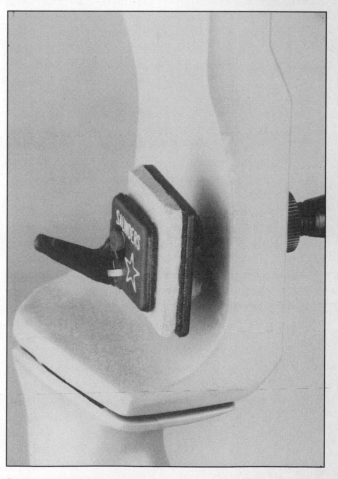

Saunders' adjustable arrow rest is a good match for finger shooters.

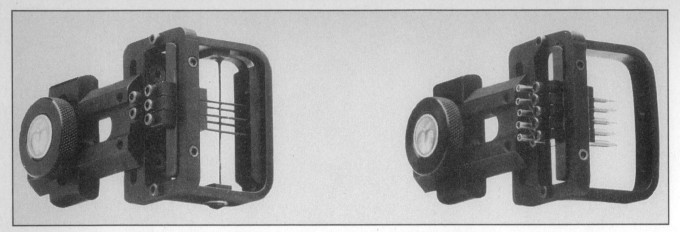

The bowhunter may prefer small gap, protected pins or crosshair sights, such as these two models from Hoyt.

Nock an arrow on the string, hold the bow at arm's length and look straight down it with the shaft on the arrow rest. Adjust the plunger and/or arrow rest so that the arrow appears to be split by the bow string. Move the plunger or rest in or out until the arrow appears straight out from the bowstring, across the rest. Then re-tighten the plunger or rest in that location.

The so-called paper test discussed further on will determine if the nocking point is too high or too low, or if the arrow rest is in or out too far. If the nock point is too low, the arrow will leave the bow in what is called a tail low attitude. If the nock point is too high, the arrow will fly out with the nock end too high. To correct either situation, move the nock point up or down as appropriate. Make only slight adjustments each time before shooting another arrow through paper.

If the arrows leave the bow flying with the tails too far right or left, the arrow rest is adjusted too far in the opposite direction. If the arrow rest is too far to the right, the arrow will fly with the nock end too far left and the rest should be moved inward toward the bow riser. For left-handed shooters, the adjustments are the opposite. If the arrows do not seem to want to fly well at all, do not be afraid to experiment to some extent. Sometimes, any change will be favorable and you can go from there.

One of the most common tuning procedures is what is known as the paper test. There are several commercial paper test frames available which are not expensive. Many archery shops and clubs have them, too. Or they are easy to construct, consisting of a simple metal or wood frame that can be hung about four or five feet from the target butts. Tape a sheet of newspaper or plain computer paper to the frame and shoot arrows from about five feet away, observing the resulting holes.

If the holes in the paper show a tear upward, rather than a three-star hole, the nocking point must be moved downward. Move the nocking point in the direction of the poor penetration; opposite the direction you want the arrow to correct. For left/right tears in the paper, the pressure point, the arrow rest or the plunger should be moved in the same direction as the hole in

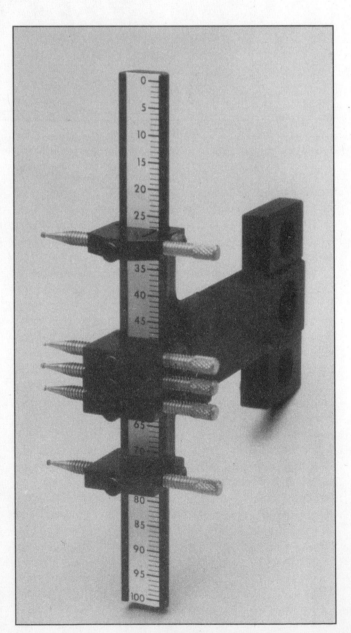

The Hoyt Pro Hunter sight is also ideal for target shooters.

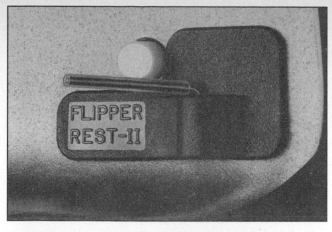

Finger shooters have used the New Archery Products Flipper Rest for years.

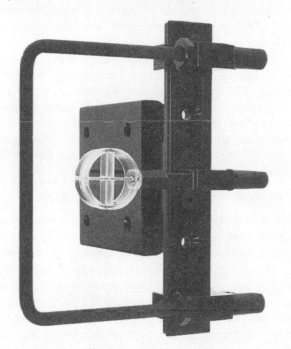

The Timberline 450 Natural Light Site has one aiming point, preferred by some whitetail hunters.

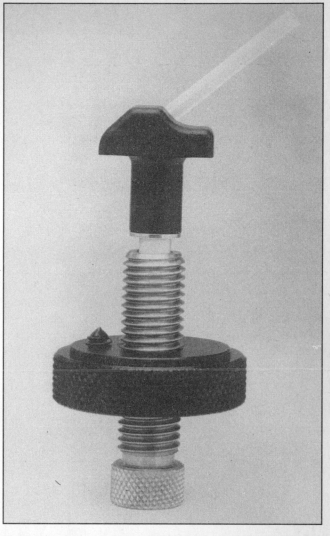

New Archery Product's PlungerRest Arrowrest Cushion Plunger System has all the adjustments many archers seem to prefer.

the paper indicates a correction must be made. Move it in or out, as the hole in the paper indicates. In most cases, a good three-point star hole should be achieved within a half-dozen arrows at most.

The paper test is not the final adjustment for good tuning, but it is an excellent starting point from which to make necessary fine tuning later, as you gain experience shooting many arrows. If you shot at targets set at the same distance all the time, no further adjustments would be necessary. However, whether shooting targets or bowhunting, archers must shoot at several distances, and most will be unknown. Some further tuning will probably be necessary as you shoot more arrows.

Some shooters will use an overdraw device on their bows. This permits the use of a shorter arrow, which acts like a stiffer spine shaft. It lightens the total arrow weight by the amount of shaft material removed. The result will be a faster, flatter-shooting arrow. However, some archers find it more

difficult to tune an overdraw bow or keep an overdraw bow well tuned. An overdraw arrow should not be more than four or five inches shorter than the correct arrow length as listed in the regular arrow chart. Remember the equipment restrictions by some national tournament associations and beware of shooting arrows too light for the bow. There is a point at which a lightweight arrow shot too many times will stress and possibly damage a bow. It will certainly produce a need for more frequent tuning.

The more you shoot, the more aware you will become of small changes and requirements for adjustments. The more you practice, the better you and your equipment will become. A new bow requires some shooting to break it in. The string will stretch slightly after hundreds of arrows and other discrepancies will soon be evident. Use the same procedures outlined above to re-tune when indicated.

Many of the above tuning techniques and procedures are outlined in instructional videos from the Precision Shooting Equipment Company with Pete Shepley and Terry Ragsdale and from Robinhood Video Productions with Frank Pearson using Browning Archery equipment.

4

Tuning Carbon Arrows
by Jeff McNail

With the introduction and blazing popularity of carbon arrows among archers throughout the world, questions have arisen about the best way to tune bows and other equipment to take advantage of these new shafts. Some have found getting and maintaining well-tuned equipment more difficult with carbon arrows than aluminum. Others have switched to carbon arrows and use nothing else for target shooting or bowhunting.

Jeff McNail is a bowhunter and target archer on the staff at the Beman Corporation headquarters in Traverse City, Michigan. McNail has been shooting a bow since he was 10 years old and successfully bowhunting since he was 15. In 1993, he placed in the top ten in the Men's Pro Division at the Las Vegas International Tournament. He also tied for 6th place in the NFAA Indoor Nationals (Men's Pro Division) and is currently ranked fourth overall in the Men's Pro Division in the State of Michigan Archery Association.

I asked him to share his experiences with carbon arrows and what follows is his report.

Jeff McNail

A FINELY TUNED carbon arrow setup is easy to achieve. I've been building and shooting carbon arrows since 1989. Since then, I have discovered a few tips for making compound bows perform quite well with carbon arrows.

The one thing I have noticed most about carbon arrows is that because they are highly responsive, shooters will sometimes mistakenly tune opposite of what is necessary. An understanding of the complete arrow system will help any archer quickly master the basics of tuning carbon arrows.

The results are rewarding. Paper tuning will help you identify and eliminate problems associated with arrow fishtailing and porpoising. Tiller tuning will help you tighten your groups, and, for bowhunters, broadhead tuning will help you align your broadhead groups with your field-point groups.

From selecting a proper spine to fine tuning for broadheads, these simple instructions will help most archers correct the flight of their carbon arrow as it leaves the bow.

Start With A Properly Spined Arrow

The first step to a well tuned carbon arrow—as with any arrow shaft material—is selecting the proper spine. Spine is the stiffness of an arrow shaft as related to arrow length and point weight. An improperly spined arrow can cause problems with arrow grouping and broadhead flight. Arrow spines are generally selected to correspond to an individual's *calculated* draw weight.

Draw weight is calculated by taking peak draw force and factoring in the type of cam or wheel used, percentage of let-off, adapter and point or broadhead weights, arrow length, string type and the method of release. Beman has developed an easy method of arrow selection by determining calculated draw weight with a bow weight calculation chart. Other manufacturers use similar charts to help archers correctly spine their arrows for the many different bows on the market.

My measured peak draw is 60 pounds, but my *calculated* bow weight is 69 pounds. To arrive at the 69-pound figure, I had to take into account that I use a mechanical release and my bow has a modified cam, a 65-percent let-off and a Fast Flight string. Other factors included my 29-inch arrow length—1-inch longer than my draw length—and my choice of a Beman standard arrow adapter with 100-grain field point or broadhead. With my 69-pound calculated bow weight, the properly spined Beman Hunter carbon arrow for my setup is the 60/80.

Build an Arrow That Meets Your Needs

The fletching—feathers or vanes, helical or straight—and fletching length will make a difference in arrow performance.

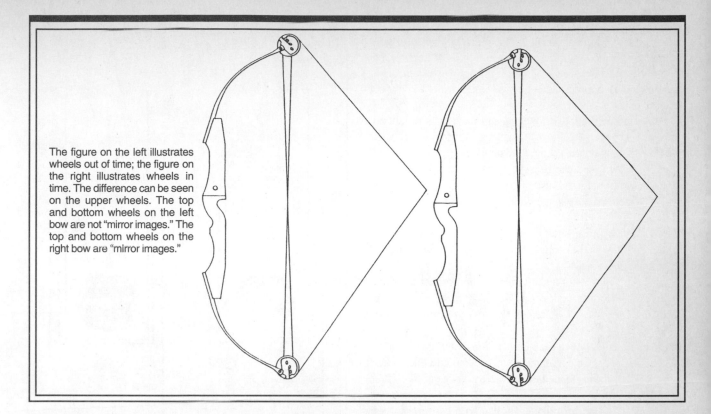

The figure on the left illustrates wheels out of time; the figure on the right illustrates wheels in time. The difference can be seen on the upper wheels. The top and bottom wheels on the left bow are not "mirror images." The top and bottom wheels on the right bow are "mirror images."

Arrow flight is affected by the balance between the fletching and the type of tip—point or broadhead—that you use. Your individual shooting style and ability will also play a factor in fletching choice. Ultimately, your optimum arrow assembly will depend on the type of shooting you plan to do.

While plastic vanes are more durable, feathers will help your arrow move faster off the bow. Because of the greater air drag, feathers will help your arrow recover and get into proper arrow flight faster than will vanes. Down-range trajectory, however, will be better with vanes, because they have less drag. Whether you choose vanes or feathers, the critical factors are size and position.

Hunting arrows typically require a longer fletching, usually four to five inches in length. The longer fletching acts as a balance to the broadhead blades and helps steer the arrow better. I use a 4-inch fletch to match my $1^1/_8$-inch cutting diameter broadhead. If I were to use a larger broadhead, I would choose a longer fletching to compensate for the additional spread of the blades.

The target shooters I know prefer the shorter 2-inch, 3-inch, or even smaller fletching. Experimentation with different vane sizes for grouping will determine the correct size for you. Typically, the longer 3-inch fletch is used for indoor shooting to provide better steerage. Outdoor target shooters prefer the shorter fletching to minimize drag in crosswinds. Because of my particular shooting style and because I like a versatile set-up, I use a 2-inch fletch for both indoor and outdoor target shooting.

On the issue of helical versus straight fletching, I find that both offer distinct advantages. While the straight fletch offers better clearance, the helical helps the arrow recover from any release errors such as torquing, hand twisting, or punching for-

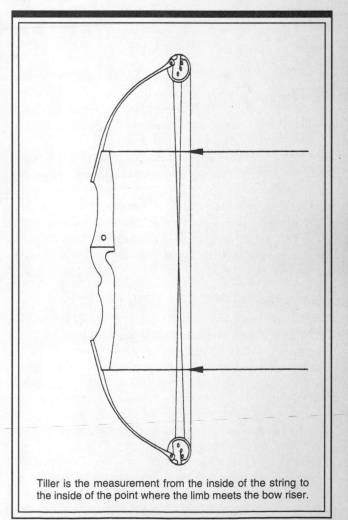

Tiller is the measurement from the inside of the string to the inside of the point where the limb meets the bow riser.

ward. Using a helical fletch will also help tighten your groups. I do offer a word of caution about too much helical. Depending on the bow setup, anything more than a two- or three-percent helical fletch may cause problems with arrow rest clearance. I personally like a three-percent helical fletch with both my center-shot and launcher rests.

Some people think that fletching carbon arrows should only be done by expert pro shops. Actually, by following a few simple steps and using the proper kind of adhesive, combined with a little patience, you can become an expert in arrow assembly in your own home in no time.

Tips to remember when building carbon arrows:

1. Prepare the carbon shaft by using a 3M Scotch Brite or similar sanding pad to roughen the shaft where you intend to put the fletching.
2. Clean the shaft with a shaft preparation product for carbon arrows—Beman makes one—or denatured alcohol on a clean cloth. *Never use lacquer thinner or acetone on carbon shafts!*
3. Clean all vanes with a shaft preparation material or denatured alcohol. Most vane manufacturers use a mould release agent that needs to be cleaned off before the vane can stick to the carbon shaft.
4. Use only a glue formulated for use with carbon shafts for adhering vanes or feathers. Glues designed for aluminum arrows will not work with carbon. Beman makes two fletching adhesives that work well with both carbon and aluminum.
5. Adapters and glue-in points should be attached with an epoxy with a rubber gel base for the best holding ability when shooting into high-density targets. A low temperature hot-melt glue can assist in making broadhead adjustments before permanently gluing with epoxy.
6. Target points have a balance pin that inserts into the carbon shaft. An ample coating of glue on the pin will provide better adhesion.
7. Gluing is not recommended for Beman nocks that have been designed to fit snugly in the shaft. Nocks can be rotated after installation by using a coin inserted into the nock throat. Be sure to hold the shaft securely near the nock while making adjustments.

Selecting and Adjusting Arrow Rests

Most of the arrow rests on the market today are adaptable to the smaller diameter carbon arrow. When choosing a rest, make certain it provides adequate clearance for vanes or feathers. Finger-release shooters must use a plunger style, springy, or similar type of rest to obtain proper flight and arrow groupings. Because my bow has been set up for use with a release, I use Beman's 3D-CLR launcher rest for target shooting. For hunting, I am currently using Beman's center-shot, prong-style rest with an adjustable spring tension.

There are a few adjustments that your bow will need after you install the arrow rest, but before your final arrow rest setup adjustments. First, wheel timing should be checked to see that the wheels are rolling over equally. If they are not in

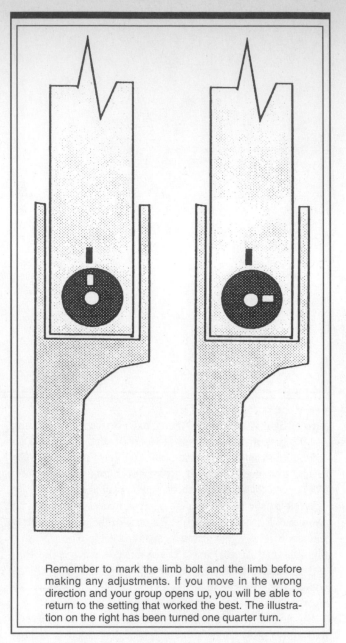

Remember to mark the limb bolt and the limb before making any adjustments. If you move in the wrong direction and your group opens up, you will be able to return to the setting that worked the best. The illustration on the right has been turned one quarter turn.

synch, consult your local pro shop to have the proper adjustments made or follow the guidance provided earlier in this chapter.

Next, set your bow at zero tiller. Tiller is the measurement from the inside of the string to the inside of the point where the limb meets the bow riser. Zero tiller is when the distance between the top riser and the string is the same as the distance between the bottom riser and the string. Tiller adjustments are made by rotating the upper and lower limb bolts. Having your tiller set at an equal distance on the top and bottom will help you make other adjustments to the bow during tuning.

When the above is complete, final setup adjustments can be made to the arrow rest. The best place to start your left-right setting is to align it with the center-shot of the bow. The easiest way to do this is by using a center-shot alignment tool. The arrow rest should be vertically adjusted until the center of the arrow is near the center of the $5/16$-inch accessory hole in the riser.

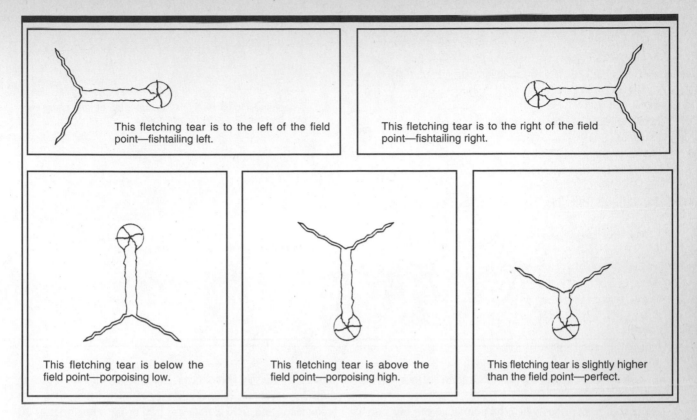

This fletching tear is to the left of the field point—fishtailing left.

This fletching tear is to the right of the field point—fishtailing right.

This fletching tear is below the field point—porpoising low.

This fletching tear is above the field point—porpoising high.

This fletching tear is slightly higher than the field point—perfect.

You will want to set the string nock at ¹/₈-inch above center—or zero on your bow square. You will note that this is less than the measurement recommended for aluminum arrow shafts. This position is a good starting point for bow tuning. The nock may be adjusted further later in the tuning process.

Carbon Arrow Weight and Balance

Broadheads come in many shapes, weights and cutting diameters. When looking for a broadhead to work with a carbon arrow, you will need to think about keeping the total weight down. I have found that 100 to 125 grains is the maximum broadhead weight that should be considered to achieve a proper balance. If you are looking for the lightest and fastest setup, you may want to try out the new adapterless, compression-lock broadhead or even a glue-on broadhead.

The cutting diameter also has an impact on carbon arrow flight. To achieve optimum results, the cutting diameter should be kept to a maximum of 1¹/₄ inches, although closed-blade broadheads should fly the same as field points.

Once you have decided which broadhead you will be using, you need to match your field points to that weight. For target shooting, choose a weight that will give you the performance you desire— fast or slow setup—without exceeding the Archery Manufacturer's Organization (AMO) minimum recommended arrow weight. Then you are ready to paper tune your archery system.

Paper Tuning to Eliminate Fishtailing and Porpoising

Paper tuning is discussed elsewhere and is one of the easiest methods you can use to determine if the preliminary adjustments you made to the bow are correct. The way the paper rips will reveal problems you may be having with fishtailing or porpoising as the arrow leaves the bow. I prefer to paper tune with my field points first, then move to a target for group testing. Only rarely do I find a need to paper tune with broadheads.

A simple paper tuning target can be made by securely attaching an eighteen-inch or larger square of paper to a frame. Position the paper no more than five feet in front of a target butt. I mark my shooting line two to three feet in front of the paper target.

Install all of your accessories and optional equipment such as quiver, bow sight and stabilizer. Then you are ready to make your initial bow adjustments. Step up to the shooting line and shoot a few arrows with ample spacing between the paper and the target butt.

Examine the paper tears and make some adjustments. If your paper tears indicate that the fletching is to the left or right of the point hole, you have a fishtailing problem. If the tears are high or low, you're experiencing what is called porpoising. The accompanying illustrations will help you understand these problems.

If your paper tears indicate fishtailing, adjust your arrow rest in the direction of the fletching tear. Shoot again and keep adjusting the arrow rest until the tear shows signs of increasing. Move the arrow rest back to the position that gave the least amount of tear.

Is your left or right tear persisting? Decrease the poundage of your bow by one full turn counterclockwise on both limb bolts. Readjust your nocking point to ¹/₈-inch above center. Shoot again and examine the fletch tear.

If the tear is reduced when the poundage of your bow is decreased, you have three options: 1) Adjust and shoot your bow at a lower draw weight; 2) Change your field point weight

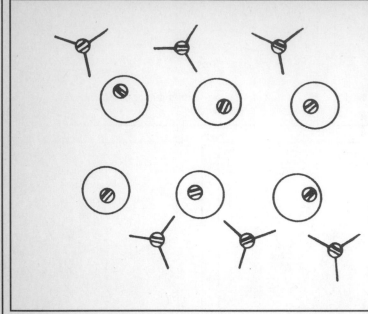

Broadheads consistently hitting upper left of field points indicate that the nocking point is too low.

Broadheads consistently hitting lower right of field points indicate that the nocking point is too high.

up or down; or **3)** Change the shaft size for a stiffer or weaker spine.

If the tear is increased when the poundage of your bow is decreased, you will need to increase your bow draw weight. Make your first limb bolt adjustment by two full turns clockwise from its current position. Readjust the nocking point and shoot again.

Did increasing your bow poundage reduce your fletching tear? If it did, you again have three options: **1)** Adjust and shoot your bow at a higher draw weight; **2)** Change your field point weight up or down; or **3)** Change your shaft size.

If you choose to shoot at a higher or lower draw weight, you can fine tune your adjustments in quarter-turn increments. Always remember that making adjustments to your limb bolts will require a repositioning of the nocking point.

For paper tears that indicate porpoising—the fletching tear appears high or low—you will need to adjust the nocking point on your string.

If you are porpoising low, raise the nocking point 1/8-inch and shoot at least three arrows to develop a pattern before continuing your adjustments.

Porpoising high may be eliminated by lowering the nocking point. I recommend making adjustments in 1/8-inch increments. If the nocking point reaches a 90-degree angle and the hole still tears high, increase the poundage of the lower limb. This is best done in half-turn increments. Each time you adjust your bow limb, you will need to readjust your nocking point to 1/8-inch above center.

For maximum arrow performance, I tune my bow with a 3/8- to 3/4-inch maximum nock high tear through the paper.

Fine Tuning for Broadheads

After you've tuned your bow to shoot field points, you can do some simple fine tuning for shooting broadheads. Slight adjustments to your nocking point and bow draw weight can get your field points and broadheads hitting fairly close to the same spot. One advantage of this type of fine tuning is that when both broadheads and field points are hitting the same spot at 20 yards, you can choose the same sight for both target shooting and hunting.

To start, you will need six arrows that are the same length and size from nock to insert. Half should be tipped with field points, the other half with broadheads that are the same weight as the field points. Your target—one suitable for broadheads—should be placed at 10 yards distance. On the target, place three dots—3-inch masking tape works well—at a distance of six to eight inches apart, left to right.

Begin shooting by using your field points to set your sight. Then alternate, shooting a broadhead at each dot and following with a field point. Evaluate the results and make your adjustments.

1. Broadheads consistently hitting upper left of your field points indicate that your nock point is too low. Move it up in small increments.
2. Broadheads consistently hitting lower right of your field points indicate that your nock point is too high. Move it down in small increments.
3. Broadheads hitting directly to the left or right of your field points indicate that your nock point is perfect, but your bow draw weight needs to be increased or decreased. To do this, adjust both limbs equally in quarter- or half-turn increments. Each time you adjust your limbs, you will need to readjust the nock to 1/8-inch above center.

Repeat the evaluation and adjustment sequence until your broadheads and field points are hitting as close to each other as possible. When you are comfortable with your adjustments at 10 yards, move back to 15 yards, then to 20 yards, repeating the process each time.

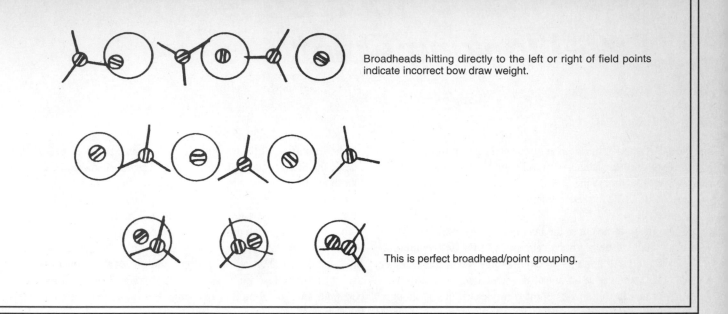

Broadheads hitting directly to the left or right of field points indicate incorrect bow draw weight.

This is perfect broadhead/point grouping.

Troubleshooting Broadhead Groupings

Once in a while you may notice that your arrows tipped with broadheads are not grouping the same as your arrows tipped with field points. This could be due to several things—a change in arrow balance, fletching contact, an off-center arrow nock or even an improperly installed broadhead.

The addition of a broadhead sometimes alters the front of center (FOC) balance. This in turn changes the spine of the arrow, which will throw off your groupings. The easiest way to correct this problem is to paper tune with your arrows tipped with broadheads.

Fletching contact with your arrow rest can cause your broadheads to fly erratically. A simple method of detecting contact is by spraying foot or talcum powder on your arrow's fletching. The powder will conveniently leave a tell-tale marker wherever contact is made.

In rare instances, you may notice that one broadhead is consistently hitting slightly higher than the others. Rotate the nock to the next vane and shoot again. This should bring your arrow into the group.

Erratic flight can also be attributed to an improperly installed broadhead. After following the manufacturer's installation instructions, check for broadhead straightness. You can do this by using a spin checker device to roll the arrow. You can also roll the entire arrow across a flat surface such as the corner of a table. The broadhead will wobble up and down if it is not on straight.

There are a couple of ways to correct the straightness problem. Double-check that the blades are on the ferrule correctly. Sometimes thread alignment can be slightly off and changing the broadhead to another arrow may correct the problem. If it is still not straight, try another broadhead.

Many shooters find they can achieve better flight when their broadhead is aligned with their vanes. This type of alignment can also help your arrow clear against the riser. If you are using an adapter and it is glued on with epoxy, you may want to put an O-ring behind the broadhead. The O-ring will make it easier to align the broadhead to the vanes.

Tiller Tuning for Tighter Groupings

Tiller tuning is an easy method of bow control developed by a few of the top compound shooters. This fine tuning will make your bow more forgiving. It is a simple method of changing the flexing or paradox of the arrow upon release. The results will be tighter grouping.

As explained earlier, tiller is the measurement of the inside limb pocket to the main string. Tiller tuning is the adjustment of the bow limbs so that the limbs are in synchronization at peak weight—the point where the bow pulls the hardest and the most force is applied to the arrow.

To start, set the upper and lower tillers at the same distance from the bow limb—zero tiller—by adjusting the limb bolts. Once you have achieved zero tiller, it is a good idea to mark them for reference. This way, if you adjust in the wrong direction and your groups begin to open up, you will be able to return to the original setting.

You will want to set your nocking point at $1/8$-inch above center and start shooting for groups at thirty yards or longer.

Starting with the top limb tiller, make slight adjustments to the limb bolt. I usually go in quarter-turn increments. This adjustment alters the speed of the limb and bow poundage and impacts the size of your groupings. One critical thing to remember: Each adjustment to the bolt will require that you reset the nock.

When you are comfortable with your groupings, reset to zero tiller and repeat this procedure with the lower limb tiller. You will then be able to go back and forth between the two, refining your adjustments on both limb bolts to achieve the best grouping.

When you have finally tuned your bow, you will find it shooting quieter, smoother and more efficiently!

4 Finding Your Constant Nocking Point

"**THE BIG** muley buck came on, turned right in front of me at six paces, checked later, and stood waiting for me to shoot. Or so it seemed. Deer to the left of me, deer to the right of me and a doe right beside me. Barely any chance to get off a shot, but why not try!

"The arrow came out of the bow quiver, my eyes never leaving the vitals of the big buck. The nock of the arrow slid onto the string, moving up to the nocking point. Who cares whether the cock feather is in or out at this distance? The bow was raised, drawn to full anchor point and released in one motion. Three jumps later the monster was down, and my biggest buck—a 6x9 non-typical—was on the ground."

As told by Bob Learn, an avid bowhunter, that happened a number of years ago. This situation could happen again, but it's not likely.

The importance of a nocking point was proven here—it is one of the few constants in bowhunting. However, there are a lot of variables.

The constants, those things that should always remain the same, include bow draw weight, which will be constant if you come to full draw each time and anchor properly. That anchor is another constant, and arrow length won't change in the field, unless you hunt with different equipment than most of us. Your arrow rest and pressure button should be set for a constant, and you should have a consistent nocking point on the string.

Recently, the same Bob Learn was running some tests on the Stotler three-piece break-down longbow. The nocking point was already on the string, since it happened to be the personal hunting bow of Jerry Dishion, the head man at

To set your nocks on your bowstring, you can use the various-sized Nok Sets made and marketed by Saunders Archery Co. or tie your own using a bobbin and thread.

Here are three sizes of Nok Sets. The small one on the right is normally used on light target-style bows, since the bands aren't quite large enough for the thicker hunter strings. These would work with a small number of Fast Flight strands. The middle one is what used to be used for hunting bows, but most of us have turned to the wider, larger nock on the left which works well on the 16-strands-plus serving found on most hunter strings.

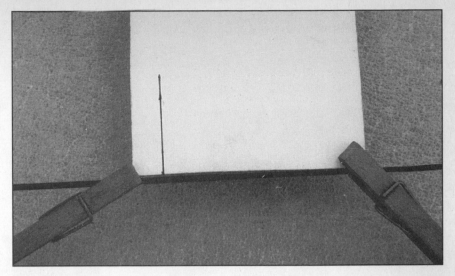

You need some method of finding a right angle to the arrow rest on the bow. This shows how to use cardboard set up with a nocking point marked at 1/2-inch. The unit is held in place with clothespins for illustration, but it gives you a starting point for your nock. You can mark the string with yellow wax pencil or masking tape.

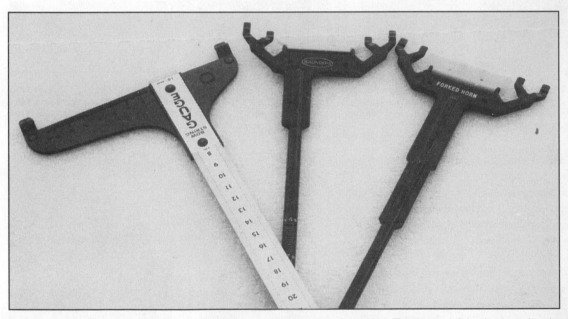

Here are three string bow squares used for marking or setting the nock position. The one on left in aluminum has its graduations in millimeters for more accurate settings. The long one-sided unit in the middle can also be used for setting the nock, a kisser or other units on the upper section of the string. This one on the right is basically used for marking nock location.

Stotler, who had supplied it for the tests. The arrow was nocked as usual, and when released, it almost missed the top bale.

"Then it dawned on me that Dishion must nock above the nock instead of below it, as I have done for years. He has his technique, I have mine. They both work," Learn says.

Many years ago, archers made their own nocking points with dental floss or light thread—lighter than serving material, at least. This worked well, but they did come loose once in a while after much shooting.

One of the first commercially made nocking points was made by Saunders Archery. It was called the Nok Set. It was a band of thin metal with a light rubber backing on it that merely clamped around the bowstring at the determined nocking point. It stayed in place until it was taken off.

"Those first Nok Sets were a bit on the small side for the 16-strand Dacron B-50 strings I usually make, but they worked," Learn recalls.

Not long after that, Saunders became aware of the bigger-string problem and made a wider, thicker nock locator that is hard to beat even today.

"Other types of string nocks have come on the market and I

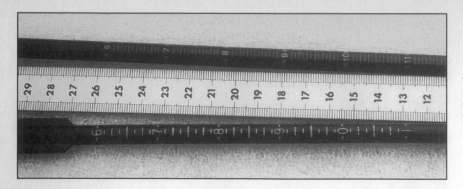

The bottom unit has 1/8-inch markings, the middle aluminum unit is in millimeters and the top unit has 1/16-inch markings for really tight figuring; they all work.

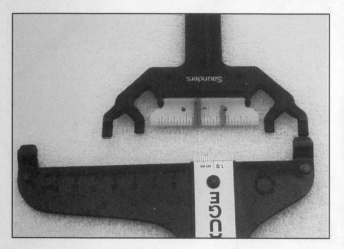

The Saunders unit at top has been marked with a felt-tip pen for easy reference to the 1/2-inch line above right angles to the string. The lower unit has a nock locator scale in millimeters. One-inch equals 25.4mm for reference in marking with this type unit.

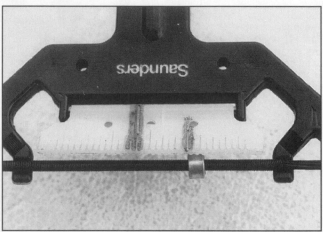

The Saunders has become a favorite unit since it is shaped round like an arrow shaft. This allows the jig to sit on the arrow rest as the arrow would and gives good positioning. The Nok Set has been placed on the string at the 1/2-inch mark and is ready for crimping.

haven't tried them all. When I find something that works as well as the Saunders, I stay with it.

"There was an early problem with some nocks in that, with the monofilament serving that became popular, it was hard to seat the nock tight, so we merely placed another Nok Set above the first to lock it in place and solved that problem."

Just where do you place the nock on the string? Recently, we picked up three different publications from manufacturers that discussed placing a nocking point on the string for constant arrow location. Two of the three failed to tell the reader where to place the nock for a particular shooting result. Do you place the arrow above or below the nock? The instructions for two didn't cover that, but the third supplied a chart that showed the arrow below the nock.

Place the nocking point where you will have a constant draw on the bowstring, but first determine where you plan to nock the arrow. Many bowhunters nock below the nocking point, but others nock above it. Either is correct, but both will get different arrow flight.

"I prefer to nock with the arrow below the nocking point. That way, I never have to take my eyes off the game or the spot I'm concentrating on. I can slip the arrow from its keeper, find the cock feather by the protusion on the arrow nock, bring the arrow nock up to the string nock without ever looking at it and draw, anchor and release without ever taking my eyes from the target," Learn says.

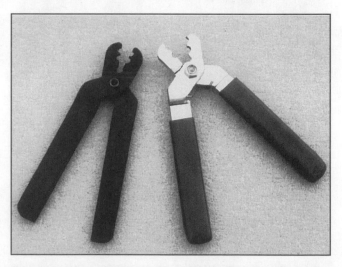

Here are two sets of crimping pliers made by Saunders. The one on the left is the older style, but they work well for all size Nok Sets. The newer unit on the right has a spring in it to hold the pliers open to make them easier to use. Note the pointed tip for removing Nok Sets or loosening them for relocation if necessary.

You may nock your arrow in a different location, and if it works for you, that is great. But try other methods, too; they might be better.

"When I shoot arrow after arrow from the shooting machine with a caliper release, I find that if I nock the arrow too close to the string nock, it will be pushed off the string

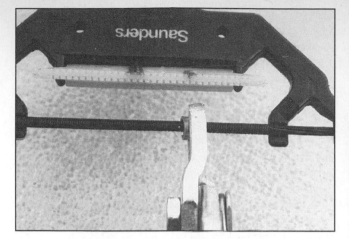

The Nok Set is held at the 1/2-inch mark, the pliers engaged and light pressure applied to crimp the nock in place. The bar above pliers merely swings up out of the way, but gives an instant reading if you move during the crimp.

This string is served with monofilament. That can often cause a bit of a crimping problem since it is so small and slick for the Nok Set. The new wide units seldom need a backup unit, but one has been placed above the set nock and will be crimped to prevent the nock from moving during shooting.

before I get to full draw. The release aid pushes against the bottom of the arrow nock, making it come off the string. I doubt this would happen in the field, but I don't use this type release for hunting and can't say one way or the other," says Learn.

Some release-aid shooters use a double nocking system, with the arrow below one nock for a constant and another nocking point on the string below the arrow nock. This can prevent the release from pushing the arrow nock and causing bad flight. This double nock works and is used in the hunting fields as well as on the target ranges.

"One of the wildest nocking points I have seen is used by a friend who seldom misses anything at which he aims." Learn says. "He uses a double-hook bow lock and the arrow nock goes between the two hooks. To use this system, he ties a slim nocking point on the string, then notches, files and fits his arrow nocks to fit it. He has great success in the field and on animal targets."

How high should the nocking point be on the bowstring? Again the directions vary from 1/8- to 1/2-inch from the right angle of the arrow rest on the bow. To put a nocking point on a string, you need a right-angle system to find the exact square setting of the rest to the string. There are many string markers or nocking point systems on the market, and Learn uses the Saunders Pronghorn.

"This gives me a right angle from the rest to the string and a choice of arrow height using the measured markings on the vertical section of the jig that goes along the string. I always start and usually stay at 1/2-inch above the vertical for my nocking point on the string."

If you don't have a nocking jig, it's not a problem. Use a piece of light cardboard, making sure the edge is straight and is at right angles to the edge you put against the string. Make a mark 1/2-inch up from the bottom edge for your nocking point. The cardboard can be used in the field if you forget to carry a nocking gauge of some sort. It really does work!

Over the years, many nocking jigs have been introduced.

One Learn used for some years was made of light aluminum and had the spaces marked in millimeters. "This is handy since the device is accurate and one doesn't have to count the spaces on the measuring bar to determine whether it is marked off in eighths or sixteenths of an inch. You do need to convert from inches to millimeters, or vice versa. There are 25.4mm in 1-inch. So, if you want 1/2-inch, you use 12 or 13mm."

If you know where to nock, make your mark on the bowstring 1/2-inch above the vertical, place a Nok Set—lightly crimped—on the serving at that point and shoot your normal hunting arrows and release system, be it a three fingers, rope or caliper system, observing the arrow flight.

If the arrows hit high from your aiming point, raise the nocking point a bit by twisting it on the serving. When you get an arrow that flies true and gives you a round ball of colored fletch going downrange, that is the correct nocking point for your shooting style and your arrows. Crimp the Nok Set down tight. You can crimp too tight, however, and break monofilament strands, so take it easy with the pliers.

If your arrow strikes low, raise the nocking point, using the same technique, until you get clean arrow flight. This, of course, assumes you have the arrow rest and pressure plunger set properly.

If you want to get fussy, there is something available called the paper test for correct arrow/nock alignment. You can learn about this by writing Easton and requesting their tech sheet on arrow/bow tuning. This approach isn't complicated, but it is time-consuming. It is a positive test.

The size of the nock on your arrow will also determine your nocking point. If you shoot cedar arrows, you will use the 11/32 nock. If you shoot the light Easton P/C carbons, they call for a nock that is quite small. Tune the nocking point for the size of the nock on your shaft or it won't function properly. This shouldn't be a problem, however, since one should never go into the field with a quiver of arrows of different sizes, spines and nocks.

If you want to try tying your nocking point, it is simple to do.

Place a piece of masking tape ½-inch above the vertical from the arrow rest. Use the masking tape as a reference, since it's difficult to mark a black string. A yellow marking crayon might work, but the tape is easy.

Using 16-gauge sewing thread or dental floss, which wraps tight and is tough, lay one end on the string and start turning the loose end around the string. Wrap up the laid string for about ¼-inch. Turn it back and make layers of thread using this small overlay procedure.

After a few solid wraps, pull the loose end tight to get it snugged up against the laid thread. Build a small ledge—enough to give your arrow a stopping point—and tie it off. You can make a big, medium or small nocking point, but a small one might slip over the snap nock system and give you a bad nocking point. Medium to large is best—and it can't be too large.

To tie off the nock, merely move up the string, make some reverse loops just as you tie off a serving on the bowstring, and reverse wrap this onto the nock or just above it. When you have one loop left on your finger, pull the loose end, drawing up the loop, to give you a solid nock. A few drops of fletching cement on the string nock will make it even more permanent.

The one drawback about this thread nock is that if you place it at the wrong spot, you have to remove it and do it over again. It's not a real problem, just a nuisance that takes a few minutes to cure.

Buy some Saunders Nok Sets, a nocking jig, pliers for crimping the metal bands and set your nocking point. Nock your arrow above, below or between the string nock as you prefer, but try them all before making your decision.

Regardless of where you place it, a nocking point on your hunting bow offers a solid position for placing your arrow when you get that big buck in front of you.

The nocking point is important to consistent, accurate shooting, so put one on your hunting bow, then practice, practice, practice! You'll get your game with a good, clean hit—and that is what it is all about!

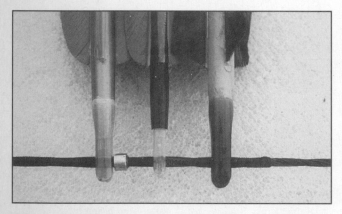

The size of the arrow nock also relates to the location of the nock on the bowstring. The nock on the left is the standard unit used on most aluminum shafts, the little, clear one in the middle is similar to those used on some of the carbon arrows now popular, and the big unit on the right is mounted on a cedar shaft for those who like shooting them. They all work, but you should only use one size when hunting.

If you want to be more traditional or don't want to carry your pliers or nocking system into hunting camp, don't despair. This bobbin filled with heavy sewing thread is always in the tackle box to repair a string serving or tie off a thread nock on the bowstring. This is an older system that still works well, especially on mono string servings. Note the section of masking tape placed as the starting point for tying the nock onto the string. It is faster this way and you can see where to turn around very easily.

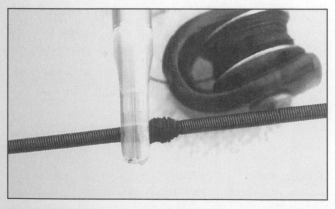

The thread nock has been tied off and is ready to shoot. Normally you should add a few drops of fletching cement to hold the threads in place, but it wasn't done here or the threads would be much tighter above the arrow nock.

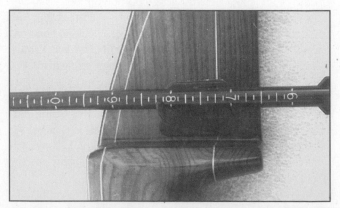

Another use for the Saunders or other type of locator unit is to measure the brace height on your bow. You can't get it into the center if the grip pivot point in this manner, but you can check it to the back of the bow after it is attached to the string. You can remove the unit from the string, place it on the grip pivot point and measure back to the string for the other type of measuring system. This shows about 7¾ inches from the wrist pivot or 9⅛ inches from the back of the bow; take your choice.

5 *3-D Target Shooting*

Whether You're Practicing For Hunting Or Tournaments, The Challenge Is For All

Archers of all sizes, ages and experience levels participate in this sport. Animal targets are set in realistic terrains at reasonable distances.

ARCHERS HAVE BEEN shooting at targets since bows and arrows were invented. Early man probably used tree stumps, bare spots on hillsides, clumps of grass and anything else they could use to hone their skills.

More modern targets have been made of straw, wood chips, cotton and ground plastic pipe stuffed into burlap bags, inexactly resembling animal's bodies. All kinds of other materials also have been used. The object was to use something that would stop an arrow, but let the arrow be withdrawn with minimum effort. The goal was not always met in actual practice. It has only been since the development and widespread utilization of the liquid foam technology used to make the targets that 3-D target animals have become universally available. Their realism and suitability for archery have helped spread the sport's popularity.

Bowhunters want to make the best, quickest and most lethal hit possible on their game. Practice with realistic targets is sure to improve any hunter's chances of success when after the real thing. There is no cut-and-dried answer as to where and when 3-D targets were first used. However, there are those who contend that the site probably was in the vicinity of Fresno, California, and the time period was in late '70s or early '80s.

In the archery circles, perhaps the most copied tournament in the world is known as the Fresno Safari. For nearly forty years, this annual event has been drawing archery enthusiasts from all over the nation. This weekend tournament is designed as a family event. Originally set up strictly as a field archery tournament under the auspices of the National Field Archery Association, the event has developed a personality of its own.

First came the targets. Instead of small targets that look like animals scattered at various distances, the Fresno Safari has long had targets big enough that even a poor shot can make a respectable score. Take, for example, the 12-foot-high elephant that has long been a feature of this shoot.

Establishing a large 3-D target course takes plenty of volunteer help and several days of hard work. This course, in Redding, California, shows annual improvements and is always well groomed for participating archers. This elk scene requires plenty of labor to set up.

Members of this club, the Fresno Field Archers, work year-round to make this shoot a success, and each member is assigned a specific task aimed at bettering the tournament. The targets are left to the imaginations of the members, and there have been some real winners over the years, in addition to that elephant. Most are cutouts posted against sturdy backing to handle the hundreds of arrows that are shot into them each day during competition. In the evening, the targets are repaired to as near original condition as possible, then draped in plastic as protection against possible inclement weather such as rain or fog.

Each year, there is at least one full-scale lion silhouette, and usually more. The more ambitious will rival the elephant by producing a life-size reproduction of a hippo or a rhino. An early eye-catcher was a full-size gorilla that a gent named Doug Walker developed and hung from a tree to try the mettle of the competing archers.

A layout such as this, of course, requires room, and the Fresno club spent a number of years sort of wandering from range to range. However, as the annual event grew bigger, members realized there had to be a better solution.

In 1958, they found 37 acres in the foothills of the Sierra Range, 40-plus miles from the city of Fresno. The club leased the land with an option to buy. Then they found they could lease an adjoining 20 acres once or twice a year if they wanted to put on a big shoot. And yet another 20 acres was available for parking and camping on a lease basis also, if needed.

The original tract was purchased and the mortgage paid off in only six years. Each year, the Fresno Safari shoot makes money for the club and uses it to improve facilities, including the addition of an enclosed playground with swings and sandboxes for youngsters too young to compete.

Mule deer and antelope may not appear together, but they often share the same habitat. The animal targets may be placed at will.

President of the Fresno Field Archers during this development period was one Harry Hinze. Like other presidents of the club, he had been elected on his ability to get things done. His platform for election was based on his plans for developing a program of added club activities. But with this ever-increasing activity had come a call for targets that would be even more demanding than the life-scale cutouts that had brought the club its fame in field-archery circles.

It was about 1985, according to the recollections of some members of long standing, that the first three-dimensional target was entered in the meet. This was an animal—admittedly somewhat crude in appearance—that had been carved

Equipment and courses for the youngest shooters are always popular with the little guys at tournaments such as Arizona's Bowhunter's Happening. Adults see that the kids have plenty of fun while they are being introduced to the sport of the future.

All archery ranges should have a practice area and provisions for novelty shoots. Foreground targets are removed before competition.

Another factor in the popularity of 3-D target archery is the possibility of substantial prize money for those skilled and lucky enough to score well. Does Gary have a great name for an archer or what?

Blocks of foam are glued together, then shaped and sanded to resemble large game animals.

An electric-powered knife cuts through foam easily. This type of labor-intensive construction is seldom seen today because liquid foam is now used.

and assembled from bits of junk styrofoam. There was some difficulty making repairs at the end of the first day of shooting, as arrows equipped with field points tended to pass totally through the bulk of the target. In short, several hundred arrows turned the target into what amounted to a shambles. However, the die apparently was cast. There suddenly was a demand for what has come to be known as 3-D targets. Tournament participants took the idea back to their own clubs, and members began to develop life-size—if not necessarily lifelike—three-dimensional animals for their own field-archery tournaments.

Early on, styrofoam tended to be used as the body agent for creatures that were carved in some semblance of game animals, but the repair problem didn't improve to any great degree in spite of efforts to coat the styrofoam with various preparations meant to keep the material in one piece. However, those individuals who saw a commercial manufacturing potential realized almost immediately that stronger materials would be needed. It was accepted, also, that instead of carving animals, the logical answer would be to cast them in moulds that would not only handle more stable materials, but would also give a more realistic, life-like appearance to these three-dimensional, full-size animal targets.

As you will read in later chapters, the foam target material is created by mixing liquid chemicals together, pouring the resulting mixture into a hard mould and waiting for the substance to cure and harden to the point that the mould is broken open and the life-size target removed.

The resulting target has a color that closely resembles the live animal and is about the same typical size. If the artist knows his business, the moulded target will have all the physical characteristics of the live animal. Further, the cured foam target will be able to withstand hundreds, perhaps thousands, of arrow hits while still maintaining its original shape. The arrows will not be too difficult to remove and will not pass entirely through the tar-

get. The challenge is to develop foam targets that will stop even the fastest carbon-fiber arrows.

As the popularity of animal target archery tournaments grows around the country, so does the development of better and faster archery equipment. The growth of 3-D target shooting has spurred manufacturers to produce better, more reliable bows and arrows, seemingly advancing further and faster than the popularity of bowhunting over the past several decades. Every manufacturer has come to realize the impact of the growth of 3-D target shooting and is attempting to meet the demand.

Archers want faster, more reliable bows that will be able to launch arrows at speeds approaching 300 feet per second. It was not so long ago that 200 fps was considered the benchmark speed for target arrows. The faster arrows are not only possible, they have become commonplace; so commonplace that some archery organizations have placed maximum speed limits on arrows to be shot at their authorized tournaments. Some officials have come to feel 300 fps is too dangerous for the equipment, shooters and targets.

The bows for 3-D shooting are more colorful than hunting bows, if nothing else. The brighter, the shinier, the sparklier, the better they sell. It is common to see bright neon-like and fluorescent colors, two-tones, three-tones, glittering finishes, multiple colors and what seem to be brand-new, freshly developed colors on bows and accessories.

With the development of better, faster bows have come improved accessories. Arrows have seen considerable improvement in the past few years. Every major arrow manufacturer now offers carbon-fiber shafts designed primarily for 3-D target shooters. The shafts are stiffer, lighter, smaller in diameter and may last longer, despite the hundreds of shots per tournament or the countless hours of practice. Many of the top professional archers are shooting carbon-fiber arrows.

Development continues by the manufacturers to find a shaft

With enough foam or bales of straw, even large exotic animals may be depicted and used for 3-D target archery.

Seen on the skyline, even a primitive 3-D lion target takes on realism.

formula with a spine that will satisfy a wider range of bow draw weights. In other words, the goal is to develop one shaft size or spine that will fly well from bows with draw weights ranging from, say, thirty-five to seventy pounds, while still satisfying the rules laid down by the major tournament organizations.

We are seeing hundreds of other products on the market for the 3-D shooter. Such things as bow sights with micro-adjustments; stronger, more sensitive mechanical releases; finger tabs; belt quivers; target points that lessen damage on foam 3-D targets; arrow rests; even shirts and shoes are available to the serious target shooter.

Long-time target manufacturers are adding plant capacity to meet the demand from their customers, and they are adding more and different animal targets. The most common targets are deer poses, but mountain goats, sheep, elk, bear, wild pigs, javelina, mountain lions, wild turkeys, and dozens of other exotic and fantastic animals are available to help make target tournaments more interesting and challenging for shooters.

Groups of club members working together can fashion a set of foam targets for tournaments and club practice. Today, the animal targets are more likely to be purchased from manufacturers.

In addition, companies that did not have targets in their line are adding 3-D targets to their catalogs for individual and tournament buyers. It has become big business.

Three-dimensional target shooting has become extremely popular with women and children, as well as with the traditional, older male bowhunters. And the sport has grown beyond merely providing spring and early summer target practice for bowhunters. Many target shooters are not—and probably will not become—hunters. Their game is, and will remain, target competition.

Another development of the sport concerns the emergence of professional 3-D target archers. With the backing of archery manufacturers and other associated supporters, target archery has found the financial maturity to offer money prizes generous enough that skilled shooters can earn $50,000 or more a year from tournament winnings. True, not many are yet able to support themselves with their archery winnings, but the numbers are growing.

Several archery groups are moving toward establishing organizations similar to the Professional Golfers' Association. While it is unlikely any archery professionals would earn as much as the top professional golfers, comfortable annual incomes are already possible. As the numbers of competitors increase, as corporate sponsorships increase and as popularity of 3-D target tournaments continues to grow, there may be increased television coverage and exposure of the sport. With that will come the big dollars that professional, spectator-popular sports enjoy. More exposure and more dollars will attract even more archers.

There is but one way to get into the sport, whether you are now a bowhunter or you have never shot an arrow. Beg, buy or borrow some mid-quality equipment and practice until you can hit where you aim. Then locate a 3-D archery tournament near you. There should be dozens within driving distance throughout the normal spring and summer months.

If there is a professional archery dealer nearby, he will know the dates and places of all local tournaments. He may even have an indoor range or an indoor reactive television shooting facility; shooting dates and times are at your convenience.

Try it. Get the family involved. This book is meant to help you get started or shoot better with the right equipment. The appeal is fun.

6 Selecting Your 3-D Bow

With Hundreds of Models Available, Choose The One Best Suited For The Task

IT MAY SEEM a bewildering and difficult assignment, picking out the best bow to shoot at bullseyes, 3-D targets, paper targets and game animals. The short, simple answer is to get a bow that best suits you and that you can afford. It is a bit like answering the question, "What is the best car I should buy?" There is no single, perfect bow for every shooter, nor for every task. You must start with a bow that fits you physically and mentally. The process may be narrowed down step by step.

Most 3-D target shooters look for a bow that will produce a fast, flat-shooting arrow. The bow must be consistent; all the arrows of a target tournament must fly the same way every shot. The bow should have a smooth, even draw that is easy on the muscles. Shooting hundreds of arrows over two or three days, the bow will probably not be set up at a high draw weight, although the requirement for a fast arrow may dictate a heavier draw. The bow must be solid, well made and comfortable for the archer, with as little felt recoil as possible. Rattles and other noise may be disconcerting to target archers, but it is not as important as it is to bowhunters. Most target archers select a bow that sports bright, shiny paint or chrome components. Perhaps it is a reaction to the dull camouflage colors one must use while bowhunting.

If you are strictly a bowhunter, the purpose of shooting target tournaments is probably to become a better hunter, a better shooter under simulated hunting conditions. Use the same bow, arrows and accessories for target work as you do for hunting. The only extra thing you may need is some additional arrows to replace those lost or damaged during hundreds of practice shots. Before you get to the point of shooting in any tournaments, though, you will want to do plenty of practice with your new 3-D bow.

Shoot a couple of local 3-D meets and you will be a better archer because of it. You'll be challenged by some unusual animal targets and shots through difficult terrain, up and down

Emery Loiselle draws the McPherson Magna Eliminator bow. It is one of the shorter bows, producing a fast arrow.

The High Country 3-D Supreme is designed for target shooting, as the name implies. It is one of the fastest bows.

The shape of the Golden Eagle Vision puts the limb fulcrums well forward of the riser.

The Jennings Uniforce is a bow using only one eccentric cam on the bottom limb, with a round pulley on top.

hills, across streams, from towers and down overgrown shooting lanes. Target shooting will not make you a better stalker or more patient on the stand, but you will become a more confident flinger of arrows. It is not uncommon for longtime bowhunters to try one of the major 3-D target events for the only purpose of improving their shooting for hunting. Suddenly, they find they are having a great time, talking and shooting with many of their hunting buddies. They are seeing the latest available equipment and they are shooting alongside some of the top competitors. They may also see their buddies winning some cold cash, finishing in the top twenty shooters of their class. Most feel that as long as they are shooting in archery tournaments throughout most of the summer months, they should get competitive and perhaps take home some of that prize money. Besides, it's a lot of fun!

As mentioned, many archers choose to shoot in the various bowhunter classes, using the same equipment as for hunting. There are no requirements that target bows be compounds, but most are. There are the occasional traditional-bows-only contests, but their numbers are small. Figures have not been accurately compiled, but more than ninety percent of all 3-D target tournaments are for any bow, and more than ninety percent of all the shooters are using compounds.

At most tournaments, archers using longbows or recurves are in the competition for the fun and the challenge, rather than for the big dollar prizes. Most of the money goes into the fund to pay Compound, Unlimited Equipment shooters. They are the most popular and reflect the highest raw scores. Traditional equipment shooters draw their share of crowds, though. To most of us, it is incredible to see longbow shooters with no sights, mechanical releases or other such equipment putting arrow after arrow directly into the vital scoring zones of the foam animal targets.

Longbows and recurves are virtually custom-made for individual archers; they are quite personal. Advice for archers about traditional bows must be general in nature; the specifics must be worked out between the shooter and the bowyer.

Some traditional archers have come from the compound bow ranks, however. They have decided to simplify and get back to tradition. They may have twenty or more years of

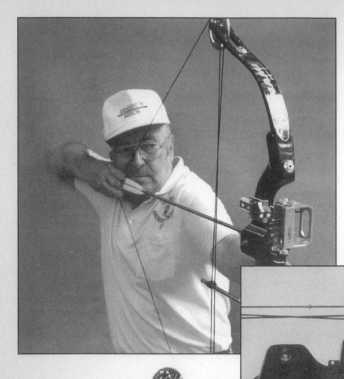

Pro Line's Tsunami has the bright, high-tech look favored by 3-D shooters.

Glossy, fade-color paint and chrome and stainless steel mark the Pro Line Tsunami as a target bow. The eccentric wheels are large.

Browning's Pro 600 target bow in jade is ideal for 3-D shooters.

experience with compound bows and simply want to experience shooting a longbow. They may feel technology has taken over and have a desire to return to something simpler in their lives. There is no doubt that a longbow or recurve hunting bow is much lighter and less bulky in the field. For moving carefully through heavy undergrowth, a lightweight longbow cannot be bettered.

Others have never used any other bow. After all, recurves and longbows were good enough for the likes of Fred Bear, Howard Hill and even Robin Hood! Choosing and using a traditional bow is highly personal. There are several fine production recurves on the market which are fine for most hunting or 3-D target shooting. Given reasonable care, one of these bows will last for years; perhaps a lifetime for most archers. A string or two might have to be replaced over a couple of decades, but nothing else, barring some sort of accidental damage. After all, there are no moving parts!

Learning to shoot a traditional bow well is much like learning to throw a baseball or hit a golf ball. There are no sights on the balls, but a good pitcher can throw one through a small opening time after time, at a speed upward of ninety miles per hour. Given a certain amount of hand/eye coordination and physical ability, all it takes is practice, practice, practice.

Watch a good longbow shooter and it appears that he does not aim at all. He draws the string back to his anchor point fast; there is no hesitation. As soon as the anchor point is touched,

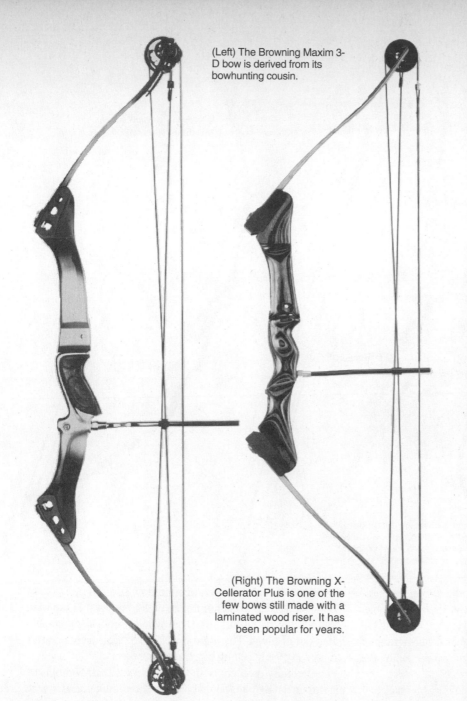

(Left) The Browning Maxim 3-D bow is derived from its bowhunting cousin.

(Right) The Browning X-Cellerator Plus is one of the few bows still made with a laminated wood riser. It has been popular for years.

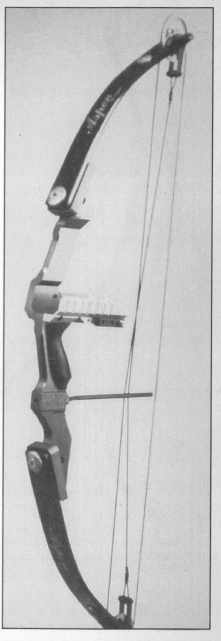

The Alpine Aspen features a machined aluminum riser in tournament colors.

the string and arrow are released. It is all one smooth, quick motion. And the arrow hits the target almost every time. Trick shooters can hit objects such as quarters, dimes and aspirin tablets thrown into the air!

Of course, they do aim. They arc aiming before they draw. They are so familiar with their equipment and have practiced enough that they know where the arrow will go with each shot.

Selecting a traditional bow is a highly personal matter. Those with enough experience—and money—will want to obtain a fine custom-built bow made to order by an experienced professional bowyer. There are dozens of makers around the country who turn out excellent longbows or recurves, one at a time, made to measure.

The compound bow, patented in 1966, literally revolution-ized the archery industry and the sport of archery. The action of the eccentric wheels at the limb tips allows the archer to draw and hold a high-poundage bow with little effort. The energy storage is in the bow limbs, stored there after being created by the archer's muscles. The average archer can shoot a bow with faster arrows than ever thought possible from recurves or longbows.

The early compound bows by Tom Jennings and other pioneers were considered ugly by most shooters; it was a few years after their invention before the design was accepted by a large percentage of archers.

Bow & Arrow Hunting magazine's technical editor, Emery Loiselle, says the cable-and-wheel system on compound bows provides a block-and-tackle effect. The eccentric wheel with its off-center axle hole acts as an ever-changing leverage system

For the more advanced shooter, the Ben Pearson Pro Classic features laminated limbs.

The Ben Pearson Blazer utilizes smaller wheels.

For those who prefer the traditional, the modern Black Swan uses a computer to help with the design. The Black Swan recurve is lightweight, using modern materials for a fast arrow.

between the bow limbs and the shooter. Furthermore, the compound bow, with its fulcrum-mounted limbs, is highly adjustable, a feature most modern archers have come to expect. Drawing the string on a compound bow provides the mechanical advantage of moving the short, stiff limbs a short distance and propelling the arrow at tremendous speed.

The eccentric wheel provides an ever-changing leverage that is in favor of the bow at the beginning of the draw, but in favor of the archer near full draw. In the strung position, the cable anchored at the opposite axle is farther from the eccentric axle than is the bowstring. The bow limbs have the mechanical advantage, and the draw becomes heavy during the first few inches of string travel. As the wheels peak near the middle of the draw, the leverage forces even out, and then start to change. Approaching full draw, the bowstring is farther from the axle and the archer gains the mechanical advantage. This is what causes the let-off the archer experiences shortly before full draw.

Most 3-D shooters and most bowhunters use compound bows. They want the most modern, highest tech, computer-assisted bow design they can buy. Manufacturers recognize the demand for the product, and they are producing bows the majority of consumers want.

Not so long ago, most compound bow risers were made of wood—laminated wood reinforced with fiberglass. These were and are beautiful, useful bows, but wood risers have gradually fallen out of favor. There are only a couple of manufacturers still making them, selling to a limited market.

The primary problem with wood risers is that, without the maximum strength that metal provides, building the riser with a window cut past centershot may weaken the bow handle. With a traditional bow, most arrows are shot off the shelf of the handle. The arrows actually bend around the handle as they are released, but recover their previous straight condition a few feet after the release. This is called archer's paradox. The shaft bends around the riser upon release, over-corrects after it leaves the bow, re-bends slightly a couple more times in initial flight, and then theoretically flies straight into its target.

Risers made of metal are produced easily with the launching area cut well past center. There is some bending of the shaft upon release, but it is not required to bend around the riser. A small amount of curving is noted by high-speed cameras, caused by the pushing effect of the string upon the rear of the arrow. The arrow rest and the string are aligned in a straight line before, during and after the release. The shoot-

The Darton Concord has a machined riser and modern looks.

The Ben Pearson Renegade features bright colors and recurve limbs.

through or centershot riser design is ideal for the archer using a mechanical release aid. Those favoring a shoot-around riser and arrow rest are advised to use a finger tab on the string hand.

Three-D bow shooters seem to prefer faster, stiffer, shorter arrows. It is easier to design in attachments for overdraw shelves that will not wobble or rattle with a metal riser. Such may not be the case with a wooden bow handle. It is a relatively simple matter to include locking detents and threaded holes in a metal riser for such things as overdraws, sights and bow quivers.

Lightweight cast aluminum, aluminum alloy and magnesium are the most popular materials for compound bow risers. Magnesium is strong, relatively easy to handle in the factory and inexpensive to produce. Most manufacturers have several magnesium risers in their line. However, in 1993, the trend toward machined aluminum risers really began to roll. All the large producers are currently incorporating the high-tech look of machined aluminum in their bows, and most have added computer-controlled machinery to produce the risers in their own factories.

Aluminum alloy is more expensive and machining takes time, skill and money to produce. However, the mould used to

produce a modern magnesium handle bow is even more expensive to design and produce. Figures of $250,000 and more for mould design have been quoted by some bow manufacturers. This cost must be recovered throughout the life of the bow in the marketplace.

Machines that can produce aluminum alloy risers and other components are standard units, available throughout the world, and can be operated by any skilled machinist. Computers assist in the design and production of bow parts from these machines. Even though the alloy may be more expensive, the actual cost of production of a machined riser is less than that of one made from cast magnesium.

The choice of basic metal in the bow's riser is but one of the many decisions any archer must consider. Another is the length of the riser. The longer the riser, the greater the axle-to-axle measurement, and the more open the angle of the string at full draw.

String angle is not as important to those shooting with a mechanical release, but finger shooters are all too aware of the amount of finger pinch derived from many bow designs.

Typically, a long riser measurement would be about 44 or 45 inches, axle-to-axle. Some new, short bows are 39 to 41 inches long. Most of those are used by mechanical release

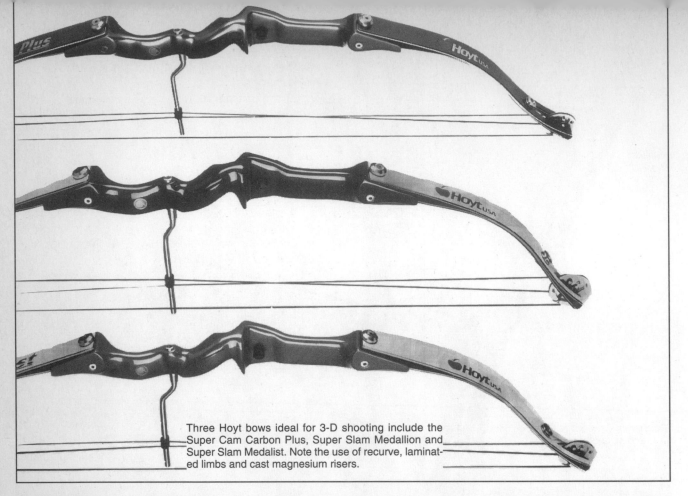

Three Hoyt bows ideal for 3-D shooting include the Super Cam Carbon Plus, Super Slam Medallion and Super Slam Medalist. Note the use of recurve, laminated limbs and cast magnesium risers.

shooters only. The shorter length and shorter brace height can produce speeds of up to 300 feet per second from arrows weighing about 440 grains. For comparison, a typical 44-inch bow might shoot an AMO standard 540-grain arrow at 200 to 245 fps.

Another design factor is placement of the limb fulcrums in relationship to hand placement. Most of the modern compound designs have the fulcrums well forward of the hand placement. This produces a more compact bow design and lower brace height.

At least one manufacturer—Golden Eagle—puts a lift or block between the riser ends and limb butt attachments. The block tends to dampen vibration between limb and handle as well as position the fulcrum a couple of inches forward of the hand. On some of these designs, the tips of the limbs become almost horizontal at full draw.

Back to the subject of riser design, some bows offer a snap-on or screw-on handle grip of wood or soft plastic. For a bowhunter, such a grip can mean comfort on cold mornings in the woods. For the 3-D target archer, it may mean less hand fatigue while shooting hundreds of arrows a day.

Compound bow limbs are most commonly made of solid fiberglass, fiberglass and carbon fibers or a lamination of wood and fiberglass. The laminated limbs are handsome on any risers, particularly on wood handle bows. Laminated carbon graphite and fiberglass is claimed to reduce vibration and recoil as well as provide a long-lasting limb. Such limbs, however, are usually more expensive. Solid fiberglass is the least expensive limb material for most bows.

On most bow designs, the highest arrow speeds are obtained from what are known as radical cams, rather than the simpler eccentric wheels. Shooters who prefer the smoothness of the wheel draw willingly give up a few extra feet per second for the smooth, quiet draw they experience with wheels. For the greatest arrow velocity, however, a bow with radical cam shape is the choice.

Early in cam history, some designs had jerky, uneven draws. The effort required to draw the bow was extreme at first, and then a distinct hump or pause was felt before let-off began. Sometimes, two humps could be felt. Today's modern cams are as smooth as most eccentrics, yielding fast arrows at comfortable draw weights. Some bows offer a choice of interchangeable cams or wheels in different draw lengths and draw weights on the same model.

The newest development in wheels and cams continues into 1995. That is the concept of a single cam on one limb and only an idler wheel or pulley on the other end. All the compounding action takes place in the single cam. The idler wheel simply changes the cable's direction. The concept certainly makes the task of tuning a bow much simpler. The two cams cannot ever get out of synchronization because there is only one on the bottom limb. Manufacturers offering these single-cam bows include Bear, Jennings, Matthews and McPherson. If they prove popular, more makers may be coming up with similar designs. Many in the industry predict that the single cam design is the wave of the future for compound bows.

Compound bow wheels and cams are made of various materials. The most common materials are either machined alu-

The York Wind Hawk Pro Signature Edition has a machined riser, recurve limbs, large adjustable cams and bright colors for 3-D shooters.

The Bear/Jennings One Cam system is the latest development for high-technology bows. The design features a single cam mounted on the lower limb and a round pulley on the upper limb.

compound bows are adjustable for draw length in 1-inch increments. Some have additional half-inch adjustments at the string or cable endings.

Another common adjustment concerns the amount of let-off possible in the compounding action of the bow. A few years ago, the most common let-off was 50 percent. The 60-pound draw weight bow required only 30 pounds of effort to hold it in the drawn position.

Recently, bows with more let-off have become the standard. Most now offer either a choice of 50 or 65 percent—or they may be adjusted to either position. Many others, particularly 3-D bows, are being offered with 80 percent let-off. Some tournament organizations have established restrictions on the amount of let-off bows may have in their contests. Some states have restricted the amount of let-off at 65 percent for bowhunting.

Some archers and designers say that better control, more consistent arrows and less wear to bow components are the results of no more than 50 percent let-off. High let-off and heavy draw weights put considerable strain on a bow's components as well as established tuning aspects.

After shooting for some time, most bowstrings will stretch enough to put the bow out of tune. Any material will stretch some small but measurable amount, but steel and synthetic polymer systems show only the smallest expansion with use. The fastest bows use synthetic strings. This material's lighter weight and inelasticity will add several feet per second to arrow speed, resulting in flatter trajectory.

Another consideration is a bow of left- or right-hand design. Any experienced archer will know whether he has a dominant left or right eye. But many beginners have no idea of the effect of trying to aim arrows for hundreds of practice shots with the weaker eye. It is not uncommon for an individual to be right-handed and left-eyed or vice versa. Learn which is the dominant eye at the start of the learning curve and practice that way to avoid the necessity of re-learning or un-learning bad habits. Drawing the bow with the weak hand may seem awkward at first, but aiming with the dominant eye will pay dividends in the long run.

Walking through and shooting for two days over a hilly 3-D course can be tiring for almost any archer. Carrying a heavy bow, plenty of arrows in a hip quiver and various other accessories can add up to several pounds. Die-cast magnesium and machined aluminum bows tend to be a pound or so heavier than a similar wood-handle bow.

For some, obtaining the best available bow is the most important factor and the price is irrelevant. For beginners, the lowest price is primary. Most of us fall somewhere in between those extremes. In 1995 dollars, new compound bow prices range from about $200 on up to more than $1,000. Most professional archery shops have excellent bow choices in the $600 to $800 range to suit the needs of serious 3-D target shooters. Sights, quivers, cases, arrows and accessories can add $300 to the price tag.

No matter the cost, there is no substitute for plenty of practice. Technology will not win tournaments; good shooting will.

minum or nylon-filled fiberglass. Over the years, all sorts of materials have been tried. Eccentrics have been made of wood, fiberglass, steel and plastic. They must be lightweight and accurately formed to provide consistent performance with every shot.

Today's modern compounds offer all sorts of draw lengths and tuning adjustments. Each manufacturer seems to use a slightly different approach to the problem. Some bows must be put in a bow press with the limbs slightly flexed to loosen the bowstring before a draw length adjustment is possible. Others are designed so the 1- or 2-inch adjustments are made with only a small screwdriver or Allen wrench while the bow remains in the strung position.

This is a real benefit to families with only one bow and several archers or for others who wish to try someone else's bow. Some archers find their draw lengths gradually increase as they become more proficient and stronger with practice. Early in the practice season, the draw length may be, say, 28 inches. After a few weeks of practice, one may find stronger back muscles mean a draw length of 28 1/2 or 29 inches. A bow that is easy to adjust makes things much happier for those shooters. Most

7

3-D Targets

Realism In Size, Color And Shape Is The Key To 3-D Targets

THE USE OF TARGETS is, no doubt, almost as old as the development of bows and arrows. Whoever invented a stick with a string to propel another stick at an animal good enough to eat probably started by practicing with something which simulated food for the table.

Archery targets can be anything within range that can accept and hold an arrow. They are concentric circles of different colors for Olympic-type archery, animal figures painted on paper or burlap cloth, tree stumps, clumps of grass, a stuffed bag high on a pole or anything else we might imagine. The important factor is that the target accept and hold the arrow in such a manner that a hit can be seen and scored. The target should not be of a material that will damage the arrow or the arrowhead, and it should allow the arrow to be removed with relative ease.

The idea of shooting at game animal images as practice for hunting is not new, either. In modern times, shortly after Saxton Pope and Howard Young began bowhunting around the world and when Pope began publishing stories about their adventures, somebody got the idea of practice. Shooting at bullseye paper targets is an excellent way to learn the sport of archery and see improvement from day to day. The colors of the target rings are easy to see at bowhunting distances, and the techniques of good arrow shooting are easily learned using standard archery targets. Bullseye targets have been, and will continue to be, used by most archers.

For decades, target animals painted or drawn on paper and backed with straw or stuffed burlap butts have been used by the National Field Archery Association for competition and practice. Originally, the use of animal target faces was for practice. In time, target competition became a goal in itself. Many NFAA shooters are not hunters and do not intend to become bowhunters. The excitement and competition of shooting at realistic animal targets are the reasons many field archers engage in the sport.

Field archery has become increasingly popular throughout the world, particularly in parts of Europe where bowhunting is not legal, as well as throughout North America. The targets are not expensive, although a sixty-target tournament

Ames All Weather Targets are printed on water-resistant treated burlap to withstand the ravages of wet weather. Although two-dimensional, these targets are ideal for practice with straw bales behind them.

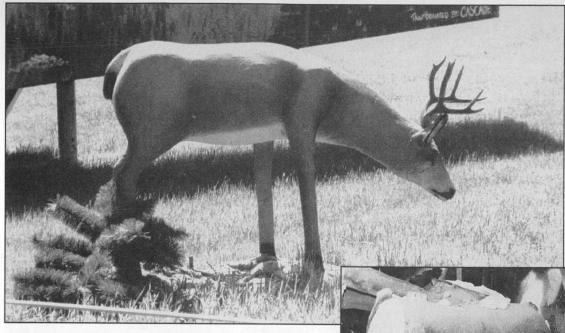

The Critter Factory one-piece mule deer target is realistic and very popular on the West Coast.

Repair sections at The Critter Factory disclose the action of expanding foam within hard moulds.

will require at least three times that many straw bales for the butts.

The animals depicted can be illustrated in any situation, position or color. They do not even have to depict real animals or legal game animals. Drawing a dragon, a woolly mammoth, an elephant or anything else takes no more skill than illustrating a whitetail deer. Kill zones or vital areas of the animals may be drawn on the paper targets for scoring the shots.

As we moved into the last decade of the century, archers began to demand more realism in their animal targets. Instead of paper target faces placed in front of straw or plastic foam butts, people began painting realistic animal images directly on rectangles of plastic foam. An easy step from there was to actually cut out the foam animals from the rectangles. Stanley Hips from Texas has been doing that for years. There is virtually no limit to the number or types of animal targets available with this technique. The targets may be placed in natural settings, complete with obstacles meant to increase the challenge to the archer.

But archers were still not satisfied with this kind of target. They demanded still more realism. This led to the development and production of thousands of three-dimensional animal targets seen in hundreds of target tournaments in all areas. These targets are anatomically and color correct, they are lightweight and moveable, and they can take hundreds of arrow hits and still remain usable.

Deer images are the most popular because deer are the most hunted animals in North America. But the 3-D target animals may be any animal depiction, including fantasy animals. Targets have been made to depict giant spiders, snakes, bugs, onions and extraterrestrials. They are limited only by the imagination and skill of the artist who designs them.

There are several manufacturers of 3-D foam animal targets today, and new ones seem to spring up every month or so. All are marketing realistic animal targets, but each has a slightly different philosophy and product.

How large a market might the 3-D target market be? Consider this: A major target tournament might have forty, sixty or over seventy targets that competitors shoot at over a period of one or two days. In a tournament with a thousand shooters—many of the large events have that many or more signed up — each shooter usually shoots two arrows per target. An easy calculation tells us that each target will have at least 2,000 arrows in it—not counting practice shots or later club shoots on the same targets. Most tournament directors will not accept the expense of replacing the larger, more expensive targets during the tournament, but most of the small animals will need replacing one or two times during the meet. A large tournament—such as the Western Trail Shoot in Redding, California, any of the larger state or regional IBO tournaments or the Bowhunter Happening near Flagstaff, Arizona—must have at least a half-dozen replacement targets for the smaller animal targets and two or three backups for the larger targets during their meets. This means a good market for the target suppliers.

On an individual basis, those archers who keep one or two targets in their backyard strictly for hunting practice might wear

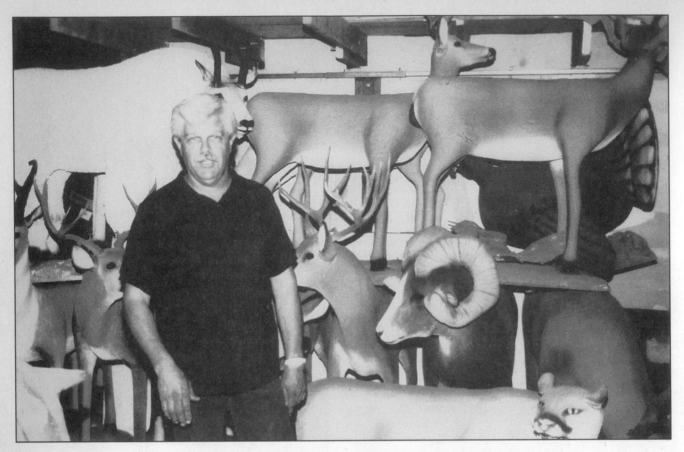

Tom Sellers is the man behind The Critter Factory in Yuba City, California. Sellers pioneered foam archery targets up and down the West Coast more than thirty years ago. Here, completed targets are ready for delivery.

out a target every year or two, especially if all his hunting buddies come around to practice.

Club shoots will use up plenty of targets in a year. As these targets become more available and are marketed more aggressively, competition should drive the price down, and more and more bowhunters will want to have one or two animal targets in their backyard ranges. The market is large and rapidly expanding.

One of the oldest manufacturers of 3-D animal targets is Tom Sellers, operating as **The Critter Factory** in Yuba City, California. Yuba City is an otherwise rather unremarkable little town in central California, but Critter Factory targets have helped make it well known to plenty of club and tournament archers over much of the West Coast. He has been at the target game for nearly three decades.

Sellers started in archery in 1965 and became a member of the local Yuba City archery club, called the Flintstones. The members had determined there was but one method of raising money for the club and that was to hold archery tournaments, using hand-painted cardboard targets. In those days, a tournament might draw seventy-five to eighty shooters.

Sellers, because of his artistic abilities, gradually became the official target painter. He painted the animal targets on cardboard, realistic enough to satisfy the needs of the tournament. Some of the members began to express the desire for more elaborate, more realistic 3-D targets. Sellers remembers

This foam-made Old Timer outside The Critter Factory illustrates the versatility of the process. Targets may depict any size or type of figure, real or imagined.

Bigfoot is a foam figure by The Critter Factory symbolizing the Redding, California, Western Trail Shoot. Relatively lightweight, it still requires six men to move it.

Mountain goat archery targets are placed in realistic settings to add to the challenge.

Elk targets sport real trophy antlers. The background is painted on plywood sheets, also protecting the campground beyond.

that he wanted nothing to do with that progression as he was responsible for a lot of the target painting. Providing the targets for his and other clubs was becoming more and more time-consuming.

Many of the club's targets were dinosaurs and other fictional characters from *The Flintstones* television program. This attracted a certain number of regular shooters to a tournament, but other local clubs were drawing 500 to 600 shooters, nearly ten times the number shooting at Yuba City.

These other clubs were using crude animal targets made of burlap and excelsior with horns tied on top to resemble elk. At another meet, someone had fashioned a burlap alligator, complete with teeth. One club constructed a gorilla target, made of carpet remnants and filled with sand. A power winch had to be used to raise and hang the target from a tree.

It became clear that the more realistic the targets, the more archers would attend the tournament. The Flintstones attendance had risen to upward of 200 shooters by the early '70s. A roofing company was using home insulation foam at the time, which proved to be just right for 3-D animals. Using this type of foam, the Yuba City club began making targets. The first tournament to see the new foam targets was a big

success for the club. All of those targets were hand-painted by Tom Sellers. Today, Critter Factory targets are still hand-painted.

As time went along, club members were building more and more targets. Archers came from afar to shoot the tournaments, and the 3-D targets became better known. Other clubs wanted some. Would Sellers build them?

Little was known about the properties of foam in those days, Sellers claims. Chemical companies were not so forthcoming as they are now in revealing the formulas used. "As 3-D archery grows in popularity and the demand for more targets increases, the chemical companies are happy to provide the materials needed for the industry," Sellers observes. "The market was too small twenty years ago to be noticed. Today, there are new foam developments, new form materials and new release chemicals available almost daily."

Most of the small clubs that wanted targets had no money. Sellers' Critter Factory agreed to finance club's target purchases. In general, Sellers would accept a down payment and provide targets worth twice that much. Later, when the clubs made a profit from the tournaments, they would pay the factory what was owed. Then, most clubs would buy more targets, realizing how effective they are in attracting shooters from all over. And that is how the business has grown.

The Critter Factory has grown many times over from its humble beginnings. Almost any archer up and down the West Coast who has shot almost any tournament has encountered Critter Factory targets. They are realistic in color, size and shape. Sellers is able to turn out replicas of any game animals from Asia, Africa or North America. He has also produced several imaginary creatures and fantasies of giant sizes. Some are more than two stories tall. They are limited only to Sellers' imagination. He makes dragons, snakes, Paul Bunyans, spiders and monsters of awesome proportions. They have become so popular that some archers have been known to travel many miles just to shoot at certain Critter Factory targets.

Sellers has designed and built a couple of special trailers to transport his products up and down the West Coast. He does not produce targets with interlocking joints so they may be

Walt Mills of Intercoastal Technologies displays the basic ingredients of the expanding foam material to make targets. The two mixtures are carefully controlled by amount, temperature, color and time before being added to hard moulds.

Intercoastal Technologies employee Loren Bostater controls the flow of liquid foam as it pours into animal moulds.

taken down and shipped via UPS or other inexpensive methods. He transports the targets to tournament and club sites generally within a one-day haul from his location in central California.

Using the same trailers, targets are returned to the factory for annual repairs and refurbishing. Even after thousands of arrow holes, the targets will look and behave as new after a trip back to the factory.

As the popularity of 3-D shooting continues to grow, more manufacturers are beginning or enlarging production. **Game Tracker**, better known for its many innovative archery hunting accessories, has introduced a line of nine different targets. The first model, the most popular at any tournament, is a whitetail deer target. Others include a turkey, a black bear, a mountain goat and a series of small varmint animal targets. From a modest beginning, the company turning out the targets, Intercoastal Technologies of Coldwater, Michigan, has grown into a full-fledged production-line operation turning out the Game Tracker targets.

The deer target is a natural gray-brown color, matching the real thing. The color is produced in the foam from which it is made. A good foam designer can duplicate almost any color to match any animal. That technique tends to minimize the amount of color touch-up work necessary for the final target. The Game Tracker targets are hand-finished with an air brush. Most of the basic colors of the animals are sprayed onto the insides of the moulds and become part of the foam targets as they are broken from the moulds. The face, ears, eyes, nose and tail look as realistic as possible. The whitetail target size is based upon an average Eastern or Midwestern whitetail buck.

The central marked target area is replaceable when it becomes shot out. This could happen during a weekend at a large tournament, but probably would not take place for a year or more on a home practice range. Scoring rings are marked in accordance with the International Bowhunting Organization (IBO) and Archery Shooter's Association (ASA) rules. The lines of the scoring rings are invisible from normal shooting distances, but are easy to locate as the arrows are being scored and pulled out. For the archer practicing at home for the upcoming deer season, the rings also provide an accurate guide to a deer's vital zones, or where the animal's heart and lungs would be located.

The larger targets break down into three body parts plus a pair of antlers for easy shipping. The package is within UPS-shippable limits. The sections are kept tightly matched by a multi-point locking system moulded into the body parts. The parts fit together with precision, leaving slight, almost invisible section lines. The interlocking tabs and slots are tight and smooth.

Most archers start assembly with the rear and center sections. The legs, feet and ground-mounting hardware are moulded in. To ease the task, slip two sections together and slide the leg sections down over pieces of steel reinforcing bar previously driven into the ground. The bars should be about a half-inch in diameter and 18 inches long.

Once the body is standing up, the head section will slide down onto the center piece. The antlers are removable and may also be used as rattlers by bowhunters. They are made of a hard material that produces a realistic sound when rubbed and clacked together. The antlers are also sold separately by Game Tracker for rattling. The antlers are packaged separately, with their metal anchors loose. The anchors are inserted into the holes in the bottom of the antler sections and aligned with the seam lines visible on the antlers. They are a tight fit; a hammer may be used to gently tap them home.

The metal anchors extend from the bottom of the antler sections. They look a bit like arrowheads. The points should be lined up with a line embossed on the deer head. They are inserted and pushed down until seated flush with the deer head.

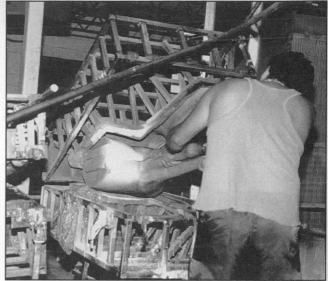

Intercoastal Technologies partner Joe Gross sprays a release agent on the surface of the mould before it is filled with liquid foam.

Intercoastal Technologies partner George Hughes removes a section of hardened foam target from the mould. Color was added before the foam was poured.

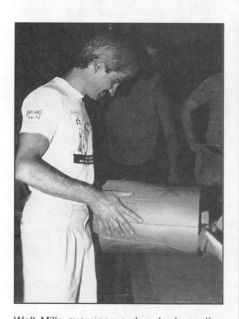

Walt Mills examines a deer body section removed from a mould. Some minor trimming will complete the target before it is packaged and shipped.

The newest target in the McKenzie Natra-Look line is the mule deer, popular with tournament directors.

The instruction sheet warns that the metal anchors must always be removed from the antlers before they are used for rattling. For such use, pull the antler sections out of the target head and remove the anchors. Some force may be required to get the anchors out. They will slip back into the antlers into the same slots of the target's head to reattach.

Inside the central scoring section is a compressed cotton core. The core is invisible, but is included to help stop fast arrow pass-throughs, especially by the thinner, slicker carbon-fiber arrows so popular with 3-D shooters. The remaining sections of the animal targets are made of a custom formulation of 7-pound ethafoam, which is highly resistant to the effects of ultraviolet sunshine rays.

A visit to the Intercoastal Technologies factory where the Game Tracker targets are produced reveals a fascinating process, amazingly simple, but highly complex and technical. The production process consists of mixing together the correct two-part epoxy-like chemicals, stirring them for a precise, specified time, pouring the thick liquid into a mould, waiting for the foam to fill up the mould and cure, and removing the formed sections from the mould.

That short description makes the whole process sound deceptively easy. If it were that easy, everybody would be doing it at home or in the garage. Production is not that easy. The body moulds must be carefully sculpted to produce a product that reflects an animal's natural lines, but without too many expensive details. The moulds must be made to turn out sections that will lock together easily, but will maintain their integrity during hard usage and weather changes. The inner surfaces of the moulds must lend themselves to modern mass-production methods. Many moulds are made of hard fiberglass, rigid enough to withstand the force of the expanding foam material as it is poured in.

The most crucial factor involved in production is the formulation of the liquid ethafoam that is poured into the mould. It has to duplicate the animal's natural color as it comes out of the mould. Colors, as well as the finished foam density, may be manipulated by the chemicals involved. It must not be too hard or too soft when hit by arrows. Too soft and arrows may pass through; too hard and arrows may bounce off the surface or may be too difficult to remove after a hit.

When the two chemical formulations are combined, the resulting mixture is not unlike the process of mixing two-part epoxy cement. The two mixtures are stirred thoroughly until they reach a uniform consistency. Here, fractions of seconds count. The time from initial mixing and pouring into the mould must be strictly controlled. The mixture must be poured into the mould fast enough to take advantage of the time factor, but slowly enough to allow air bubbles and pock-

A typical 3-D target is shipped in three sections, easily assembled. The center scoring section may be replaced when shot out by arrows.

ets to work their way out of the mould as the liquid expands and begins to harden.

The amount of time the foam remains in the mould is also carefully monitored to produce the best target. Air vents are built into each mould so that air can escape ahead of the expanding and hardening foam. The vents are closed just as the foam reaches the top level of the mould. Each step must be carefully monitored and regulated.

The mould material has to be lightweight enough for easy handling, while still able to withstand hundreds of pours. A releasing agent is used on the inner surfaces of the mould so the target sections may be easily removed when the time arrives. Some moulds are made of aluminum for greater strength, but the metal is more expensive than fiberglass.

Designing and producing a prototype is one thing; designing a production line to turn out hundreds of product units is something else again. The task is to satisfy the needs of the marketplace at the time needed. Walt Mills is the man behind the Game Tracker target facility in Coldwater, Michigan. Coldwater is in the heart of some of the best whitetail deer hunting habitat in Michigan. Mills' background is in the production of hard plastic parts for the automotive industry. He also happens to be an avid and successful bowhunter. Many of his associates, partners in the target production company, are also bowhunters. They have first-hand knowledge of what the game animals are supposed to look like.

Mills and his crew have the experience to formulate the foam material to the correct consistency, density, color and weight. They designed the automated production system that turns out targets on an assembly line basis.

The Game Tracker whitetail deer target has a realistic appearance when seen at bowhunting distances. The bone and muscle outlines and physical proportions have been researched and duplicated within production considerations. It will withstand plenty of arrow hits before the center section must be replaced.

The latest from Delta Industries is a realistic strutting turkey. Scoring markings are found on both sides, plus front and rear of the bird. This turkey target features a beard on the target chest.

Delta Industries' deer target is clearly marked with IBO scoring rings.

This Delta deer target is shipped in four sections: main body, two leg pieces, and head and neck section.

Among the best-known 3-D targets are those from **McKenzie**. They are called Natra-Look, a play on words, but for good reason. The targets are lifelike in size, color and configuration. There are about a dozen different models, including several deer poses, two bear models, an elk, antelope, javelina and wild turkey.

The large, alert deer target is packaged in three sections, all in a single, shippable box. The target includes a head section, a center section with IBO-approved scoring markings and a rear section. The single-leg, front and back construction presents added strength and fast, easy setup. A pair of whitetail-looking antlers and a pair of steel reinforcing bars are included.

The body sections slide together by way of two interlocking tabs and slots. The middle and rear sections are of the single leg construction, each with support tubing moulded in. These pipes or tubes fit over the 20-inch-long rods that are pounded into the ground as supports. The three body sections fit together well, thanks to the interlocking design. From afar, the section divisions are invisible.

The simplest approach is to drive one rod into the ground about where the target is to be placed. Assembling the two body

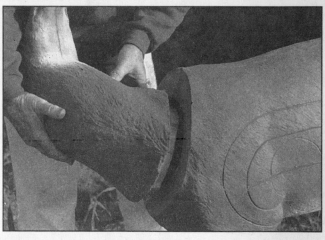

Target sections are twisted and locked in place during assembly.

sections will indicate the location of the second rod. If the ground is not too hard, the rod can be manipulated or tapped until the second tube is slipped down over it.

The target may be used to depict a doe, or the antlers may be pushed down onto the head for a buck. The antler locations are marked on the target's head section. The antlers may be removed and replaced at will.

When the target area is shot out, the entire center section is replaced. All target center sections for the deer models are the same. The front sections with head and neck are interchangeable for different poses. This simplifies things and saves money for the manufacturer and the archer.

McKenzie targets are made of a substance called Elasta-Foam. Described as a new, improved, tough and flexible material, it was developed specifically for McKenzie's Natra-

Look targets. The material improves the life of the target when shot with broadheads or field points. Shooting may be done from either side, as both are marked with scoring circles. The dense, elastic material lets arrow holes re-seal themselves when a shaft is pulled out. Each mid-section scoring zone is reinforced with a 6-pound Dow ethafoam core that is moulded into the body. It will stand up to hundreds of tournament arrows.

The deer target is a gray-brown color, with painted details around the tail, ears, eyes and nose for a realistic appearance. From a typical shooting distance, the scoring markings are not visible and the animal target looks quite realistic. The sculptor responsible for the design knows a bit about animal anatomy.

The large deer target stands 36 inches high at the shoulders. The body measures 56 inches long. Medium deer are 34 inches at the shoulder and 45 inches long. The elk target is 55 inches high at the shoulders and 78 inches long. The standing bear target is the largest McKenzie has to offer, 60 inches tall and 18 inches wide in the chest. Smallest is the javelina target, 21 inches at the shoulder and $30^1/_2$ inches long. The newest targets are a realistic-looking strutting wild turkey and a large coyote. Both contain the IBO-approved scoring zones on each side.

The three deer body sections and complete target are light enough in weight to be moved easily. The target is simply pulled up and off the ground rods. The rods may need some persuasion if the ground is hard, but should pull right out if the soil is soft and moist. McKenzie offers an optional metal shooting and display stand for their targets. The stand may be used indoors or out and is said to work as well on uneven ground as on level. It is adjustable for all targets except the elk.

McKenzie targets were designed originally to aid bow-hunters in realistic pre-season practice. Beyond that, they have become popular with 3-D shooters, many of whom never have—and never will—hunt live animals. They are the targets of choice among such organizations as the IBO, ASA and NFAA. A group of Natra-Look targets in realistic terrain—among trees, brush and grass—becomes challenging for any archer.

Natra-Look targets are protected by U.S. patent and copyright laws and are manufactured in compliance with all federal EPA regulations.

Delta Industries is another name known to many archers. The company manufactures several archery accessories, including bow quivers and hunting decoys. The new Delta Elite 3-D targets offer genuine realism to challenge shooters at club and regional tournaments, as well as archers who want something more in their backyards. Delta's targets are produced of tough urethane foam that closes and heals when the arrow shafts have been removed.

The targets have the familiar IBO scoring rings on both sides of the animals for greater flexibility when shooting. For backyard practice or large tournaments, markings on both sides will double the life of any target.

Delta offers a choice of mid-section styles. Shooters may order the target with a replaceable core that can be pushed out of the center section when it has been shot out. It is normally held in place with friction. If many shooters are not hitting the scoring zone, the entire center section can develop too many holes. This center section may be replaced instead of only the core.

Delta offers optional center sections with or without the marked vitals. Without the vitals, the targets are called the Competition Series. Each has a 6-pound ethafoam core moulded into the center section.

The new whitetail deer targets are available with the head and neck positions depicting different buck attitudes. The rear and center sections are the same for all three targets, but the

McKenzie's bear target is mounted on a portable steel stand that may be used indoors as well as out.

This Browning wild boar target shows a realistic, fearsome head.

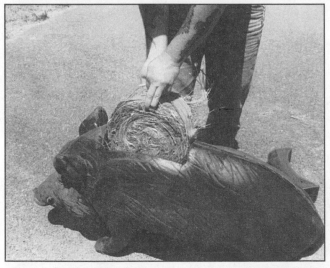

Browning's Paragon targets feature an arrow-stopping, replaceable round Saunders grass matt section inside the vital area.

head positions represent a buck in rut, a buck sneaking or one on alert. It is possible to buy all three complete targets or one body and three different head and neck attitudes for home practice.

Early in 1994, Delta introduced targets representing Dall sheep, desert and Rocky Mountain bighorn sheep, as well as a strutting turkey and a coyote. The turkey has IBO scoring markings on both sides, as well as on the front and rear of the target. The tail is detachable for easy shipping and transport. The turkey also has a 6-pound moulded-in core—which is

invisible to archers—inside the target to help it withstand hundreds of hits. The strutting turkey target also has a realistic-looking beard on the front that would appeal to any trophy hunter if it were real.

The Delta deer target is easy to assemble with a simple twist-lock formed in the foam mould. The bodies are made in lifelike colors, sizes and contours. The larger targets break down into four parts that fit into a single carton for easy shipping. Delta targets are seen at a number of club shoots as well as large tournaments around North America.

Stanley Hips—long known for his hand-painted targets on foam blocks and sheets—has added the familiar moulded foam 3-D targets to his product line. The sample target that was shot by our test crew was a little javelina. The target is easily transportable and offers a real challenge for archers trying to place an arrow in the vitals. Stanley Hips is from Texas, so it seems appropriate that the javelina target is one of his choices.

Browning recently entered the 3-D market in a big way. In addition to several attractive and effective bows, their new targets have been carefully designed by people who know game anatomies, sizes and colors. The foam targets are all sculpted and hand-painted for maximum realism. The Browning targets are called Paragon. They are marketed primarily as aids for bowhunting practice, but should be seen soon at many archery tournaments.

Interestingly, Browning targets are produced from a water-blown foam manufacturing process. The process cre-

Stanley Hips offers a small javelina target.

This Browning Paragon black bear target is popular with practicing bowhunters.

ates high-density urethane foam without any environmentally harmful CFCs. The resultant foam stops the fastest graphite and carbon arrows—even those shot from overdraw-equipped bows.

Another important, unique feature is a Saunders spiral-wound grass core located inside each target, within the vital zone. These cores are the same type as found at most major Olympic archery tournaments around the world. The Saunders matts are much larger for that type of shooting, of course. The matts are famous for their arrow-stopping ability and their durability against hundreds of arrows.

The cores are easy and inexpensive to replace when necessary. The grass cores are inside a cavity accessed from the top of each animal target. The grass disc is covered and protected by a contoured foam closure on top and is held in place by wooden rods. For broadhead practice, the grass cores may be replaced by foam discs.

Another product available from Browning is the Paragon target repair kit. Shot-up sections of targets are easily and quickly repaired using the two-solution, epoxy-like mixture, not unlike the production material earlier described. An instructional videotape is available with the repair kit to demonstrate how repairs are accomplished.

Browning's Paragon target line includes a mule deer, a realistic-looking bighorn sheep, a raccoon, a whitetail deer, a wild boar, a wild turkey and a black bear. Each animal

This less-expensive American Whitetail target combines front and back legs.

This Morrell target assembles easily. Scoring rings are marked on the center burlap-covered section.

A special feature of the Morrell target is the ease with which arrows may be removed. Material inside the burlap center section releases arrows far easier than foam material.

includes the familiar vital scoring zone to meet IBO and ASA requirements.

Arkansas' **Morrell Manufacturing** offers an unusual target called the Eternity 3-D. The patented design has a vital area intended to stand up to more than 10,000 arrow shots. The area is covered by a burlap blanket, the same color as the foam body. Inside the blanket is a special bag in the body cavity that will catch and stop any arrow without damage to the bag. The burlap outer surface is self-healing, as are most other targets, and any arrow is easily removed with a two-finger pull. The burlap and arrow-stopping bag are held in place with hook-and-loop fasteners. The two foam target body sections are bolted in place underneath the belly of the animal. The bolts and nuts are invisible to the archer.

The rest of the Morrell body sections are made of urethane foam. A realistic set of antlers adds to the lifelike appearance of the target. The Eternity 3-D target looks a bit odd when examined up close, but from a distance of twenty yards or so, it presents a most realistic appearance.

Timberline Targets has a set of foam targets that includes a rutting whitetail, alert whitetail, sneaking buck, mule deer, antelope, bear, caribou, elk and moose. All are made from high-grade urethane foam and have replaceable marked vital

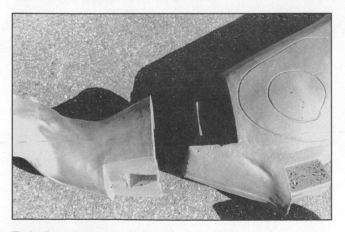

Timberline target sections fit together with tight tolerances.

zones. Each target is shipped in four sections, with a nice, authentic-looking set of antlers. The main body sections are marked with the typical scoring rings for tournament and bowhunting practice.

American Whitetail is another manufacturer of top-notch 3-D targets. Their deer target is shipped in three sections in a single carton. The three sections lock together by means of key ways and tabs moulded into the body sections. The sections are the head and neck, front legs including the main center body section, and the rear section with back legs. The replaceable center body section is marked with IBO-like scoring rings.

One of American Whitetail's targets, the Powermax 3D200, is the largest 3-D target available. It is patterned after a 240-pound North American whitetail buck. The target measures 56 inches long, 11 inches thick and 37 inches at its back. The three sections of this giant break down for easy shipping, and the sections are connected by means of a dado joint for lock-up.

Similar to many other 3-D targets, the whitetail buck is designed to stand up, using the moulded-in tubing in the legs. These legs are slipped onto sections of steel reinforcing bars hammered into the ground. Reinforcing bar sections are included with the target. They have been ground down on both ends to remove any burrs or sharp edges left when they were cut to length. The smooth tips let the steel slip easily into the tubing. It is a nice touch by the manufacturer.

In Minnesota, the **Swanmar Company** offers a basic deer target made of an outer fabric of 10-ounce burlap backed by a woven poly material with quad stitching and stuffed with cotton and polyester fibers. The target is sewn to resemble a life-size deer and is three-dimensional for practice from any angle. The material inside the burlap permits two-finger arrow removal, no matter how fast the arrow travels or of what material it is constructed. Two metal rods are pressed into the ground and the target is hung about a foot off the ground for use. The body size matches an average whitetail deer and the target is moved easily from one location to another. There are no breakable parts.

Swanmar burlap bag targets are ideal for bowhunting practice and feature easy arrow removal.

Morrell Eternity targets are also available as simple bags to hang or shoot on the ground.

A further new development from Swanmar is the Pottinger Magnum Plus CAT System. The patented system has the potential to produce drama and excitement for spectators and shooters alike. All bowhunters will agree that they would rather miss an animal entirely than make a poor shot. The Magnum Plus provides a remote indication when an arrow actually penetrates one of the vital organs. The target contains sensors that are shaped, sized and placed in a realistic manner inside the body cavity to simulate the heart and lungs. The simulated organs require the shooter to adjust the impact point depending upon the angle of the shot. A rear quartering shot requires an arrow which enters the body behind the area normally associated with the heart/lung of a regular target face. The arrow must penetrate forward into the body to score a good hit.

When a good hit is made, an electrical impulse is sent to a computer display unit normally located near the shooter. The unit signals to the shooter and to spectators that a good shot has been made.

As with a live animal, it is possible to hit both the heart and the lungs with the same arrow. A slight variation either way and only one or the other is penetrated. Sensor construction is designed to let the vital area be filled with arrows, but a better shot could result in a better hit. If an arrow does not produce a killing shot, there is no indication that a fatal hit was made. If a well placed arrow is removed from the target and another arrow hits in the same spot and angle, the second will score the same as the first.

The sensors are not damaged when hit by an arrow. However, if the second arrow angle changes slightly and it misses the recessed organ, it will not show a score. No judgment calls are required and scoring arguments become non-existent. Only the target electronically scores the arrow.

Many manufacturers have come to recognize the growing market for realistic 3-D foam targets for hunting practice and archery competition. The market is growing rapidly as more and more archers discover the fun and challenge of the sport. There are sure to be more.

8 3-D Target Shooting Contests

Three-dimensional target shooting is always a family sport, with ranges and provisions for children and adults of all skills.

Hundreds Of 3-D Tournaments Are On Tap To Test Skills And Offer Fun

THERE ARE HUNDREDS of 3-D target tournaments around North America each year, spring through fall. There are—or will be—dozens more during the winter months, indoors and out. The computer-generated, interactive video systems beginning to show up in professional archery shops around the country are sure to become popular in places where weather or terrain prevents archers from venturing outside. Add up all the large big-money shoots, the regional and state championships, the International Bowhunting Organization, the Archery Shooters' Association, the National Field Archery Association, the club shoots and informal, friendly range competition, and the total opportunities may well soar into the thousands.

New contests are being organized every week, and the older, well-established tournaments grow larger each year. They grow larger in numbers of participants and in the monetary amount and number of prizes offered. One aspect feeds on the other: The more entry fees paid, the larger the prize money pot; the more dollars available for successful shooters, the more people who will sign up. Children and other amateurs have plenty of trophy chances for recognition and rewards. Contestants include bowhunters who want to tune up their shooting techniques before the opening of early deer seasons, as well as target archers who do not intend ever to nock a broadhead-tipped arrow. Hundreds of men, women and children are being drawn into archery through the lure of 3-D target shooting and the competition it offers.

Generally, the tournament season begins in April or May in most parts of North America. Because of the warmer weather, the first meets take place earlier in the south than up north. In places such as Florida, the Gulf Coast, southern Texas, Arizona and Southern California, the weather is usually friendly enough that some tournaments are on the schedule as early as February, when most of the rest of the country may still be snowbound.

One of the larger, early tournaments is the **Western Classic Trail Shoot** in Redding, California. Redding is in the northern part of the state, only about an hour's drive from the Oregon line. The tournament, established in 1984, is usually scheduled for the first weekend of May. It draws upward of a thousand shooters from all over California, Oregon, Nevada and Arizona, as well as dozens of pro-class shooters from coast to coast.

Sponsors and money shooters have pushed total prize money to a minimum of $50,000 in recent years. Add manufacturers' contingency prizes, and the best and luckiest pro shooters can earn themselves fat paychecks for a weekend of fun and games. There are hundreds of additional trophies and merchandise prizes available for archers in every class.

Big cash and merchandise awards are not the only incentives drawing archers to Redding each spring. One of the most appealing aspects of the Western Classic is the location and the range. The range, just west of downtown Redding, is owned by the local sponsoring Straight Arrow Bowhunters Club. Club members work all year to improve and maintain the archery courses across the rolling hills, grassy slopes, wooded canyons and hilltops. Most of the year, this area of northern California is relatively dry. But plenty of snow in the winter and the usual spring rains make the tournament site green, cool and inviting in early May.

The club offers self-contained camping areas within walking distance of the ranges and hundreds of travelers take advantage of that. There is enough shade, available water and snacks at the club's shack to satisfy all the campers.

Those who wish to stay in nearby Redding will find plenty of hotels and motels only fifteen minutes or so from the range. The Sacramento River runs through the center of downtown Redding, and Lake Shasta and Mount Shasta are only a few freeway miles north of town. The area is famous for its river, stream and lake fishing and boating and offers some great mule deer hunting later in the year. Most members of the local archery club trace their interest in target shooting back to their bowhunting interest.

The tournament courses are set up with seventy lifelike targets from The Critter Factory, a manufacturer located about 100 miles south of Redding, in Yuba City. Tournament director Larry "Grizz" Grigsby believes one factor that has made the Redding contest so popular is the unusual

At most 3-D tournaments, the meet officials try to place realistic animal targets in realistic habitats and backgrounds. The elk targets are full-size and natural in color. The antlers are trophies from elk. Here, archers are scoring and pulling arrows from targets.

Real antlers on foam targets replicate sparring bull elk. The young and female elk in the scene will cost the archer penalty points if hit.

and realistic-looking Critter Factory targets. All the targets are set in realistic settings and habitats; some are highly challenging. Grigsby claims many shooters travel hundreds of miles just for the challenges the terrain and targets present.

There usually are about 300 money tournament shooters registered annually, but most shooters at the meet are there for the fun, rather than the money. Many families are in attendance, with mom, dad and plenty of small children shooting in their own classes, touring the range together. It is wonderful to watch the little guys, who have their own distance stakes from which to shoot. The little ones seem thrilled when their arrows hit anywhere on the realistic targets.

All target yardages are marked, and NFAA equipment and class rules apply. The Western Classic is also part of the Professional Archers' Association professional point tour.

There are several categories at various skill levels in which archers can participate. These include family classes, man-wife events, singles, three children's age groups, seniors and guests. The Money Shoot classes include Bowhunter Freestyle Limited, a Bowhunter Team event and a Freestyle Team event.

Some participants will earn prize money from their own class, as well as from their team scoring. It is possible to earn $5,000 or more, depending upon manufacturer premiums and the number of shooters in a class. Money Shoot payoffs are paid down through 20th place in men's Freestyle, Freestyle Limited, Bowhunter, Bowhunter Freestyle and Bowhunter Freestyle Limited. Women's payoffs are in the Freestyle and Freestyle Limited classes. All Western Classic Money Shoot champions receive an Easton-sponsored trophy along with their top prize money.

Forty-five targets are shot on Saturday, with twenty-five more ready for Sunday. Each day, shooters have a shotgun start. That is, groups of shooters begin at the same time in the morn-

Two foam mountain lions lurk behind a real oak tree against a painted background. The plywood background also serves as an arrow stopper to protect other shooters.

ing at each of the targets. This way, groups of shooters move from target to target throughout the day, utilizing time and space most efficiently.

Grigsby and his fellow club members do their best to prevent shooters from bunching up at any target, although there may be delays at some targets. Shooters are afforded shady rest and refreshment areas at most targets throughout the course. However, when the group with the really hot shooters—those pros who win the big money—show up at any open target area, they are sure to draw a crowd of spectators.

According to Grigsby, the object is to move as many shooters through the seventy targets as rapidly and smoothly as possible. "We want to keep the tournament moving rapidly each day," says Grigsby. "Furthermore, we have enough new targets for each area to make sure all competitors have a chance at fresh, non-shot-up targets at most stations. When we see a target with too many holes in it, we quickly replace it with a new 3-D animal target. We have radio communications throughout the course, and our club workers can have a target replaced with a new one in a matter of minutes, no matter where it is on the course."

Each shooter shoots two arrows at each target. A hit within the marked spot on the target is scored at eleven points. The shooter gets ten points for a hit that is in the kill zone, but outside the marked area. Eight points are awarded for hits anywhere else on the 3-D animal target. A miss is no points. On the longer ranges, shorter distances are marked for children and other select groups.

In 1992, more than 900 shooters were registered for the tournament, shooting at sixty targets. Ten more targets were added in 1993, and nearly 1,000 shooters registered for the event. More novelty shoots are added each year, many on the Friday before the official tournament begins.

Competitors shoot through the lunch hour as no lunch break is called at the range. However, plenty of food and refreshment stops are located at various spots throughout the range. On Saturday, the club house serves breakfast, lunch and dinner. On Sunday, lunch and dinner are available.

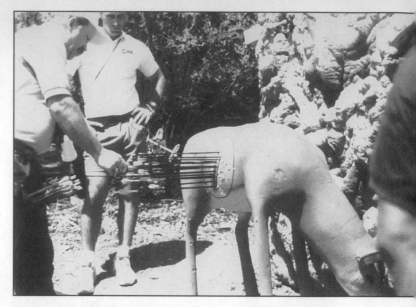
The top tournament shooters will put all the arrows into the scoring circle of the foam target. The arrows are clearly marked with each archer's identification.

Tournament shooter Dee Wilde seems pleased with his arrow placement and score. In this case, some of the background was made of foam, which is much easier on arrows than the real rock at right.

Local club members and families prepare and serve the delicious food.

Grigsby and his crew arrange several auctions, raffles and novelty shoots throughout the three days of the event. Each year sees improvements to the range, the shooting lanes and the manufacturers' display area. It is grassy, shaded and comfortable for exhibitors and visitors alike.

Any event of this type—archery or otherwise—must depend on thousands of man hours of volunteer work. Club members pitch in with plenty of labor and donated services. Grigsby is a big man with a bushy beard. Almost as big as a grizzly bear, he

has a wonderful sense of humor and a dedication to archery and to the mission of the Straight Arrow Bowhunters Club of Redding.

In 1975, Grigsby, then thirty-six, was living in Redding, but was not a member of the local bowhunting club. He had just obtained a new bow and wanted to try it out. He had heard about a range not far from town and proceeded there. He happened to hit a weekend when the club was having one of its shoots at the range. One of the first persons he met at the range was a man who began coaching Grigsby. He became nationally competitive within one year.

That skill level was not all good news. Grigsby began participating in all the local tournaments he could find, and he was winning most of them. But he was putting too much pressure on himself to continue to win. He heard about a 3-D animal shoot in South Lake Tahoe in which the targets were built by the Critter Factory. They were the first such targets he had ever seen.

Grigsby remembers: "I took one look at that tournament and said 'Wow.' I never had so much fun before. I couldn't get enough of these 3-D target shoots. I proceeded to win the tournament there three times. It was like nothing any of us had ever seen before.

"Several of us club members put our heads together and asked ourselves why we couldn't do the same thing in Redding. We had tried almost everything else to increase attendance at our shoots; we offered gift certificates and everything else we could think of. But our targets looked nothing like these new ones we were seeing. Ours looked like lumps of wet paper about halfway through a tournament. Nobody wanted to come back for a second time.

"I talked to Tom Sellers of the Critter Factory. I told him we had no money, but would like to try some of his targets in Redding. At the time, we were passing the hat among ourselves just to get enough money to hold a tournament.

Many 3-D archery tournaments, such as this one near Flagstaff, Arizona, include areas for manufacturers to display and sell equipment. The event draws thousands of shooters and spectators.

Tournament shooters may be grouped according to ability, past scores, shooting classification or merely by chance or friendship. Everyone has fun.

"Sellers had four or five extra targets on his trailer at the time. Sellers loaned us the targets he had, just to use them for our next club shoot, already scheduled." In the meantime, Sellers was offering to sell the five extra targets at a deep discount, just to get Grigsby and the Redding group started.

"It was a deal I couldn't pass up," recalls Grigsby. "I hauled those five targets back to Redding and set them up on the range. At the time, I had no authority or standing with the club, but I was so excited about the targets, I set them up and we had a practice shoot at the range. All the members loved them, and we included the targets in our next shoot.

"We had a hundred more shooters that year than we had ever had before. That convinced us we were onto something with these targets. We even made some money at the shoot that year. We decided that if we could invest the profits in more targets, we could put on a fourteen-target shoot.

"Sure enough, that shoot saw an additional 100 shooters at the tournament. We soon learned that the more of these real-istic Critter Factory targets we had, the more shooters would show up. We would soon grow from 150 shooters to nearly 1,000 registered archers for the weekend. The growth is directly attributed to the 3-D animal targets. We found that the more targets we put out, the more shooters would register. We could raise our entry fees enough to pay for the targets without diminishing the number of shooters, too. This was leading to the large cash and merchandise awards we see today."

As time went along, Sellers was calling Grigsby on the phone every time he was passing through with an extra target or two on the trailer. Grigsby would meet him off the freeway, look at the targets and buy them for the club. Each target was unique.

"Within two years, the shoot had developed into a twenty-eight-target tournament," Grigsby remembers. "Within five years, we had forty-two targets. We learned that people were registering for the next tournament a year ahead of time. More

Some tournaments have the distance to the targets marked on the aiming stakes. At other locations, the archers must guess at the range.

and more were showing up for our target shoot. Ten years ago, we enlarged the tournament to two days in length. We continued to see that the more we put into the tournament, the more people wanted to be a part of it."

Sign-ups seemed stalled at about 400 shooters per two-day weekend. Grigsby thought that the addition of larger cash prizes might again result in increases in shooter numbers. He approached dozens of manufacturers from around the country who were attending a major tradeshow in Las Vegas. He had no professional standing at the time, but asked anybody who would listen. Grigsby came away with ten sponsors that first year, each of whom wanted to bring their own product displays to the tournament.

Grigsby says, "I believe these archers who win tournaments all over the country should be paid as well as professional golfers. The money we raise and pay out to the pros helps the sport of archery. It makes it worth their while to travel to Redding for a good tournament. The money shooters must pay upward of $350 in entry fees, but the family shooter can pay only about $20 to shoot the same course, right behind the pros. Each enjoys the tournament and has plenty of fun.

"We have a plan to put four or five of the top shooters in a group of double that many amateurs and families. The pros will watch each other and keep one another honest without too much outside monitoring. But it lets the families who shoot for fun mingle, talk and shoot with archers from around the country whom they have read about. It makes everybody happy, including our sponsors. We seem to have the best of both worlds."

Grigsby finds much of the growth of the tournament is due to word of mouth. An individual or two may shoot the tournament one year, return to his home club and spread the word. The next

One of the benefits field archery and 3-D targets shooters enjoy is the beautiful terrain. Tall timber helps conceal the target on this range.

year, most of the club members will be sending in their entry fees early to take advantage of the discount.

"They know we try to make them happy," says Grigsby. "We treat everyone fairly, we offer good food, a great range, a comfortable place to stay and camp out; we have an honest tournament, and I believe those things are what make our tournament so attractive. Every dollar we make from the shoot we plow back into the range and the targets. We look forward to greater success in the future.

"Today, the Straight Arrow Bowhunters Club may be one of the richest clubs in the country, but it didn't get that way overnight. We have put a lot of work into making the tournament and the club what it is today."

The Western Classic is successful, but there are many other terrific archery shoots around the country, offering plenty of

Many archery tournaments feature several novelty shoots which are not part of the scoring. These are often operated as fund-raisers for educational, fraternal or hunting organizations.

appeal. One of these is the tournament held near Mormon Lake, Arizona, in mid-July. "Arizona in July?" you ask. Too hot? Not a bit, and that is part of the story.

The lake itself is the largest natural, unenhanced lake in Arizona. It is located about twenty miles south of Flagstaff in the mountainous northern part of the state, at altitudes above 7,000 feet. In July, the days are usually clear and crisp, the nights cold enough to require an extra blanket or two for those camping out at the range. It is in the midst of tall timber and also in the middle of some of the best elk habitat in the country. It is not uncommon to see individual elk crossing the road at night, visible in passing vehicle headlights, with good-size herds grazing along the shores of the shallow lake.

The town of Mormon Lake has a year-round population of about fifty. But when the Arizona Bowhunters Association puts on its **Bowhunter Happening**, the population swells to 5,000 or more, including shooters and their friends and families. As the nearest motels are more than twenty miles away, most archers manage to park their RVs or set up tents within a mile or so of the ranges, in the local forest service boundaries. The usual safety restrictions apply, but there seems to be room for everybody without overcrowding.

The Bowhunter Happening dates back to 1980. It has grown to its present size and level of success through the hard work and dedication of hundreds of Arizona bowhunters and other archers.

The tournament has followed a similar pattern as other large meets around the country. The targets began as painted cardboard, moved through colorful printed target faces mounted on straw bales and hand-painted foam silhouettes, to the hundreds of 3-D foam animal targets of today.

Many of the targets at the Mormon Lake novelty shoots are fantasy creatures, ranging from seven-foot quail to huge, hairy mammoths or full-size elephants and other exotic game. The object is to offer plenty of fun and challenge to the hundreds of shooters who come from all over the Southwest to participate.

No doubt, one of the primary reasons anyone would travel to the area at that time of year is the beauty and atmosphere of northern Arizona. It is but a short drive to the Four Corners and the American Indian art and cultural centers of New Mexico and Arizona. Flagstaff boasts Northern Arizona University with all its cultural and educational advantages. And it is nice to simply enjoy the high country and scenery of that part of the South-

Tournament trails are carefully marked and controlled with safety in mind.

Late in the day, the exhibitors' area is crowded with archers at the Redding, California, Western Classic Trail Shoot.

west. If a nonresident, one might take a look at the possibilities of a bowhunt later in the year. For whatever reason, the area is a wonderful place to visit.

The Bowhunter Happening represents the single annual fund-raising effort for the Arizona Bowhunters Association. Proceeds generated from the shoot are used to support vital wildlife and enforcement activities of the Arizona Game and Fish Department, the U.S. Forest Service, the Bureau of Land Management and other conservation-related groups in Arizona. Projects funded by the ABA play a major role in enhancing the image of bowhunters in the state of Arizona and elsewhere. The ABA also realizes the critical importance of positive public relations in the '90s, and the tournament is one of the steps toward that goal.

Shooting classifications follow the familiar IBO rules—the Bowhunter Happening is IBO-sanctioned. Archers may register for Traditional Class using recurves or longbows and any arrows. The Barebow Class is for compound shooters who do not use sights or mechanical releases. Those shooting Freestyle use compound bows with no more than five sight pins and no mechanical release aids. The Unlimited shooters use compound bows and at least mechanical release aids.

More than 2,500 archers sign up to shoot the scenic courses each year. Usually, Mormon Lake features five twenty-target non-competitive courses as well as the competition course, also made of up twenty 3-D targets. The crowds in attendance range upward of 11,000 people, many who are simply spectators or supporters of the shooters.

In addition to the competitors, dozens of retailers, manufacturers and distributors of archery products display their wares in the 25,000 square-foot circus-type tent erected near the archery ranges. With the possibility of the not-infrequent summer thunderstorms, the exhibitors' tent is one of the favorite places to be in July.

These two Western 3-D tournaments are only a sampling of the hundreds of events taking place across North America.

On any given weekend in the spring or summer, there are dozens of meets being held, from the small club tournaments to major events such as the ones at Redding and Mormon Lake, drawing thousands of archers who shoot for fun or profit. There are dozens of older tournaments, originally affiliated with such organizations as the National Field Archery Association (NFAA), that now include or feature realistic foam 3-D targets instead of the painted paper target faces fastened to straw bales.

Each range and tournament has its own distinctive competition, geography and appeal. Some are set up on prairies, some on hills, some with heavy forest paths cut for shooting lanes; others offer only grass or brush as obstacles. Some are through lush, green vegitation; others are laid out across deserts. Each course is different, but shooters may shoot with confidence knowing that fellow archers in other states and other matches are following the same rules.

Beginning in the Midwest where the organization is still the strongest, the International Bowhunting Organization (IBO) now holds events in most states. It is expanding rapidly into the West, the Mountain States, the Northeast and other parts of the country. More meets are added each year. Some are older events whose sponsors recently affiliated with or joined the IBO; others are under the guidance of local IBO-affiliated clubs. It is by far the largest and most important tournament-sponsoring group to be found.

Another 3-D-sponsoring group is the newer Archery Shooters Association (ASA). As of 1995, about a dozen large tournaments are under ASA supervision, but the organization is expanding as rapidly as possible. The ASA has its origins in the South, but is attempting to grow into other areas of the country.

More detailed discussions of the IBO, the ASA and other sponsoring 3-D target organizations follow this chapter. Read archery magazines and check with local archery pro shops or ranges for the details and dates of other local tournaments.

8 The International Bowhunting Organization

The appeal of most IBO archery tournaments includes natural shooting areas—up and down hillsides and through trees and brush—just as in actual bowhunting situations.

Truly a family sport, the young archer can get help from dad or other adults in most tournament groups. This little one is showing good shooting form.

THE INTERNATIONAL Bowhunting Organization (IBO) has been in the forefront of 3-D target archery shooting, competition and equipment development for more than a decade. When formed, the group standardized the shooting and equipment rules, making competition among distant archers possible. Its influence has exploded from several small tournaments held in three Midwestern states to an international governing body with local, state, provincial and national championships. Tournaments in Mexico and Canada have been held, and Canada already has its own national championship. Plus, archers in other countries have expressed interest in the program.

There are far more amateur shooters than professionals, but with the support and sponsorship of a dozen major manufacturers, cash and trophies worth more than a quarter of a million dollars are distributed at the annual IBO World Championship tournament.

Membership in the organization has surpassed 30,000, backing the IBO's claim of being the largest bowhunting organization in the world. The IBO and 3-D targets, now so familiar to us, originated to give bowhunters an opportunity to practice shooting before the opening of deer seasons in the Midwest. Clearly, the group has gone beyond this mission.

The preamble to its reference manual states:

Since its creation in 1984, the International Bowhunting Organization (IBO) has made several strides forward. The first of these was to create the Triple Crown of bowhunting. This consists of three national shoots in three different states using identical rules and classes, and climaxing in the crowning of 14 National Champions of different ages, sex and equipment levels. This event has grown in popularity each year. In 1989, the IBO created the IBO World Championship. This is a series of sanctioned preliminary qualifying shoots in several states. The World Championship was shown on ESPN TV.

IBO animal targets may be placed in realistic settings, like this group of mule deer. An arrow in the wrong target may result in scoring penalties.

The IBO has been instrumental in implementing a State Bowhunter Week in several states and has endorsed the National Bowhunter Educational Foundation (NBEF) program for bowhunter education to further perpetuate the heritage of bowhunting. The IBO is part of the WLFA Bowhunting Defense coalition, created to protect the sport nationwide.

The purpose of the IBO is to:

Promote, encourage and foster the art and sport of bowhunting, bowhunter education, act as a liaison for the betterment of bowhunters, to function as a clearing house for essential bowhunter information, to assist and foster the conservation and preservation of wildlife, and to adhere to the basic ideal of the International Bowhunting Organization; the unification of all bowhunters.

There are several types of memberships. The most common and numerous is an individual membership, which is for one year. Membership entitles the member to compete for a national award and receive a subscription to the magazine that publishes the IBO Newsletter.

A family membership is also for one year and can include every family member age 13 and older. Family members may participate as individuals, with the same benefits and obligations.

Local bowhunting clubs can also become members of the IBO. If the club has at least ten members who are individual IBO members, it becomes eligible for insurance through an IBO agent.

There is no sanctioning fee for membership clubs to hold an IBO-sanctioned tournament, but the club must follow all IBO

Kim Sehr from Mitchell, Indiana, won first place at the 1993 IBO World Championship, taking home a purse of $5600. She scored a perfect 200 in the event and shoots professionally for Xi Compound Bows.

rules and shoot all of the IBO classes; no exceptions. They must also publicize the classes they will have and the number of awards being offered. If a club wants to vary any of the IBO rules, the variation must be published.

Non-membership clubs wishing to hold IBO-sanctioned shoots must also shoot all IBO classes and abide by all IBO rules, in addition to paying a sanctioning fee.

In both cases, if a representative from the IBO is desired at a match, the local club must pay travel expenses to have the nearest representative attend.

The IBO has several general equipment rules:

* For all adult male classes, maximum draw weight is 80 pounds; for youth and women, 60 pounds.
* Arrows shot must weigh at least 5 grains per pound of peak bow weight.
* If sights, stabilizers or V-bars are used, they must extend no more than 12 inches from the forward edge of the bow nearest the point of attachment.
* Overdraw devices may be used in any class.
* There is no limit to the number of sight pins on the bow.

The following classes are recognized by the IBO:

Male Compound Aided—This calls for a compound bow with fixed sight pins, shooting with a glove, finger tab or bare fingers.
Female Aided—Women may shoot a compound, recurve or longbow with fixed sight pins, shooting with a glove, finger tab or bare fingers.
Male Compound Unaided—This class calls for a compound bow with no sighting device. A rest and plunger are all that may reside within the sight window. There must be no markings on the bow or the bowstring that could be construed as sighting marks. The bow must be shot with a glove, finger tab or bare fingers.

Carefully laid-out shooting lanes allow many hundreds of archers to shoot on a course at the same time. Equipment rules are strictly enforced.

Colin Booth shot first place at the 1993 IBO World Championship in the Male Bowhunter Open division. As a member of the Xi Compound Bow professional shooting team, Booth is a popular winner of may local tournaments.

Female Unaided—Women may shoot a compound, recurve or longbow with no sighting device. A rest and plunger are all that may reside within the sight window. There must be no markings on the bow or the bowstring that could be construed as sighting marks. The bow must be shot with a glove, finger tab or bare fingers.
Male and Female Bowhunter Release—This involves shooting a compound, recurve or longbow with or without a sight. If a sight is used, it must have fixed pins. The bow must be shot with some type of mechanical release aid.
Male and Female Bowhunter Open—These archers shoot a compound, recurve or longbow with movable sight, scope or laser sight. The archer may use any type of release aid, glove, finger tab or bare fingers.
Male Recurve Aided—This class calls for a recurve or longbow with fixed pins. It must be shot with a glove, finger tab or bare fingers.
Male Recurve Unaided—This class calls for a recurve or longbow with no sighting device. A rest and plunger are all that may reside within the sight window. There must be no markings on the bow or the bowstring that could be construed as sighting marks. The bow must be shot with a glove, finger tab or bare fingers.
Youth Aided, 13-17 Years—This class uses a bow with fixed pins, movable sight or scope. It must be shot with a glove, finger tab or bare fingers.
Youth Release, 13-17 Years—This class uses a bow with fixed pins, movable sight or scope. It must be shot with some type of mechanical release aid.
Youth Unaided, 13-17 Years—The bow in this class must have no sighting device. A rest and plunger are all that may reside within the sight window. There must be no markings on the bow or the bowstring that could be construed as sight marks. It must be shot with a glove, finger tab or bare fingers.
Cubs, Through 12 Years—These youngsters may use any type of equipment or style as previously described.

Tournament shots may be uphill or down, simulating many bowhunting situations.

Peewee Class—This is for shooters 8 years and under, shot at a maximum of 15 yards, any style equipment. It is suggested by the IBO that tournament officials announce a scheduled starting time and all shooters be present to begin shooting at one time. A separate range of 10 targets should be set up for this class only. The range may be just an open field with shooting stakes in a straight line and targets at unknown distances up to 15 yards.

Traditional Longbow Class—Besides the regular IBO rules, the traditional bow used in this class can be up to 90 pounds of draw weight. In addition:

1. Adult males shooting the Traditional Longbow Class will use a longbow defined as: A bow, when strung, the string touches only the nocks of the bow limbs. At the shelf, the bow shall be cut no closer than 1/8-inch to the center line of the bow. In case a bow cut for centershot is found, it may be requalified by adding a leather pad to a thickness that will meet the rules. Cushion plungers or mechanical adjustments shall not be permitted.

2. No sights, stabilizers nor counterbalances shall be allowed. Attempts to circumvent this rule by building bows with massive or weighted handles/risers shall disqualify the shooter.

3. Arrow shafts shall have a minimum of 125-grain points.

4. Arrow shafts shall be identical in length, weight and color, except for normal wear. Arrow shafts shall be restricted to wood.

5. Strings shall have a single color middle serving and no marks.

6. One single nocking point only is permitted.

7. One or two nock locators—which may be snap-on type, shrink tubing, thread or dental floss tied or served on the servings—are allowed.

8. Arrows should be shot from the shelf or hand with no elevated rest. Only a piece of leather or similar material 1/8-inch or less thick shall be allowed on the arrow shelf.

9. One anchor point only is permitted.

10. An archer shall shoot only with a Mediterranean release; that is, with one finger above and two fingers below the arrow.

This group of mule deer targets, built by The Critter Factory, is posed in a natural setting on the Redding, California, course.

Professional Class (Previously known as Manufacturers' Class)—Any shooter who shoots in this class during the tournament calender year must remain in the class for the entire shooting calender year. The entry fee is $125 at each leg of the Triple Crown National Championship, with $100 going into the cash purse. A National Championship Triple Crown Team award will be issued by the IBO at the third leg. There will be no additional entry fee for the team competition. There will be no team awards at each individual leg of the Triple Crown. A team will consist of three shooters with the same three shooters at each leg eligible for a National Award. Entry fee for the World Championship is $230, with $200 of it going into the cash purse. There is no team competition at the World Championship. The number and places paid and amounts paid is determined by the number of entries in each event.

Many women shooters score as well as men in IBO tournaments. Manufacturers recognize the women's market with plenty of first-class bows and equipment.

Brush is cleared along an access road to provide a shooting lane to a deer target.

For competitors in all classes, clickers, Fine-Line-type sights and levels are permitted. Fixed pins are defined as pins that are set at a predetermined distance and are not to be moved while on the range. String walkers with marks on the string will be considered aided. No markings are to be added to the finger tab or glove. All unaided classes will be defined additionally as having a string with nothing other than a nocking point.

All protests must be made to the Protest Committee in writing on the protest form and accompanied with a $50 protest fee. The fee will be returned if the protest is upheld. The Protest Committee may rule on any problems or items not specifically covered in the rules. All decisions are final unless a written appeal is received by the IBO at the business office within five days of the incident.

Tournaments with IBO sanctions or sponsorships use the familiar 3-D foam animal targets with the vital areas marked on the sides. Most target manufacturers now label their products as IBO-approved or at least complying with IBO scoring rules.

For national-level competition, IBO scoring gives 10 points for an arrow shot inside the circle of the vital area. The score counts if the arrow at least touches the line. Eight points are scored when the arrow is in the vital area, but not inside the circle. Five points are scored when the arrow strikes anywhere on the remainder of the animal, at least touching the body color. All glance-offs, misses or hits on the horn or hoof area score no points.

For IBO-sanctioned tournaments, the meet may use the national scoring system described above or a slightly different version—the 10-point ring scores the same, but for hits in the vital zone, not in the 10-ring, 6 points are scored; the rules for misses are the same.

Targets are set at unmarked distances at yardages up to 50 yards maximum. The target vital areas must be free from obstacles, and the target distinguishable by shooters. Shooters in the Cub class shoot at 30 yards maximum. The targets are to be either two-dimensional or the more familiar three-dimensional types. The two types may be mixed on the course.

Shooting stake colors are white for Cubs and fluorescent green for all classes except adult male classes. Males have fluorescent orange stakes.

No binoculars, cameras or range finders are permitted on the course, whether used or not. Any violations of these rules will be grounds for disqualification.

As stated earlier, arrow weight must be at least 5 grains per pound of bow shooting weight. For the IBO, total shooting weight is defined as the maximum forward thrusting weight applied to the arrow. Five grains are allowed for scale error and differences between scales. Arrows cannot be equipped with blunts or broadheads.

Working rules of the IBO have been adopted to cover various items during the life of the organization. These rules, according to the IBO, have been used to help establish certain guidelines necessary to better define the basic shooting rules or interpret the intended meaning of the shooting rules. Some of the following rules are for the Triple Crown events only; some pertain to all shoots.

1. Once an archer starts shooting a side or round, he or she must finish with the assigned group, unless otherwise directed by a shoot official.
2. All scorecards will be shuffled, and groups busted. A group with three or four friends or family members plus one outside person is considered busted, provided the outside person is one of the two scorekeepers for the group.
3. Pictures of targets may be posted at registration areas or shooting stakes, or copies may be given to shooters as they begin the event.
4. Double scoring is required.

The Redding, California, tournament course includes a couple of lightweight bridges across steep canyons.

5. Targets must be scored by both scorers before any arrows are touched. Early pulls or handling will result in a score of zero. Repeated offenses will result in the guilty shooter being disqualified.

6. Stakes farthest from the target are to be shot first, unless otherwise directed by the shoot committee.

7. Any arrow released accidentally or deliberately will be considered shot and scored as zero. Any arrow dropped that can be recovered while touching the stake may be re-nocked and shot.

8. All scorecards will be kept by the host club.

9. Fine-Line-type sights are allowed as fixed pins.

10. Circular sight pins are permitted if all the circles are the same size.

11. All scorecards must be legible and complete to be accepted. Scorecards are the responsibility of the shooter. Inaccurate totals may result in the elimination of that shooter's card. No duplicate cards will be issued.

12. Shooters must touch the stake with some part of his or her body while shooting.

13. Any discussion of yardages before arrows are scored will be grounds for disqualification.

14. Anyone competing in any IBO-sanctioned event who alters without authorization, mistakes or falsifies a score shall be disqualified, and shall remain ineligible to compete in any other subsequent event for one year.

There is a two-minute maximum shooting time per target. The time begins when one shooter releases his or her arrow. The next shooter must touch the stake and shoot before the two-minute time is reached. Each group is responsible for the shooters within that group. If other groups point out the time to a group, it is the archers' responsibility to speed up and stay within the allowed time. After a range officer warns a shooter once, the second time will result in a disqualification. If other groups protest, an entire group may be disqualified.

In cases of equipment failure or if any one shooter in a group needs to leave the range for any reason, the entire group must leave the range together. They must report to a range official as they leave and when they are ready to re-enter the range. The official will escort the entire group back to the target they were

Most IBO rules call for a 10-point score in the central ring and 8 points outside the first, but inside the second ring. Five points are scored for anywhere else on the target animal.

to shoot next. Any shooter leaving the range alone will not be allowed to re-start. The range official will determine the amount of time necessary to make the needed repair. The time element will not be abused. Equipment may be re-checked as the group returns to the range.

At the target, a pass-through is defined as an arrow that leaves both an entry and exit hole in the target.

As children grow older, there are provisions for advancing in class by age. Any time after the final day of the current World Championship that the child becomes 9, 13 or 18 years of age, he or she will advance to the next age level of competition, from Peewee, Cub or Youth.

At any IBO shoot, alcoholic beverages may not be carried or consumed on any range or practice area.

As of 1995, not every state and province in North America has IBO tournaments, but most have. Certainly each of these political divisions has some bowhunters, and prospects are good that, in a few years, no area will be without sanctioned 3-D target meets. The International Bowhunting Organization is working hard to bring about that day.

8 The Archery Shooter's Association

Wayne Pearson (center) is the founder and driving force behind the Archery Shooter's Association. Sue Ray and Randy Chappell show off their professional winnings at one tournament.

WAYNE PEARSON STARTED the Archery Shooter's Association in 1992; his love for archery and a recognition of the need for a professional tournament tour were his stated motivations.

"Several years ago, at my tournament in Valdosta, Georgia, we had 1700 shooters. I saw a potential to develop a tournament tour similar to the Professional Golfers Association," says Pearson. "I knew we had to have television to be successful. I could supply that, and we can handle up to 2,400 shooters at any one event. There are a lot of archery shooters out there who want to make a living with bows and arrows. I think it is possible.

"I had a goal of having 40 states represented at the shoot in Valdosta. When we reached that goal, I formed an association and, in 1993, we went on tour."

Pearson is the host of two well-known national television outdoor series. *Outdoor Trail Magazine* is nearing its tenth year in production and is syndicated through various broadcast stations and cable networks. His other program, *Ultimate Outdoors With Wayne Pearson*, is broadcast over ESPN July through December.

Pearson hunts with gun and bow, and is a fine shotgun clay target competitor. He has taken several trophy whitetail with bow and arrow, and he has a number of Pope & Young Club

trophies on his office walls. He is also an avid wild turkey hunter.

In 1991, Pearson became involved with the Hunter Education Association through a third TV show, *Outdoor Classics*, and began to provide youngsters who have successfully completed hunter safety courses the chance to win hunting trips with a parent or guardian.

His love of archery began through bowhunting a decade ago. In 1989, he began his Bowhunter Championship 3-D archery tournaments. These were immediately recognized as well-organized archery tournaments. The formation of the Archery Shooter's Association was a direct result of these earlier tournaments. In the second year of its existence, the ASA provided the largest cash paybacks in the history of competitive archery.

With a potential to reach more than 100 million households through his outdoor television programs, Pearson's efforts with 3-D target archery may soon reach the masses.

At ASA tournaments, shooters are divided into two basic categories: professional and amateur. The professionals pay an entry fee of $250—as of 1994—per tournament. Most professionals have sponsors, either bow companies or some other industry manufacturer. Participation—winning—can lead to big money. As of July, 1993, Virginian Randy Chappell had

93

pocketed more than $20,000 from archery tournaments. A single win at a tournament in Gainesville, Florida, was worth $8,500. He had the potential to finish the year with an income of $50,000 to $75,000. As of July of that year, the total payback for 52 pros at five tournaments had exceeded $120,000. The total pot was more than $816,000 for the year on the Pro-Am tour.

The amateur shooters pay an entry fee of only $20 per tournament, but still compete for cash. Dollars for the amateur tour shooters exceed $700,000 for the year, based on a full field of 480 shooters. At a recent Federation Classic, more that $11,000 was paid out in nine classes to lucky and skilled amateur shooters. Amateurs and pros who compete in the Pro-Am Tournament Trail must belong to the ASA. As of 1994, a membership fee of $20 for an individual, $25 for a family and $400 for a lifetime membership was charged.

Archers shoot at McKenzie 3-D foam targets, with no targets set at ranges of more than forty-five yards. Targets are stationed in a clean hunting environment, and yardage is unknown to the competitor. Scoring is slightly different than other familiar tournaments. A heart shot scores 12 points, an inner kill circle 10, the main kill circle is good for 8, a wound shot will get the archer 5, and a miss is worth zero.

Equipment restrictions for professional shooters are simple—arrow speed cannot exceed 280 feet per second with an 80-pound draw weight maximum. For the most part, the same general rules apply for amateur shooters. Approved binoculars may be used, but range-finding devices are not permitted.

The Federation Amateur Tour is designed for those archers who can't travel to all tour events. A federation tournament is held on a state-wide level with four state-qualifying tournaments in each state. Based on 400 shooters at each event paying a $20 entry fee, there is a payback of $32,000, divided

Women shooters have a place in the ASA tournament ranks; many receive sponsorship assistance.

Two different types of bows and different sights, but both ladies shoot Jennings equipment.

Much of the ASA's beginnings occured in the southeastern part of the U.S. Most of the early tournaments were in Florida and Georgia.

Several established tournaments around the country are aligning themselves with the ASA to attract more shooters.

among classes. That amount increases as more shooters sign up.

An archer may shoot in all four state qualifiers. However, a shooter's final qualifying score will be based on one qualifier over the four separate events. The top 50 percent in each class will qualify for the ASA Federation State Championship match. The top five shooters from each of the nine classes then qualify to compete at the national tournament. The top five from the national tournament qualify for the ASA Classic in Valdosta, Georgia. In addition, the top male and top female at the national tournament are allowed to compete against the professionals for the big money prizes. More than 10,000 archers compete annually on the federation level, according to Pearson.

Major sponsors of the ASA series of tournaments include Easton and Loggy Bayou tree stands. In addition, there are nearly sixty other sponsors, including most of the major bow manufacturers. It is Pearson's plan to make the ASA tournaments a television event, starting with eight televised events and perhaps expanding to a thirteen-week schedule. As it has done with other sports, major and minor, successful television exposure could lure additional sponsors and increased prize money for the shooters.

Pearson's goal is to establish at least $1 million per year for the ASA tournaments. In addition to the Pro-Am Tournament Trail, ASA has developed a plan to sanction local archery clubs to qualify participants for a Federation Tour that will crown state and national champions. Based upon full sign-ups at every ASA tournament, the tour may award up to $744,000 to amateur archers.

The promotion of archery and bowhunting through national television air time is not the end of Pearson's support. For four years, Pearson has donated a minimum of 10 percent of the registration fees from the Bowhunter Championships in Valdosta—more than $16,500 per year—to support the National Archery Association of the United States and the U.S. Olympic Archery Team. He has also earmarked a portion of all ASA Pro-Am registration fees for the Save Our Heritage Program, an effort to maintain and increase the number of persons involved in hunting game.

The nine amateur classes are Men's Open; Men's Unlimited; Men's Limited; Barebow Compound; Traditional; Ladies Unlimited; Ladies Limited; Young Adult, 15-17; and Youth, 12-14.

The **Men's Open** class allows any safe bow-and-arrow combination to be shot in the tournament. The **Men's Unlimited** class calls for use of a mechanical release aid and fixed sight pins on the bow. **Men's Limited** calls for fixed sight pins, fingers only and any arrow point. For the **Barebow Compound** class, archers shoot no sights, fingers only and any arrow point. The **Traditional** class features recurves, longbows, stickbows, no release aids, no sights, no stabilizers, no overdraws and no added weight to the bow.

The **Ladies' Unlimited** calls for any type of sight, a mechanical release aid and any arrow point. The **Ladies' Limited** allows for any type of sight, fingers only and any arrow point.

The **Young Adult** class is for those 15 to 17 years old, shooting whatever equipment they bring to the tournament. The **Youth** class is for those 12 to 14, shooting whatever they choose.

The ASA shooting rules are as follows:

A. All targets will be 3-D targets set at approximately forty-five yards, but unmeasured. The Pro-Ams and North American Championship targets will be McKenzie Natra-Look targets.

B. Archers will shoot in groups of not less than three nor more than six to be able to turn in an official score.

C. One arrow per target will be shot from a painted stake. Stakes will be white for adults, male or female; red for young adults, traditional barebow shooters and ladies unlimited classes; blue for youth shooters.

D. Shooters must touch the stake with some part of their body while shooting.

E. No archer may practice on any part of a course to be used for tournament shooting. Special practice targets will be supplied; no other targets may be used for practice except those supplied.

F. One group shall not hold up the following groups while looking for arrows. Each archer should carry enough arrows to continue shooting the tournament.

G. An archer leaving the range for any reason other than equipment failure may be privileged to return to his or her group and complete an unfinished round. He or she will not be privileged to make up any targets missed in the interim.

This youngster was inspired to build his own bow and arrow. It may be awhile before he turns pro, but youngsters everywhere play their part in the ASA tournaments.

H. In the case of an equipment failure verified by a tournament official, the archer may have the needed time, with a maximum of 45 minutes, for equipment repair or replacement. Then, in the presence of the tournament official, the archer will be allowed to shoot the targets missed. This occurrence of repair or replacement may not happen more than once in the tournament.

I. No archer may compete in more than one class.

J. An 80-pound maximum bow draw weight shall be enforced.

K. There shall be a maximum arrow speed of 280 feet per second, with a three-percent plus or minus margin of error.

The ASA general rules are as follows:

A. There will be absolutely no time changes or class changes.

B. Any participant who is late or does not start with the assigned group at the correct target will not be allowed to shoot. No exceptions and no excuses!

C. Shooters must be on the range for equipment checks 30 minutes before the shotgun start. No spectators will be allowed on the range until after the shotgun start.

D. Talking to spectators while shooting will not be allowed.

This McKenzie whitetail deer target is marked in accordance with IBO and ASA scoring rules. The ASA scores slightly different from the IBO. See the text for details.

Shooters benefit from the support of manufacturers such as Bear/Jennings Archery of Florida.

E. Overdraws will not designate class/shooting style; sight or release type will be the determining factors.

F. Each shooter will be assigned a shooter ID number. This number must appear on all scorecards. It will be the shooter's responsibility to know the number.

G. Scorecards will be color-coded to match the color on the board at the beginning of each range. Shooters must pick up cards as they go onto the range and mark them with a legible, printed name exactly as it appears on the entry form, complete with the shooter ID number. Groups shooting together must turn in cards together.

H. Range finders will not be permitted.

I. Alcoholic beverages may not be carried onto or consumed on tournament grounds.

J. Binoculars will be allowed, but may be checked by a range official for ranging marks.

K. Littering the grounds will not be tolerated. Anyone seen littering will immediately be disqualified from the tournament.

L. Any grievance must be registered with the tournament director in writing and accompanied with a $50 protest fee. All decisions of the protest committee will be final.

M. All winners and/or anyone protested will be subject to a polygraph test.

N. Video cameras will not be allowed on the ranges until the final day of the tournament.

O. All shooters must attend a safety meeting held one hour before each start time.

It would seem Pearson is serious about the ASA and its role in archery's future. He says a dress code, similar to that established by the Professional Golfer's Association, will be enforced during ASA-sanctioned target tournaments. At press time, some of these rules seemed to be in a state of change. Potential tournament shooters should check with their local ASA state representatives or tournament officials for the latest guidelines.

Can a shooter actually earn a decent living at archery? The answer shows up in the first place purses for men's and women's professional divisions. In the qualifying rounds, the first place shooters, either sex, may take home $10,000 each, assuming there are 300 pro shooters in the meet. At the ASA Classic in Valdosta, the top man and woman will receive $45,000 for first, $10,000 for second place and $6,500 for third. The remaining purses work their way down to twentieth place, earning $500 in the Classic. Add in some product endorsements and contingency shooting awards, and it would seem that the top shooters might earn comfortable incomes.

The ASA relies on McKenzie Natra-Look 3-D targets for most tournaments, as outlined in the rules. Antlers are easily replaced or removed.

8

NFAA Shooting Styles and Equipment Rules

THE FIRST SET of rules for the National Field Archery Association was published nearly 30 years ago. Since then, each time they have been revised, they have gotten longer and more detailed. It seems that the people who have governed the NFAA have attempted to cover nearly every eventuality and new equipment development in all that time. Each time there is a question or dispute by a member concerning an infringement or change, a decision must be made, and that decision is incorporated into the next publication of the constitution and by-laws of the organization.

The most important part of the rules deals with equipment that may be used by certain archers in certain classifications. It is important, because many archery tournaments rely upon the NFAA rules, even though the event may not be an officially sanctioned contest. But the breakdown of classifications and equipment is logical and is followed by many shooters and other organizations.

Altogether, the Constitution and By-Laws of the NFAA runs nearly 200 pages and covers everything from membership, officers, directors, committees, fees, shooting rules, instructions for conducting tournaments, awards and hundreds of other specifications. Copies are sold by the NFAA headquarters to those who are interested.

Because of the universality of the styles and equipment rules, we shall include only that portion of the by-laws here. The reference to FITA (*Federation Internationale de Tir a l'Arc*) is the organization responsible for target archery competition around the world. It is under the auspices of FITA that the sport of archery takes place in the Olympics. Recently, the NFAA and the NAA (National Archery Association) have agreed to share responsibilities for the development and conduct of target archery in the United States. Thus, some field archery events are sanctioned by FITA.

ARTICLE II

A. General

1. A conventional bow of any type may be used provided it subscribes to the accepted principal and meaning of the word "bow" as used in archery competition, i.e., an instrument consisting of a handle (grip) riser and two flexible limbs, each ending in a tip with string nock. The bow is braced for use by a single bowstring attached directly between the two string nocks only. In operation it is held in one hand by the handle (grip) riser while the fingers of the other hand draw, hold back and release the string.
2. Compound bows may be used, provided: a) Basic design includes a handle riser (grip) and flexible limbs. b) Total arrow propelling energy is developed from a flexing of the materials employed in limb construction. c) Weight reduction factor is of no consequence. d) Bows which develop any portion of arrow propelling energy from sources "other than the limbs" shall not be allowed. This is not to be construed to mean that compound bows which employ other sources of arrow propelling energy, not specifically listed in this paragraph, will be allowed. e) The cables of the compound bow shall be considered as part of the string and all applicable string rules except color requirements shall apply.
3. The maximum peak bow weight allowed in NFAA competition shall be 80 pounds.
4. This Paragraph Is Applicable Only To Competition On Unmarked Distance Tournaments: The use of a range finder is prohibited. At no time shall any device be allowed that would in any manner be an aid in establishing the distance of any shot. No archer may refer to any written memoranda that would aid in determining the distance to the target.
5. Any device that would allow the mass weight, or the draw weight of the bow, to be relieved from either or both arms, at full draw, shall be declared illegal.
6. All overdraws shall be designed in such a fashion as to prevent the arrow from falling off the rest, endangering other competitors.
7. All equipment rulings must be accompanied by an example of the item in question to the assigned committee and for examination by the Board of Directors prior to voting.

B. Barebow

1. Archers shooting Barebow style will use bow, arrows, strings and accessories free from any sights, marks or blemishes.
   a) String will be made of one or more strands. Strands will be of one consistent color of the archer's choice. The center serving on the string will be served with one layer of any material suitable to use, but material will be of one consistent size and one consistent color. Placement of a nock locator on the serving will be permitted.
   b) No written memoranda shall be allowed.
2. An adjustable arrow plate may be used to control the space between the arrow and the face of the sight window.
3. The use of stabilizers shall be permitted.
4. One consistent nocking point only is permitted.
   a) Nocking point shall be held by one or two nock locators, which shall be snap-on type, shrink tubing, thread or dental floss, tied or served on the serving. Nocking point locators shall not extend more than one-half-inch (1/2-inch) above or below the arrow nock when at full draw.
5. No mechanical device will be permitted other than one nonadjustable draw check and level mounted on the bow, neither of which may extend above the arrow. Note: Mechanical type arrow rests and cushion plungers are legal.
6. Releases other than gloves, tabs, or fingers shall be deemed illegal.
7. All arrows shall be identical in length, weight, diameter and fletching, with allowance for wear and tear.
8. The ends or edges of laminated pieces appearing on the inside of the upper limb shall be considered a sighting mechanism.
9. No device of any type, including arrow rest, that may be used for sighting, may be used or attached to the archer's equipment.
10. The pylon (string clearance bar) will be allowed in this style if it is not located in the sight window.

11. Any part of the arrow rest extending more than 1/4-inch above the arrow is deemed illegal in the Barebow style.
12. An arrow plate extending more than 1/4-inch above the arrow is deemed illegal in the Barebow style.

C. Freestyle
1. Any type of sight and its written memorandum may be used.
2. Any release aid may be used provided it is hand-operated and supports the draw weight of the bow.

D. Freestyle Limited
1. Any type of sight and its written memorandum may be used.
2. Release aids shall be limited to gloves, tabs and fingers.

E. Competitive Bowhunter
1. This style of shooting is for those with heavy tackle equipment used during hunting activities. Junior Bowhunters shall not be recognized.
2. No device of any type (including arrow rest), that may be used for sighting, may be used or attached to the archer's equipment.
3. There shall be no device, mechanical or otherwise, in the sight window except the arrow rest and/or cushion plungers.
4. Any part of the arrow rest extending more than 1/4-inch above the arrow shaft is deemed illegal in the Competitive Bowhunter style.
5. An arrow plate extending more than 1/4-inch above the arrow is deemed illegal in the Competitive Bowhunter style.
6. No clickers, draw checks, or levels will be allowed. No laminations, marks, or blemishes may appear in the sight window.
7. A string of suitable material with a center serving and end servings of the same or different color than the string may be used. One consistent nocking point only is permitted. Nocking point locators shall not extend more than one-half-inch (1/2-inch) above or below the arrow nock when at full draw. Any marks, ties or string attachment to the string (except brush buttons and silencers properly located) shall invalidate its use in this division.
8. One anchor point only is permitted.
9. An archer must draw and anchor the bowstring with one finger above and touching the arrow nock, with the remaining fingers below, with the middle finger touching the bottom of the arrow nock, the third finger if used, touching the middle finger, or an archer must draw and anchor the bowstring with fingers below the arrow nock, with the top finger used, touching the arrow nock and all other fingers below touching each other with no gap between any fingers.

   Finger position may not be changed during competition. In cases of physical deformity or handicap, special dispensation shall be made.
10. Releases other than gloves, tabs, or fingers shall be deemed illegal.
11. Each time an archer shoots a round, all arrows shall be identical in length, weight, diameter and fletching with allowances for wear and tear.
12. The Field Captain, or his counterpart, shall be the final authority regarding equipment and style eligibility, and may reclassify at his discretion.
13. Brush buttons, string silencer, no less than 12 inches above or below the knocking point, and bow quiver installed on the opposite side of the sight window, with no part of the quiver or attachments visible in the sight window, are legal. One straight stabilizer, coupling device included if used, which cannot exceed 12 inches at any time, as measured from the back of the bow, may be used in the Competitive Bowhunter style. No forked stabilizer or any counter balance will be legal.
14. The following broadhead standard will be followed whenever broadheads are authorized for tournaments:
    a) Male—7/8-inch cutting edge width (minimum).
    b) Female—3/4-inch cutting edge width (minimum).
15. Arrows must be equipped with a minimum of 100-grain point assembly(s) for men, 75 grains for women. This means the point and its components must weigh a minimum of appropriate grains, or if an insert is required to attach the point to the arrow, the assembly must be removable for verification.
16. Any device for lengthening or shortening the draw length of an archer shall be prohibited.
17. An archer will not be permitted to change the draw weight of the bow during a round.
18. The pylon (string clearance bar) will be allowed in this shooting style if it is not located in the sight window.
19. No written memoranda shall be allowed.
20. All official NFAA rounds shall be considered official rounds for the Bowhunter style of shooting, and further all classification shall be based upon the Field and Hunter rounds.
21. During a round, no adjustments may be made to the Bow and its related equipment unless an equipment failure is recognized.
22. Camouflage bows will be allowed.

F. Freestyle Bowhunter
1. A sight with a maximum of five fixed horizontal reference points and a maximum one fixed vertical reference point that must not be moved during a round. Reference points are to be of straight stock from point of anchor to sighting point. Hooded pins or scopes with glass cannot be used. The maximum sight extension measurement shall be 5 inches, measured from the back of the bow at the center of attachment to the furthest pin, as measured on a horizontal plane. Electrically lighted sights are illegal.
2. Release aids will be permitted.
3. A kisser button or string peep sight will both be permitted. They must be installed and secured so as not to be moved during a round.
4. It will not be mandatory in this style of shooting to provide for other than one division for men and one division for women.
5. Pinguards will be allowed in this style of shooting providing there are no marks or blemishes which can be used for sighting purposes.
6. There shall be no device, mechanical or otherwise, in the sight window except the arrow rest and/or cushion plungers. Any part of the arrow rest extending more that 1/4-inch above the arrow shaft is deemed illegal.
7. No clickers, draw checks or levels will be allowed.
8. A string of suitable material with a center serving and end servings of the same or different color than the string may be used. One consistent nocking point only is permitted. Nocking point locators shall not extend more than 1/2-inch above or below the arrow nock when at full draw. Brush buttons and string silencers properly attached will be legal.
9. One anchor point only is permitted.
10. Each time an archer shoots a round, all arrows shall be identical in size, length, weight and fletching with allowances for wear and tear.
11. Brush buttons, string silencers, no less than 12 inches above or below the nocking point, and bow quiver installed on the opposite side of the sight window, with no part of the quiver or attachments visible in the sight window, are legal. One straight stabilizer, coupling device included if used, which cannot exceed 12 inches at any time, as measured from the back of the bow, may be used. No forked stabilizer or any counter balance will be legal.
12. Arrows must be equipped with a minimum of 100-grain point assembly(s) for men, 75 grains for women. This means the point and its components must weigh a minimum of appropriate grains, or if an insert is required to attach the point to the arrow, assembly must be removable for verification.
13. An archer will not be permitted to change the draw weight of the bow during a round.
14. No written memorandum shall be allowed.
15. During a round, no adjustments may be made to the bow and its related equipment unless equipment failure is recognized.

G. Freestyle Limited Bowhunter
1. Same as Freestyle Bowhunter except for these restrictions:
   a) Release aids will not be permitted.
   b) An archer must draw and anchor the bowstring with one finger

above and touching the arrow nock, with the remaining fingers below, with the middle finger touching the bottom of the arrow nock, the third finger if used, touching the middle finger, or an archer must draw and anchor the bow string with fingers below the arrow nock, with the top finger used, touching the arrow nock and all other fingers below touching each other with no gap between any finger. Finger position may not be changed during competition. In cases of physical deformity or handicap, special dispensation may be made.

H. Traditional

1. This style of shooting is for those who wish to compete with the recurve or longbow.
2. No device of any kind, including arrow rest, that can be used for sighting, will be used or attached to the archers' equipment.
3. There shall be no device, mechanical or otherwise, in the sight window except the arrow rest, arrow plate or plunger button.
4. No part of the rest or arrow plate may extend more than 1/4-inch above the arrow.
5. No clickers, drawchecks or levels will be allowed. No laminations, marks or blemishes on the face of the bow in the sight window will be legal.
6. The string may be of any color but must have a single color center serving. One single nocking point is permitted. One or two nock locators may be used. Brush buttons and string silencers, properly placed, may be used. Any other marks or string attachments will be illegal.
7. One anchor point only is permitted.
8. The archer shall touch the arrow when nocked and drawing the arrow with the index finger against the nock. Finger position may not be changed during competition.
9. Gloves, tabs or fingers shall be the only legal releases.
10. Each time an archer shoots a round, all arrows shall be identical in length, weight, diameter and fletching with allowance for wear and tear.
11. No stabilizer or counter balance may be used.
12. There shall be no restriction on the bow draw weight. Arrows must have 100-grain minimum point assembly(s) for men and women.
13. No written memorandum will be allowed.
14. Bow slings are permissible.

All RIC rulings for this style of shooting that are in conflict with these new rules (1992) shall be rescinded.

I. FITA COMPETITOR'S EQUIPMENT
(As listed in the January 1,1994, edition of the FITA Constitution and Rules)

7.3 COMPETITORS' EQUIPMENT

* This Article lays down the type of equipment competitors are permitted to use when shooting for FITA purposes.
* If it becomes necessary for an archer to use equipment which has not been inspected by the judges, the onus is on the competitor to show this equipment to the judges before using it.
* Any competitor found to be using equipment contravening FITA rules may have his scores disqualified.
* First are given the general regulations that shall apply to all disciplines. Then follow the special extra regulations that apply only to certain disciplines.

7.3.1 COMPETITORS' EQUIPMENT GENERAL REGULATIONS
7.3.1.1 For the Olympic Division, the following items are permitted:

* A Bow of any type provided it subscribes to the accepted principle of the meaning of the word Bow as used in Target Archery, i.e., an instrument consisting of a handle (grip), riser and two flexible limbs each ending in a tip with a string nock. The bow is braced for use by a single string attached directly between the two string nocks only, and in operation is held in one hand by its handle (grip) while the fingers of the other hand draw, hold back and release the string.

* A Bow String may be made up of any number of strands of the material chosen for the purpose, with a center serving to accommodate the drawing fingers, a nocking point to which may be added serving(s) to fit the arrow nock as necessary, and to locate this point one or two nock locators may be positioned, and in each of the two ends of the bow string a loop to be placed in the string nocks of the bow when braced. In addition one attachment is permitted on the string to serve as lip or nose mark. The serving on the string must not end within the archer's vision at full draw. A bow string must not in any way offer aid in aiming through a "peephole" marking or any other means.

* An Arrow Rest, which can be adjustable, any movable pressure button, pressure point or arrowplate may all be used on the bow provided they are not electric or electronic and do not offer any additional aid in aiming. The pressure point shall be placed no further than 4cm back (inside) from the throat of the handle (pivot point) of the bow.

* One Draw Check Indicator, audible and/or visual, other than electric or electronic, may be used.

* A Bowsight or a Bowmark for aiming is permitted, but at no time may more than one such device be used.

* A Bowsight attached to the bow for the purpose of aiming which may allow for windage adjustment as well as elevation setting is subject to the following provisions:
  It shall not incorporate a prism or lens or any other magnifying device, leveling or electric or electronic devices, nor shall it provide for more than one sighting point.
  An extension to which the Bowsight is fixed is permitted.
  A Bowmark is a single mark made on the bow for the purpose of aiming. Such mark may be made in pencil, tape or any suitable marking material.
  A plate or tape with distance marking may be mounted on the bow as a guide for marking, but must not in any way offer any additional aid.

* Stabilizers and Torque Flight Compensators on the bow are permitted provided they do not:
  Serve as a string guide;
  Touch anything but the bow;
  Represent any obstacle to other competitors as far as place on the shooting line is concerned.

* Arrows of any type may be used provided they subscribe to the accepted principle and meaning of the word Arrow as used in Target Archery, and that such arrows do not cause undue damage to target faces or buttresses. An arrow consists of a shaft with head (point), nock fletching and, if desired, cresting. The arrows of each competitor shall be marked on the shaft with the competitor's name or initials, and all arrows used for the same end of three or six arrows shall carry the same pattern and color(s) of fletching, nocks and cresting, if any.

* Finger Protection in the form of finger stalls or tips, gloves, or shooting tab or tape (plaster) to draw, hold back and release the string are permitted, provided they do not incorporate any device to help hold, draw and release the string. A Separator between the fingers to prevent pinching the arrow may be used. On the bow hand an ordinary glove, mitten or similar item may be worn. An anchor plate or similar device attached to the finger protection (tab) for the purpose of anchoring is permitted.

* Field Glasses, telescopes and other visual aids may be used for spotting arrows. Ordinary spectacles as necessary or Shooting Spectacles and sunglasses. None must be fitted with micro-hole lenses, or similar devices, nor marked in any way which can assist in aiming. The glass of the non-sighting eye may be fully covered or taped, or an eye patch may be used.

* Accessories are permitted such as bracers, dress shield, bow sling, belt or ground quiver, tassel, and foot markers (See also Article 7.3.2.1.)

7.3.1.3 For the Compound Division, the following equipment is described.

Generally speaking all types of additional devices, unless they are electric or electronic, are permitted within the limitations given below:

* A Compound Bow, where the draw is mechanically varied by a system of pulleys and/or cams. The peak draw weight must not exceed 60 pounds. The bow is braced for use by either a single bowstring attached directly between the two string nocks of the bow limbs, or attached to the bow cable, as may be applicable to the particular design. Cable guards are permitted.
* A Bowstring of any number of strands of the material chosen for the purpose, with a center serving to accommodate the drawing fingers or release aid. A nocking point may be fitted to which may be added serving(s) to fit the arrow nock as necessary. To locate this point, one or two nock locators may be fitted. In addition, attachments are permitted on the string to serve as a lip or nose mark, a peephole, a peephole "hold-in-line" device.
* An Arrowrest, which can be adjustable, any movable pressure button, pressure point or arrow plate on the bow provided they are not electric or electronic. The pressure point shall be placed no further than 6cm back (inside) from the throat of the handle (pivot point of the bow.)
* Draw Check Indicators, audible and/or visual, other than electric or electronic, may be used.
* A Bowsight attached to the bow, which may allow for windage adjustment as well as elevation setting, which may also incorporate a leveling device, and/or magnifying lenses and/or prisms. An extension to which the bowsight is fixed is permitted. Electric or electronic devices are not permitted.
* Stabilizers and Torque Flight Compensators, provided that they do not:
   Serve as a string guide;
   Touch anything but the bow;
   Represent any obstacle to other archers as far as place on the shooting line is concerned.
* Arrows of any type may be used provided that they subscribe to the accepted principal and meaning of the word Arrow as used in Target Archery, and that such arrows do not cause undue damage to target faces or buttresses. An arrow consists of a shaft with head (point), nock, fletchings and, if desired, cresting. The arrows of each competitor shall be marked on the shaft with the competitor's name or initials, and all arrows used for the same end of three or six arrows, shall carry the same pattern and color(s) of fletching, nocks and cresting, if any.
* Finger Protection in the form of finger stalls or tips, gloves, shooting tab or tape (plaster) to draw, hold back and release the string. A Separator between the fingers to prevent pinching the arrow may be used. An anchor plate or similar device attached to the finger protection (tab) for the purpose of anchoring is permitted. A release aid that must not be attached in any way to the bow nor incorporate electric or electronic devices may be used. On the bow hand an ordinary glove, mitten or similar item may be worn.
* Field Glasses, telescopes and other visual aids may be used. Ordinary spectacles as necessary, or Shooting Spectacles and sunglasses. None must be fitted with micro-hole lenses or similar devices nor marked in any way which can assist in aiming. The glass of the non-sighting eye may be fully covered or taped, or an eye patch may be used.
* Accessories are permitted such as bracers, dress shield, bow sling, quiver, tassel and foot markers. (See also Article 7.3.2.1)

7.3.1.4. For the Barebow Division, the following items are permitted:
* A Bow of any type, provided it subscribes to the accepted principle and meaning of the word Bow as used in Target Archery; i.e. an instrument consisting of a handle (grip), riser and two flexible limbs each ending in a tip with a string nock. The bow is braced for use by a single bowstring attached directly between the two string nocks only and in operation is held in one hand by its handle (grip) while

the fingers of the other hand draw, hold back and release the string. The bow must be bare, except for the arrow rest as mentioned below, and free from protrusions, marks, blemishes or laminated pieces which could be of use in aiming. The inside of the upper limb shall be without trade marks. Integrally fitted Torque Flight Compensators are permitted provided that they are not fitted with stabilizers or added weights.
* A Bowstring of any number of strands of the material chosen for the purpose with a center serving to accommodate the drawing fingers, a nocking point to which may be added serving(s) to fit the arrow nock and, to locate this point, one or two nock locators, as well as at each end of the bowstring a loop to be placed in the string nocks of the bow when braced. The serving on the string must not end within the archer's vision at full draw. The bowstring must in no way offer aid in aiming through a peephole, marking, or any other means.
* An Arrowrest, which can be adjustable, a movable pressure button, pressure point or arrow plate on the bow provided they are not electric or electronic and do not offer any additional aid in aiming.
* Arrows of any type which subscribe to the accepted principle and meaning of the word Arrow as used in Target Archery, and which do not cause undue damage to target faces and buttresses. An arrow consists of a shaft with head (point), nock, fletching and, if desired, cresting. All arrows used at any one target (i.e. numbered target) shall carry the same pattern and color(s) of fletching, nocks and cresting, if any. The arrows of each competitor shall be of the same length and marked on the shaft with the competitor's name or initials.
* Finger Protection in the form of finger stalls or tips, gloves, shooting tab or tape (plaster) to draw, hold back and release the string, provided they do not incorporate any device to help hold, draw and release the string. A Separator between the fingers to prevent pinching the arrow may be used. On the bow hand an ordinary glove, mitten or similar item may be worn. An anchor plate or similar device attached to the finger protection (tab) for the purpose of anchoring is permitted.
* Field Glasses, telescopes and other visual aids may be used, ordinary spectacles as necessary, or Shooting Spectacles and sunglasses. None must be fitted with micro-hole lenses or similar devices nor marked in any way which can assist in aiming. The glass of the non-sighting eye may be fully covered or taped, or any eye patch may be used.
* Accessories such as arm guard, dress shield, bow sling, quiver or tassel. (See also Article 7.3.2.1)

7.3.2 COMPETITORS' EQUIPMENT SPECIAL REGULATIONS
7.3.2.1 For Field Archery:
* Field glasses, telescopes and other visual aids may be used at any time to spot arrows. The field glasses must be of standard design, however, and may not have scales of any kind on the lenses or incorporate any other means for evaluating distances.
* For competitors of all Classes the following equipment is not permitted:
   Range finders or any other means of estimating distances that are not covered by the current rules regarding competitors' equipment;
   Any written memoranda apart from notes concerning the competitors' normal sight marks or the recording of the present personal scores;
   Any electronic storage device.
* In the Barebow Division competitors may not use:
   Sights;
   Draw check indicators.
* In the FITA Forest Round, all arrows must be numerically marked and shot in ascending order.

9

Home On The Range

Practice Is What Builds Scores—A Backyard 3-D Target Course Will Help!

EXCLUDING APARTMENT dwellers and condominium residents, virtually every other archer should have room for at least one practice target somewhere in his yard. Some of us who reside in less congested areas have sufficient open space for several 3-D animal targets on our properties, creating mini-field courses.

Those who live in apartment buildings or condominiums may have trouble locating the open space required for a range, but perhaps a neighbor or friend can help. A local archery club or retail dealer also may offer places to shoot. More and more firearms dealers are recognizing the growth of archery and offer small practice ranges alongside or behind their places of business for those who want to shoot a few arrows. Some offer league-type shooting competitions for a nominal fee. Many archers find they will shoot more arrows when a little friendly competition is involved in addition to routine backyard practice.

With a little luck, some planning and adequate space, the imaginative archer can lay out a safe course of up to a dozen 3-D animal targets in realistic settings. The amount of area available may range in size from a twenty-yard driveway with a safe backstop to an acre or more for those who live in the country. The more space available, the easier and more exciting the task will be.

With a large enough backyard, the only restriction will be the cost of a dozen 3-D animal targets. As of early 1995, most foam animal targets were retailing for around $130 each. At that price, a dozen targets would put a strain on the recreational budgets of many individuals, although discounts through clubs or dealers may be available. A small group of archers may wish to pool their efforts and resources and share the cost of eight or ten targets to be placed in the largest yard.

Safety, of course, is the most important consideration for which every archer must plan. Safety is the utmost priority when shooting into a couple of straw bales in front of the garage door or through a complicated, realistic 3-D course of a half-dozen targets. When setting any target, one must *always* examine the background—the area behind the target. What is behind it and how far away is it? Is there even the most remote possibility that an errant arrow might fly past or over the target

The backyard target range takes advantage of existing terrain to put target animals in realistic situations.

Trees and brush will add challenge to shooting 3-D targets.

Artificial antlers sold with most deer targets will help the practicing bowhunter avoid "buck fever" during the season.

and into a building or onto another's property? Will other humans or animals be endangered? If the possibility exists, the location of the target or the shooting angle to the target must be changed.

Another recognized consideration involves conservation of arrows and other equipment. After all, arrows are an expense, and those that become broken or lost can add up to several hundred dollars a year, if the archer is unlucky or careless. These days, $50 for a dozen arrows is considered average. Some arrows approach a price of half again that much.

If possible, the backstop area should be free of large rocks or other impenetrable objects. An arrow that strikes a rock will most likely be destroyed. Invariably, if the shaft is aluminum, it will be bent beyond repair or have the head insert jammed back into the shaft so far as to split or bulge the shaft wall. A carbon arrow will likely be split with such an impact and will also be irreparable.

But that involves only monetary damage; you can always buy more arrows. A ricocheting arrow can prove dangerous to the archer who shot it, as well as to others in the area—even a damaged arrow can fly hundreds of feet.

Ideally, soft, clean sand might be the best backstop, but only a few of us have that luxury behind any of our personal shooting areas. Tall, thick grass or weeds works well, although there is the continual risk of losing arrows. Still, the high grass will usually slow arrow flight quickly, bringing the missile safely to a stop.

In some situations, it might be good to place a stack of straw or excelsior bales behind the 3-D targets. The important thing is

Targets such as Browning's wild boar may be placed in front of or behind tree trunks to add variety to backyard practice.

to ensure that the backstop will stop any errant arrows. In a perfect world, all the arrows will hit the target, but misses do happen. Practice safety with those arrows.

Most tournament courses are spread across ten, twenty or more acres, running through woods, across meadows, up and down hillsides. A national tournament, such as one put on by the National Field Archery Association, might cover fifty acres. The course must be laid out so groups of archers will be safe from flying arrows to the side of and even behind tar-

This little scene might depict a doe in heat with several interested bucks after her. Practice rules may put one or more targets off-limits.

There are small foam targets available that depict smaller game such as raccoons and opossums. Put them in realistic situations for a challenge.

gets. These protections can be in the form of backstops, obstacles or extra distance.

The home 3-D layout will certainly not have as many archers on the course as would established tournament grounds. Instead of laying out the backyard course so the shooter must move from target to target, from one shooting lane to another, the animal targets may be situated so several are shot from one or two locations on the property.

Imagine a flat, grassy area measuring 100 yards square. If your backyard looked like that, you might stand precisely in the middle and have someone place eight or ten 3-D animal targets at various distances and at equal radiating angles. The archer would stand at the hub of the imaginary wheel with the targets at the ends of the different-length spokes. One, two or several shooters could stand in the center, keeping their backs to one another, and shoot a round of targets by simply rotating slowly from one target to the next. Presuming safe backstops have been constructed and nobody else will be entering the yard, such an arrangement would be safe.

Such an area would be safe, but boring. One could have a few trees to break up the plain appearance of the scene and create a degree of challenge. One could even add some folds in the terrain. By means of dirt berms, one could put in a few valleys, hills, canyons and more trees. The area would soon resemble a typical 3-D target course. This will continue to be a safe area from which to shoot, as long as all archers stay in the center and enter and leave the course at the same time. This would be ideal for a small range setup.

Most of us cannot financially afford to change our backyards to the degree outlined above, but the idea is to establish a safe area from where several targets can be shot without much movement by the archers. If the area is flexible enough, the 3-D targets can be moved slightly from time to time to vary the course. An animal may be positioned within a grove of small trees or in a cleared lane through brush. The distances might also be altered with each practice session.

Should a single shooting point not be possible, the backyard might well lend itself to two or three shooting locations instead of one. Considering the sameness—and the resulting boredom factor—a single shooting point may eventually prove to be lacking in fun at practice time.

After shooting a few ends, even a large range can become boring; all the targets have been shot from exactly the same angle and height. The archer tends to become too familiar with the distance and the vital zones of each target, if they have the typical IBO scoring areas on them. The challenge and practice value may be reduced due to overfamiliarity with the range.

A number of other backyard range configurations can be constructed, depending upon the local terrain. One alternative is a walk along a hillside. A dirt hillside would be ideal for the butts. There might be room for two, three or more targets set at the bottom of a hill or bank. The shooter could walk along a straight line, taking a shot or two at each target. If there is room, the targets may be set at different distances. If space is limited, let imagination simulate different ranges and use smaller targets or smaller vital/scoring areas instead of longer distances.

At the risk of repetition, constantly keep safety in mind when shooting in a walk-along target area. For instance, the archer might be able to shoot at two or three targets from a single position before moving on to another location. Arrangement of your 3-D targets in a limited space can be interesting and challenging, but be careful that the arrow trajectories do not cross from one location to the next. Do not plan the shooting lanes in such a way that a careless shot from one location might possibly cross into the shooting zone of another shooter several yards away.

Those who lay out tournament courses with sixty or seventy targets are acutely aware of arrow trajectories at maximum distances and angles. In a tournament situation, the challenge is to offer enough safe shooting room for hundreds of archers at the same time. The same considerations should be given in developing your home range.

The ideal home situation might be an L-shaped or U-shaped hillside. Several targets may be placed at the bottom of the slope. The shooter could take a shot at two or three targets from one position before moving left or right to engage another couple of targets. A miss will put the errant arrow into the hillside without danger to other shooters or bystanders. While shooting in this situation, one must not permit people or pets to stand atop the hill. Even relatively slow-flying arrows have been known to ricochet dangerously after striking a rock or other hard object. As indicated earlier, a ricocheting arrow is a danger in itself!

Laying out a course around a hillside and walking around the base is another practical possibility, but if more than one person is shooting the course, shooters should stay together in a single group. One would not want to be on the opposite side of a hill shooting at a target while another archer is coming to a full draw, even with the apparent protective bulk of the hill between them.

Given any specific piece of backyard, the essential ingredient is imagination. Look over the terrain and decide on the best way to lay out a short, challenging course. Even one 3-D practice target can add spice to what otherwise becomes routine practice sessions.

If you can't afford the hundred bucks or so for a factory-manufactured 3-D animal target, there are several homemade possibilities. Who says you have to practice with only a 3-D target?

With enough space, the backyard range may include several deer and other animal targets. The hillside in the background will stop errant arrows.

Typical black bear habitat will be in shadows in dense growth areas, seldom in the open. Pay attention to the target background.

Shooting from one hillside down into a valley with another hillside behind is an ideal situation. The far hill should be free of rocks and other solid objects.

In this situation, the archer may practice a stalk through the stream bed and shoot from several distances.

Put up your old bullseye practice target in a new, interesting location. Get away from the golf-course-like yard and put the target between two tree trunks or partially hide it in some brush. Shoot down an embankment, if you have one. If you have a tree that will hold a treestand, put up the stand and shoot from there. Incidentally, even during practice, one always should wear a safety belt when in a tree stand. Back-yard target practice is no exception to this rule. Furthermore, wearing the belt will add realism to bowhunting practice. As hunting season nears, be sure to wear all your hunting clothing during some practice sessions. Practice is the time to find out if the added bulk may interfere with good arrow flight.

If you have none of these natural surroundings, you can still put up some artificial barriers or erect obstacles around the bullseye target. Mentally add some score points for the toughest shot and subtract points for putting the arrow outside the imaginary scoring zone. A couple of bent or damaged arrows can be used as zone markers.

Lacking even a foam bullseye target, consider reverting back to a homemade cardboard animal target. These have been in use for decades by field-archery shooters. You can make your own out of brown cardboard, which is almost the color of many North American deer, thus adding realism to the target.

Mark out a rough outline of the animal's kill zone, invisible from twenty yards away, but which is useful for scoring in shooting practice. Such cardboard targets are easy to mount on straw or wood shavings bales, and they cost almost nothing.

Whether your backyard course is simple or elaborate, keep in mind that the most important factor is safety. It is imagination that adds challenge and variety to your archery practice. The more fun it is, the more you will want to practice—and the more your target scores or your bowhunting results should improve!

10 *Practice Can Be Fun*

Archers Who Practice Enough Are Almost Assured Of Success In Hunting And Target Shooting

ARCHERY PRACTICE can be tedious. It may be downright boring at times, but it does not have to be either of these. Practice can be exciting, rewarding, fun, stimulating, inspiring and exhilarating. And it can lead to success at the season's archery tournaments with monetary rewards. Enough of the right kind of practice also will help the bowhunter fill that whitetail deer tag or put a bull elk trophy on the wall.

To develop the proper arrow-shooting techniques, virtually any type of target will do. The important thing is to follow the basics of good style when executing each shot. In theory, it does not matter what kind of targets or butts into which one shoots the arrows. However, because we all get bored from time to time, most of us need some sort of diversion and variety in our activities to keep our interest at peak form.

Yes, Olympic target shooters in many countries shoot at bullseye targets hour after hour, day after day. We have seen this particularly in the Far East. The Koreans win a lot of Olympic medals using that kind of archery practice. Most of us would reject that kind of boredom.

One way to spice things up and prepare for bowhunting at the same time is to practice on 3-D animal targets. The average archer will get just as much bow and arrow time at the range as the above-mentioned practice method, but will have a lot more fun. Any 3-D animal target will do, as long as it is marked with tournament-type scoring rings. The rings are visible only when close and when pulling arrows. They cannot be seen from shooting distances, but the lines encompass the average animal's vitals. That is what makes this type of practice so valuable to the bowhunter.

The target is the same size and color of the actual game animal, and the hunter gets practice placing his arrows in the vital organs for a quick kill. The archer will also become familiar with how a deer or other game animal looks from different distances. This should increase the hunter's range-

The new McKenzie Aim-Rite 3-D target is designed and sold primarily for bowhunter practice. The whitetail deer target is anatomically accurate and has a replaceable plug at the vital area.

Field points or broadheads may be used for practice with the Aim-Rite target. Most shooting will be with field points for extended target use.

The flexible foam plug of the Aim-Rite may be replaced when it is shot out. Both sides of the target may be used to increase the serviceable life of the target.

estimating skills, which is vital to the success of every bowhunter.

In the middle of 1994, just before the early deer seasons, McKenzie Natra-Look Targets came up with a new 3-D animal practice target and a matching training program for bowhunters or archery competitors. The target is typical of McKenzie—realistic in size, shape, color and detail. It has a replaceable plug where the deer's vitals would be. The target is called an Aim-Rite, and the replaceable core is made of durable, flexible foam. The target can be shot from either side to prolong its range life.

The good news for most archers is that it is intended to retail for less than most targets made for tournaments, but has most of the same features as other McKenzie 3-D targets. The Aim-Rite includes a set of supporting steel rods—actually sections of concrete reinforcing bar—synthetic antlers, an order form to

obtain additional replaceable plugs and a written training program.

The target is shipped in two pieces to remain within the size restrictions of most parcel shipping companies. The weight is no problem, as it tips the scales at no more than 25 pounds. The Aim-Rite measures 34 inches to the top of the shoulders and is 47 inches from nose to tail.

The target, notes McKenzie, is intended to be used with field points, but broadheads may be used sparingly. Broadheads will shorten the life of the replaceable plug in the vitals area. The frugal archer will restrict broadhead-shooting sessions to final practice days, just before the opening of deer season, after shooting plenty of field-point arrows.

The target is quick and easy to set up, similar to most other 3-D animal targets. The front and rear legs of the deer have sections of hollow tubing moulded into the legs. The tubes are

Most 3-D foam targets, including this wild boar by Browning, are marked with a scoring/vital area not visible from a hunting distance.

sized to accept two reinforcing bar sections, without too much space.

To easily establish the distance between the bars, McKenzie suggests first placing the target on the ground and then pounding the bars about halfway into the ground where the tubing openings line up with the rods. A little adjustment of distance and angle of the rods may be necessary as the target is slipped down onto them. The head section is slipped down on the standing body. The archer may have to use a bit of pressure to get the target settled down into position.

The included antlers may be used to make the target a buck or left off to depict a doe. Either way, the target practice is the same. The antlers are pushed down into the head at marked locations. Once the antlers are pushed down as far as possible, basic assembly of the target is complete.

As mentioned, practicing with a 3-D target has several benefits. Whether or not you are a bowhunter, the realistic deer target adds variety and fun to the practice session. If you are a tournament shooter, there is no better way to practice than with a target that is similar to what you may encounter at the next club meet.

If the next hunting season is what you look forward to, practice with a 3-D target is the best way to train. In addition to improving your archery proficiency, you will learn about field range estimation, how best to shoot through or past natural obstacles and improve your knowledge of deer anatomy.

More often than not, knowledge of where to place an arrow is at least as important as the ability to get the arrow to the target. One of the purposes for the design of the McKenzie Aim-Rite target is to improve the archer's understanding of deer anatomy, or at least the whitetail deer's anatomy.

In the written training program, the manufacturer states:

The Aim-Rite target comes fitted with a plug that represents the largest, most lethal area to shoot. If the plug area is hit from the broadside position, the shot will hit lethal organs—primarily the lungs. The plug is positioned clear of what would be bones or organs that may only cripple the deer when hit. There are other areas that would be lethal if hit correctly. However, it is not recommended to consider these areas, because the margin for error is too great. When hunting, the ethical hunter should look for the highest percentage of possibility for a quick-killing shot, even if it means passing up a shot at the animal.

Most bowhunters will agree with that advice, no matter what the game. We must all recognize our obligation to pass on shots in the best interest of the animal.

The instructions accompanying the Aim-Rite target also state:

To practice with the Aim-Rite target, we suggest you start as simply as possible from a range of 10 yards. Set the target on level ground and pace off ten steps. Aim for a spot within the vital plug and shoot. It is extremely important that you aim at a spot on the animal. One of the biggest mistakes a hunter will make is simply aiming at the animal. This leads to misses or, at the least, poorly placed shots. Concentrate on determining where the most lethal area is on the intended target and aim for that spot, even if it is only a tuft of hair. Aiming for that spot will help your concentration and your technique. This dramatically increases the possibility for a successful shot.

Shooting from only 10 yards has a couple of benefits for the archer. At the start, you will become more familiar with the equipment you are using. This may be especially important if you have new gear or if you have done some re-tuning of older equipment since the last hunting season. This goes double for the beginning archer with all new gear.

The archer will also become familiar with shooting at a single spot in the vital area. Do not only look at the marked-out vital area as the place to shoot an arrow. Keep shooting at your chosen spot on the vitals until every arrow is hitting that spot in the plug. When that becomes routine, you will have established your maximum effective range at 10 yards. During your next hunting trip, you should not attempt any shots at live game beyond that range.

Most of us will want to extend our maximum effective range beyond 10 yards before the start of the season. Pace off another five yards from the target and commence shooting at the spot on the vital area. Continue shooting arrows, using your best concentrated technique, until you begin to tire.

When the muscles become overtaxed, arrows will not hit the plug as consistently as before, and you are likely to make shooting errors. Depending upon your eyesight, the plug may begin to lose some of its visible outline. That is not all bad, because it will force you to concentrate on a spot on the animal where you must imagine the vital area to be, rather than a marked plug. But perhaps the best thing to do is put away your gear and shoot another day.

When you return to the practice range, plan to begin the next session at a distance just a little short of your longest accurate shots the last time out. This technique will lend a bit of a psychological boost. You will see more confidence and accuracy with the first few arrows of the new practice session. After all the arrows are flying well at this slightly shorter distance, move back another five yards to the previous session's best range and keep shooting.

At some point, every archer will learn his maximum effective range. It cannot be stretched at any particular stage of the shooter's development and level of equipment. In many parts of the country, the average successful shot at live game is less than 25 yards. In other areas, the average killing shot may be a few yards more, but not many.

It is true that many game animals have been taken at considerably longer distances, but a responsible bowhunter should never attempt a shot at a live animal beyond what he knows to be accurate with every arrow. Plenty of archery tournaments feature 3-D targets at much longer ranges, but these are foam animals, not live animals.

Once the maximum effective range is established, the archer should continue to practice at various distances within that maximum distance. The archer may set up stakes or place some sort of marks in the dirt at several known distances within that range restriction. Move from distance to distance and shoot plenty of arrows at each location. Try several slow, deliberate shots and some others with a fast look, fast draw and fast release, as if a deer had suddenly appeared in front of your stand.

This type of practice will help you become familiar with which sight pin or crosshair color belongs to which range. Make sure you memorize the colors for each distance and don't ever change them. The practice will also help program your muscles, nerves and brain to coordinate a shot quickly at any one of the ranges encountered.

The process described may take a couple of hours, or it may take several weeks. The process depends upon many factors such as your experience, equipment, age, dedication, general health, the weather, instructions or coaching available, and dozens of other factors.

The more you practice at known distances, the better archer you will be. At this point, you may wish to go no further with your skills. The serious bowhunter or tournament shooter,

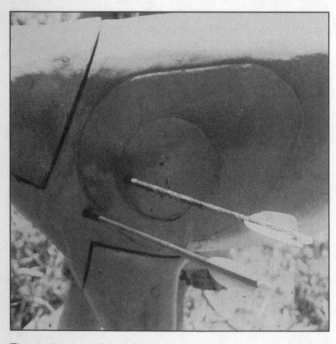

The scoring rings of the 3-D target let the archer adjust arrow impact into the lethal area of the animal.

Most 3-D targets have replaceable plugs or replaceable center sections when the scoring area is shot out. This model is from Game Tracker.

Delta's whitetail deer target has three scoring rings marked on the sides. They may be used to improve archery scores or for bowhunting practice.

Even the small javelina target from Stanley Hips is marked with scoring rings that may be used for bowhunting practice.

though, will move on to unknown-distance shooting. In the wild, marked range stakes are rather rare.

McKenzie realizes most bowhunters will agree that "the ability to determine distances is usually the greatest challenge an archer will face. A wrong guess can send the shot either high or low, out of the animal's vital area."

Archers can spend a lifetime perfecting their range-estimation skills. It seems to come easier for some than others. There would seem to be no question that extra target practice—concentrated practice—will make the task easier and more accurate.

McKenzie offers two techniques for estimating range: the halfway system and the end-to-end method. The latter has to do with picking an object or mark between you and the target. It should be an object at a known range. Then estimate how many times the known distance must be multiplied to reach the target.

One method many of us use is to picture imaginary 10-yard markers on an imaginary football field. Most of us are confi-

dent we can estimate a point 10 yards from where we stand or sit. From there, it should be easy to guess how many multiples of that 10 yards will be required to reach the target. Plenty of practice at known ranges will have a confidence-building effect when it comes to unknown-distance shooting.

The other method McKenzie refers to is the halfway system. The archer looks at the target and imagines an object about half the distance to it. Then the distance estimate of that object is doubled to the target. If you pick a tree or rock that you guess is 20 yards away, you can estimate that the target is 40 yards away.

In a given hunting situation, 40 yards may be past your maximum effective range, and the shot should not be taken. But the only way to determine that fact is through enough practice. With plenty of practice, both of the above-mentioned range-estimating techniques will be enhanced.

Your first 3-D or field tournament, and any deer hunt, will teach you that few, if any, archery shots are across flat terrain, with no obstacles, at known or easily determined distances. Most shots are through small openings in the cover, uphill or downhill, or a combination of all the above. If you do not have challenging terrain in your practice area, take some time to set up a few teaching situations for more realistic practice. You might drive a stake or two down in front of your target to simulate a tree trunk that is partially hiding the deer.

If you have no hills, but do have a tree and a tree stand, put up the stand, using all your safety equipment, including a safety strap. Practice shooting the target from the stand, as you might in a hunting situation. This kind of practice will not only help you when hunting from a stand, but will also let you get general downhill shooting practice.

Be particularly careful when practicing uphill shots. Be certain you know what is beyond the target and beyond the hill. If an arrow should fly over the hill, you must make sure there will be no animal, human, structure or some equipment that might be struck by the arrow. If that possibility exists, do not shoot from that angle or location; find another practice range. Use the same precautions when hunting or when shooting a target match. Always be sure of what is above and beyond the target before you release any arrows.

Practicing in your backyard range is helpful to prepare for the hunt. However, there are few deer that will wait for you to get into a good shooting stance and carefully draw and release the arrow. Deer will always surprise you with their appearance. They will be at an angle, distance and situation that you did not anticipate.

The archer must practice shooting from sitting and kneeling positions, as well as from the perfect target-shooting stance. Twist your upper body into awkward positions while on the practice range. If you have a tree stand, shoot from different angles at your chosen target. Your established maximum effective range may change when you shoot from something other than the perfect position. The only way to learn about it is to continue practicing.

Another thing to do is shoot in other than perfect target-practice weather. Hunting season will not be warm and sunny with no wind. You will probably hunt during inclement weather, and you should practice, at least during the pre-season, in whatever weather nature provides where you live.

Wear comfortable clothing for most of your archery practice, but remember that during the hunting season or even during winter target tournaments, you will be wearing your hunting togs. Put in some time practicing while wearing the same clothes you will wear during the hunt. Put on camouflage clothing, including gloves and headnet, if you are likely to need them during the season. A thick, long-sleeve coat will change the way you draw and release when compared to a T-shirt and shorts. Make sure the heavy sweater or coat does not contact the bowstring. Your arm guard will probably need some adjustment when you put on long sleeves. That will have an effect on arrow flight. Find all this out during practice, not when a world-class whitetail buck walks past your stand.

McKenzie points out that "any change in technique, no matter how small, can have a major impact on your shot and its effectiveness."

Top archery competitors—field archers, Olympic archers, 3-D target champions and successful hunters—know the sport is as much a product of mental preparation and concentration as it is physical prowess. Good archery practice helps physically, for sure, as well as increases the mental understanding of shooting arrows and having them strike where you aim. Confidence in your abilities is essential.

Visualization is important to archery success, according to the champions. The techniques of visualization are taught to most athletes in the Olympic training program, especially the archers. The archer mentally "sees" the arrow flying to and striking the target spot. The bowhunter imagines the game animal approaching the stand. With some mental practice, the hunter will watch the deer as it moves and stops and eats. You will improve your chances by mentally going through each step as you get into position, nock an arrow, draw the bow, aim, release and follow-through. Visualize the arrow making a clean, lethal hit on the precise spot you picked. Use this technique for each arrow. It will intensify the results of your practice many times over and will result in more hunting success

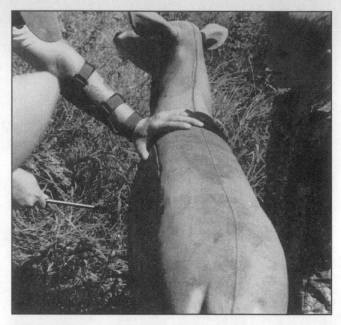

At touching distance, the scoring rings are clearly visible, but cannot be detected from 20 yards and beyond. Any 3-D target may be used to improve shooting, adding variety and interest to practice sessions.

and better tournament scores. Train your brain to master the necessary discipline to make each arrow count as if it were the only arrow.

Competing in 3-D archery tournaments is excellent practice. No matter how casual your approach to the game, there will be a certain amount of mental pressure during the meet. Use the mental techniques of visualization for each and every shot to improve your scores and your hunting practice. You will have one chance per target to determine the range and the best spot at which to aim. Concentrate on every arrow just as you do with your practice target.

Not every beginning archer has or can afford a 3-D animal target. Look to your local archery club or professional equipment dealer. Many have access to practice ranges with plenty of targets at little or no charge for usage.

Tournaments are great because many of your competitors will have similar skills and experience levels. They will be able to offer tips and ideas that will help you improve. And you can do the same for them. Many shooters will have the latest equipment for you to examine and discuss before you invest. You will have plenty of fun, gain experience and meet new friends and hunting partners who love the sport as much as you.

The McKenzie Aim-Rite is designed specifically for practice. But you can use any 3-D target for concentrated backyard practice, using the techniques outlined above. Most foam targets have the approved vital area outlined for scoring purposes. These lines make good practice guides, similar to a bullseye target. The more diverse the practice target, the greater the challenge, and this will make you a better archer.

A little extra target practice will bring more benefits than you might have thought possible.

11 Make Your Own Arrows

This Time-Honored Activity Will Save Money And Provide Satisfaction, But It Takes Patience

A transportation case filled with bowhunting gear, including a matched set of arrows; the hunter is ready for deer season.

IN THE BEGINNING, the first archer may have cut a stiff reed or sapling, sharpened one end and used it as an arrow. In time, it was learned that some sort of chipped stone with sharp edges on one end and feathers or leaves on the other made the missile fly better and become more lethal at the end of its flight. It was also learned that one type of wood stick flew better and more accurately, and lasted longer than others. The word got around, either because someone was on the wrong end of an archery attack or because a friend was the hunter/soldier in the next cave. After all, one would want to make arrows just like the guy's next door so he could experience the same success.

Since then, many improvements, changes and modifications have been applied to arrows, making them more efficient and lethal. The hunter who returned home with no game because of a broken arrow shaft soon learned to change materials, or he and his family soon died out. The bow-armed soldier was either victorious in battle or he became a slave or, worse yet, dead. There was plenty of incentive to improve.

The evolution described may have taken thousands of years. It has been only about the length of a long lifetime ago that most archers quit making their own arrows and began buying them to order. About a half-century ago, arrows began to be offered on a production basis. They were turned out in a factory production line in dozens of different lengths, colors, spine weights, diameters, finishes, nocks, points, fletching and materials. Arrows may be purchased at professional archery shops, some sporting goods stores, swap meets, gun shows or through sporting goods catalogs and specialty mail-order companies. Most arrows shot by modern archers are purchased ready-made, ready for the hunting woods or the target course within minutes of delivery and unwrapping.

Correct arrow selection is essential to archery success. The many variables and requirements for the right arrow are discussed in Chapter 4. For now, though, we shall attempt to describe the techniques of arrow construction, one by one, to obtain the best arrow flight.

Until the middle of the 20th century, arrow shafts were made of wood or other natural substances. No doubt, somebody, somewhere, experimented with bone, sinew, bronze, brass, copper, iron and combinations of those as each became available. There is no evidence that anything other than wood gained any prominence among soldiers or hunters until the invention of aluminum.

In the late 1930s, James D. "Doug" Easton developed a process that could be used to turn aluminum tubing into precision-engineered arrow shafts with the tightest of tolerances and quality controls. Today, the Easton Company continues to dominate the production and manufacture of aluminum arrow shafts, used by millions of archers all over the world for hunting, target shooting and fun. The process still remains a secret held by Easton and has yet to be duplicated anywhere, although many manufacturers have tried. Today, any mention of aluminum archery shafts is a mention of Easton.

Aluminum dominated the market for several decades, although there continued to be a demand for wood arrows among traditionalists and hobbyists. But while the market for wood shafts may have remained the same in numbers of arrows sold, the overall demand was growing many times over, mostly for aluminum shafts. They became the standard throughout the world.

There is still a demand for wood arrow shafts, and it seems to be expanding a bit as some archers return to more traditional equipment. However, rather than remaining the least expensive shaft available, the old favorite—the Port Orford cedar shaft—has become more and more dear. This particular wood is found only along the Oregon coastal region and has become less economically sound to cut and produce.

Furthermore, logging restrictions and forest fires have reduced the number of cedar trees that may be cut for the purpose. In many parts of Oregon, the logging and lumber industry has all but disappeared.

Other woods have been tried, and some have found favor. Any stable, tight-grained wood may be formed into the shafts for arrows, but most have not found the popularity Port Orford cedar has enjoyed for so long. New traditionalists everywhere are experimenting with available local trees to determine their suitability for arrows. After all, the longbow archers of England and most Native Americans did not have access to Port Orford cedar—and they shot thousands of arrows!

As we near the end of the 20th century, technology continues to progress, and aluminum and wood are not the only materials used for arrow shafts. In Europe and elsewhere, carbon fiber is being used for all manner of industrial processes, including the

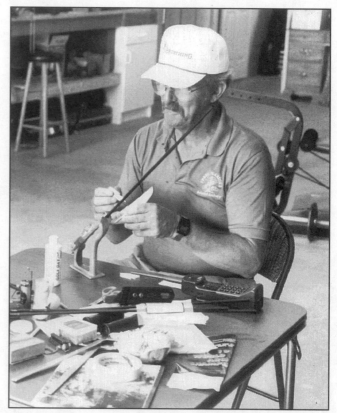

Frank Pearson, champion professional target archer, prefers building his own arrows. He works on other projects while the glue dries on the fletching, reducing the boredom factor.

This finished fetching job is as clean and neat as any factory product. A field point and the nock have yet to be installed.

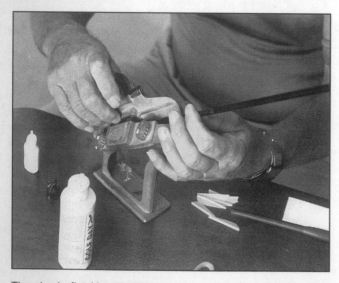

The simple fletching jig has virtually remained unchanged after decades of use. Shafts, fletching materials and glues have changed, but the process is the same.

Wood is the oldest material used for arrows. Still popular, many archers prefer to make their own arrows, especially when shooting traditional-type bows. The tools needed are simple and last for years.

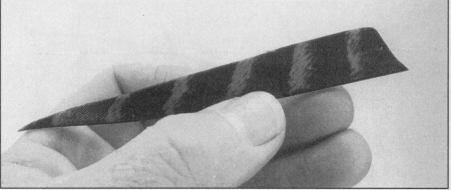

Naturally barred turkey feathers have been popular with those who make their own arrows. Feathers may be cut and trimmed to many sizes and shapes.

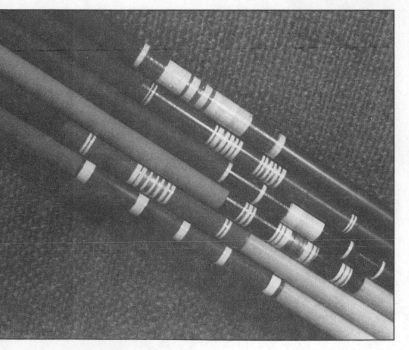

Cresting is the time-honored process of identifying individual arrows. The colors, widths, patterns and numbers of rings around the shafts are unlimited.

aircraft industry. Arrow shafts of all-carbon fiber and of aluminum with carbon wound around it have found broad acceptance. The all-carbon arrows have been particularly successful in the past couple of Olympics.

The all-carbon arrows do not bend like aluminum arrows. If they are manufactured straight, they will stay that way. They are smaller in diameter, stiffer per given length and therefore lighter in weight. They fly faster from the same bow. However, some carbon-fiber shafts sell for far more than aluminum, although the marketplace is making adjustments in cost. As stated, carbon arrows do not bend, but they can split and shatter. Under normal use, a good carbon-fiber shaft will last for years. However, if one should strike a solid object—such as a rock, a hard tree stump or the wooden frame holding the target—the fiber strands will separate and crack apart. Use caution when checking for cracked or damaged carbon shafts. The tiny slivers of fiber can stick into the skin and/or break off under the skin and become quite painful. Such shafts must be discarded; they cannot be repaired.

Easton developed the aluminum/carbon arrow. The technology is the most advanced to be found. The shaft is made of smaller-diameter, thinner-walled aluminum tubing which is wrapped in carbon fibers. This produces a stronger, thinner, stiffer arrow with the characteristics of both materials. The

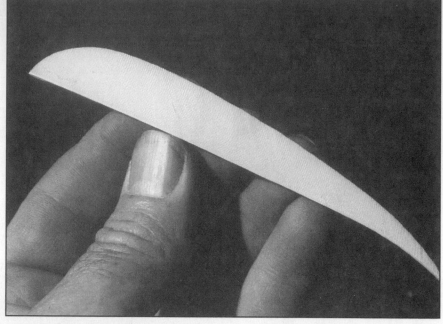

This feather fletching has been dyed a bright color to let the archer follow the arrow's flight more easily.

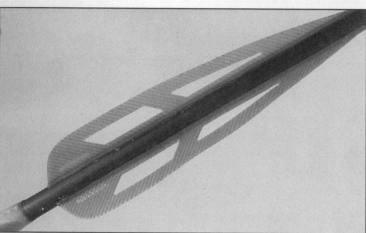

The archer who builds his own arrows can do things like cutting vents in the fletching, or glue on extra long or short vanes or feathers.

result is a measurably faster, but more expensive, arrow. The aluminum/carbon arrow is for the more advanced archer and should be tested before money is laid out for a dozen or two.

Any of these arrow materials may be purchased ready-to-shoot, complete with target or field points, fletching and nocks installed. They will be cut to the ordered length and produced with the proper spine for the bow to be used. The manufacturers of these shafts—Easton produces all three types—publish arrow selection charts to help the archer purchase the shaft most likely to perform well in a specific bow. Every archery shop has copies of these arrow charts, and they are reproduced by manufacturers each year. Selecting the correct arrow is at least as important to success as choosing the right bow. Give it plenty of thought and consideration.

As mentioned, most archers buy completed arrows. There are, however, several reasons why many archers still build their own arrows. The primary reason is cost. Once the home shop is equipped with the inexpensive, basic gear to produce arrows, a dozen can be produced for about half the cost of those from mail-order or pro-shop sources. The home production equipment will last for decades, with routine care.

Other reasons archers like to make their own arrows is that it is fun and satisfying. The process may be slow, but one can build arrows while studying or reading or between football plays on television. Shaft spine weights, lengths, fletching styles, fletching lengths and fletching materials may be experimented with as the archer works toward optimum arrow flight.

Furthermore, the skills acquired when making arrows will come in handy when one needs repairs in the middle of a tournament or when miles from the nearest archery shop during hunting season.

Some arrows are better suited to specific uses, but each type, if carefully selected and crafted, may successfully be shot from almost any bow. We asked Bob Learn to look into at least one of each type of arrow shaft and build several arrows from each. Learn has nearly four decades of experience at all aspects of archery. He is one of those who never got out of the habit of making his own arrows, from the earlier days of building arrows for his longbows and recurves to the most modern, high-tech compounds. The following special projects reflect his findings.

Lofty Canadian Pines

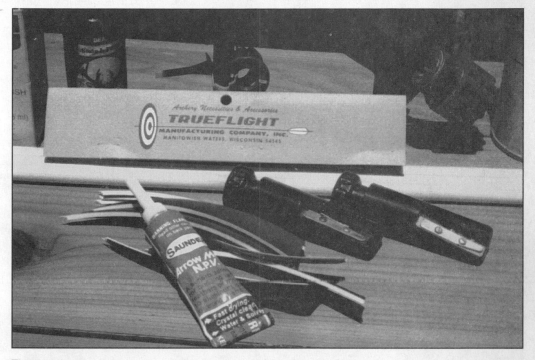

The supplies needed to construct pine arrows include sorted pine shafts, some fletching cement such as Saunders', two tapering tools for the nock and broadhead tapers, feathers such as TrueFlight in the shield configuration, a fletching jig, some wood stain, wood finish and a can of spray paint for shaftment coloring.

WOODEN ARROWS HAVE been around for many years. Wood was probably the first arrow material used when man started flinging shafts at game long ago. Wooden arrows have remained popular, despite the new materials currently available. The wooden arrow hasn't changed much over the years, but there have been a few variations.

In times gone by, when archers wanted to shoot wooden shafts, they merely ordered a few dozen—or maybe hundreds—of Port Orford cedar shafts. They were available in three grades—premium, select and mill-run. The first two grades were a bit rigid in shaft selection by the distributor, and shafts were matched in spine and weight. Premium-grade arrows were the highest quality; they were excellent arrows. The select grade were just a touch less matched in spine and weight, but still made great hunting arrows. Mill-run was just that. A hundred mill-run shafts with a spine range from, say, 60 to 65 pounds were purchased. These shafts mostly fell in that range, though there were a few wild ones from time to time with respect to spine and weight. We sorted, matched and constructed good hunting arrows and used the ones we liked for the game being hunted.

Today, if you try to find Port Orford cedar shafts, you will have a bit of a problem—this material just isn't that available.

Consequently, different makers of arrow shafts have been searching for a good arrow wood to replace cedar.

"Recently, a dozen pine arrow shafts came to my shop, and I was asked to make them up for bowhunting," reports Bob Learn, our Man of All Work. "This was simple to do, but I was also curious as to spine, weight and how they would shoot. One needs more than a fletching jig to work up wood arrows. You could invest in or make a spine tester to check the bow weight with which you could use the arrows. You probably already have a grain scale, so the only new additions would be a tapering tool to cut the nock taper at the top of the shaft and a broadhead taper for the front end. These are simple tools usually utilizing a razor blade for the cutting edge; merely replace the blade when it becomes dull."

First, the pine shafts were placed on the spine tester. The fine-edged grain of the wood must be placed against the window of the bow to obtain the stiffest section of the shaft.

"If you drop the weight on the shaft and rotate it, you will note the spine change as you do this. Pick the fine or close grain and set it so it will work against the window of the bow.

"These few pine shafts I had varied from 53 to 57 pounds in spine weight, giving a 55-pound average. I prefer to have 10 pounds or more spine weight above the draw weight of the

Taper about 10 inches from the nock end and wrap it tightly so there are no bleeds. Spray the upper shaftment to seal it from moisture and provide a good gluing surface. Shafts are also easier to find with the bright red coloring.

bow I shoot. For example, for a 55-pound-draw recurve, I like at least a 60-pound spine or, better yet, a 65-pound spine for heavy broadheads. The pine shafts would work with light broadheads or field points shot from the 55-pound bow weight."

Next, Learn placed the shafts on the grain scale and found they varied quite a bit. Three shafts scaled 425 grains, one 420. The others weighed between 340 and 380 grains. That is quite a spread in weight, but Learn had no knowledge regarding the grade of these arrows. They could have been first, second or mill-run in quality.

Three shafts were selected for straightness by spinning and set aside for work-up. Of the other shafts, one or two really bounced when spun over the thumb for straightness. "This is no problem, since you can bend these straight with a small amount of time and energy. We have always had to straighten most wood shafts anyway," Learn reports.

The nock end of the pine shaft was turned, using the tapering tool, and masking tape was applied 10 inches from the nock end and wrapped around the shaft at this point. A can of spray enamel was used to paint, seal and color this upper section called the shaftment. This does three things. It seals the wood from moisture, the bright color makes it easy to find, and it offers a good gluing surface for the fletch glue.

The Martin jig puts a nice full-curl left-wing helical on the shaft with the bronze-dyed feather from TrueFlight. The single jig works great; it just takes longer.

After the paint dried, he positioned a nock on the taper, aligning the grain with the nock so the stiffest section of the arrow was against the window of the bow. It was glued in place.

For this project, the $^{11}/_{32}$ nock was used, since these shafts were $^{23}/_{64}$, and there isn't a nock made in the $^{23}/_{64}$ size. We called a few distributors and none knew of any place to buy $^{23}/_{64}$ nocks. Then we called a nock maker and learned there is no current plan to tool up to that size.

When the nock had set on the shaft, Learn merely fletched this arrow shaft as he would any arrow. He chose to use three 5-inch, left-wing, bronze, shield-cut feathers from TrueFlight, since this was more of a primitive arrow and the feathers looked good against the red of the shaftment dip. He set the Martin single-fletch jig for a full left-wing helical and did one fletch at a time until he had all three arrows constructed.

When the fletch glue has cured, the arrow is cut to length and the broadhead taper attached. This is a slip-over attachment without the screw-in system used for aluminum arrows. Add 1-inch to the desired draw length to obtain the correct arrow length when the broadhead is attached. For this project, the Martin cut-off tool was used, since it works quite well on pine shafts.

The length was set at 30 inches to obtain the 29-inch draw arrow that Learn favors with broadheads. The ends were cut, and the sections set aside; the tips were shaped using the tapering tool with the shallow angle to match the angle on broadheads and field points. This is pre-set when the tool is purchased, so

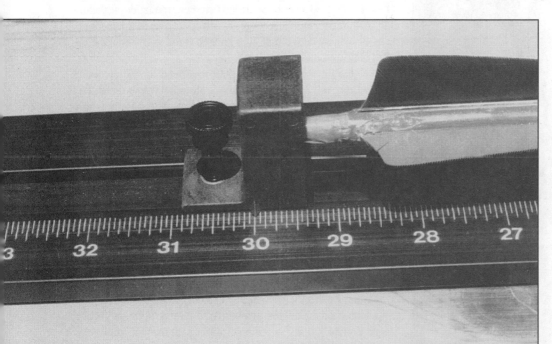

When the fletch has dried, set the cut-off saw for the length needed. Remember, this isn't the same as aluminum, so you must allow extra length for the taper. This is set for 30 inches, which will give 29 inches, a normal draw length for hunting arrows.

Using the fine-toothed saw on the unit, these shafts can be cut exactly to length. After cutting, insert the shaft into the five-degree taper tool and cut the taper.

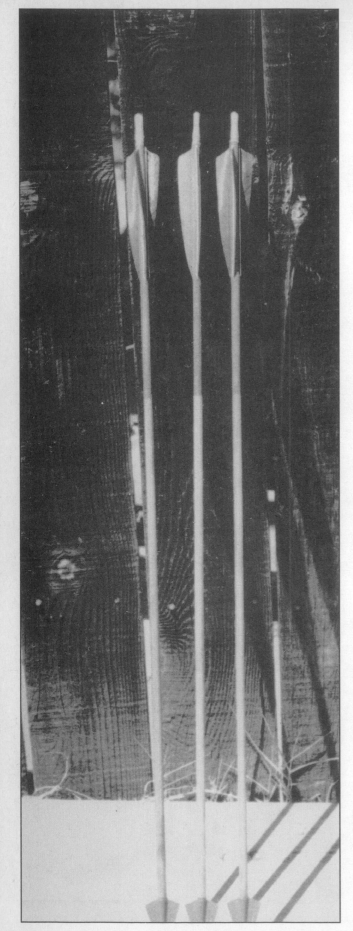

the taper is merely cut until the end of the shaft at the point is reached.

The next step is to seal that lower end of the shaft against moisture. If the wood is not sealed, the arrows will absorb moisture on humid days, which will make them heavier than normal and cause them to warp.

"First, I wood stained the lower section a darker brown. It looked great after two applications that were allowed to dry," Learn reports. To finish the lower section, there are several methods. It can be sprayed with polyurethane, applied with stock finish from Birchwood-Casey to seal it, or coated several times with a good floor wax such as TreWax, which contains carnauba, a tough, hard wax that holds up well. TreWax was chosen for these arrows.

When the lower arrow section is stained, the taper on the tip can also be stained. This gives a neat package that leaves no lines of white wood, which will happen if the shafts are tapered after they are stained.

The final phase was to add the broadhead of choice, or in Learn's case, a 125-grain field tip for shooting into target butts. This point was added using Ferr-L-Tite hot-melt cement. Don't get this cement on your fingers when it is flowing, since it must be pulled off, and it will often take skin with it. Once the cement has cooled, the new pine arrows are ready to take to the range for test shooting.

In Learn's case, a Bob Lee Custom bow was braced and taken to the butt. A pine arrow was nocked, brought to draw and sent flying downrange to the ping-pong ball he uses for a target.

"The arrow flew all right, but it was off to the side. The arrow's spine was a touch light for this bow. Even after a few more rounds, the ping-pong ball hadn't been skewered on the arrow, but it did a lot of swinging around on the string to which it was attached due to near misses. Will it hit a rabbit, coyote or deer? You bet it will, but I would prefer a bit heavier spine for a heavy broadhead," Learn concludes.

"Pine arrows," Learn contends, "will shoot as well as most archers. If you shoot a compound, you can use them, but be certain to obtain the right spine when ordering the shafts. These shafts would work well with a lighter broadhead. So order up a dozen or so pine arrow shafts, do your homework on them, and you should have some fine shooting arrows that are more than good enough for small game and stump shooting. If you plan to hunt deer, they are fine for that also. Like the 30-30 lever-action rifle, wood shafts have been around for many years and have taken many big-game animals, probably more than hunters care to admit."

The finished arrows with a Black Diamond Delta attached will down anything you care to shoot them into; well almost. They work up easy, look good and fly fine, but could be a bit heavier in spine for most hunting bows.

11 AFC V-Max 2400 Carbon Arrows

The AFC V-Max shafts arrive with the oversleeves ready for broadhead/field point adapter use as well and some faint, light-colored oversleeve nocks. The 2400 series is the correct spine for a 55-pound recurve.

THE CARBON ARROW has made its entry into the bowhunting and target archery scene with a strong surge. One company new to the arrow scene, but an established industrial corporation from France, is AFC, Aligned Fiber Composites.

AFC markets three types of bowhunter shafts. The Carbon Camo is a carbon arrow that has been camouflaged. The camo wears off in time, but only after a lot of bale-thumping. The average archer need not worry about that if he intends to use them only for hunting.

Another AFC shaft is the V-Max, a black carbon arrow shaft. This has basically the same spine as the Carbon Camo, but without the camo covering. The third model AFC markets is the Max-II. This bowhunter shaft has the same sizes and tolerances of the other two, but is less expensive.

All of the above shafts are available fletched with feathers or vanes or as bare shafts for the archer to assemble. The AFCs are available in sizes 2200, 2300, 2400 and 2540 to accommodate the draw weights of compound and recurve shooters. All assemble easily and quickly.

To make a set of AFC V-Max 2400 shafts into arrows, an adjustable fletching jig is needed so the smaller-diameter shafts will fit the clamp and the alignment can be set to obtain correct fletching. A must is a high-speed cut-off saw to bring the length

of the full-length shaft to the correct measurement. If you don't have one of these saws, you might talk your local archery shop into whacking off the end of a dozen or so shafts for a reasonable consideration.

Another option for cutting carbon shafts is the fine-tooth saw and jig that Martin Archery offers through dealers and catalogs. This has an accurate ruler with a thumb-screw to hold the shaft in place once the length has been set. The fine-tooth saw is used to first score the outside of the shaft before the actual cutting begins. Without the scoring, there is the risk of fraying the carbon fibers of the shaft as it is cut. This fraying possibility is the reason tubing cutters or other such tools must not be used on carbon arrows. Once the shafts have been cut to length, you are ready to fletch.

The first step is to place the oversleeve nock on one end of the shaft. It is good practice to use the end closest to the brand name and spine designation logo for later reference. You should roughen the outer half-inch slightly with fine-grit sandpaper or steel wool so the glue and oversleeve will adhere to the shaft.

AFC suggests temporarily attaching the oversleeve nock with a touch of rubber cement so the nock can be twisted to its best setting after some trial shooting and tuning with the arrows.

The nock slips over the end of the AFC carbon shaft for a snug fit. One archer used rubber cement as suggested, but the nock kept turning. A cleaning and application of fletching cement on the nock end solved the turning problem. This might become a problem later if nocks need to be changed.

Some like to line up the cock feather with the brand logo; it looks better to have them aligned.

Once the nock is in place and the glue almost firm, place the shaft in the jig and adjust it for the type of fletch pattern preferred. I usually make all my arrows with a left-wing feather fletch, 5 inches long by about 1/2-inch wide.

When a feather or vane is placed in the clamp, be certain the quill of the fletch will set properly on the tiny carbon shaft. It only takes a few moments of working with the jig's adjustments to get them lined up correctly.

Most of this set of test arrows can be fletched with a Martin composite-type fletching jig that allows right, left and straight fletching, as well as a full helical in right and left. Place the nocked shaft in the jig and a feather in the clamp, and position the clamp on the shaft as if it were being glued. Check the back tip of the fletch vane or feather and move the adjustable clamp slides until front and back are in contact with the shaft. If the front has a bit of overhang, adjust it back onto the shaft. Carbon shafts are of small diameter compared to cedar or aluminum shafts, but they will take a helical fletch.

When the clamps are adjusted, add fletching cement. We used Saunders fletching cement on this project, as it has always proven reliable. Run a bead of cement down the quill at the base of the clamped fletching, place it in the magnetic clamp section and seat it on the shaft. Wait the recommended drying time, rotate and repeat until all three feathers or vanes are glued to the shaft.

A carbon shaft must be cut 5/8-inch longer than an aluminum shaft to allow clearance for the oversleeve at the arrowhead. Our normal 29-inch arrows came out 29 1/2 inches long so the oversleeve would not contact the arrow rest at full draw.

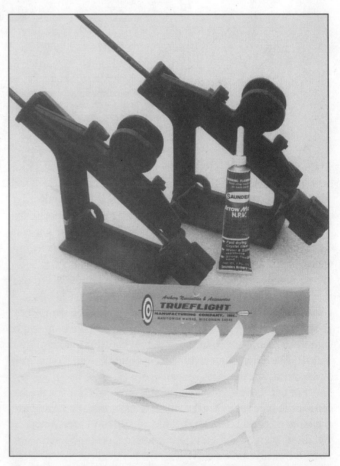

The nocked V-Max was placed in the Martin fletching jig, adjusted to the very small diameter of the shafts and set for a slight left wing angle. The fletching will be TrueFlight white cock feathers with some bright green hens, very colorful and bright. The cement used for this project was Saunders N.P.V.

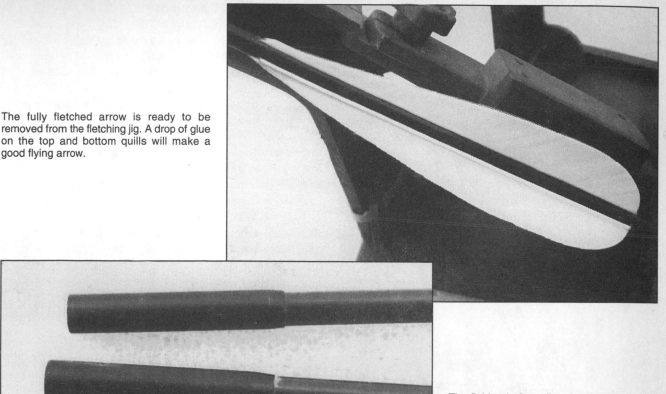

The fully fletched arrow is ready to be removed from the fletching jig. A drop of glue on the top and bottom quills will make a good flying arrow.

The field point/broadhead adapters are set using epoxy. These are oversleeves rather than inserts, but they do the same thing. Lightly sand about $1/2$-inch of the shaft end, mix slow-curing epoxy and dab it on the shaft. Push the oversleeve gently on the shaft, making sure you have cement on all points. Allow it to cure for at least one day before shooting.

After all the shafts have been cut, mix up a solution of two-part, slow-drying epoxy cement. Wipe the head end of the shaft with a cloth or paper towel soaked in alcohol to remove any dust or skin oil. Place a dab of epoxy on the arrow shaft, slip the sleeve on the shaft and slowly rotate to obtain proper adhesion of the sleeve to the shaft.

The oversleeve may be fitted with a field point to prevent any of the epoxy solution from gumming up the threads when it dries. This slow-curing epoxy should be cured for about twenty-four hours before the arrows are shot.

The instruction sheet that comes with the AFC shafts mentions the slight ledge behind the oversleeve on the point adapter. They suggest running a bead of glue around the base on that ledge. While the glue is still soft, sprinkle some baking soda on the glue. Rub the baking soda around to fill in the transition to the slight ledge. We tried it, and it worked.

The finished V-Max 2400 arrows, spined for a 55-pound-draw recurve at 28 inches of draw, weighed 460 grains each when finished. This included the three 5-inch feather fletchings, the oversleeve, nock and 125-grain field point. That is less than the AMO standard arrow for this bow weight, but within the limits of what the International Bowhunter's Organization (IBO) regulations permit.

We used a Groves takedown 55-pound recurve bow to see how the arrows shot. The target was a ping-pong ball suspended in front of straw bales. We missed by a bit too much on the first set. This isn't uncommon when shooting new arrows. We had no way to adjust the shelf or side pressure because there was no arrow rest on the bow. A second round of arrows had us hitting the string three times, but we were aiming for the ball on the end of the string.

A small moving target really forces one to concentrate on the target. With the second arrow of the third round we sent the ball flying around on its tether string.

The Martin Firecat compound was also set at 55 pounds. Switching between a recurve and a compound will give you fits every time. Both bows may be the same draw weight, but they will handle differently. After a few familiarization rounds, the Firecat was doing its thing, as usual.

Shooting from the shelf presented no problems. We didn't change the nocking point on the string as additional tuning might require. The Firecat had a launch ramp already in-

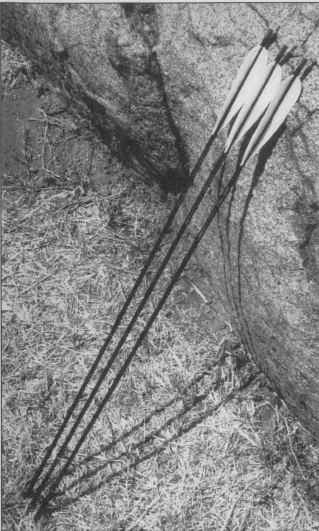

stalled—one of those V-shaped ramps. It presented no problems with the small-diameter arrow shafts. If you use a set of prongs or other type rest, you may have to adjust them for these small shafts. You also might find you need to lower your nocking point on the string to compensate for smaller measurements.

Before you pack your hunting gear and head for the game trails, check to see if your favorite bow quiver will hold these slender shafts. Some will, but some will not; the rubber holding fingers will be too far apart. Most bow quivers made in the past few years have provisions for both sizes of shafts. If not, it may be time to get a new quiver to go with the new arrows. Check at home, not in camp on opening day.

The AFC V-Max shafts performed well from our bows. One precaution: Shoot only carbon shafts if you set up a bow for them. Carbon arrows and aluminum arrows have a different feel, even when shot from the same bow. When everything is tuned for V-Max 2400 arrows, give them a long run for best results.

(Left) All ready for the hunting field, 3-D tournament or backyard shooting, these AFC carbon arrows will give good performance if you tune your bow properly. Flex the shaft from time to time to be certain you don't have any cracks. If you do find a break, set it aside and don't continue shooting it.

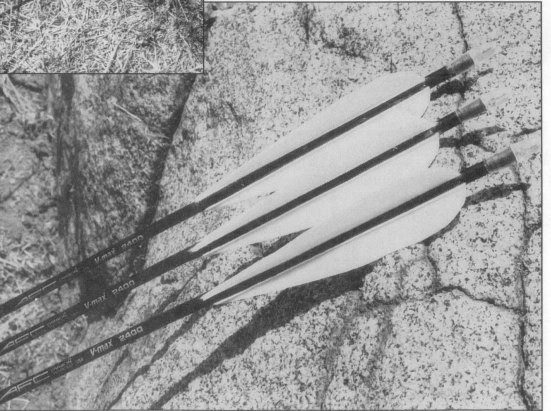

The fully made AFC V-Max carbon arrows are ready to shoot. The field point was oversized, but that is simple to replace with a smaller size from the local shop.

Beman Carbon Hawk Arrows

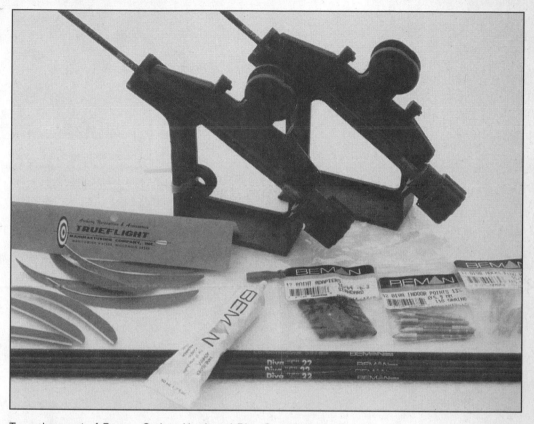

To make a set of Beman Carbon Hawk and Diva C shafts into arrows, you need a set of fletching jigs, cement of the proper type and some feathers of your desired color and style. You also need overserts for the points on the Hawks and target points for the Divas, along with nocks and epoxy.

BEMAN ARCHERY has been manufacturing arrows for the bowhunter and target archer since 1986. The carbon arrows were made in France and shipped to the United States, where they are distributed by Beman Archery Corp. Today, all Beman products are made in Michigan. Archers may purchase fully constructed arrows or components to make preferred-style arrows for hunting or target shooting.

We ordered a set of the new Carbon Hawk arrows, made primarily for the bowhunter, but also used by target archers, mainly in 3-D tournaments. This double-duty shaft is set up with a polycarbonate nock and can be purchased only with the slip-over style insert system for field points or broadheads, which makes it versatile.

In addition to the components necessary to make Carbon Hawk arrows, the shipment also included six already-made-up shafts in the Diva C configuration. The Diva C is designed for target shooting only. In most cases, bowhunters use them in 3-D tournaments or on local practice ranges. These arrows came with 4-inch, slightly offset feather fletching and a bullet-style outsert for the target head. The shafts were not cut to length.

The archer should do that at home in order to match individual draw length. Also included were six bare shafts with arrow components.

The Carbon Hawk and Diva C shafts rely on similar guidelines when constructing arrows. Any variations are indicated as such. Beman includes an instruction manual that points out the correct procedures and differences which apply.

Attaching the nock is simple with the Beman system. These large nocks are made of polycarbonate material, the stuff used for bullet-proof glass. The nock merely slips onto the arrow shaft; it is that simple. Beman recommends lightly sanding the end of the cut section with 400-grit sandpaper to eliminate any chance of lifting some carbon fibers. The fit is tight in the nock-to-shaft attachment.

Sand the shaft end, then clean the shaft with some denatured alcohol to remove any graphite residue. The alcohol will also remove any finger or hand oil left from handling the shafts. This may sound trivial, but the oil from your hands can result in a loose fit on many archery items, and this is one of them.

When setting the nocks in place, align the Beman logo on the shafts with the string. It makes a neater package this way, but has no effect whatsoever on performance. Check the alignment of the nock to be certain it is not picking up any fibers before it is pushed down over the end of the shaft. This takes a bit of pressure, but each nock smoothly slips on with a touch of pressure.

Beman does not recommend using glue. The nocks stay put when shot and give the advantage of being able to rotate for adjusting alignment if needed.

We chose a set of three-fletch, 5 inches long, from True-Flight for both sets of arrows. This is a popular pattern for fletching hunting arrows. We planned to use a set of Martin Archery jigs and had two of these on hand to speed up the process. The fletching was set for a left-wing helical to match the feathers. Each clamp was readjusted for these small-diameter shafts.

We used three white fletch feathers on the Diva C and one white cock feather with two orange hen feathers on the Carbon Hawk. One of the unglued feathers was positioned in the clamp, which, in turn, was placed on the shaft with the clamp index set at the cock feather position. Look at the front and back edges of the fletching to be certain they are both contacting the small

TrueFlight feathers were chosen for the Carbon Hawks—one white cock feather and two orange hen feathers. These are 5-inch, left-wing, parabolic die-cut feathers.

shaft. Adjusting the clamp is not a problem—loosen the adjusting nut, move the clamp until the tip of the fletching feather is on the shaft and tighten the nut.

Clean the shaft area with some denatured alcohol. Do *not* use

The nocks for the Hawk and Diva are different sizes and can't be interchanged. Target points are all that can be used on the Diva, since it is a target arrow, while overserts and target, field or broadhead points can be used on the Hawk.

The Beman spine designations of 55/65 and C22 denote spine and type of shaft.

Note the length of the overnock on the Hawk. On the Diva, make the clamp ride up on the fletch. To offset this, you can cut the notch in the clamp to make it fit snug or pull the fletch below the clamp and press the quill to the shaft for good contact.

lacquer thinner, MEK or other strong solvents, as they may damage the resin in the arrow shaft. Beman stresses this precaution. Use only denatured alcohol—ordinary rubbing alcohol found in drugstores.

Beman glue does not contain toluene or MEK, for the same reason mentioned regarding shaft cleaning. Checking the various glues on hand, we found they all contained one or the other of the not-recommended chemicals. We found Beman glue at a local archery shop.

With the arrow in the jig and set for the cock feather position, the shaft material clean and the clamp set for proper adjustment for the fletch and shaft size, we ran a bead of Beman glue down the base of the feather quill and placed it on the jig, making certain the clamp was correctly against the shaft. Beman notes that their nock is a bit longer than others. It is an outsert

style and may interfere with the clamp at the rear of the fletching. We had the choice of either cutting that section from the clamp or pulling the fletch down far enough to allow the quill clearance.

Setting the timer for 20 minutes, compensating for temperature and humidity, we allowed the glue to set. We repeated this procedure until all arrows were made up.

After fletching the shafts, they must be cut to proper length. This requires a high-speed cut-off saw used by bow shops or a fine-tooth hand saw such as the one sold by Martin Archery.

Before cutting the shaft for length, proper draw length must be determined. The Carbon Hawk may work at your standard draw length, if you are in the habit of cutting your hunting arrows 1-inch longer than draw length. However, this might not allow enough length for the oversleeve used for the replacement point system, so add 3/4-inch more.

The Diva C types are target arrows and should be cut 1/2-inch longer than usual. This allows for the slight channel found on the bullet target point outsert on the carbon shaft. The channel prevents abrasion when hitting and being removed from targets. Avoid using an arrow which is too short. If that is the case, the lip of the outsert or oversleeve on the inside edge of the arrow point might catch on your arrow rest.

Beman recommends their 24-hour epoxy cement for both types of arrow tips—the outsert/oversleeve for the Carbon Hawk and the target point on the Diva C. Again, sanding with 400-grit paper to rough up the surface of the shaft for better adhesion is advised. Wipe with alcohol, allow to dry and mix the epoxy. Spread the epoxy on the shaft ends. Slip on the points with a twisting motion to get a good smear of epoxy on all the joining surfaces. Be sure to follow the time restraints to properly cure the epoxy cement.

The finished Carbon Hawk arrows weighed 436 grains with 125-grain field points. The 4-inch-fletched Diva C arrows came in at 365 grains, using the 110-grain target points. The 5-inch-fletched Diva C arrows were 5 grains heavier at 370 grains. That 5 grains could have been from the extra inch of feathers or merely from more epoxy, but that weight difference was averaged.

The Diva bullet target points on the left have a slight lip on the upper end that goes over the shaft for protection when shooting into butts. The two Hawk arrows on the right have oversleeves that will accept any of the 8-32 points you want to use. These points are attached with Beman 5-minute epoxy or a similar method.

The Carbon Hawk will accept any type of threaded broadhead. Beman has a new series of broadheads, made for their shafts. The Diva C can be used only with the target point, but it has an oversleeve that will accept a standard nock.

To test the finished arrows, we chose a Lee Custom recurve bow set at 55 pounds of draw and a Martin Firecat compound bow, also set at 55 pounds. The standard arrow chart indicates the Diva C 22 is just right for the compound bow. The listing for recurves stops at 52 pounds, but the Diva C 22 shot well from the recurve. The Carbon Hawk at the 55/65 spine listing was a touch on the heavy side for the recurve.

The recurve indicated average speeds of 181 feet per second (fps) for the Diva C 5-inch-fletched arrows; 178 fps for the 4-inch fletching. The Carbon Hawk arrows, with their added weight, clocked 167 fps. These didn't look right for that bow, and later, we found out why.

On the compound, the Diva 4-inch fletched arrows clocked 211 fps; 209 fps with the 5-inch. The Carbon Hawk arrows traveled at 195 fps from the Martin Firecat.

We knew the Lee Custom recurve was faster than it recorded and the blame is on pilot error. Never chronograph when tired. Setting up the same Custom Chronometer Speed Tach to prove it, we hit 195 fps from the Carbon Hawk, 209 fps from the 5-inch-fletched Diva C and 211 fps from the Diva C with 4-inch fletching. All shots were made at 28-inch draw length.

While shooting the test arrows, we saw only a round ball of feathers going downrange. There was no flirt, porpoise or wobble of any kind. Both bows had been set up for standard aluminum arrow diameters and we hadn't changed the nocking point on the bowstrings. The Lee was shot off a rug rest on the shelf, and the

The Hawk with two-colored fletch in full left-wing helical will hold any broadhead downrange and keep it on track. Most bowhunters prefer the helical system.

The Diva C with a look at the full left-wing helical put on with the Martin fletching jig. It really rolls around the shaft and gives excellent guidance.

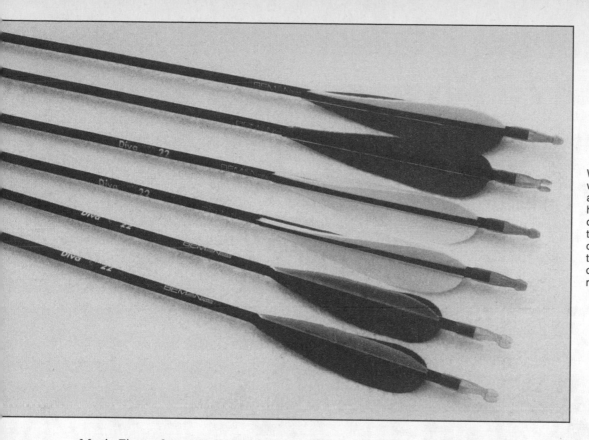

When all fletch has cured, you will have three sets of arrows almost made. The upper two have Carbon Hawk shafts with orange/white fletch, the middle two have all-white 5-inch fletch on Diva C shafts, and the lower two have two blue feathers with one yellow cock feather, as made by Beman.

Martin Firecat from a V-channel Martin rest. That defied all basic rules which say one should change the nock point and retune the rest for smaller shafts. We didn't do either, but had great arrow flight, anyway.

Beman arrows shoot great and fly well. We didn't cut the fletching jig clamp for the longer nock and had no problems fletching. As recommended by Beman, we didn't glue on the nocks and had no problems.

Beman has a variety of carbon-fiber shafts from which to choose: three hunting arrows, two target types, some fish arrows, crossbow bolts and some arrows for school and summer camp shooting. Beman also has a choice of broadheads, stabilizers, arrow rests and other items. They recommend checking arrows after shooting.

When we used the shooting machine, it put almost all arrows into one spot and they slammed together at the target with no problems. One thing about the carbon arrows: They are either straight or broken; they never stay bent!

These three arrows are set up on end, but you only get the curve on the one directly in front of the lens. All Beeman arrows fly well.

11 ▶ Easton Classic XX75 Arrows

The new Classic pattern by Easton shows little difference from the natural wood it is patterned after. This is a mix of the Easton Classic and regular wooden arrows that have been stained on the main sections of the shafts. Which are the real wooden shafts?

MANY OLDER BOWHUNTERS began hunting with traditional wooden arrows usually made of Port Orford cedar from Oregon. Today, Port Orford cedar shafts are difficult, if not impossible, to obtain because of logging restrictions and other economic considerations. However, some traditional archers still rely on wooden arrows they make for themselves.

Easton Aluminum's engineers and product developers have not forgotten the look of wooden arrows and have produced a lookalike—their Classic pattern. The popular XX75 shafts are made of aluminum, but have a beautiful wood-grain pattern. We worked with a set of Super Lite XX75 arrows in 2213 shaft spine, and they flew as well as they looked.

The comparison of these shafts with some actual wood arrows seemed interesting. "I had some larch, cedar and birch arrows that had been made up over the years," reports our field man, Bob Learn. "I laid the woods alongside the new Classic pattern Easton shafts and found it difficult to tell the difference solely by appearance. One might not be able to tell them apart in a photograph."

The logo on the Classic pattern is easily seen and read. One of the things Easton has done recently is make the logo, which names type of shaft and size, much more readable; you don't need a magnifier to see what shaft size you have.

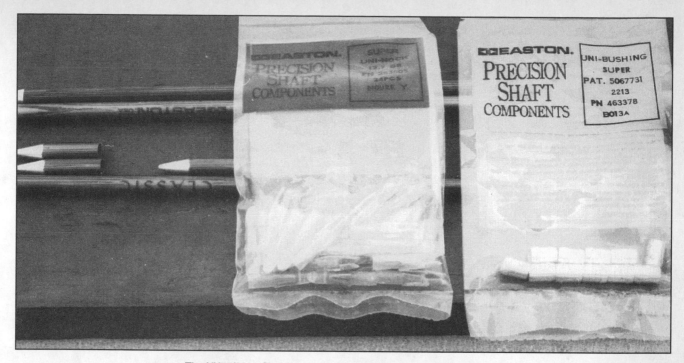

The XX75/2213 Classics come with a swaged nock just like the older styles. We incorporated part of the new Uni Bushing/Super Nock system; three of the test shafts were cut and this new system applied.

It does seem ironic. Doug Easton spent years perfecting the aluminum arrow, lowering the cost and raising the quality to the point that bowhunters came to prefer aluminum in the field rather than traditional wooden arrows. We all know how well he succeeded. Now we have turned full circle—Easton aluminum arrows have deliberately been made to look like wood.

All of us have our druthers. We'd rather go fishing than do yard work. We'd rather go hunting than work. Many of the dyed-in-the-wool traditionalists would rather go down fighting than use an aluminum or carbon arrow on their longbows and recurves. If you walked out with a set of these Easton Classics in your back quiver, no one would bat an eye until they picked one up.

Bob Learn received a dozen of the Classic XX75s in 2213 size and made up three in the traditional manner and three in the modern mode.

"I dug out my favorite fletching jig, a Gebhardt Multifletcher that will produce six shafts at a time," Learn reports. "I combined this with the left-wing helical jig in each station and made up some arrows in almost no time. The left-wing clamps were pulled out and cleaned of old glue before being set up on the jig for the Classics. This jig has been set up for years for a full left-wing helical as tight as I can wrap it around a large shaft such as the 2213. Long ago, I worked for some time to get the maximum helical fletching perfected from this jig. I do not plan to change it for any reason."

There are two ways to nock any of the Easton shafts. Many of the older-style shafts, such as the XX75, are manufactured with a swaged nock on one end. That system has been satisfactory for many years. We can't ever remember having a crooked nock swaged on these shafts.

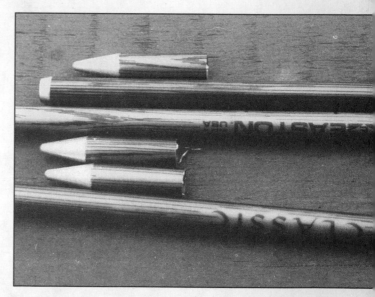

The shafts must be cut over an inch back from the swaged end in order to insert the Uni Bushing since the swaging process runs up the shaft a bit.

The second method is to use the newer Uni Bushing and Super Nock system. Learn chose to cut the nock ends of the shafts to his specific length to keep the logos on the shafts in similar positions on all arrows. He inserted the Uni Bushing after first chamfering the cut-off end to facilitate the fit.

"I had to tap the Uni Bushings lightly to fit them snugly into the shaft tubing. Using the included polycarbonate applicator, the Super Nock is fitted into the Uni Bushing. The bushing and nock are in place without the use of glue or cement. I asked Easton about hot-melt glue on the Uni Bushing. Easton recom-

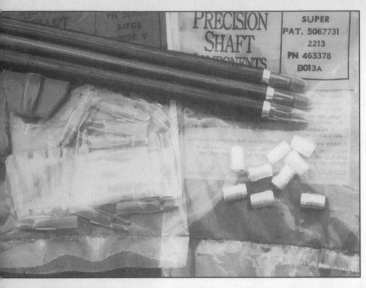

The Uni Bushing has been installed on these three shafts and the Super Nock inserted using the tool provided.

mends its use, but I wanted to see the results of shooting an arrow without any cement at the nock. The fit is quite tight," Learn recalls.

The other three arrows were made in the standard manner using $5/16$-inch, ruby-colored nocks from Arizona Archery. These nocks are undersized by design.

With the arrows made using the Uni system, a slight collar around the upper end of the shaft, below the nock, will be visible. The 2213 shaft size calls for an $11/32$-inch nock. Using the $5/16$-inch nock, Learn observed a slight rim of bright metal when installing the smaller nock. Otherwise, it was almost impossible to tell the difference between arrows using the different systems.

The Uni Bushing and Super Nock system has another advantage if they are not cemented in place. The Super Nock fits so snugly that one may have to use the little tool supplied by Easton to rotate the nock to any other position. This may be necessary to compensate for any contact by the fletching as it passes by the arrow rest and riser.

The Gebhardt Multifletcher was put into use for this project since six arrows can be made at one time. For years, it has been set for a full twisting left-wing helical fletch that flies very well. The feathers from True-Flight in left-wing brown and bronze were used for the guidance system.

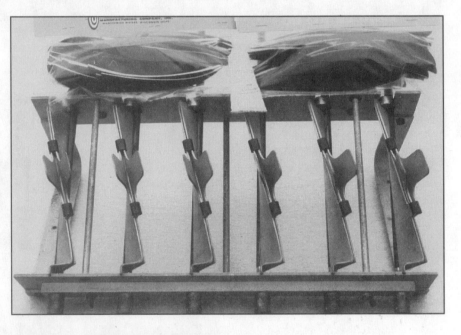

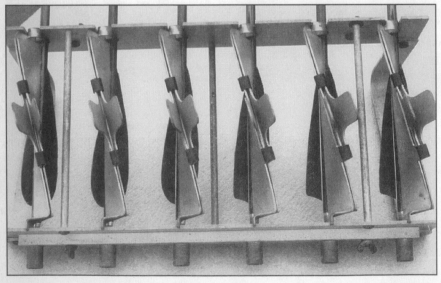

The first group of fletched shafts have the new Uni Bushing and the parabolic fletch, visible on the jig below the clamp. Those on the right have the old-style swaged nock and shield-fletching cut.

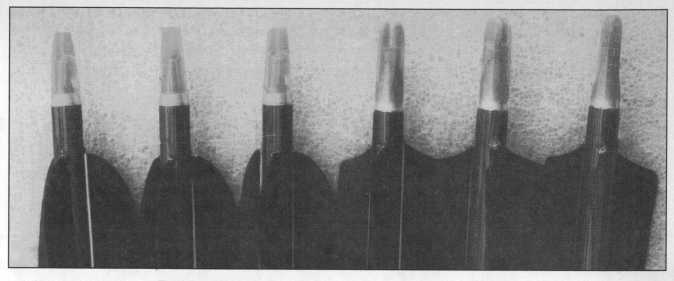

The finished arrows all have the point insert on the lower end. The three on the left have the Uni Bushing/Super Nock; the three on the right have the swaged Arizona Archery nocks.

Learn prefers to shoot from the shelf of most bows, rather than use an arrow rest. TrueFlight has a fantastic fletching that can be obtained in light or dark shades. The lighter-colored fletching was used for the cock feather. The two hen feathers were in a darker shade of brown. This made a contrast in brown tones that Learn felt looked great with the wood pattern of the Classic shafts.

Years ago, we shot what was called a shield cut on our feathers. It came out in a flare from the nock, then curved down to the forward end. These are still made by TrueFlight. We ordered a few of the shield-cut feather fletchings and a few of the standard parabolic pattern feathers in order to try out both.

The three standard-nock swaged Classics were fletched using the shield-cut brown feathers. The Uni system shafts were fletched using the parabolic feather fletch pattern. This was about the only way we could tell the new from the old.

The feather fletching was wrapped on the shafts in a full helical configuration and the glue was allowed to cure. The shafts were taken to the Easton high-speed cut-off saw and cut to Learn's 29-inch hunting arrow length. He normally measures 28 inches, but adds 1-inch for broadhead clearance on hunting arrows. Standard RPS inserts were put into the shaft using Ferr-L-Tite hot-melt cement, and the shafts were ready.

The finished arrows with the swaged nock shafts each weighed 435 grains, including a 125-grain field point. The Uni system arrows each weighed 450 grains. The extra few grains were attributed to the bushing. An extra 15 grains of arrow weight should make little difference to any archer.

A compound bow set at 55 pounds of draw and a standard recurve at 55 pounds each sent arrows zinging to the target with equal speed and accuracy. Changing over from recurve to compound, and then back again, isn't recommended for best shooting results, but the arrows flew perfectly.

"I made up the arrows and I knew the shield cut had the swaged nock while the parabolic fletching had the Uni Bushing/Super Nock system. The more I work with this newer system, the more I like it. I need only one nock for shafts with a spine of from 2018 to 2519.

"The Classics fly well with either of the two systems. I could feel no difference between grain weights. The arrows didn't flirt, porpoise or wiggle in any way, but flew like a little, round ball of brown feathers directly to the target."

If you try a set of the Easton Classics, you will probably agree that they look and fly extremely well. That is part of what this game of bowhunting is all about.

The Delta quiver is filled with the six Classic shafts that have been made into great-shooting arrows using two processes. They look great, perform well, as all Eastons do, and could fool many of the traditional bowhunters, if you like to do that sort of thing.

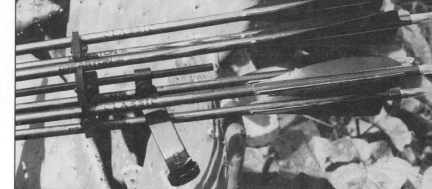

Easton XX78 Super Slam Arrows

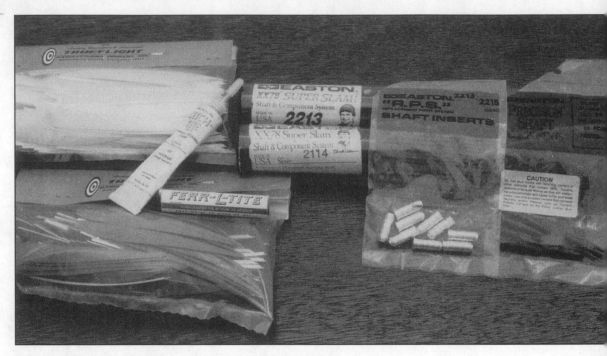

All you need to make a couple dozen arrows from the new Easton XX78 arrow shafts—the shafts in your specific spine type, RPS inserts for broadheads, Super Nocks, fletch such as this from True-Flight, cement for fletch and inserts.

The XX78 Super Slam shafts come in clear plastic tubes with the size imprinted on a slip inside. These are capped and have a foam insert to keep them from falling out.

EASTON ALUMINUM has long been the leader in construction and engineering of aluminum arrow shafts. They have been at it for many decades, continually upgrading and devising new products. They have always produced arrows designed for target archers and recently introduced their XX78 Super Slam arrows for bowhunters.

The Super Slam is an entirely new arrow. It is made from an ultra-strong 7178 aluminum alloy to give greater bend resistance and toughness for a better hunting arrow. This shaft material and the finished product were in engineering processes for more than a year. Jim Easton, president of Easton Aluminum, and well-known bowhunter Chuck Adams worked on producing a newer, tougher arrow strictly for bowhunters. The basic idea for the name of the Super Slam was in reference to Adams' feat of becoming the first bowhunter to collect a specimen of each of the twenty-seven recognized big-game animals of North America.

What will the new XX78 do to the existing arrows on the market, such as the much-favored XX75? The latter is still made, but this newer XX78 will be offered in all hunter bow weights in standard sizes such as 2018, light and superlight sizes like 2016 and 2114, as well as all the other sizes for heavier-draw hunting bows.

The sample set of XX78 Super Slam shafts sent for test purposes came in a round, clear plastic tube with replacement

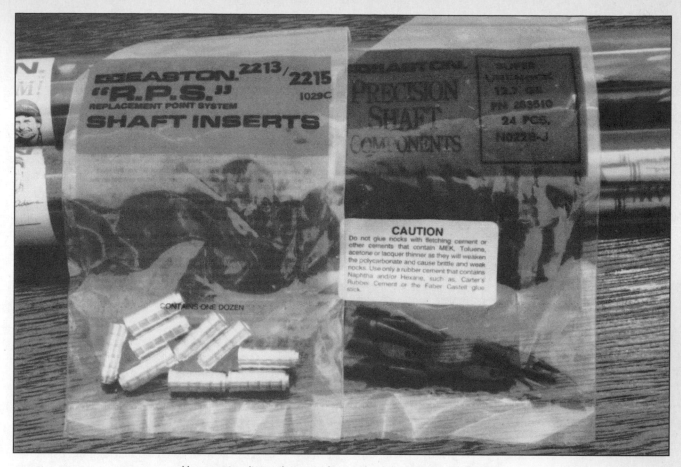

Here are two items that must be purchased separately—the shaft inserts for the RPS system, which are standard and are selected to fit the shaft size, and the Super Nocks.

point system inserts and some instructions. The archer must use his own nocks or buy a set of the new Easton Super Nocks.

The color of the XX78 is light tan with camo colors in hard-anodized Easton finish. The color is light enough to show any blood left on it from a hit on game. Most bowhunters like to examine blood color to determine shot location. Bright red means a solid hit, frothy pink means through the lungs, and so forth. Trailing can be easier if you know how hard the animal is hit. This camo should prove no problem for that purpose.

The appearance of the XX78 shows little difference from any of the many millions of shafts Easton has produced over the decades. The nock end, however, is different. The aluminum shafts we have used over the years have had a swaged end to accept the nock when making up arrows. This swage is put on by machine at the proper angle and is part of the arrow system. The XX78 has no swaged nock taper on either end of the shaft.

What the XX78 has is a Super Uni Bushing, developed by Easton. What they have done is make an old idea much simpler. The Super Uni Bushing is a press-fit ring of aluminum put on at the factory. This results in uniform nock alignment. And they won't come out; we tried to pull one out, but mangled the shafting instead.

If you prefer to use the standard aluminum tapered nock adapter, you can purchase special inserts from your dealer—Super Uni Extensions—and use your preferred nocks. Insert the extension into the Uni Bushing and glue on your nock.

The other nock this system works with is Easton's Super Nock. This nock varies from the usual in that it has a stem at the bottom of the nock that inserts into the Uni Bushing to give a solid, straight nock/arrow alignment. This Super Nock is injection-moulded from super-tough polycarbonate—the same stuff from which they make bullet-proof windows.

The Super Nock system isn't totally new in concept. Gordon Plastics once made what they called the Nocksert, which was used with their fiberglass arrows years ago. They used injection-moulded nylon, but there was a different stem size for each shaft size. The Uni Bushing offers one stem size for each of the various sizes of Super Nocks—a good idea that makes life simpler.

The Super Nock is made to hold on your bowstring with 5-pound pressure, found to be the ideal. The Super Nock may not be new by about thirty years, but it is simple and fast and is offered in various colors. The Super Nock and the Super Uni Extension are not included with the XX78 shafts; just the RPS insert for field points or broadheads.

Assembly of XX78 Super Slam arrows is the same as with any other system. First, place your Super Nock in the Uni Bush-

The logo is imprinted on each shaft and is much easier to read than the old system, which had a faint imprint legible only with a magnifying glass.

ing. Keep a pair of pliers handy, as you may need them to help with a snug fit. You can add a drop or two of rubber cement, but super glues or fletching cements should not be used on the Super Nock, since it might dissolve it and cause it to seat untrue in the Uni Bushing. Should you try to position the Super Nock in the shafting by pressing it on a table, you will probably bend one or both of the nock's ears.

Easton now makes a slick little gadget that has several uses, the main one being to aid in inserting the Super Nock into the Uni Bushing. Our unit is bright orange in color, is made of polycarbonate and has a hole in one end that fits over the Super Nock, a vertical section fitting into the nock ears. Place the gadget on the Super Nock and, using the ears on each side of the

gadget, put even pressure on the Super Nock to insert it correctly. If you prefer not to glue the Super Nock, leave it clean. This insert gadget can then be used to rotate the inserted Super Nock on the shaft for proper alignment of the fletch to the arrow rest for proper clearance. Twist the nock on the shaft to change alignment slightly for true clearance.

After the Super Nock is in place, fletch the shaft in a normal manner, using feathers or vanes on the fletching jig. Don't forget to clean the shaftment with Ajax and water to remove body oils or other contamination from the shafts so the fletch will adhere properly.

With the fletching finished, cut the XX78 to the proper hunting draw length. This is one place where that high-speed shaft-

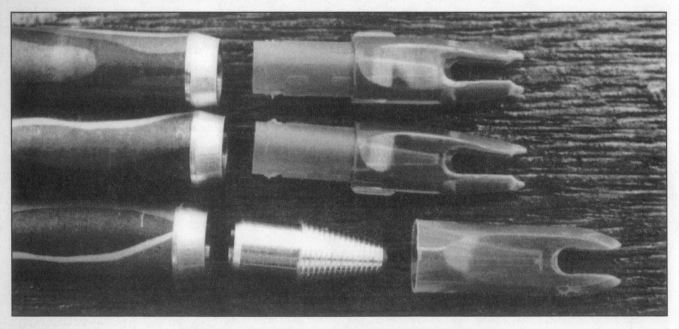

There is a choice of the Super Nock with an index notch for cock feather location or the Super Uni Extension of aluminum that will allow use of standard nocks. Either system fits into the factory-installed Uni Bushing on the shaft.

Use a good-quality cut-off saw for cutting arrow length to keep it straight and true. This is an Easton unit that has been used for many years and still works great.

cutting saw is invaluable. After cutting, chamfer the inside of the tubing to remove any slight burrs, and then place the RPS insert in the end of the shaft.

If you have made up a few dozen or so arrows with your own fletching system, you will have no problem with these at all. We made up several sets of arrows using a three-feather fletch, 5 inches long and ⅝-inch high, practical for both hunting and target shooting. With a properly cleaned shaft, these TrueFlight feathers should be part of the arrow for a long time. We weighed several field points to be certain they all were the same 125 grains in weight.

The best way to find out how the new XX78 Super Slam arrows would perform was to shoot them, so several sets were taken to the target butts for a session. The Super Nock fit well on the 16-strand Dacron string, and as usual, the Easton shafts flew true.

When we fletched these arrow sets, fletching of various colors was used to make it easy to identify different sizes and spines. One set had two black hen feathers and one white cock feather. When these flew downrange, it appeared that the arrows were flying crooked due to the rotating fletch. The arrows were definitely straight, however. In fact, Jim Easton claims the XX78 Super Slams are the straightest hunting arrows made.

Testing different spines and weights, the arrows flew as they should. Using the same aim point, which is hard to do instinctively, the heavier shafts flew low, the lighter ones high, and the standard weight hit the middle.

Our Man About the Shop, Bob Learn, recently resurrected an old shooting machine he'd made years ago. This machine is ugly, but efficient and accurate to a fault. With the bow strapped into the machine drawing 28 inches, Learn shot his first XX78 at the butt. The second XX78 slammed in alongside the first. The third slammed into one of the first two and hit the Super Nock. This cut an ear off one side of a nock to stop any further testing with the machine. What do you do when you bend, break or somehow manage to damage one of these Super Nocks? For us, the problem was simple. We had not glued them in, so it merely took a hefty tug with a pair of pliers and the Super Nock came out. The seating gadget was again used to insert a new Super Nock, and the arrow was ready to shoot immediately, since there was no drying time for any glue.

If you use glue, you could probably break the slight film of adhesive by using the insert tool to twist the Super Nock in the Uni Bushing, thus breaking the bond of glue to metal.

After cutting all your shafts to length, deburr them with the tool set onto the saw frame or use a hand-held unit. If you don't deburr, you can't fit the RPS insert into the shaft.

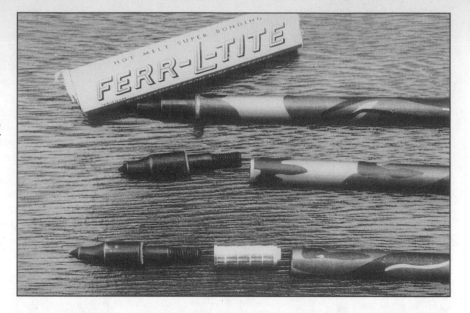

Use a good hot-melt cement such as the proven Bohning Ferr-L-Tite and cement your inserts onto the arrows.

Another thing we liked about this system was the simplicity in aligning the nock with the cock feather. Using the insert tool, we merely rotated the Super Nock until alignment was proper. That was it!

Easton Aluminum's XX78 Super Slam series should be a hit with bowhunters. The maker has a complete range of hunting sizes to fit every style of shooting, and using the RPS system, you can use all your field points and broadheads as usual—no changes there. If you are a diehard and have a favorite nock you've used since the age of ten, you can still use it with the Uni Bushing and the Super Uni Extension.

Give the Super Nock a try. We found it fit well, didn't come off at any time during testing and hugged the string without compressing it too much. There was no snap as the nock left the string in flight, as might happen when a nock fits too tightly.

We didn't try to destroy the XX78 Super Slams by shooting into a granite rock—that would destroy any arrow. The usual way aluminum arrows are damaged, however, is by ricocheting off something, rather than being shot into it.

The XX78 is a good idea that should prove as popular as Easton's proven XX75 and other shafts made for bowhunters.

The finished arrows with Super Nocks and 5-inch full left-wing helical feather fletch. This is the normal arrow makeup and nothing was changed for this test system.

12 Compound Bows

Some May Look More Complicated And Technical, But The Principle Is Still The Same—Store Energy

ALL BOWS, REGARDLESS of the type, have something in common—they all are simple mechanical devices designed to transfer and store human muscle energy into a set of bow limbs and impart that stored energy to an arrow as the bowstring is released.

There are many factors involved in that storage and transfer—technical, physical and emotional—but the object is to accurately propel a sharpened missile to a target. Thousands of years ago, the primary targets were food animals or enemy soldiers. Today, most targets are still game animals, but they are two- or three-dimensional depictions of game animals or painted circles used to test one archer's abilities against another's.

All the complex wheels, cams, strings, cables, yokes, nuts, bolts and other high-tech devices attached to or a part of the compound bow are intended to make the process easier on the human muscular system and produce a more accurate arrow, but the energy must still be provided by the archer. The energy is stored in the bow limbs until released by the shooter.

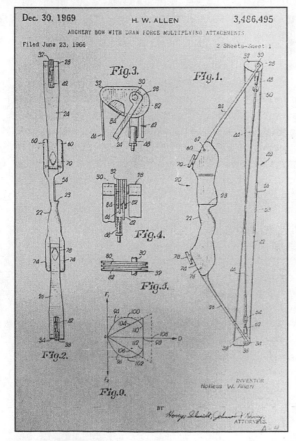

The original drawings from which the patent for compound bows was granted is dated December 30, 1969. The design is still valid, although improvements have been made.

This is H.W. Allen, the man who held the patent on the invention of the compound bow. His heirs received millions in royalties after his death.

Before the development of the compound bow, recurve bows, such as this beauty from Browning, were what most archers used.

(Below) One of the early developers and promoters of the compound bow has been Tom Jennings. He continues to advance the design and technology for Bear and Jennings bows.

In modern compound bows, the movement of the limb tips may be only 2 or 3 inches from resting to full draw. On a traditional recurve or longbow, the bow limb tips will move several more inches as energy is stored and released. Less tip movement is not what makes the compound bow so popular; it is the let-off, or compounding action, of the eccentrically shaped wheels at the limb tips. The mechanical action allows the archer to hold a bow at full draw, ready to release, but requires the archer to hold back less than half of the bow's draw weight.

In other words, if a traditional longbow is rated at 60 pounds of draw weight, the archer must pull back and hold the full 60 pounds at the established draw length in order to shoot an arrow. But with a compound bow—also rated at 60 pounds of draw weight—the archer is required to hold back only 30 pounds or less, depending upon the amount of let-off designed into the eccentric wheels. These wheels are sometimes called cams, energy wheels or modified cams, depending on the terminology favored by the specific manufacturer.

So, the average archer can shoot a compound bow of higher draw poundage because the bow can be held at full draw for a longer period of time. If all other aspects are the same, the higher the bow poundage, the faster the arrow. A faster arrow will fly in a flatter trajectory with less chance of a miss, even if the range is slightly misjudged.

Holding and shooting many arrows from a 60-pound longbow or recurve bow, which happens during a target tournament, can be tough on the muscles, leading to misses late in the day and even sore or injured muscles. One might shoot the same number of arrows from a compound bow and not experience these same effects.

The archer must still exert the same amount of force and muscle effort to draw both types of bows, but the holding weight is far less on the compound. The longer the archer holds back the arrow and string of a longbow, the more strain is put on the muscles. And if the archer attempts to pull the string back past the rated draw length, the amount of effort tends to build exponentially. The same effect may be argued regarding a compound bow, but when the rated draw length is reached, a distinct and abrupt stopping point is felt by the archer.

Incidentally, drawing any bow past its designed draw length is not recommended. While the possibility of breakage is remote, it can happen. Releasing an arrow from a bow drawn past its rated draw length will usually result in erratic and unpredictable arrow flight.

Getting a bow back to full draw is generally easier with a compound bow than a traditional bow because the muscles must overcome the draw weight only momentarily. The draw reduces by 50 percent or more as the bow's wheels or cams move into the let-off phase. The effort is modified further because momentum is on the archer's side as the arrow is pulled back. The peak weight is encountered for but a fraction of the time and length of the full draw. It is not only easier to transfer the energy from the muscles to the bow limbs, when compared to a same-draw-weight longbow, but it is usually possible to draw a heavier draw-weight compound bow.

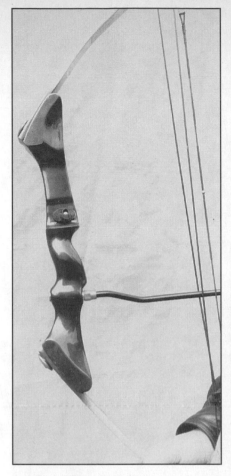

This Browning youth bow is typical of a riser made from cast magnesium. The material is lightweight, smooth and attractive.

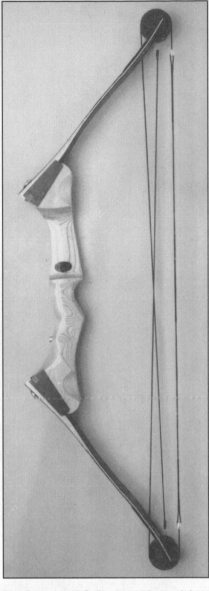

The Browning X-Cellerator, with wood riser, continues as one of the few still in production. It is still an attractive, popular bow.

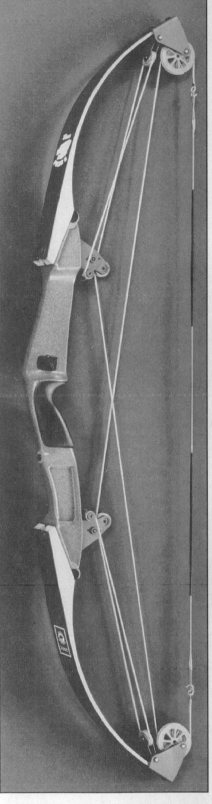

In the earlier years of compound development, bows with four, six or more wheels and pulleys were not uncommon. This is the Bear Polar II.

With the muscle energy stored in the bow limbs, the next step is to release the string and arrow, letting the stored energy transfer to the arrow and fling it through the air to the target. Thus, the muscle energy is now at or in the target! And it didn't take all that much effort.

Since the development and patent of the compound bow by Hollis W. Allen in 1969, this style of bow has passed through several changes in size, materials, construction techniques and, most importantly, public acceptance. Despite nearly three decades of change, Allen's basic design still looks a lot like today's most modern compound bows.

The original Allen patent bow had two of what looked like cams at the ends of the limbs, today commonly called eccentric wheels. Compound bows went through phases during which four wheels, even six wheels, were considered the ultimate in high-tech. Today, most bow manufacturers have settled on designs with two wheels, although there is a strong trend toward

(Above and right) Tom Jennings developed the Unistar bow a decade ago, with the compounding mechanism at the center of the mass rather than at the limb tips. The draw-length adjustment is on the pylon-mounted Unicam at the riser.

Martin Archery's riser is machined aluminum for strength and light weight. Note the high-tech look of the machined metal with sharp angles and flats.

compound bows with only one action cam; the second wheel is simply a center-mounted pulley to wrap the cable around the end of the other limb.

Along the way, Tom Jennings experimented with a single compounding cam action mounted on a pylon in the center of the bow riser, rather than at the limb tips. The wheels at the tips were, again, pulleys. Jennings called that a Unicam. It was a smooth-shooting bow, but the pylon on which the single cam unit was mounted seemed to add too much mass weight to the bow. It was removed from the lineup after a few years of production and a couple of modifications. Technology of the Uni-

cam bow led to further experimentation with the design by Jennings and others, however.

During a discussion of new developments and compound let-off a couple of years ago, Jennings mentioned that there were some considerations with regard to the amount of let-off a set of wheels or cams might develop. Jennings said he had experimented with bows that had more than 90 percent let-off, but they had several serious drawbacks.

True, with a 90-percent let-off bow, it might be possible to hold only 6 or 7 pounds at full draw while shooting a 60-pound-draw bow. A hunter might be able to hold 6 pounds back for hours at a time!

However, with that kind of let-off, the string is actually slack when the bowman is at full draw. There might not be enough weight pulling on the string to allow some mechanical releases to activate—to pull the string out of the jaws and let the arrow go. Jennings said that with a 90-percent bow let-off, the arrow literally has to be pushed forward slightly to get the string to release.

As of early 1995, most bow manufacturers have settled on 50- to 65-percent let-off for most of their new bows. Many compounds have provisions to allow archers to change their bows from 50 to 65 percent at will, without altering any other settings such as draw length or draw weight. There are several bows offered that are standard with 80-percent let-off. However, some states and other governing bodies have legislated that compound bows can have no more than 65-percent let-off when used by bowhunters.

Not every arrow shooter seeks the most let-off possible in a compound bow. Some archers prefer the feel of the heavier weight at full draw. They may prefer a bow with only 35 percent let-off. It can be held back longer than a traditional bow, with less strain on the muscles, and some believe the extra holding weight permits a smoother, more accurate release.

Part of the decision-making process archers must use when arriving at a chosen let-off depends upon the amount of draw weight built into the bow. A youth bow with a maximum draw weight of, say, 35 pounds, might function best with no more than 50-percent let-off. A strong bowhunter using an 80-pound bow might prefer a 65-percent let-off. Some target archers prefer a lesser let-off percentage, especially those shooting with a finger tab and not using mechanical releases.

Adjustable draw-length changes are also features of compound bows. With a longbow, the draw length may be changed by simply drawing the string back a farther or lesser distance. However, well-designed standard bows are built to function at their optimum at specific draw lengths, and anything more or less will result in less efficiency and poorer accuracy.

The draw length of a good compound bow may be changed without affecting draw weight or let-off. Draw length of many modern compounds may be changed by removing a couple of lock screws and slipping a movable cam section within the wheel, and then replacing the screws. There are numbers or letters at the settings to ensure balance at each end of the limbs. One does not even have to use a bow press to let the string go slack. Some earlier compound designs required the use of a bow press, a tool difficult to come by in the hunting fields.

Why adjustable draw length? One reason is that each archer's draw length does not stay exactly the same from year to year, especially a beginning archer. From the start, most rookie archers' draw lengths will increase from $1/2$- to 1-inch as muscle strength and condition improve with practice. As the important back muscles get stronger, the distance the string hand can be drawn back and held in place may increase to a degree. Or some injury or illness may force a shortening of one's draw length. Some archers may find that arrows made of different materials may result in slightly different draw lengths.

Another reason for adjustable draw lengths—particularly when the discussion turns to younger archers—is that children will grow. A good youth bow can be relatively expensive, and it makes sense that a bow should grow with the child. Typically, many compound bows designed for youngsters have a draw length range of from 25 to 28 inches. Others may have a range of 27 to 30 inches. Whatever the range and whatever the reason,

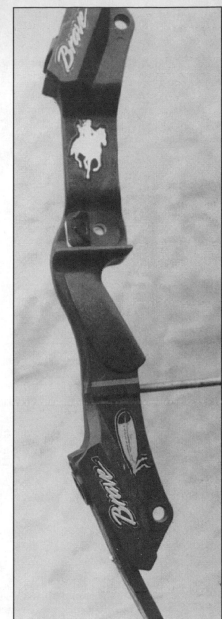

A small youth-size bow, the Golden Eagle Brave is made of fiber-reinforced plastic. This material is practical on low-draw-weight bows only.

an adjustable draw length can be of genuine benefit for most archers.

Another common feature found in all compound bows is draw-weight adjustment. These adjustments are made by simply turning the limb bolts at the base of the limbs in or out. Turning the bolts down as tightly as possible, usually with a large-size Allen wrench, will set the bow at its maximum draw weight. Loosening the bolts—it is absolutely essential that each bolt be turned in or out exactly the same amount—will reduce the draw weight. The amount of gain or loss per turn is usually noted in the manufacturer's instruction booklet or printed on the face of the bow on the specifications label.

There is a weight-change range for each compound bow. A decade or so ago, the typical draw-weight adjustment would be over a range of 10 pounds. Today, most bows have an adjustable range of at least 15 pounds and many have a 20-pound range. The best bows will not change draw length or wheel alignment during draw-weight adjustment.

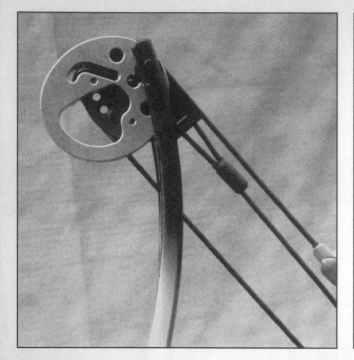

Here is the side of a Browning cam bow showing the three draw-length adjustment holes. Changing draw weight is as simple as moving bolts on both ends to new marked holes. The cam shape is smooth-drawing.

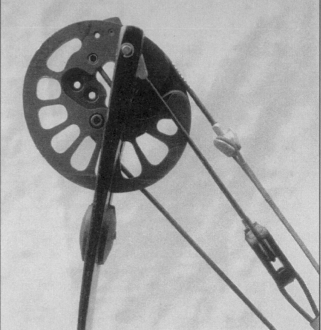

The large wheel on this Martin bow is marked with 65-percent let-off. The wheel is clean and smooth-drawing.

The advantage of weight changes are many, especially with beginning archers. Most develop back and arm muscles to the point that they can pull considerably more weight than when they started shooting. A higher draw weight, within the archer's physical abilities, will produce a faster, flatter-flying arrow. The flatter trajectory will somewhat obviate errors in distance estimation for the bowhunter as well as the unknown-distance target shooter.

Arrows are expensive and, sometimes, increasing or decreasing draw weight has the same effect as shooting a stiffer or weaker-spined arrow to improve arrow flight. That way, the same arrows may be used for practice, rather than junking a set of $50 shafts. Most archers experiment with draw weight adjustments to get the best arrow flight. Higher poundage is not always the answer to arrow-tuning problems, however, and the highest draw weight may produce the worst accuracy with some arrows.

Each bow and arrow setup must be carefully shot and tuned. The same setup will not perform the same for different shooters. The shape of the shooter—build, arm strength and length, height, weight and dozens of other factors—will have an effect on arrow flight. Each combination must be evaluated by the person shooting that setup.

The most common material for the bow handle—also known as the riser—has been wood. Early compound bows used wood for the handle of the bow, but now there are only a few modern compounds still made with wood risers. Lightweight, strong, inelastic metals have taken over the assignment. Cast magnesium and aluminum alloys are the most common materials used for bow handles today, and the trend is toward machined aluminum for the highest-tech bows.

Wood bows are attractive and warm looking, of that there is absolutely no debate. However, even laminated wood presents challenges for the manufacturer when it comes to consistency and water repellency. The most important drawback to wood bows is that the material cannot be shaped so that the arrow window, the cut-out where the arrow rests before it is shot, permits a true centershot. The arrow must always bend around the bow handle as it is shot, rather than fly straight in front of the bowstring. This is not a problem for traditional bows, longbows and recurves; the arrow always curves around the handle. But modern compound shooters have come to expect a centershot design with the arrow rest area cut out to allow the string and arrow to be shot from the bow on the same horizontal plane.

Magnesium and aluminum do not have the same restrictions regarding shape and size. They are, however, usually more expensive than wood. The magnesium castings must be perfect with no invisible air bubbles or gaps that would weaken the finished riser. Machined aluminum alloy bars may be more expensive than cast magnesium, but the high-tech look has become considerably more popular with bow buyers.

Manufacturers have learned that they can control the production process more closely using machined risers. Today's computer-controlled machines are expensive, but one machine can turn out thousands of risers or other parts and can operate twenty-four hours a day, seven days a week—and on the builder's schedule, not the casting supplier's. Judicious and artistic machining will produce a lightweight, strong, attractive product that is appealing to most archery buyers. The metal risers may be brightly colored for the target-shooting crowd or fin-

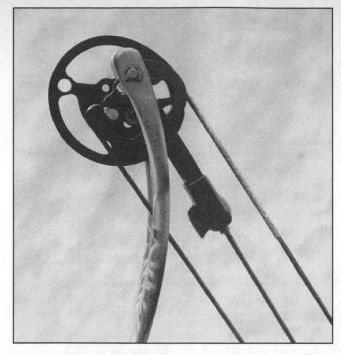

Minor tuning adjustments may be accomplished at the cable ending below the cam on the Jennings bow.

All compound bows feature adjustable draw weight. This bow is set at the lightest setting. Closing down the limb bolt will increase draw weight effort.

ished in dull, non-reflective camouflage colors to appeal to bowhunters.

Wood was also the chosen material for the limbs of the compound bow when it was invented. Today, several modern bows feature limbs of laminated wood and fiberglass; usually several kinds of wood. The fiberglass offers waterproofing as well as longer life and consistency. Other bows feature limbs of all-fiberglass material or fiberglass and carbon fiber. Aluminum and spring steel have been tried for compound bow limbs, but now are no more than museum oddities.

Most modern compound bow limbs are relatively short; they may be 15 to 20 inches long. The typical compound bow measures from about 38 to 44 inches, axle to axle. Youth bows and some special designs have shorter or longer limbs. The typical limb is about $1\frac{1}{2}$ inches wide, sometimes flaring out wider in the middle of the limb. The butt end—the part that connects with the riser—is usually a bit thicker, and the limb may taper toward the tip. Most compound limbs are reinforced slightly in the area of the wheel axle. Most have an elongated V-section cut out near the tip to accommodate the wheels and axle assembly; most also have a reinforcing button at the bottom of the V to reduce possible splitting when under stress.

The various limbs are manufactured and tested for draw weights because they must match one another within a small tolerance. Slight adjustments help to balance less-than-perfect limb matches, but the stiffness and bending curves should be as close as possible. As with the handles, the limbs are finished according to their anticipated use. They may carry bright, shiny tournament colors or one of the many camouflage patterns. This does not have any effect on the bow's shooting capabilities.

The limbs may be straight or recurved, following the design concepts of thousands of years ago. While there may be some

Sweeping recurve limbs are popular on some compound bows.

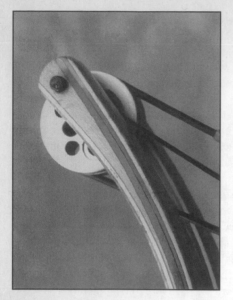

This older model Martin bow limb is still attractive with laminated wood and fiberglass construction.

This light-drawing youth bow has a wheel made of plastic.

This aluminum wheel on the Jennings bow indicates adjustment procedure and cable attachments. The wheels are lightened by machined cut-outs.

arrow speed advantages to a traditional bow with recurve limbs, there seems to be little difference when placed on modern compounds. The difference may only be cosmetic or aesthetic. A look at typical bows from the same manufacturer that produces straight and recurved-limb bows on the same riser, with the same tackle and other components, will reveal little or no difference in performance. The draw weight, draw length, percentage of let-off, arrow speed and arrow trajectory will be the same for each bow. The shape of the limbs will be the only difference between the bows. The choice between the two seems a matter of personal preference.

Modern compound bow designers seek out the strongest, lightest weight and non-elastic material possible for bowstrings. Depending on the intended use and final draw weight, the bowstring is made of several strands of material carefully laid down together and bound by serving thread and string wax. The number of strands can vary from fourteen to more than twenty. Heavy-draw-weight hunting bows tend to have more strands than bows shooting lighter-weight target arrows.

For years, Dacron string material was the most popular, and today, it still finds plenty of advocates. It is lightweight, strong and stretches little after it is broken in with many arrows.

A newer material, commercially known as Fast Flight, is gaining favor with manufacturers and shooters all over the world. Some manufacturers have gone so far as to make all the tackle, including what would ordinarily be steel cables, with Fast Flight string. The jury is still out on that decision.

Plastic-covered steel cables are favored for the rigging and tackle that does not come in contact with the arrow. Fast Flight has the advantage for strings, as it is lighter in weight and is claimed not to stretch at all, even during wide temperature changes. However, the string material, while plenty tough, can be cut by an inadvertent broadhead blade, while the steel cable will withstand plenty of abuse—accidental or otherwise.

The average compound bow for hunting may be expected to weigh 4 to 5 pounds. A few smaller bows will be less than 4 pounds; most archers prefer the lighter weight as they stalk through mountains and heavy woods after wild game. The given weight may be compared with a typical longbow that tips the scales at just about 1 pound, ready to shoot. As explained in a later chapter, simplicity and lighter weight are the primary appeals to archers who switch from compounds to traditional bows and equipment. Four pounds may not sound like much weight, but it will seem like 40 pounds at the end of a long day in the Rocky Mountains or the thick forests of the South.

The other disadvantage some archers ascribe to the modern compound bow is exactly that which appeals to others—high-tech mechanics. There are several moving parts on a compound bow, each requiring diligent adjustments and maintenance. Anything mechanical is subject to breakdown—screws can come loose, axles may need lubricant, cables can stretch, rust may form, parts can become lost, etc. Every component must be examined on a regular basis and readjusted as necessary.

Compound bows are here to stay; industry designers are coming up with improvements every year. The arrows fly faster and the bows are easier to shoot and adjust. Without compound bows, archery would not be nearly as popular as it is today. Compounds are what have driven the sport during past the three decades.

The single-cam concept is the hottest trend for the late '90s. Predictions are that nearly every manufacturer will introduce a single-cam compound bow well before the century has ended. Lighter, more durable materials are being used in the research and development departments of every manufacturer. Other breakthroughs are just around the corner. Stay tuned.

13 Traditional Bows

Thousands Of Years Ago, Different People In Different Places Invented The Bow— It Has Changed Little Since

Perhaps some early bow developers and shooters may have had equipment similar to these primitive models.

THE BOW, AS we know it, still is basically a stick and a string. We do not know exactly where or exactly when the tool was developed, but it probably happened in several parts of the world and evolved over hundreds of years. Most likely—based upon what scientists have told us—the bow was first invented as a device to help early humans hunt down and kill game because it made gathering food easier. It became a weapon to be used against other humans in a later age.

All that is conjecture. Nobody knows for certain how it all came about, and it seems unlikely anybody will ever know the exact history and development of the bow. However, the fact remains the bow is basically a device that stores human muscle power in a bent stick or section of bone until that energy is released and imparted to a slender, pointed stick, propelling it forward at great speed to strike a target.

Energy from the archer's back and arm muscles is used to draw the bow, and that energy is stored in the limbs of the bow. Some energy is lost due to inertia, vibrations and friction as the bow is drawn, and more energy is lost as the string is released and the energy is imparted to the arrow.

All the developments in compound bows and improvements to materials in traditional bows, strings and arrows merely make it easier for humans to draw and hold the arrow back until it is released. Improved materials will make the bow less likely to break and help ensure each shot is uniform. Stronger, lighter materials may be used for the bow limbs, reducing friction. Certain bow and string materials will help reduce the amount of shock or recoil the archer feels when releasing the arrow.

New, synthetic string material has little elasticity, reducing the need for constant tuning as the bow is shot and perhaps reducing the amount of vibration in the setup. The bow can be built to a lighter weight; the arrows straighter and more consistent with each shot. But the physical actions of shooting an arrow are the same as they were when early man began to gather his food.

Perhaps the most familiar traditional-style bow is the English longbow, similar to those the legendary Robin Hood and his Merry Men used in Sherwood Forest. These were rather

The typical longbow shooter must put plenty of muscle into the draw and release the arrow. There is no chance to relax until the arrow is away.

(Below) The recurve bow shooter may cant the bow slightly to the side as an aid to aiming and drawing. The arrow is shot off the shelf, and the cant helps prevent arrow drop-off while aiming.

large, heavy-draw-weight bows that required considerable muscle strength to draw and shoot. Surviving examples are 5 to 6 feet long, with draw weights of 80, 90 and even 100 pounds. No doubt, some were even heavier than that. Only the best and strongest archers would be permitted to shoot those bows, but they must have been effective. The English long-bowmen were instrumental in winning several battles against foes that had more soldiers, more horses and, sometimes, better tactics.

Some of these ancient longbows, still available for study, indicate the archer experimented with the basic design. While today's traditional longbow shooter prefers to "shoot from the shelf," there were some early attempts at moving the arrow rest closer to the center of the bow. Shooting from the shelf means the arrow is rested on the bow handle itself or on top of the archer's hand. One assumes those early shooters wore some sort of leather glove to protect their hands, as the feather fletching passed across the top of the thumb and fore-finger.

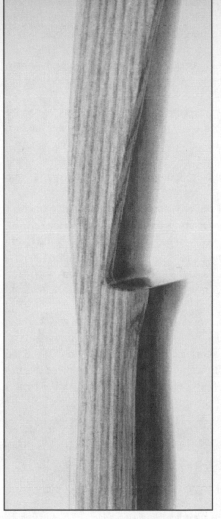

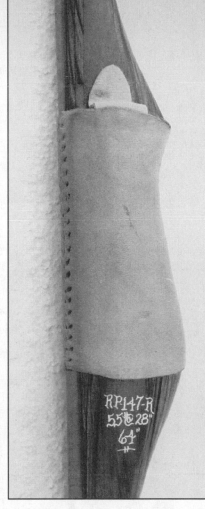

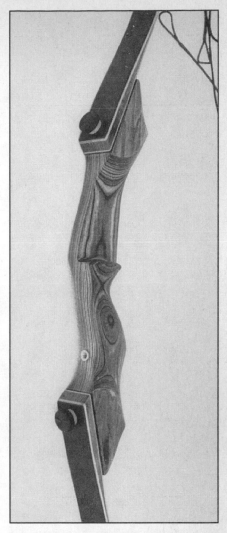

The Martin Bushmaster is an example of a modern traditional bow with a laminated handle, permitting considerable cut for the arrow. Later, the cut will be lined with leather.

Rancho Safari's traditional longbow is rated at 55 pounds draw at 28 inches. A soft leather grip is sewn on and a soft leather arrow rest is in place above the grip.

The Jeffry Raven takedown bow is marketed by PSE Archery. The riser is of contrasting laminated wood layers and is cut almost to center. Here, the bow is not strung. Thumb bolts hold the limbs in place.

Other longbows are built to have wider or narrower handles, depending on the hand of the archer. Some archers have left the wood of the handle bare, with nothing on it; others have added leather, cloth, woven grass, beads or some other softer material wrapped around the handle for a more comfortable grip. In modern times, a leather wrap is the most popular.

Most modern longbows and recurve bows have a slight cut in the riser that is lined with one or two pieces of leather to ensure the arrow is drawn across the bow at exactly the same spot each time. Some English longbows had the handle area narrowed slightly before adding the leather grip to present a uniform dimension across the surface.

The original English longbows, and many bows since, were made of English yew wood. In time, so many English yew trees have been cut down and split to produce staves for bow manufacture that there is a shortage of old yew trees throughout the world. The few remaining yew trees in England are now protected.

To aggravate the situation further, breakthroughs in medical research indicate substances extracted from the yew tree help battle certain types of cancer. Until synthetic chemicals are developed, the remaining yews growing in the United States may be in danger of final extinction.

Of course, yew trees do not grow everywhere in the world. Bows have been made from almost any kind of tree in many parts of the world. The early builders used whatever kind of wood that happened to be available. Bows have been built of all kinds of wood, even fashioned from standard cedar 2x4s in modern times. The wood grain does not have to be straight, either. Bows of straight, flawless, tight-grained, unblemished wood may be a relatively modern development. There are plenty of examples of old bows—and new bows built by makers who follow the old, traditional ways—with knots, discolored sections, crooked grain and all sorts of cosmetic "flaws" that shoot fast, straight arrows as accurately as any modern compound bow.

Wood is not the only material that has been used for bows.

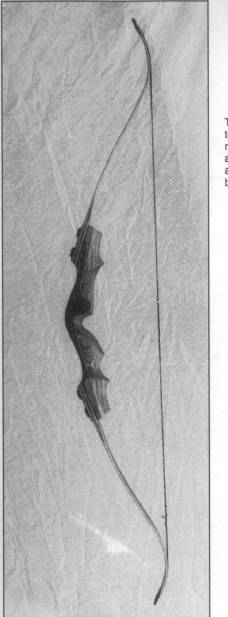

The Bob Lee Custom takedown recurve offers another approach to a fast, traditional bow.

They have been and still are made of metal, horn, bone and any other material that would bend, then smoothly and rapidly return to its original shape. No doubt, amid all this construction and experimentation, many bows cracked, broke, warped and allowed the next week's meals to get away. But survival provides a way of figuring out what works best, no matter what the odds.

The earliest bows were simple, one-piece designs, the entire tool made from a single stave of wood. Many popular modern longbows are made the same way. Somewhere along the time line, bowyers discovered they could produce bows that could be taken apart and reassembled in two or even three parts—the takedown bow.

The modern takedown bow has a riser or handle in the center, plus upper and lower limbs that are attached to the riser by bolts or straps. The takedown has the advantage of being transported easily in a compact package. It must be designed so that, when assembled, it fits together exactly the same way each time, so draw weight, draw length and arrow flight are identical each shot.

Many, if not most, modern Olympic-type target shooters utilize three-piece takedown bows. When traveling great distances by airplane or surface means, a takedown may be the only bow permitted by some carriers. The three-piece tournament bow is more often a recurved limb bow, rather than a longbow.

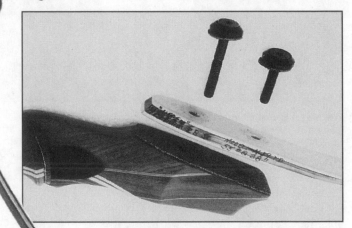

(Above) Upper and lower limbs are marked on the Chastain Wapiti bow. It is specified for 55 pounds and 28 inches of draw weight. The limbs are locked in place by two large limb bolts.

(Below) Chastain's Wapiti takedown recurve bow breaks down into a compact package for transport.

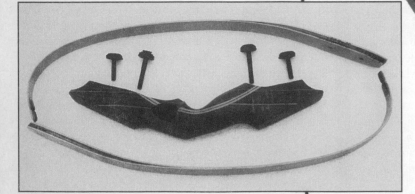

(Left) The Jeffry Raven's laminated limbs curve gracefully with the bow string nocked. The recurve is considerable, offering an extra impulse to the arrow as it is released.

One of the early modern takedown designs—patented by the late Fred Bear in 1948—utilizes what is called a latching hinge. Earlier designs had hinged, two-piece takedown construction, but Bear's model featured several screws to lock the two pieces in the same place each time. The latching system also kept the bow together in case of a broken string. Fred Bear did not, however, invent the first takedown bow. There are historical references to similar designs as long ago as 300 years. Some of the designs are still valid.

Various methods of joining the two or three sections include a sliding sleeve and socket system, requiring a precision-built oval-shaped metal sleeve and piston; round socket and sleeve designs with indexing marks to ensure precision fitting; various hinge designs and screw-in designs that required the parts to lock down exactly the same with each assembly. All designs must be precision-fitted and maintained to be successful. Usually, the joints are covered with leather, fabric, ivory, wood or some other material to cover and hide the metal fittings and protect the archer's hands.

The most traditional of the longbows have no shelf or cutout on the handle on which to rest the arrow. Early illustrations show the arrow resting on the archer's hand as the string is drawn and released.

Many of today's longbows and recurves feature a small cutout in the riser just above the grip. This small shelf usually is covered with soft leather to protect the bow material as well as to cushion and reduce wear on the arrow fletching.

Some bowyers break the leather shelf into two parts. One portion is on top of the grip; the other is higher up on the bow's riser. The gap between the two pieces of leather is intended to allow the fletching to pass through without touching any of the bow, while the arrow shaft slips along across the leather shelf. Many longbow shooters swear by this particular arrangement.

The recurve bow design is not as old as the longbow configuration. As far as we know, the Turkish recurves, made of sinew, horn, tendon glue and wood, date back 500 or more years. They were short in overall length, lightweight and portable, and shot fast arrows over great distances. The Turkish recurves were strictly weapons of war. When strung, the short limbs were under a great deal of stress; it must have taken superior strength for archers to employ them in battle. Examples are found in museums and collections around the world.

The modern recurve design dates back only about half a century. It remains popular today among bowhunters and target archers everywhere. Modern laminating and mass-production manufacturing techniques enable producers to provide thousands of archers with consistent, reliable and accurate bows. Experimentation and improvements to recurves have resulted in a faster, lighter bow. Most of the modern recurve limbs are made of laminated woods and fiberglass, often several layers of each. Typical modern recurve bows have shorter, stronger limbs and much longer handle riser sections than typical longbows. The riser may be of wood, laminated materials or even a lightweight metal such as magnesium or aluminum.

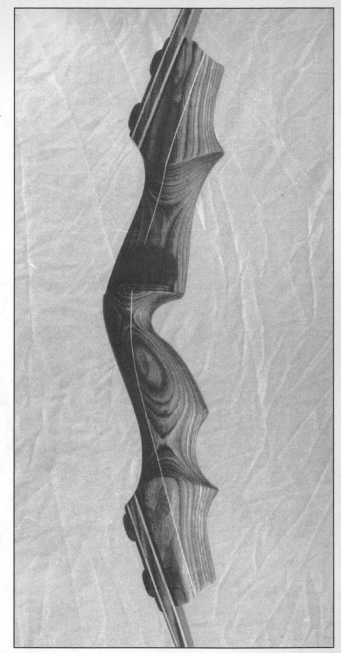

The Bob Lee Custom presents an interesting lamination pattern in the wood riser. The formed grip places the archer's hand well forward in a high-palm position.

Using metal for the handle permits the designer to cut the area near the arrow rest past the center of the bow. The riser can be designed to allow the arrow to be drawn and shot in line with the string. The arrow does not have to bend around the handle as it is released, as is the case with all longbows and wood-handled recurves or compounds. Attempts to cut out the handle past center using wood, even strong laminated wood, leave the handle riser section considerably weakened and subject to breakage. Metal bolts or steel pins through the handle to strengthen the area have been tried, but the efforts have been unsuccessful.

All modern traditional bows—longbows and recurves—are built to provide their rated draw weight at a specified draw length. The most common draw length is 28 inches. That length has become almost standard for this type of bow. If the bow is built correctly, the listed draw weight will be found at the draw length, not before and not after. Poorly made bows that don't comply with these rules demonstrates erratic arrow flight and/or draws that are rough or otherwise difficult for the archer.

Because a traditional bow must be held at its full draw weight to shoot and does not have the relaxing let-off found on compound bows, most archers are happier shooting a bow of less draw weight than might be possible with a compound. An archer who might be comfortable with 70 or 80 pounds of draw on a compound with 65-percent let-off might be better off with 50 or 55 pounds of draw when shooting a longbow or recurve. Furthermore, the draw length of a compound probably will be an inch or two more than that for a traditional-type bow.

Most archers shooting traditional bows will release the arrow as soon as the string is drawn back to the anchor point, rather than holding at full draw for several seconds—or minutes—as with a compound bow. Some shooters find a shorter anchor point easier to deal with when shooting traditional bows.

In addition to lighter, faster limbs, many modern recurve and longbow makers are adopting the most advanced materials for the bowstrings. For years, Dacron was the standard. It still is found on many bows, but other synthetic materials have been developed in recent years that do not stretch with use, which results in less re-tuning for the archer and more energy imparted to the arrow as the string is released.

Some archers say these non-elastic strings cause more hand shock, but others feel that, when the bow limbs come to an abrupt halt in their forward motion as the arrow leaves the string, there is less recoil and bounce in the hand. The trend among compound bow manufacturers is to use more and more of the non-stretch string material.

Those who shoot longbows and recurves feel there are several advantages to them, beyond the traditional values of using a wonderful tool invented thousands of years ago. The weight of a traditional bow is about one-fourth that of a typical compound with the same draw weight. Without any sights or quiver attached, a modern longbow can weigh a pound or less. Even a typical takedown recurve with sights, a stabilizer, arrow rest and a bow quiver will tip the scales at less than 2 pounds. A comparable compound will be between 4 and 5 pounds.

For the bowhunter, a longbow is easy to carry all day and is simple to maneuver through heavy brush or trees. With practice, a traditional archer can pull an arrow quickly from his back quiver, nock it on the string and get off a shot. Early man did it for thousands of years, managing to feed himself and his family or tribal group with the same type of equipment.

There are virtually no moving parts to wear out or break. In time, the bowstring will have to be replaced, and there is always the danger of inadvertently cutting the string with a broadhead blade when miles from camp—but that is a potential hazard every archer faces. Most traditional hunting bows are quiet to

Martin Archery offers a bow quiver and mount for those who prefer to hunt with their arrows close at hand.

shoot if string silencers are used. Many traditionalists feel the spirit of their hunting ancestors lives on in them through their simple longbows.

Traditional bows—longbows in particular—require considerably more practice before the archer is proficient. The muscles must be strengthened and toned to accomplish a smooth, quick draw with each and every shot. Without sights or an arrow rest, the archer must shoot hundreds of arrows before accurate, tight groups become the rule. Practicing with a traditional bow is much like learning to throw a ball or learning golf. There are no sights on the ball, but most American kids have learned to put the ball into a rather restricted target zone with every throw. The same holds true for archery. The muscles, eyes and brain must be programmed with plenty of practice.

When Fred Bear was alive, he always would put on

Flight shooting is a specialized part of archery. The goal is long distance without regard to accuracy. The powerful one-piece recurve bow is small, utilizing a forward handle with a central channel for the arrow to shoot through the riser. Great strength is required for this activity.

impromptu shooting demonstrations when he appeared at hunting or equipment consumer shows. Bear shot left-handed. He would hold his recurve bow with an arrow nocked and look at his intended target. Then he would explode into motion, quickly drawing back the string, touching his anchor point and immediately releasing the arrow. The movement was almost a blur; the arrow inevitably would be seen next in the center of the bullseye. He did not seem to aim, as he might if the bow were equipped with sights, but he did not miss. Bear was aiming subconsciously as he looked at the target before drawing. It required a lot of practice.

There are several manufacturers mass-producing longbows and recurves, although most of today's traditional market is with the latter. Production longbows are available, but most longbow shooters have custom-made bows produced by

bowyers who build the bows to order, one at a time. Many of these same makers also can turn out recurves built to customer order.

To obtain the best recurve or longbow from either type of manufacturer, the archer must know the exact draw length and anticipated draw weight. The specifications should be understood thoroughly and discussed with the bow seller. An experienced, dedicated bowyer or retailer will ask the right questions and make sure the buyer is satisfied with the purchase.

As mentioned, longbows and recurves are built to produce their specified draw weight at a particular draw length. As the bow is drawn, the energy required to bring the bowstring back rises at a fairly steady rate until the listed draw length is reached. The farther back the bowstring is drawn, the more difficult it becomes. When the listed draw length is reached, the listed draw weight also should be reached. Typical specifications might be 50 pounds draw weight at 28 inches of draw length.

Given enough strength, it is possible to continue to draw the string and arrow well past the specified draw length. However, most bows will become far more difficult to draw past that point. Each inch requires far more effort to pull back than required until that point. The phenomenon is called stacking. Carelessly made traditional bows will begin to stack before the specified draw length is reached, an undesirable situation. A bow scale placed on the string will indicate that the bow is exhibiting the specified draw weight at the desired draw length, but it is far too difficult for the archer to achieve.

A longbow or recurve buyer, especially one dealing with a custom bowyer and high prices, should test the new bow. Shoot several arrows and be aware of how it draws and holds upon release. The buyer should not accept a bow that stacks before the nominal draw length is reached. Any legitimate bowyer will want the archer to be satisfied with the new bow, as that will lead to more business. Complete satisfaction is the goal of the legitimate businessman, large or small.

Overall, longbows and recurve bows are more efficient than compounds, based on measurements using the same draw length, draw weight and arrow. However, at the same shooting specs, a compound will move the same arrow faster, even though it is less efficient. The compound stores more of the muscle energy from the archer than do traditional bows.

No matter what new materials and technologies are developed in the next decade, or even the next century, traditional bows are not likely to change much from what they have evolved into over the past several thousand years. Recent years have seen more archers who learned on and took up the sport using compound bows. Increasingly, more and more of them are trying and shooting longbows and recurves, just as their predecessors did. They are attracted to the simplicity and beauty of the equipment, and they can relate to their ancestors who used the bow and arrow as survival tools, not sporting implements. Many average archers are attempting to build their own bows using primitive tools and tested techniques. Traditional bows will always have a large role to play in the sport of archery, no matter what high technology might offer.

13

Ancient Bows And Their Modern Uses

Sinew has been applied to the back of an ash bow, but is not completely dry. When dry, sinew will reduce deflex and increase reflex.

Limb tip with an ash overlay applied over the sinew. Strands of sinew are glued together on the limb.

WHEN TALKING about primitive archery and the equipment used by early people, we must talk about backed bows as well as self bows. Primitive peoples used a number of different materials in building their bows, learning to rely on what was available. In different parts of the world, our ancestors found a variety of materials from which to make bows and arrows. Most of the time, it was a matter of using what people had on hand, rather than getting the best material from somewhere else in the world, as we are able to do today.

Most modern bows—at least the ones most often seen—are backed with fiberglass. Primitive bow makers probably would have loved to have had fiberglass and modern glues available to them. It would have made bow building a whole lot easier.

Even though our ancestors were stuck with using the materials at hand, they made some really effective equipment out of some less-than-perfect materials. They learned how to use what they had, either by itself or in combination with other natural materials.

In general, early bows were made of whatever wood was available in the immediate area. We have evidence that a few bows used more than one type of wood in their construction. If necessary, the bows were backed with animal products such as sinew or rawhide, with sinew the most common. Though there are several theories as to why primitive people used backings on their bows, most subscribe to the "it was the eas-

iest way to get a shootable bow and have dinner on the fire pit" theory.

The use of a wood backing was not common practice until the past few years, but has become popular as a means of reducing breakage in a self bow when the main bow wood is not as tough as the bow maker would like. Perhaps the bow has been built without regard for the grain of the wood, keeping the back of the bow in a single growth ring of the tree.

Woods used for backing are usually strong and stringy, and therefore less likely to break when the bow is drawn—hickory, ash, bamboo and sometimes locust wood.

The work involved in backing a bow with wood is a lot more complicated than using sinew or rawhide. Using wood, the process is basically one of lamination, gluing a thin layer of wood onto the back of the bow. The most challenging part is getting both surfaces flat enough to bond well. One of the most popular combinations is backing an Osage orange bow with hickory wood.

On the other hand, sinew has been used as a backing material since the beginning of archery. Horn bows used in Europe and Asia were either backed with sinew or used sinew in some other part of the bow construction. Countless examples exist of primitive wood bows utilizing a sinew backing.

For those asking, "What exactly is sinew?" It is the tendons from various parts of an animal, sometimes called "silver skin." The most useful tendons are found in both front and rear legs and along the backstrap of every mammal. There are tendons in other parts of the animal, but they are small and of not much use, except for lesser primitive projects such as tying feathers onto arrows.

Any bow built without manmade materials such as fiberglass can be sinew-backed whether longbow or recurve. The important thing to remember is that the sinew always will pull the bow into a reflex position when it dries. A common expectation is that putting sinew on a wood longbow will make it a recurve.

This bow has sinew backing on the handle area. This unusual design has an arrow shelf cut into the bow above the handle.

A closer view of a sinew-backed limb tip.

This is not true. Recurve limbs have a deflex and a reflex curve, not just a reflex. If you want to end up with a recurve, you have to start with a recurve. If you back a longbow with sinew, it still will be a longbow, no matter how much reflex is added by the dried sinew.

Though the backstrap tendon of an animal is the best one to use for achieving a smooth, nice-looking backing, it is the most difficult to obtain in a large enough quantity to back a bow. The leg tendons are the more commonly used. The most sought-after are the rear leg tendons from large grazing or browsing animals such as deer, elk, moose and buffalo. They are strong and large, so the bowyer can get a lot of backing out of each one.

I've tried all of these and find elk to be the easiest to use, though moose tendons seem to have a finer-grain sinew, thus the finished job looks better. I also like buffalo sinew, but it is not as easy to obtain; I've been able to get only a few from time to time.

No matter the type of sinew or its origin, it has to be dried thoroughly after being removed from the animal. If you plan to use the sinew from an animal you hunted or from a local butcher/meat packer, you will need to dry it yourself. Yes, beef sinew also will work as backing material. If you're buying sinew from a supplier, though, it already should be dried, or it will develop some bad odors.

The best way to dry it is to lay it outside on an old window screen with the screen supported so air can circulate all around it drying the tendon completely through. This usually will take from several days to a week, depending upon the thickness. As it dries, it will begin to turn an amber color. You will know it is dry when it has become completely amber and translucent. If it has any spots in it that you cannot see through, it is not yet dry enough.

One big caution: Depending on where you live, you may find that every stray dog, cat, coyote, bear and mountain lion will

think it is a free snack. You will want to find a way to protect your drying sinew, or you may become the most popular guy in town to these animals.

If you are going to back a bow with sinew, drying is only the beginning and by far the easiest part. Once the sinew is dry, it has to be separated into thin strands and glued onto the back of the bow in intertwined layers. This sounds easy, but it is a rather difficult procedure.

Separating the dried sinew into thin strands is no picnic. It has to be thoroughly hammered to break down the bond between the individual strands so they separate. Keep pulling them apart until they are no thicker than the size of one strand

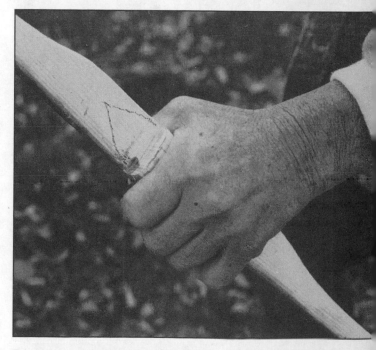

This self-bow handle area is carved to fit the shooter's hand.

of bowstring material. The thinner the strands when applied to the bow, the smoother, tighter and stronger the backing will be.

As you separate the sinew, notice that individual strands can be broken by hand. Not to worry. When several thousand strands are glued together, they are unbelievably strong.

There are several ways to hammer the sinew to separate it. The early Native Americans pounded it between two rocks. It was about the only material they had that was sturdy enough. It was effective, but an unbelievable amount of work. If you want to use rocks, I suggest you find several smooth ones, one that is of pretty good size and has a fairly flat side plus a couple of smaller ones to do the pounding. If you try this method, you will soon find out why I only demonstrate it and do not recommend it. By the way, it is a good idea to keep your fingers from between the rocks.

When I hammer sinew, I use a piece of hardened "traditional" tool steel plate and a smooth finishing hammer. If you do not have access to hardened steel, you can use a hardened shop anvil or a short section of railroad track. Don't use any old piece of steel, because, if it isn't hardened, the hammer will dent the soft steel and create sharp edges that will cut the sinew. For the same reason, make sure you use something with a smooth face to hammer the sinew. Your purpose is to strip it, not cut it. Use a hammer with a smooth face, rather than one with ridges cut into it, such as a framer's hammer.

When you finally have the tendons stripped into thin strands, you will need to sort them into groups. These groups will be glued onto the back of the bow in an interlaced pattern. If you tried to back a bow with the individual strands, you would yourself become primitive before you finished.

Both modern and primitive tools for pounding/splitting elk sinew.

I assemble six to eight strands in a group and place them between the pages of an old magazine. I then roll the magazine up and rubber-band it. This tends to press the sinew and straighten it out so it will lay on the bow more evenly.

Gluing the sinew onto the bow can be a real mess. It requires some planning to get through the job without gluing everything in sight. The only glue to use is powdered hide glue made by boiling down animal parts such as hide, tendons and hooves. It has been the glue of choice for this operation for hundreds of generations of bow makers. Luckily, it is available commercially in powder form, so you don't have to make it yourself.

Hide glue must be heated and kept at 120 to 130 degrees F. Safety is essential throughout the procedure. The pot of warm water on the right is ready to clean up the mess. Sinew is dipped in glue and squeezed to remove the excess.

First strips of sinew are placed along the centerline of the bow as subsequent strips are overlapped. Everything must be smoothed down. Each group of sinew is placed and smoothed as work progresses.

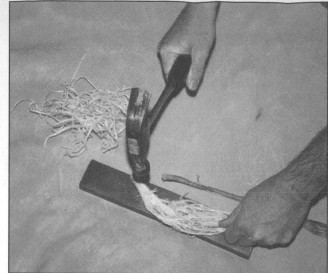

Rocks were used to strip this piece of sinew, although this is doing it the old, hard way.

Using a hammer and piece of tool steel is a much easier method of splitting sinew for backing.

I use a homemade double boiler—a pot and bowl—to get the glue ready. I also keep a pot of warm water at the side to wash excess glue off my hands from time to time. To apply the sinew, dip several strands into the hide glue and work the glue into the strands with your fingers. Make sure you squeeze the excess out of the group before laying it on the back of the bow. The sinew then is pressed onto the bow and smoothed out to remove excess glue. It only requires a minimum amount to hold the sinew. If you leave too much glue, the bow will make cracking noises when you draw it; it is only the excess glue cracking, but it can make you a bit nervous.

Start applying the sinew at the middle of the handle and work out toward the edges of the bow and to the tip. The joints between groups are alternated in a manner that is similar to laying bricks. This creates a strong, interlaced backing. Since the length of sinew, after being stripped out, can be as short as 6 inches, it may require several groups of sinew to completely cover the back of a bow.

In most cases, backing is used to prevent breakage. However, sinew backing can be used to increase bow performance. As the sinew dries, it shrinks and pulls the bow into a reflex curve, which will add a little to the draw weight. If it is done properly, it can help the performance,

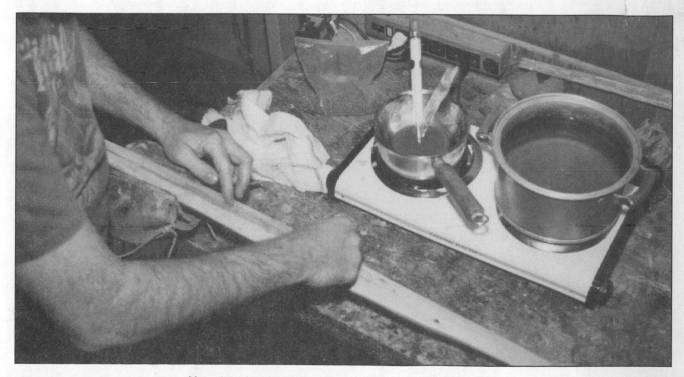

More sinew is stripped along the bow limb and smoothed down. The job can be messy.

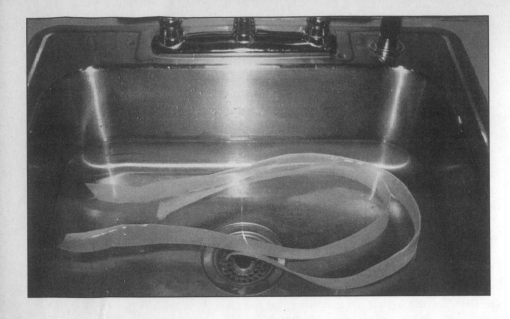

If rawhide is used to back the bow, it is first cut into strips and soaked in warm water until soft enough to work.

but it is easy to use too much sinew and make the bow sluggish.

When it comes to performance, there is no difference between a well-made self bow and a well-made backed bow. Performance can be attributed to the material or basic construction of the bows in question. Any difference comes from the design, the piece of wood that was used, and the skill and care of the person making the bow.

Many people building their first self bow ask, "Do I have to back it with sinew?" The answer is no! Backing should be used only if you have cut through the tree growth ring on the back of the bow or if the bow wood is weak. There are people who subscribe to the theory of backing every bow, just in case. That seems like a lot of unnecessary work to me.

There is one other type of backing that I have not talked about yet—rawhide. Rawhide backing on an English-style self bow made of yew wood is almost a necessity. With this type of bow, both the sapwood and heartwood are used, the sapwood becoming the back of the bow.

Sapwood is soft and can be dented fairly easily if bumped on a rock or other hard object. If dented, the bow most likely will break at that spot. As with sinew backing, rawhide is applied wet and allowed to dry before the bow can be shot. Since rawhide becomes quite hard when it dries, it will protect the sapwood from damage. I know the frustration of bumping a yew bow on a rock and denting the sapwood. It's not a fun experience. You might as well say bye-bye to the bow.

I have heard of ordinary tanned leather being used as a backing, but I'm not sure what that would accomplish. Tanned leather is soft and has little tensile strength by itself. I guess it might have a level of psychological help for the novice bowyer.

There is a special thrill that cannot be described when it comes to hunting and taking an animal with a primitive bow. It has to be experienced to be appreciated. Primitive archery is not for everybody, but for some people there is nothing else. It is the most difficult style of archery to semi-master.

I said semi-master, because if you ever think you have mastered it, you soon will become bored. Then you would have to find a new sport. Maybe you could become a Paleolithic spear chucker and use an atlatl to hunt woolly mammoths.

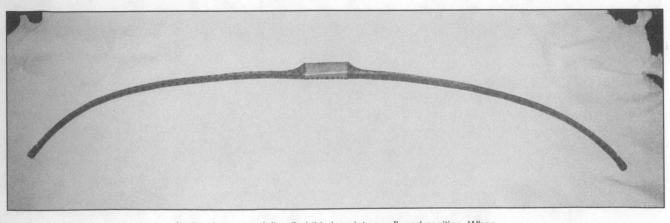

As the sinew cured, it pulled this bow into a reflexed position. When strung, it will be a longbow, not a recurve. Sinew and limbs were covered with rattlesnake skin to make it waterproof.

14 Major Archery Companies

They Came From Varying Backgrounds, But These Pioneers Started The Ball Rolling!

WHEN ONE LOOKS down the list of today's major archery tackle and bowhunting equipment manufacturers, it is obvious they come from many backgrounds. Some came from the aerospace industry after military aviation downgrading forced them to find other endeavors. Others are major sporting goods outfits who diversified such as Browning, whose founder, John M. Browning, designed military pistols and machineguns.

But when one delves back into the development of archery as a sport in this country, it quickly becomes apparent that the bona fide target archers and bowhunters of the first half of this century were the real pioneers. In pursuing their sport, they saw the needs of themselves and others. Equipment design, development and manufacturing followed their lead.

The Pioneers

As early as 1922, Doug Easton was crafting custom wood bows and cedar arrows in the farming community of Watsonville, California. An avid target archer, he was able turn out tournament-grade cedar arrows which he shot in the championship tournaments of that era. However, he found himself frustrated with the inconsistency and lack of uniformity in his wooden shafts.

Easton decided to do something about it. He was convinced that consistently straight, uniform arrow shafts were impossible to manufacture—even from Port Orford cedar, a straight-grained wood grown only in the Oregon coastal regions. Thus, he turned his attention to aluminum.

Easton was not a highly educated man. He had no advanced degree in engineering; in fact, he had no college degree at all. However, he did have an understanding of machines and how they worked. Thus, he was able to design and build machinery that would take aluminum pipe an inch or so in diameter and, through several specific operations, draw it down to arrow shaft

Doug Easton, and the company that bears his name, revolutionized arrows and arrow shafts. Today, most of the aluminum arrows used throughout the world are of Easton aluminum. Easton developed the production technique, which never has been duplicated.

Ben Pearson is another modern archery pioneer who successfully moved from the sport or hobby of archery to the business of archery. Pearson Archery still lives on in Pine Bluff, Arkansas.

diameters. For many decades, the design and inner workings of these machines were kept secret, and no other company was able to match Easton's work.

He began manufacturing his first aluminum arrows in Los Angeles in 1939. There were problems in the beginning, but he worked them out one at a time. Aluminum arrow shafts tended to bend under stress, so an arrow straightening machine was developed. This mechanism also was useful in checking straightness for quality control when Easton began to market the shaft in bulk.

Easton's instincts about aluminum arrows proved correct, and in 1941, after a California archer, Larry Hughes, won the

national target championship with a set of Easton arrows, there began a trend that changed traditional archery and the rest of the sporting world forever. In 1970, James D. Easton, Inc., applied the aluminum technology to ski poles, baseball bats and ice hockey sticks.

Doug Easton passed away in 1972 and his son, Jim, took over as company president. There have been many expansions in the empire since, including purchase of the Hoyt Archery Company. Jim Easton served as archery commissioner for the 1984 Olympics.

In 1925, twenty-seven-year-old Ben Pearson read an article in a Boy Scout magazine about how to make your own bows and arrows. Near his Arkansas home, he located a good piece of hickory and hand-carved a crude longbow with an 80-pound draw weight

Pearson competed unsuccessfully with this overweight bow in local tournaments, but gradually improved little by little, eventually winning the Arkansas state championship.

He had met several archers in Pine Bluff who were passionate about archery, but who resented the tedious tasks involved in making and repairing their own archery tackle. In that era, there were no archery shops and no store-bought supplies available.

Pearson moved his few belongings—including his bow and arrows—to Pine Bluff where he became a part-time bowyer. He organized one of the nation's first archery clubs, supplying members and other archers with bows and arrows, as well as handling repairs. He did this sort of work at night, since he was employed by Arkansas Power & Light during the day.

The Great Depression of the 1930s proved a boon to Pearson. He lost his job, but the idleness offered the chance to continue handcrafting archery tackle. Soon he was able to mass-produce bows that almost anyone could afford, even in that era of universal poverty.

In 1938, a visiting Oklahoma oilman, who also was an archery enthusiast, inspected some of Ben Pearson's work and was sufficiently impressed that he offered to back the bowyer in his own archery tackle manufacturing company. On March 19, 1939, Ben Pearson, Inc., was founded.

Throughout his career in the archery business, Ben Pearson made a point of spreading his own enjoyment and passion for the sport to young people. A Pearson-owned camp near Blanchard Springs, Arkansas, was a popular place for young people to learn the ins and outs of archery, and Pearson taught hundreds of children himself.

Ben Pearson died in 1971 at the age of seventy-three, but the company has continued, bearing his name and following his philosophies.

It has been said that "in 1929, when Fred Bear started hunting with bow and arrow, all the bowhunters in Michigan would fit into a Model T Ford."

Born in Pennsylvania in 1902, Bear left behind a boyhood of hunting and trapping, then a stint in the cavalry, to migrate to Detroit when he was twenty-one. He worked in the automotive industry until he met Art Young. Young had been taught bowhunting skills by Ishi, who had been found in the California mountains in 1911 and was the last primitive Indian in America.

Bear and Young huddled in the former's basement workshop, where Young taught the young novice how to make bows, arrows and bowstrings fashioned from linen thread. In the woods near Detroit, Young helped Bear learn instinctive shooting skills that were to serve him so well in later life.

In 1933, at the height of the Great Depression, Bear and Charles Piper each came up with $300 to start Bear Products Company. Their specialty was silkscreening advertising banners for auto dealers. However, off in one corner, Bear had set up a shop where he handcrafted archery tackle and sold it to friends and other archers who had heard of it via word of

Fred Bear may be the best known name among the modern pioneers of archery and business. He hunted with Art Young, built bows in his basement and eventually founded the Bear Archery Company, now operating in Gainesville, Florida.

mouth. In six years, this segment of the business had become successful enough that Fred Bear knew he could support himself as a custom bowyer. Soon thereafter, Bear Archery Company was launched.

Bear had bowhunted first—and unsuccessfully—in 1929; in fact, it was six years before he took his first game animal, a whitetail deer. Nonetheless, he was instrumental in promoting a bowhunting season in Michigan in 1936. Later, his trophies taken in far corners of the world numbered in the hundreds.

As a target archer, he won the Michigan State championship three times during the '30s, then barnstormed the sports show circuit, exhibiting his shooting skills in such major urban areas as Chicago and St. Louis.

From this beginning came the industry giant we know today as Bear Archery. Corporate headquarters were moved to Gainesville, Florida, prior to Fred Bear's death on April 27, 1988 at the age of eighty-six. Arlyne Rhode of *U.S. Archer* magazine said, "His memory will live on in the things he invented and the people he helped."

The bowhunting and target archery exploits of the three men profiled here are legion and legend; entire books have been written about them. But there were other pioneers of that era, working away in small workshops or garages, developing accessories and items that eventually would make archery easier and more interesting. They should not be forgotten.

And with the wide range of new materials and theories being introduced today, pioneers still are being born in this sport. There will be more in the future!

However, it was the vision of the Doug Eastons, the Ben Pearsons, the Fred Bears that, during the second quarter of this century, brought archery from what was considered a primitive pastime to the status of a modern multi-billion-dollar industry!

Besides being used to test bow prototypes and accessories, the Bear Archery Proving Grounds at the company's headquarters are open to the public.

Appropriately enough, this 15-foot high bear is one of two that "guards" the entrance to Bear's Gainesville, Florida, headquarters.

ONE OF ARCHERY'S oldest bow manufacturers is also one of its most progressive. Founded in 1939, Bear Archery is quite aware of its heritage, using the past as a signpost for the future.

Backed by a reputation for quality, Bear Archery continues design experimentation and innovation. In a highly competitive industry where rivals also build quality bows, excellence in design is not enough.

What is enough was the late Fred Bear's basic philosophy: "We want to make the best archery equipment we can and sell it at a fair price."

To maintain and achieve that goal, the company made wholesale changes in its physical plant in 1990-1991. Equipment that had changed only marginally since the 1930s was scrapped and replaced with state-of-the-art machinery. Assembly lines that owed their heritage to the automobile industry were replaced with three-person cells, each cell fully assembling a single bow. Each cell member can work at any one of the three-cell workstations.

Instead of a productivity philosophy that measures success in terms of units produced per hour and per day, Bear strives for quality in every bow produced.

"We can still do as many bows as ever," said Roy Clark, manufacturing/engineering manager, "but it's not the most important statistic."

What is important is quality control. Quality standards at Bear are tighter than normal safety tolerances. The machinery, machine operators and assemblers are better than they actually have to be, Clark explained. One benefit of this is that the company's quality control department becomes, in effect, its training center, because all the trained employees are already quality controllers in their own right.

Bear management also believes in a manufacturing operation system known as Build-To-Order. By keeping a relatively small inventory of assembled bows and components on-hand, Bear can pare back its inventory investment to a minimum which increases overall profitability and gives the company greater flexibility without sacrificing responsiveness.

The inside of Bear Archery's 165,000-square-foot manufacturing and assembly facility is dominated by a series of wall murals depicting archery and bowhunting throughout history.

Bear's thoroughly modern, state-of-the-art facility is organized so as to be employee-friendly and therefore highly efficient and productive. This approach is in keeping with the company's dedication to the most advanced of world class manufacturing principles.

All of Bear's mass merchants, distributors, pro shops and mail-order customers are asked to order sixty to ninety days in advance. Bear manufactures exactly what is needed for each order. From its inventory, the company can handle last-minute orders and emergency resupplies for customers who run out of a particular bow or accessory.

Bear offers a wide range of accessories and manufactures an ever-increasing percentage in-house. This follows in line with the Build-To-Order system and is made possible by the fact that "we know we do a good job, so we can bring much of the process in-house, for everything, every step," said Clark.

In a way, this cutting edge approach to archery manufacturing is nothing more than a return to the company's roots. Bear Archery was founded by the legendary Fred Bear, who learned to make longbows and recurves from Art Young. Young, along with Saxton Pope, is credited with resurrecting bowhunting as a sport in the 20th century. In 1952, Fred Bear introduced the Grizzly, the industry's first truly mass-produced bow. Forty-one years later, the company brought out the Super Strike, a compound bow with the revolutionary single cam that Bear Archery calls the OneCam system.

In a little over half a century, Bear Archery has grown from a $600 investment for a few machines and a shed to house them into a multi-million-dollar company housed in a custom-built, 165,000-square-foot plant. This large, modern facility—which also houses the impressive Fred Bear Museum and Fred's office and workshop—has space for Bear Archery not only to continue to grow, but also to manufacture in-house ever more components and accessories.

From its original home in Michigan to its present site in Gainesville, Florida, Bear has increased its line of products from the one or two stick bows offered in the '40s and '50s to the fourteen models offered today, including three youth bows, four recurves and two crossbows. Five of its compound models are available as 3-D/target bows. Bear's broad range of accessories includes broadheads and points, arrow rests, sights, overdraws, quivers, release aids, stabilizers and more than fifty other products.

By the time Fred Bear died in 1988, the company he founded had perhaps grown and diversified more than this progressive giant of the industry had dreamed it would. Obviously, Fred Bear is a man who can never be replaced. However, Bear Archery is fortunate to have the services of another industry legend, Tom Jennings, the man who popularized the compound bow.

The Jennings Compound Bow Company was acquired by Bear in 1983 and was moved from California to Florida. Bear Archery designs, manufactures and markets Jennings bows as a separate line of fourteen hunting and competition models. The definite distinction between the two lines is maintained by having design features unique to each.

Change is ever present in the archery industry, but change for the sake of change is not the way to go, say Bear staffers.

"The most important thing is what the consumer wants; he drives this train," said Gary Simonds, vice president of engineering and product development. "The bowhunter drives the train by the simple expedient of knowing what capability he needs, then demanding that the industry meet those needs."

Among the developing needs, Simonds predicts, are newer, better, different accessories; stronger, lighter, more durable materials; and maybe a significant, but not necessarily revolutionary, change in the shape of the compound bow, one made possible by progress in design, engineering, manufacture and materials. The most immediate and noticeable change will be the switch to single cam, which Simonds expects to be the industry standard in two to three years.

Looking at today's compound bow and comparing it to the Osage orange wood string bow Fred Bear carved and hunted with in 1929, it is perhaps a little hard to conceive of a Bear Super Strike XLR or a Jennings Carbon Extreme XLR as a "primitive" device.

But primitive doesn't mean lack of quality or care in manufacturing. Nor does it imply that bows are inefficient. What it does mean is that bows are thousands of years old and haven't really changed an awful lot. Which should tell you that the basic, ages old design was pretty good to begin with.

Perhaps that explains why a company with the rich and storied past of Bear Archery can be a legend with a future.

Bear employee Rita Lesene inspects Bear Panda youth bows before they are packaged for shipment.

Bear employee Judy Deneault applies the finishing touches to the under-coating of a Bear Performance+ competition handle.

Fred Bear with one of the Museum exhibits, a polar bear posed in a natural habitat setting with one of its prey, a seal.

The exhibits in the museum include not only such trophies as these bears, wolves, goats and sheep, but photos, artifacts and simulated natural habitats.

The Fred Bear Museum

If there were one place that could be said to properly embody and enshrine the heritage of bowhunting, then that place would have to be the Fred Bear Museum in Gainesville, Florida.

The museum, open to the public every day except Christmas, is in the Bear Archery, Inc., manufacturing facility. From the second floor of the museum, visitors can gaze from large picture windows onto the production line below where thousands of modern compound bows and accessories are made daily. This visual link between archery's past and present is an important part of the museum's mission.

The company's founder, Fred Bear, had a simple philosophy about archery: "We want to make the best archery equipment we can and sell it at a fair price." But according to museum director Frank Scott, there is a corollary to Bear's motto: "And we want the consumer to make a profit; his profit is the recreational use of that equipment."

It is to the recreational use of archery equipment that the Fred Bear Museum is dedicated.

Bear was one of four men to take a deer when his home state, Michigan, opened its first bow season in 1936. By the time of his death in 1988, he had taken more than 100 big game animals, many of them world records at that time. He traveled all over the world and hunted just about everything—deer, elk, moose, bear, lion, tiger, elephant, antelope and Cape buffalo. Besides bringing home trophies, he brought back a wealth of carefully cataloged artifacts from primitive cultures extant and extinct. His love of hunting took him throughout the United Sates and Canada as well as Africa and Asia.

The ever-growing accumulation of Bear's hunting trophies, photographs and artifacts first became a museum that opened in 1967 in the Winter Sports Park of Grayling, Michigan, Bear Archery's original home. In 1980, the museum followed the company to Florida and was housed in a custom-designed facility opened in 1985. Though larger than the Michigan museum, this one was still not large enough for all that Bear brought home from the hunt.

Many still photos taken of Bear's hunting trips are incorporated into the museum exhibits along with meticulously preserved trophies in recreated natural settings and auxiliary displays of native tools, weapons, clothing and accessories. Many of the animals are posed in full mounts, looking as they would in their natural habitat.

A 1991 addition to the museum is a soundtrack. The trophies and artifacts are grouped into twenty-four exhibits, each with its own visitor-operated audio station. At the push of a button, visitors can enter the ever-allur-

Fred Bear Museum director Frank Scott stands beside the bronze plaque immortalizing Fred that stands at the Museum's entrance.

Just the way he left it in 1988, Fred Bear's office at the Bear Archery Company's headquarters is now a shrine. Shown here is one wall with its accumulation of pictures, plaques, bows and mementoes.

Two visitors stroll through one of the galleries of the Museum.

ing world of the big game hunter, hearing about how and where and when Fred Bear took the animals in the exhibit. The recordings, like the exhibits, are not meant merely to show off the trophies, but rather to educate visitors, especially young people, about the animals, their preservation and conservation, their habitat and about bowhunting.

Among the 50,000 yearly visitors are numerous Scouting and school groups. Just as Fred Bear did when alive, the museum reaches out to youngsters to help them gain an appreciation of nature and its wonders.

Nor is the museum a static affair. Because Bear's treasure trove of trophies and artifacts is greater than the space available, Scott is able to change exhibits adding previously undisplayed items and taking others out of view.

An outgrowth of Fred's belief in natural resources management and an adjunct to the museum is the Fred Bear Sports Club. Begun in 1972 as a small group of celebrity hunters, it has grown to be a broad-based, worldwide organization dedicated to clean air, clean water and the natural beauty of an unlittered countryside.

Its members believe in the intelligent management of wildlife, support fish and game laws, and abide by the rules of fair chase. The club even sponsored one of the first television nature programs, "The American Outdoors," which ran all over the country, telling the story of bowhunting. It is a story that Fred Bear dedicated himself to telling. With his prodigious energy,

he made more than twenty wildlife and hunting films, many of which later aired on television.

Another example of that energy is Fred Bear's office. Though not a formal part of the museum, it is as much a shrine to the legendary sportsman as is the museum. The office remains exactly the way it was the last time Fred was in it. On the walls are the plaques, photos and mementoes of a lifetime of service to archery and to bowhunting.

Bear's desk is as neat and orderly as the man himself. It is where he sat when he pioneered archery as a business and where he would, even after becoming the head of a multi-million-dollar-a-year concern, hand-address the letters and cards that he always pecked out on his own portable typewriter.

Adjacent to the office is the workshop where Bear labored on new products, crafting bows, parts of bows and accessories. His well-used, but meticulously cared for, tools are arrayed on the walls, within reach of his workbench and his lathe.

The office is shown only during VIP tours. "And to remind future presidents of this company where we came from," said museum dsirector Scott. "I can't visualize this office being used for anything else."

The office, like the museum and the Fred Bear Sports Club, is a fitting tribute to one of archery's legends.

"We miss him, but we don't grieve for him," said Scott. "We remember him for the tremendous influence he had on millions of people."

Bingham Projects

Gary Peterson (left) and Charles Rowe examine some of the full-size drawings and instruction sheets intended for Bingham Projects bow construction.

ARCHERY ALWAYS HAS been sort of a do-it-yourself activity. In the thousands of years prior to mass production, every bow and every arrow was made by the person who used them. The archer—probably using a stone ax—cut down an appropriate tree, shaved and sliced it into shape, let the wood dry and cure, then finished a new, custom-made bow. The same procedure had to be followed to make arrows for practice and for hunting or warfare. No two bows were alike, but all followed some general guidelines that had been developed through generations of trial and error.

Today, after most of the trials and most of the errors have been segregated, most archers simply buy a new bow off a dealer's shelf. But there are those who wish to challenge themselves further. A new compound bow may be flawless in design and construction, and every component may work without a hitch, but some want to try to make their own special bow. Modern man can chop down a tree and make a bow and arrows, but there are somewhat easier and more practical solutions to the problem.

Bingham Projects has been operating out of a modest home in Utah for more than three decades. The company has been supplying longbow, takedown recurve, one-piece recurve and youth bow kits and components, complete with plans and instructions of varying levels of difficulty, to bowyers all over the world. Today, the business is bigger than ever. Edmont Bingham and Gary Peterson, son and son-in-law of the company's founder, continue to operate the business from Bingham's converted basement and garage, offering every part and element necessary to construct any of several models of traditional bows.

The bow-building kits marketed today by Bingham Projects include everything required for the rank beginner or the experi-

Bingham warehouses hundreds of wood pieces for bow riser construction, both single piece and laminated blocks.

enced bowyer to construct an attractive, good-shooting bow. Detailed instructions and clear, full-size drawings are necessary ingredients for any project to be successful. Every bow kit includes a full set of instructions and drawings, the effectiveness of which has been proven over many years—and with many bows.

In modern times, most bow limbs are made from laminates composed of wood and fiberglass that are held together with strong, modern epoxy cement. Depending upon the type of bow one may want to build, Bingham can provide all the laminating materials, glues and cements, along with drawings and instructions, to complete the chosen bow. Bow limbs from short recurves with easy draw effort for small children to the strongest hunting longbow can be accommodated with the materials offered.

Three-piece takedown recurve bows are also part of Bingham Projects' available kits. This one has unfinished riser.

Peterson holds a finished longbow, made from the company's components. Bows may be made to any draw length and weight.

Gary Peterson lays out the various thin strips of wood for bow limb laminations. Such thin strips are difficult to find, otherwise.

Wood for all types of bow risers is stocked on shelves that fill the company's warehouse area. Any shape or type—two or more laminates, plain or fancy risers—are among the possibilities. For newer bowyers, semi-finished wood risers to match the chosen bows can be supplied by Bingham. For those with the skills or the curiosity, and the tools with a home workshop, laminated blocks may be the choice.

Gary Peterson declares that only the best components are selected for Bingham Projects bows. Lengths of straight, cured and dried wood, carefully stored and shipped, are the hallmarks of the handles and limbs. Limb laminations are precisely cut and stored until ready to ship. They are painstakingly packed to avoid shipping damage before being directed to destinations throughout the world.

Peterson says only the best epoxies are included with the wood and fiberglass materials. Instructions are clear in specifying exactly which type of cement is to be used on each portion of the project.

Most bows to be constructed require careful curing of the epoxy cement under controlled temperature and humidity conditions. Bingham includes additional kits and instructions for building a heat box that will serve as a laminating press. The press uses ordinary light bulbs to maintain the temperature necessary to cure the laminated cemented limbs. The good news is that the box may be used for as many more bows as the archer may wish to construct in future years. Printed instructions show the bow builder exactly how the

press and box are to be constructed to hold the limbs in the proper shape for the bow.

Peterson and Bingham are proud to show off some of the bows they and others have made from the Bingham kits. Whether recurve or longbow, each is a fine example of what a traditional bow should look like when finished.

At one time, Bingham Projects turned out semi-built bows that the archer finished. Sandpaper and finishing materials, plus the bowstring and some adjustments, were the few necessities required to produce a customized bow at home. However, the business has grown beyond that stage, says Bingham, and only the bow kits now are offered.

This family-operated firm also sells the components for making arrows that will match the bows being built. Everything from shafts, nocks, fletching and finishing materials are offered.

Why would the average archer go to so much trouble for a bow? The low cost is one of the reasons. The prices are far below what one might pay for a finished, professionally-made, custom traditional bow. Custom bows from some professional bowyers, in 1995, were selling for $300 to $700, with others costing considerably more, depending upon the materials and special options included. A simple kit is far below these costs. Furthermore, builders find a certain satisfaction in constructing and shooting bows they've crafted themselves. It is an easy possession to show off at the target range or in hunting camp.

The Bohning Company, Ltd.

After manufacturing dozens of different sizes, colors and types of fletching, Bohning exposes the product to plenty of sunshine and outdoor weather conditions. Results are recorded for later consideration.

AS WITH a number of other archery-oriented manufacturing entities, Rollin Bohning had been a long-time avid archer and bowhunter before he started The Bohning Company, Ltd. Again, it was an instance of seeing a need in a hobby and going on to develop a successful business enterprise.

Rollin Bohning was a research chemist by profession. With that background, he became unhappy with the lack of a proper adhesive for bonding broadheads to hunting shafts. A year later, in 1947, after endless hours and days of testing and research, the chemist/archer had developed what has come to be known as Ferr-L-Tite. This liquid cement quickly came to rank as the leader in attaching points to the then popular Port Orford cedar arrows.

In 1948, when Doug Easton's relatively new aluminum arrow shaft was just beginning to find favor with target archers, buyers were finding it difficult to make fletching adhere to the aluminum surface. With this knowledge and the understanding of Easton Aluminum, Bohning went back to the drawing board—or mixing bowl, if you will—and eventually came up with a concoction he advertised and sold as Fletch.

Since that era, the formula for the original Fletch-Tite has been modified several times in a continuing effort to give superior bonding strength. In recent years, the company has developed other grades of Fletch-Tite, with the express aim of keeping up with the needs of the manufacturers of finished arrows. With the various arrow shaft materials now being sold—several types of wood, fiberglass, graphite, aluminum

and combinations of most of these—this sort of continuing research is no small operation!

Since the design of the longbow, beeswax had been the material used on bowstrings. However, Rollin Bohning took a long, hard look at this nature-produced wax and felt that, as far as the new synthetic materials being used for bowstrings were concerned, he could improve upon the old standby. He dared a face-off with Mother Nature and began laboratory work and testing. Eventually, he found that, by combining a number of other waxes and natural oils with beeswax, he was able to produce a much better product.

With this information and positive testing, Tex-Tite Bowstring Wax was placed on the market. As with the other Bohning products, Tex-Tite still is being constantly upgraded, the formula changed and reworked to meet the changes in bowstring materials.

It was not until the early 1950s that Rollin Bohning completed two years of research and development of a product that has found a wide range of uses beyond the archery industry. This was called Hot Melt Ferr-L-Tite and still is the Lake City, Michigan, company's most popular product.

Prior to 1952, archers and fishermen had improved only slightly on the techniques of Native Americans when it came to water-proofing feather fletching and flies. The Indians used bear grease on their fletching, according to some sources, or nothing at all. Archers and anglers learned to dissolve a little paraffin in gasoline for waterproofing. The gasoline would thin the paraffin so it could be applied to the feather fletching or trout flies, and when the gasoline evaporated, it left a thin protective coating. The concoction that Bohning developed was a lot easier and simpler to use. It was known as Dri-Tite, when introduced in 1953. Eventually, an aerosol version was introduced.

Throughout the 1950s, Doug Easton was urging the research and development of a lacquer that would adhere to his aluminum shafting without complicated preparation of the metal or equally troublesome application. Rollin Bohning and his son-in-law, Colby Johnson, hearing of Easton's plea, launched into further research. In 1958, they brought Fletch-Lac finishes to archery shops and sporting goods emporiums. Since the original development, these finishes have been improved frequently with a variety of spinoffs. The Bohning enterprise today markets dye coats, camo coats, cresting lacquers, metallic dye coats and a line of textured Fletch-Lac. The last-listed formula has been used by several top bow manufacturers for painting bow limbs, as well as for application to metal bow handles.

By the early '70s, the business had expanded to include a full-time research chemist and two consulting chemists. This meant that Rollin Bohning could give up hunkering over his test tubes and Bunson burner. He went into semi-retirement, designating Colby and Martha Johnson as chief administrators for the growing company.

Also during the '70s, the company began to receive a growing number of requests and assignments from bow manufacturers to develop a good coating for expensive bows that deserved proper protection from weather and natural and human destructive forces. There probably is no way of protecting against the human forces, but for other types of damage protection, the Bohning chemists created a product marketed as Bohning Bow-Tite. According to company chemists, this product is made from a combination of natural and synthetic waxes and hardeners that can be applied easily to the bow and other archery products for a weatherproof finish.

During this same period, Bohning personnel began to study and test materials for better plastic fletching or vanes, as they are called. Such vanes were being manufactured in various colors at that time by several companies, and Bohning's chemical staff felt there had to be a superior material. Today, plastic fletching is the accepted rule for most major archery tournaments and, thus, constitutes a constant, stable market. A great number of materials and designs were reviewed in Bohning's Michigan laboratories until, in 1976, the company decided it was time to market their own vanes. The following year, the first Fletch-Tite vanes were sent out for evaluation. Experienced, knowledgeable archers called upon to try the early runs expressed what has been called "fantastic interest," and this new product became part of the Bohning line.

Of interest is the fact that the Bohning team also recognizes product needs beyond the archery field from time to time and takes them on. The Christmas tree is an example. In 1978, the company found that there was a need for a good, competitively

Bohning is able to create virtually any color for its products. Computer-controlled machines carefully monitor color mixes.

priced Christmas tree colorant. This colorant, sprayed on trees in the early fall, enhances the appearance of trees that begin to yellow later in the year. Additionally, it contains an adhesive which helps seal in moisture, thus keeping trees fresher in the home during the holiday season.

In 1989, the assets of a small golf manufacturing company were acquired, starting off the firm in a new direction. A tool and die shop also was started to handle outside work—and add sales to the Bohning enterprise. Nonetheless, archery still remains the firm's foundation and true love.

In October, 1987, a new management team—Larry Griffith, John Kleman and Gordon Shackleton—took over the day-to-day affairs. This allowed Colby Johnson the time to investigate new products, conduct research and development, and handle product testing. One result of this new restructuring has been a line of bow quivers that includes five models meant to cover the entire spectrum of bowhunter needs. From this approach has come a host of new products that either have been introduced or will see dealers' shelves in the coming months. Included are two new vanes. One is a transparent, flourescent urethane vane; the other, a wide base, high production type. A third vane is a limited edition camouflage type of a non-glare material.

An entirely new quiver system will be introduced with the Sidewinder quiver holder, and a new adhesive, Bond-Tite, is easier to use than so-called super glues in attaching vanes and fletching to carbon or aluminum arrow shafts.

Rollin Bohning

Other upcoming products include a new bowfishing kit that already is being marketed, a universal arrow pad that is being sold to arrow manufacturers, an inexpensive bow square and a product called the Apex C/A nock for arrow makers working with composite shafts.

The Bohning Company is coming up on half a century of service to archers of all types.

Bohning utilizes plenty of special equipment during the manufacturing process. Tim Dehn (left), a factory supervisor at Bohning's Michigan plant, discusses operations.

Attendance at many consumer and trade shows is a part of Browning's aggressive marketing plan.

Twenty-four-karat gold-plated bow risers are locked away in a vault until ready for shipment. The bows are intended for collectors and dealer displays, although they could be shot.

THE COMPANY, KNOWN simply as Browning these days, is moving ahead in its determination to remain a leader in the archery industry. Headquartered in Morgan, Utah, the firm continues to create dozens of innovative archery designs, while increasing its support for professional archers and tournaments, and participating in archery events all over the world.

The company seems to be adding to and upgrading its manufacturing facility continually, with modern machines and production capability. Browning employs many of the top designers, developers and archery industry leaders. By recent count, Browning has been granted more than two dozen patents in recent years, and more are pending.

Innovation and advanced technology are what Browning archery products feature. Each new bow or accessory introduction seems to advance the art of shooting or manufacturing bows. Yet, they are one of the few companies still offering a wood-handle compound bow, the X-Cellerator. For bowhunters, the laminated riser results in a natural camouflage pattern. Target archers will opt for the attractive pattern produced by the many layers of wood laminations. The rest of the bow is as modern as any other. Many archers prefer the natural feel and warmth of a wood-riser bow, and the X-Cellerator enjoys brisk annual sales.

All work—from concept and design, manufacture and assem-

Browning's archery construction facility includes modern computer-controlled machines.

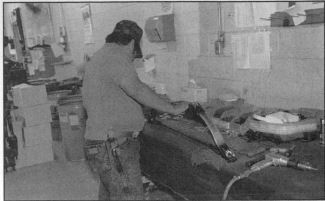

Bow assembly still requires plenty of hand work to complete.

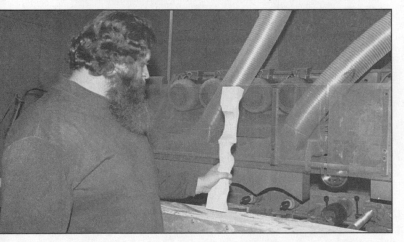

Browning is one of the few companies still offering wood-handled compound bows, made of laminated wood at the factory.

bly, to finished product and shipping—is done at the Morgan plant. The nearby original corporate headquarters building was a hunting lodge in the early days of the Browning company and looks like it. Part of the original building is home to the administrative and corporate employees, while bow and accessory construction is done in the modern factory facilities. The surrounding area is great deer, elk and other big game hunting habitat, a fact not lost on any of the Browning employees. There are plenty of game trophies displayed on the walls of the headquarters building to attest to their many successes. Many of the employees are experienced bowhunters, talented tournament shooters or both.

Bows for bowhunting as well as target shooting are featured among the many products. In addition to bows, arrows and 3-D targets, Browning offers a complete line of accessories. These include overdraws, arrow rests, sights, mechanical releases, stabilizers, quivers, roller guides, cable guards, bow carriers, string silencers, bow cases, training videos and even flashlights. Also of interest to the hunter is a line of folding and fixed-blade knives, boots, hunting clothing, 3-D foam targets for practice and tournament use, as well as a complete selection of carbon arrows, marketed under the Browning Mirage name.

In addition to the wood-handle bow model already mentioned, Browning bows are available with the most modern machined aluminum risers as well as the more familiar cast magnesium.

Perhaps one of the most unusual compounds in the Browning line is a machined aluminum riser bow that has been 24-karat gold-plated. The bow is called the Frank Pearson Signature bow, named for one of the best professional archers in the United States. Pearson has been the number one professional in the country three times, has won the National Field Archery Association title once and the Professional Archers Association championship twice, and is the holder of five international championships.

Samples of the gold-plated bow are kept in a locked vault at the Browning factory. They are collector items, and several Browning dealers around North America have purchased them strictly for display purposes.

The bow is beautiful to behold. Though shootable, most will be strictly for display at archery shops. If the price of gold goes up, the bow will be a good investment for the future.

As Browning moves into the 21st century, advanced technology is the watchword. The newest, most advanced design is the Mantis compound bow. It features a new riser that is one solid piece of forged aircraft aluminum machined to close tolerances and into attractive lines. It is called the Power Riser, and even the limb pockets are forged by machines at the Morgan plant. The sight window is 6 inches high, and an overdraw-ready arrow shelf has plenty of cutout area for wide broadhead clearances.

The limbs of the Mantis are recurved and made of seven layers of graphite and Kevlar to help dampen vibration and recoil. The Whisper Plus cams produce plenty of speed with little vibration and have a let-off of 65 percent. Draw length adjustments are in 1/2-inch increments.

One of the chief architects of the high-tech movement at Browning is designer Marlow Larson. He is the developer of cam roll-over timing, a system that Browning calls the Axle Synchronizer, a patented feature found on the Mantis and other bows. Larson is a competitive shooting archer and winner of several major tournaments. He knows shooters' needs and always is innovating new ways to help archers. His successes in competition and in the field as a bowhunter have led him to

173

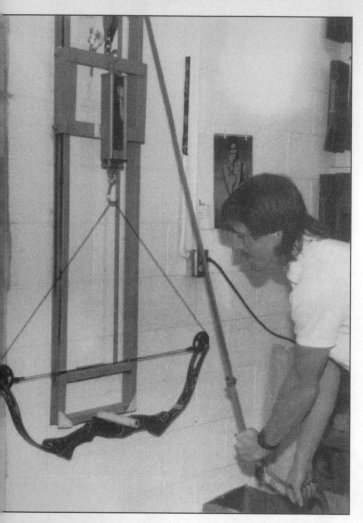

Each bow is tested after assembly and before shipping to dealers.

design many of Browning's bows, bow components and accessories.

One of the problems with any compound two-wheel bow is that, when roll-over is out of synchronization, correct timing is most difficult. An out-of-tune bow always will be inaccurate and is unacceptable to target shooters and bowhunters alike. The Axle Synchronizer allows micro-adjustments of cable length for precise tuning of the cam roll-over without requiring a bow press to relax the bowstring. The cams themselves are indexed for tuning. They let the archer first recognize when there are timing problems, then correct them on the spot, even in the field.

Youth bows are not neglected by Browning. Two models with low draw weights and shorter draw lengths are offered. Adjustable draw lengths are available from 19 to 24 inches for the Micro Midas SSD, as well as 20- to 22-inch or 23- to 25-inch draw lengths for the Spitfire. They seem ideal for youngsters getting started in archery, keeping pace with their growth and strength for several years.

For many years, Harry Drake has led the progression of world records in flight shooting. He was involved in the development of Browning's new recurve takedown bow limbs, the Olympian and Apollo. Limb choices are high-modulus carbon graphite or carbon ceramic Kevlar materials. Both models are available with wood core and fiberglass construction, with a choice of 66- or 68-inch limbs. The new bows are designed primarily for traditional Olympic-type target shooters.

Browning does not ignore the 3-D target shooter, either. The company recently added a complete line of realistic foam targets. The Paragon targets include a mule deer, whitetail deer, black bear, raccoon, bighorn sheep, wild turkey and wild boar. Each has a replaceable vitals section filled with a choice of cores to withstand plenty of practice.

Browning has several sets of camouflage clothes designed for bowhunters. There are insulated and uninsulated jackets, parkas, hats, trousers, bib overalls, gloves and rain gear. The camo pattern includes several variations and color combinations of Mossy Oak camouflage. Some are lined with waterproof Gore-Tex, and some have outer surfaces of soft, quiet fleece. There should be something in the line to fit the needs of the hunter in any season or habitat.

One of the slickest new archery tools contains a knife blade, common-size Allen wrenches, a nock crimper and remover, screwdrivers, and open-end and broadhead wrenches. All the tools fold down into a stainless steel handle to be carried in a nylon pouch.

With the plant expansion and modernization in Morgan ongoing, and the advances in technology continuing at Browning, the company is determined to remain a leader in the archery industry.

Browning's foam 3-D archery targets are made of water-blown urethane that does not produce environmentally hazardous CFCs. Targets include deer, turkey, bear and wild boar.

14

Darton Archery

Hale, Michigan, is the home of the Darton Archery production and administrative facilities. It is in the heart of good whitetail deer country and is easily accessible to visitors wanting plant tours.

BACK IN 1950, Ralph Darlington figured he could manufacture quality leather accessories for the sport of target archery and do it well. Admittedly, he had a leg up, for his company, Container Specialties, contracted leather work for General Motors.

With this background, Darlington founded Darton Archery in Flint, Michigan. It wasn't long before he was turning out leather quivers and other accessories for a ready market. In 1964, the company's main thrust changed from the manufacture of archery accessories to turning out recurve bows.

The resulting success led to Darton's relocation in Hale, Michigan, in 1968. As Rex Darlington, now president of the company, recalls, "We wanted to get closer to the heart of Michigan's fabulous hunting region and find the space for future expansion." At that time, the plant was producing fourteen different bow models, ranging in price from about $20 to more than $200.

Alloy risers and laminated wood limbs were introduced to the recurve line in 1969, and in 1974, Darton introduced its first compound bows. Two years later, with the success of the compound line, the recurve bows were discontinued.

It was this Michigan company that upgraded the compound scene in 1980 by introducing magnesium wheels. Three years later, the company introduced the Mark I cam; this was the predecessor of the respected Darton Lightning Mark II cam. Darton's success continued through the decade of the '80s and was capped in 1989 with the Darton Lightning being lauded as the "world's fastest bow" following its win in a Hocking College IBO competition. It followed up by winning the same competition in 1990 and, again, in 1991.

"In 1992, the competition was cancelled due to a lack of participation," according to Chip Klass, Darton's marketing director. "We were the only ones to show up!"

Another major step for the Michigan manufacturer also came in 1989, when a die-cast magnesium handle with a second centershot hole was introduced. This bow still is marketed as the Darton Excel model.

According to a lot of shooters—especially shooting families with archers in several age and size brackets—there always seems to be a shortage of youth models. With this knowledge at hand, 1990 was the year in which Darton introduced the Thunderstick, a compound bow designed and built specifically for the youth market.

Over the years, there have been many other changes and innovations at Darton Archery. In 1977, for example, they introduced solid glass bow limbs; in 1986, the designers incorporated limbs in their compounds made of a graphite laminate. In 1991, Darton also introduced Timberland Forest camo and Woodland Forest camo clothing to their expanding product line. The following year, a new graphite composite was used in bow limbs. Topping the accomplishments for that year was the fact that the Lightning model was found to produce the best force draw curve in the archery industry! This same model was awarded the highest rating by the Archery Manufacturers Organization for its velocity rating of 242 feet per second!

In 1993, Darton introduced machined magnesium handles on three of their bows, the Concord, Falcon and Electra. This was an industry first and earned the company the International Magnesium Design Award. Taking this concept still further, in

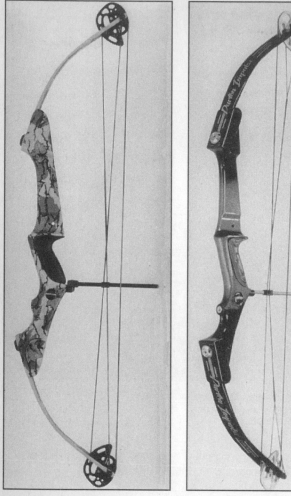

The Darton Renegade uses innovative Mark III cams. Darton says it is the first hatchet-cam bow to produce the draw characteristics of energy wheels. Arrow speeds of 310 fps are claimed with a 60-pound draw and IBO restrictions.

The 1995 Darton Impulse bow claims an AMO specs arrow speed of 247 feet per second using Mark II cams. Draw lengths available are from $24\frac{1}{2}$ to $30\frac{1}{2}$ inches, with draw weights of 40, 50, 60 or 70 pounds. Normal let-off is 60 percent.

Archery is becoming a more family-oriented sport, according to industry findings, and Darton expects this trend to continue with the growth of bowhunting and especially 3-D target archery. Members of the marketing team that includes Chip Klass and sales manager Neil Parr intend to ride the crest of this interest to the company's advantage.

"Darton foresees a bright future for the archery industry as a whole," Klass states, "and is committed to continuing its leadership in archery technology advancement. In fact, the entire Darton team is committed to leading the archery industry into the 21st century by continuing its quest for excellence in innovation, quality and superior product performance."

One's first impression is that Chip Klass has laid out a goal for the rest of this century. Only time will tell whether those goals are achieved or not. However, at this writing, it would appear plans have been hatched for launching a continuing campaign that will pursue the aforementioned goals. The Hale, Michigan, plant now consists of some 42,000 square feet and maintains a work force made up of approximately seventy highly experienced employees. Darton's bows and other products now are distributed through national sales networks as well as selected pro shop retailers.

"Darton's conservative marketing approach throughout the years has allowed this company to enjoy consistent growth," Chip Klass confides. "We have refused to allow ourselves to grow too quickly at the expense of quality. Our customers demand dependable, high-quality performance products, and this is what we are striving to provide."

1994, they incorporated a new die-cast magnesium handle on their Action series of youth bows. This lineup includes the Scout, SuperStick and Explorer models.

As for 1995, this annum found the company redesigning the machined magnesium riser and introducing the Darton Hurricane model. Early in the year, the 1995 Darton Impulse bow had achieved a new record-setting velocity of 247 feet per second—five feet faster than the record set in 1992 with the Darton Lightning.

"But even better," according to Chip Klass, "is the fact that of Darton's eleven bow models for 1995, six of them have IBO velocity ratings of over 300 feet per second!"

Numerous other developments and improvements in the Darton line in recent years have led to the corporate claim of being the leader in performance bow design.

"This is demonstrated," Klass insists, "by the fact that Darton bows are unmatched in both speed and efficiency."

Inside the plant, Darton's new CNC machine is producing machined magnesium bow risers.

14 *Easton Aluminum*

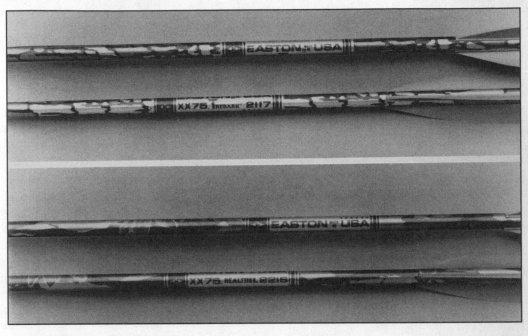

The Easton company was founded on and continues to dominate aluminum arrow shaft production throughout in the world. The shafts are available in hundreds of spines, colors and patterns.

IT HAS BEEN twenty-four years since Doug Easton passed away and his son, Jim, assumed the duties as president of James D. Easton, Inc. Old-timers in the industry recall the father as a man devoted primarily to the sport of archery and to turning out the best aluminum arrow he could.

"Doug Easton was a lot happier in the back of the plant, fiddling with the machines he had invented, than he ever was behind a stack of ledgers," one of those old-timers is quick to declare. The machines that he had designed and built were meant specifically for drawing aluminum pipe down to arrow shaft thickness. Parts of the process still are secret.

While the ecologists of today might shudder at the thought, Doug Easton recognized Port Orford cedar—an adequate, cheaper and traditional shaft material—as his greatest competitor, and prior to his death, he would purchase Port Orford cedar in Oregon, have it trucked to Los Angeles and burn it in his fireplace during the California winter!

Observers of the '50s and early '60s were amused by this effort to wipe out a competitor. Today, of course, Port Orford cedar, with its straight grain and superior strength, is in short supply, but that shortage has been created more by weather, fire and the replacement of forest acreage with homes than by Doug Easton's minor effort.

The 56,000-square-foot plant built in Van Nuys, California, in 1968, did not devote itself totally to arrow shaft production. In fact, even before the plant was built, Easton began fabricating aluminum tubing for ski poles. In 1970, the company entered the team sports market with aluminum Little League and softball bats.

"Jim Easton had a part in developing these markets," says an acquantance of that era. "Archery was Doug's sport. Archery was Jim's sport, too, but he was interested in a lot of others and saw the potential."

In the decade following the introduction of the baseball bat, the company developed a lightweight, high-strength bat for high school and college baseball; entered the mountain dome tent tubing market; and had the first aluminum ice hockey stick approved by the National Hockey League.

Archery had not been forgotten, however. In 1983, the growing company purchased the Hoyt Archery Company. Founded by Earl Hoyt, an internationally known archer, the company manufactured quality bows and archery accessories. That same year, the Easton aluminum/carbon composite arrow shaft was introduced. In 1984, Jim Easton served as archery commissioner for the Olympic Games.

Other acquisitions in the sports field followed. Easton Sports, Inc., was founded as a subsidiary. A composite company for making arrows shafts was founded in San Diego, and Easton began making mountain bicycles through another subsidiary. A distribution center was opened in Salt Lake City, and the Van Nuys headquarters expanded, as the company entered the golf shaft market.

In 1989, Jim Easton took time out to serve as president of FITA, the international governing body of Olympic archery.

Visitor Charles Rowe (left) looks at aluminum shaft material in the Salt Lake City plant. Randy Schoeck is Easton's marketing services director, showing some of the millions of shafts in production.

The aluminum shaft manufacturing process includes swaging down the tubing end to accept the arrow nocks.

Part of the way through the manufacturing process, an Easton worker feeds aluminum into a special machine that cuts them to a specified length.

The following year, the Easton Sports Lab was created in Van Nuys by what had come to be known as Easton Aluminum, Inc. In 1991, Easton Sports Europe was established

This California-based company has played a key role in the development of a U.S. Olympic Training Center in San Diego, funding construction of the Easton Archery Complex. Half of Easton's $500,000 grant goes toward the archery range, with the remaining $250,000 dedicated to developing a youth archery program in San Diego County.

Today, Easton has something over 1,000 employees worldwide involved in manufacturing, marketing and distribution. Other than Van Nuys, there are company operations in Salt Lake City, San Diego and Burlingame, California. On the international scene, Easton operations are located in the Netherlands, Australia, Mexico and Canada.

Virtually from the beginning, Easton has produced aluminum items for national defense. A little known fact is that Easton engineered and produced the thermal shroud for the seismometer used on the first Apollo lunar landing!

Since 1941, when Larry Hughes won the National Archery title using Doug Easton's aluminum arrows, the sport has been what amounts to a stronghold for the corporation. After all, since archery was reintroduced as an Olympic medal sport in 1972, the vast majority of all medals have been won by archers using Easton shafts. In the past decade, top archers who have served on the Easton/Hoyt advisory staff have included such target champions as Darrell Pace, Rick McKinney, Jay Barrs and Denise Parker.

In the bowhunting world, Chuck Adams, Jim Dougherty, Dwight Schuh and dozens of others have carried Easton arrows and Hoyt bows on world-wide hunting expeditions. In 1992, Chuck Adams worked with Jim Easton to design and create the XX78 Super Slam arrow shaft and component system.

The Easton Sports Development Foundation was established in 1981. This is a non-profit organization established to support and encourage youth archery programs across the nation, to include the Olympic Youth Archery Program and the Junior Olympic Archery Development Program. By providing archery equipment support and certifying instructors across the country, the foundation is playing a major role in putting archery back in summer camps and recreational programs.

Through the Easton foundation, the company is able to continue its long-time commitment to supporting not only elite archers who endorse the company's products, but to help beginners as well. It is the corporate stand that, from the ranks of those youngsters and teenagers, will come America's future archery champions.

Easton's mission statement is simple and to the point:

"To be the world leader in supplying high-performance sports equipment and components. To innovate, develop, manufacture and market all types of high-quality sports and recreational equipment and components that utilize our unique engineering and manufacturing capabilities and offer the consumer distinctly higher performance products."

Aluminum arrow stock tubing receives thermal treatment in huge ovens during the manufacturing process.

14 C.W. Erickson's Manufacturing, Inc.

C.W. Erickson's new building addition houses all aspects of the business.

A NATIVE OF Minnesota's Twin Cities, Curtis W. Erickson's first nine years in the world of business were spent with a drug-store chain, where he ultimately became manager of one of the company's stores in St. Paul.

"I was devoted to the idea that I would work may way up the corporate ladder and one day be president of the chain," he recounts now with a trace of a grin. "Then the upper management changed. It wasn't long before it became evident that they didn't like me and I didn't like them. I lasted six months before I quit and started looking around for my own business."

Archery and bowhunting had been Erickson's first love on the recreational scene for years, and it was only natural that he would look at the possibilities there.

C.W. Erickson's Manufacturing, Inc., was established in 1983, and the first product was a new concept in climbing tree stands. The business was started in a 26x40-foot pole building on Erickson's 10-acre hobby farm near Buffalo, Minnesota.

"Settling on a tree stand was my first mistake," Erickson recalls. "After ten years in the retail business, I certainly should have known better, but I spent all of my available funds in developing the tree stand and tooling up to make it. When the stands started rolling off my one-man production line, I had no money for advertising or promotion.

"Besides, in those days, bowhunters tended to think of a tree stand as three pine boards nailed to the limbs of a tree. In that era, they weren't ready to spend $300 for a climbing stand, no matter how safe and efficient it might be."

Putting the tree stand on the back burner, Erickson looked around for other possibilities. "That was where my retail experience did come into play," he recalls. "In trying to sell my tree stand, I had visited a lot of archery shops.

"In a lot of situations, the owner had simply moved from his basement or his garage into a store front. He had plenty of space for racks and even shooting lanes, but there was nothing attrac-

About 90 percent of Erickson's work is done on the premises.

tive about his displays of bows, arrows and accessories. The manufacturing of special archery-oriented displays and fixtures was pretty limited at that time.

"My own belief is that, if you are going to be professional in any business or industry, you need to look professional. With that premise in mind, I designed a number of displays, fixtures and other equipment that would show off those $300 to $400 bows in a professional, eye-appealing manner."

Erickson also designed equipment that aided in organizing shooting lanes and helped to make daily routine in the pro shop a bit easier for the operators. In manufacturing five different types of dealer bow display racks, a pair of bow presses for stringing the cables of compound bows, as well as coming up with a paper target tuning rack, and bow and arrow stands for shooting lanes, the Minnesota manufacturer had a line that would afford any shop a true professional look.

In 1986, Erickson also designed a tree stand bow rest that would hold any type or style of bow—compound, recurve or stick type.

"I saw many useful accessories coming on the market," Erickson says, "that were very fancy and, in turn, cost a lot of

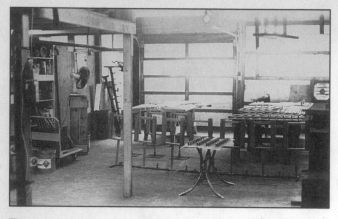

The new building has room for cutting, drilling, grinding, welding, painting and assembly of Erickson's products.

After painting, each product is inspected before packaging and shipping.

money. I also saw a lot of bowhunters like myself who loved the sport, but just did not have the money to spend on many of the fancy, high-buck accessories.

"From my college days, I remembered the old KISS theory, which translates to 'keep it simple, stupid,' and I set out to design a number of practical accessories that are without frills, but are functional and affordable to the average bowhunter."

As a result of a good deal of thought and experimentation, followed by careful development work, Erickson's manufacturing company now turns out a double-duty safety belt that can be used in a tree stand, but once your deer is down, it can be reassembled for use as a game drag. Today, the Minnesota factory's staff also turns out three types of tree stand bow rests and a bow sling that allows one to have both hands free. The sling is adjustable to fit any style bow. Made of 2-inch webbing, it is lightweight and easy to get on and off the shoulder.

Other products produced in the Minnesota factory include a utility belt that can be used with a bow holster, extra packs, knives, saws, ad infinitum. There also is an item called the CWik Draw bow holster that attaches to the belt and relieves the pull of the bow while standing or walking. A tree stand protector can lock your stand in place and also can double as a game drag.

Other items are in the mill, and Erickson continues to build professional displays for pro shops and shooting lanes operations. All of this, of course, has outgrown that original building, and in 1993, Curtis Erickson built a 50x72-foot addition to the plant and added a new computer system.

"With the assistance of the computer, we now can perform 90 percent of all manufacturing in our own facility. That includes cutting, drilling, grinding, welding, sewing, painting, assembly packaging and shipping," Erickson reports. "And when that's done, we use the same computer for our bookkeeping. This, of course, lowers our cost and affords us more control over our production."

What does the future hold for C.W. Erickson's Manufacturing, Inc.?

"Our goal is to be a major supplier of functional but affordable bowhunting and camping equipment," Curtis Erickson declares. "And we want to be the accepted specialist when it comes to providing pro shop fixtures and equipment."

Finished products are inspected and packaged to fill customer orders.

C.W. Erickson's production schedule provides plenty of business for local shipping contractors.

14 Fine-Line Archery Equipment

Sam Topel, general manager and son of Fine-Line's founder, exhibits one of the first models of bow sights developed by his father. It was primitive, but effective.

KEN TOPEL, the founder of Fine-Line Archery Equipment, retired in early 1994, but not before he had made a mark on the sport of archery that is not likely to be forgotten. His innovative ideas led to the first crosshair bow sight, the first self-aligning peep sight and the first quiver that adjusts to arrow length.

"Ken has given the archery industry some of its most innovative products," said Sam Topel, the founder's son and current general manager of the company. "His ideas have been generated from a strong engineering background with extensive personal field testing."

A life-long outdoorsman and bowhunter, the senior Topel missed two shots on what was certain to have been a record book buck. That was in 1972. This missed opportunity—coupled with the fact that he had not found a sight he felt was accurate nor rugged enough to meet his personal demands—led him to design the Hunter Crosshair bow sight.

When completed and taken afield, the sight caused instant excitement among fellow bowhunters. As a result, Fine-Line was started in 1976. "I always wanted the best equipment, because my hunting time was so valuable," Topel said at the time. "I figured everyone else wanted the same thing."

Since the original crosshair bow sight, Fine-Line has developed and marketed three self-aligning peep sights, the Hunter bow quiver, a low-cost honing guide for sharpening broadheads and a relatively new item called the Ultra Crosshair bow sight.

The heart of the Fine-Line effort is a modern building, clean and efficient in design, tucked away in the rain forest in the rural reaches of Puyallup, Washington.

With his son, Sam Topel, now in charge, Ken still is doing development research and product testing. That's one way of saying the senior Topel is doing a lot of bowhunting. The company's most recent product, the Ultra Hunter crosshair sight, was designed specifically for fast 3-D and hunting bows. How good is the crosshair sight? According to Sam Topel, "The Hunter sight was so good that it was banned for use in National Field Archery Association tournaments." The contention was that the sight gave those archers using it an unfair advantage.

"Incredibly, the ban still remains in effect," Sam Topel says. "We think the whole point to any sighting system is to give the shooter the accuracy required to be consistent and, without shooter error, hit the target!"

With a sight design adapted from the firearms industry, the original Hunter sight measures $1^1/_4$ inches wide and $4^1/_2$ inches high. The Ultra Hunter is a full inch shorter in height, but is shipped with a 6-inch extension bar and a 3-inch dovetail mounting bracket for mounting a bow quiver.

Designed with the aid of computers, this latest addition to the Fine-Line product array features a double row of horizontal sight lines, allowing closest placement on the fastest bows. "Once set, the settings for windage and elevation are locked down and will not vibrate loose," Sam Topel insists.

Like the two versions of the crosshair sight, the Fine-Line Hunter bow quiver also is patented. It differs from other quivers in the fact that the arrows are held in place by their nocks rather than by the usual rubber slots that grip the center of the shaft. The whole unit weighs only 12 ounces and is rigged to adjust to any arrow length.

There are three types of patented peep sights: the original peep design which still is being produced, one called the Zero II and the Pick-A-Peep, the newest addition.

The original Fine-Line peep sight was designed to align its aperture on the string by means of a length of latex tubing. One end of the tubing attaches to the back of the peep sight, the other to the face of the bow limb by means of a flat, adhesive-backed plate.

The Zero II peep model is lighter in weight, because a section of the latex tubing has been replaced by braided nylon cord. The hooded aperture incorporated on both models measures only .050-inch and has been given a matte non-glare finish to cancel possible reflections.

Sam Topel examines the newer Fine-Line bow sight in its modern packaging. Products are manufactured and shipped daily.

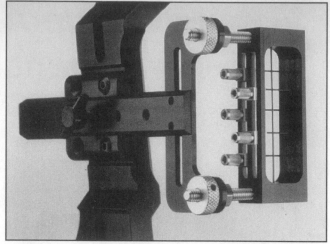

The Fine-Line crosshair bow sight has found acceptance with target archers as well as bowhunters. The product is solid, resists corrosion and has adequate adjustments.

The Fine-Line design, manufacturing and shipping facility is located a few miles from downtown Puyallup, Washington. There is plenty of deer habitat nearby.

Modern computer-assisted machines are a part of the Fine-Line manufacturing process.

The Pick-A-Peep, also patented, offers archers seven choices of aperture size. These sizes are quickly interchangeable, which means that the target archer or bowhunter can select the aperture that he or she feels will suit a particular shooting style, purpose or field condition.

The Pick-A-Peep comes with slides that are installed easily into the peep housing by sliding them into a special groove where the aperture is locked into position. Apertures on these interchangeable slides range from .030- to .065-inch.

Sam Topel reports that many archers—especially bowhunters—tend to install two sights, combining the crosshair sight with the peep type. This, it is felt by some, gives them more versatility and latitude in the field where a single shot on a trophy buck may be the only chance. All of these sights mount easily, have little weight and can be used on both right- and left-handed bows.

The Fine-Line honing guide is an excellent means of sharpening broadheads as well as other types of small blades. The aluminum, corrosion-resistant guide locks the blade at the prop-

er angle so that the edge can be passed over a hone or any other type of sharpening stone.

In the modern but hard-to-find Washington State plant, an extensive—and expensive—array of sophisticated computer-controlled machinery is utilized in building the Fine-Line products. According to Sam Topel, this aids in the precision design of each component followed by equally precise production. This eliminates poorly fitting parts that would have to be rejected, adding to production expense, in final assembly.

"The key to accurately producing components from aluminum bar stock is in the tools and jigs we've designed and built here at Fine-Line," the general manager explains. "The jigs are crucial and are monitored closely before actual production."

How does the founder, Ken Topel, feel about all this modernization?

"Sam runs the company," he says. "The rest of us who own stock in the firm kind of dump things in his lap and go off hunting."

And that's the way it goes at Fine-Line Archery Equipment.

High Country Archery

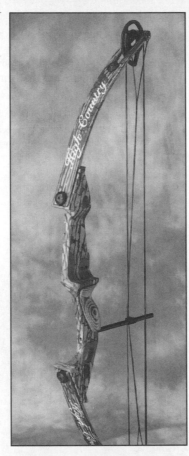

The High Country Archery Excaliber bow is one of the fastest shooters available for bowhunters and 3-D target archers.

THE CURRENT SUCCESS of High Country Archery seems to be the direct result of planning and work by Spencer Land. He is the owner and guiding hand for the company, which also owns American Archery. The companies operate out of the unlikely town of Dunlap, high in the hills of south-central Tennessee. Dunlap is reached by a long, winding and steep narrow road up into the mountains from Chattanooga and would not seem to be the place for a high-tech manufacturing facility. However, the High Country installation is surrounded by several modern international manufacturers of other products.

Spencer Land apparently knew what he was doing when he moved the company from Idaho to Tennessee. He had grown up in northern Arizona and had been a bowhunter most of his adult life. He purchased High Country, but was not satisfied with the situation and facilities he found in Idaho. While he was looking around for a new location, the officials of Dunlap and the state of Tennessee made him an offer he did not want to refuse. The area wants businesses such as an archery equipment manufacturer to move into the area, hire workers and be successful without polluting the air or water.

When the company was moved, some of the key employees made the transfer to Tennessee while others have been hired locally. Land made the offer to most of the long-time loyal staff in Idaho. Those who took him up on the offer to move sing high praises for the new location, noting the relaxed lifestyle, mild weather most of the year, good schools and easy access to transportation and communications centers nearby. Not the least important for bowhunters are the excellent hunting opportunities in Tennessee and other nearby states with reasonable non-resident fees. The lifestyle is pleasant, and the location is quite near many of the company's customers in the South.

High Country has installed the most modern computer-assisted machines to help design and manufacture the components needed to build fast-shooting, high-tech products.

The Tennessee company's bows and equipment have found acceptance and a large following among the 3-D target tournaments around North America, especially those conducted by the International Bowhunters Organization (IBO). Many of the top money-winners of the series of tournaments shoot High Country equipment—and Spencer Land understands what that can mean to the company.

Success is a two-way street. High Country supports the IBO contests with prize money and sponsorships for many of the top competitors. Land is convinced his relationships with 3-D target shooting is good business. It seems to pay off, as he spends a great deal of time traveling to and from the sites of many of the most prominent target tournaments around the country.

An example of the company's current thinking in bow design and purpose might be the model called the Excalibur. This particular model features a riser machined from aircraft-grade aluminum; the machining is done at the Dunlap factory.

Spencer Land is the man behind High Country, moving the factory from Idaho to Tennessee.

The Excalibur uses cams that can produce official arrow speeds of 242 feet per second with a 30-inch draw length, and 60 pounds of draw weight, shooting a 540-grain arrow. The bow is available in either High Country's bright competition colors or in the maker's own Treeleaf camouflage pattern. It is a bow designed for either bowhunters or target archers and has proven popular with both categories.

Bows are not the only product of High Country Archery, however. The company produces and distributes a full line of accessories, including machined aluminum overdraws for right- or left-handed use, one- and two-piece bow quivers, plus a full line of bow sights for both hunters and target archers.

As Land has observed, one of the added benefits to having the giant, efficient CNC machines in the factory is that almost anything can be machined. The machines must be programmed and operated, and High Country has those necessary skilled employees on the payroll. Once the machines are set, tested and running, they may produce sight bodies, cams, overdraw parts or complete bow risers. Not only are the components turned out at one location, but the company has control of their quality and quantity on the spot, at all times. Delays or errors may be corrected immediately; shipping times and distances are no longer factors.

Spencer Land is a savvy, aggressive businessman, as well as an experienced archer and bowhunter. He makes it a point to remain close to his customer base so he can keep continually informed of new trends and changes in the marketplace. Land surrounds himself with informed, active people to advise him and help carry out production and business decisions. He understands his customers and is willing to give them what they ask for. It is a combination that should bring High Country Archery continued success and, eventually, a degree of fame for Dunlap, Tennessee.

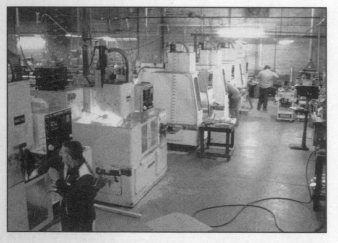

A look inside the High Country factory reveals the latest modern CNC machines, able to turn out production archery components.

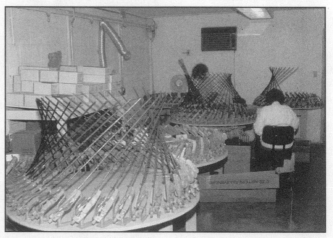

Arrows are a large part of High Country. The production line turns them out on order from dealers around the country.

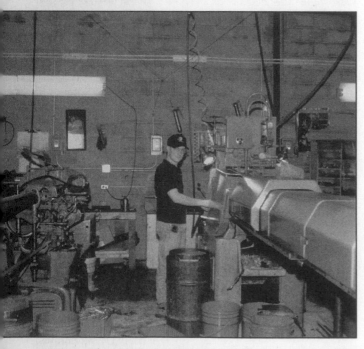

There are plenty of skilled hands in and around Dunlap, Tennessee.

The five-pin Ultra Sight is made from aircraft aluminum and is available in High Country's Treeleaf camouflage finish.

Hoyt USA

Hoyt is never a company to hide its light under a bushel basket. It always has a large display at trade and consumer archery shows around the country.

HOYT USA IS a relatively new name for an old-line company. It was known simply as Hoyt Archery during the years that Earl Hoyt started the enterprise, then ran it with his wife, Ann. Both were target archery champions, and in those early days, initial emphasis was on supplying quality target bows to competitors.

After the company was purchased by Easton Aluminum, it was known for more than a decade as Hoyt-Easton. With a change in corporate structure, the company—though still an element of the Easton empire—came to be known by its Hoyt USA handle.

Easton had moved a great segment of its arrow manufacturing to a facility in Salt Lake City, Utah, and the Hoyt division was moved to the same city, where production could take advantage of several entities, including the sophisticated distribution network.

Many decades ago, archery champion Earl Hoyt took the opportunity to trade in his expertise and knowledge of what it takes to become a top archer, by turning out bows on a custom basis in a small shop in Missouri. Today, manufacturing is a mass-production effort, with computers being used to design and even build the bows.

As mentioned, in the beginning Hoyt bows were meant primarily for the target archer, and they made a lasting reputation on the target ranges of the world. However, it soon became evident that bowhunting was a coming sport; before long, there were far more bowhunters than target archers coming to full draw in this country. As a result, in recent annums, emphasis has been on bows for the camouflage set rather than the white-dressed shooters on the target competition line.

"Today's archery world is full of bows," a company spokesperson acknowledges. "There are bows from many different companies; there are faster bows, forgiving bows, longer bows, shorter bows, expensive bows with machined risers, bows to fit the tightest budgets. There are bows of every description, color and brand, and the choice seems to be endless."

Well, in 1995 alone, Hoyt USA has added to what may result in buyer confusion. In this one year, the company added three new compound bow risers, a new compound limb design, two new eccentrics, a new yoke system, five new anodized colors for competition bows, a new youth recurve model and a hunting recurve as well.

Other additions for this single marketing season are four new bow sights, ProCoat competition colors, a recurve hunting bow case, two new stabilizers meant specifically for 3-D animal targetry, a new anodized camouflage pattern, four new Micro-Adjust rest systems and a new machined riser cable guard system.

Among the late offerings are the new Defiant riser, which is meant for speed. It is machined from a solid aluminum billet and has radical, swept-back reflex geometry. This bow is being made in four slightly different configurations—the Defiant Supreme, FastFlight, Excel and Heat. All are offered in either natural form or HiddenLeaf camo. For the first three bows, draw weights vary from 50 to 80 pounds, while the Heat's draw ranges from 60 to 80 pounds. Draw lengths vary slightly, and various cam and wheel options are incorporated.

The Flashpoint Excel is a new variation on an established line. Designed primarily as a hunting bow, it features 16-inch

Bill Krenz, now with Hoyt in Salt Lake City, was a well-known bowhunter long before he entered the business world. He demonstrates construction procedures at Hoyt's factory.

Bow limbs are inspected after they are painted and have the Hoyt logo applied.

dual-laminated limbs and has an overall length of 39 inches. It utilizes what Hoyt calls an M Cam and has draw-weight options covering a range of 50, 60, 70 and 80 pounds for draw lengths of 25 to 31 inches. This one also is available in HiddenLeaf camo or even something called Gray Chameleon.

Internationally recognized bowhunter Chuck Adams is on the Hoyt evaluation staff and has taken a liking to a trio of bows called the Mystic line.

"New bowhunters, even those on a limited budget, should look for a bow that provides reliable and consistent performance in all hunting situations," Adams advises. "The Mystic brings together the quality one deserves, the performance needed and the value required."

These bows feature a magnesium midsection and independent limb pockets. Thus, this becomes one of the lightest weight compound bows around. The Mystic Excel has Dual-Lam limbs, while the Mystic Rebel XT and the Mystic Rebel are equipped with 16-inch solid fiberglass limbs.

A need that every archery company is seeking to fill is the youth bow market. Hoyt USA is no exception. Two brand-new models, the Magic and the Magic XT, were introduced early in 1995. These are compound models that cause Chuck Adams to comment: "My first archery experiences would have been more enjoyable and successful had these been available when I was a kid."

Each of these bows measures 33 inches in overall length and has solid fiberglass risers of 14 inches. Draw weight choices are 20, 30 and 40 pounds. The big difference is in the type of wheels used by each.

There are other new models as well, but a view of what might be expected of Hoyt bows in the immediate future is reflected in recent competition accomplishments.

The 1994 IBO world championships, the largest archery tournament held anywhere in the world that year, was the culmination of an entire season of heavy-duty 3-D competitions.

In the men's pro division, Bobby Ketcher used a Hoyt SuperStar bow to win; Wayne Risner took second place with the same bow model. In the women's pro division, Sherry Cartright won the world title by shooting with a Hoyt Flash-

Point; Joella Bates, the third placer, also was using a Flash-Point.

In the men's bowhunter release competition, Fletcher Cummings shot a FlashPoint to win, and the world champion in the open youth division was Blaine Homistek who launched his winning arrows with his Hoyt SuperStar.

"Accuracy is the secret," according to Bobby Ketcher. "My bows are fast, but it's even more important that they're super accurate."

Chances are one would have to go quite a long way to find a better recommendation for a product than that type of word-of-mouth advertising!

Hoyt bows are assembled from component parts according to computerized instructions from customers.

Hydraflight Archery Products

Charles O. Waller, president of Eason & Waller, manufacturers of the Hydraflight stabilizer, has a background of precision manufacturing for the aerospace industry.

HYDRAFLIGHT ARCHERY Products, which manufactures and markets the Hydraflight Adustable Hydraulic Shock Stabilizer, is perhaps best described as a direct descendant of the aerospace industry, since the stabilizer was developed by the engineering department of Eason & Waller.

"Eason & Waller has been in the aerospace and aircraft parts manufacturing business for nearly forty years," according to the company's president, Charles O. Waller. He insists that the careful manufacturing techniques and tolerances necessary to the space industry are utilized in production of the stabilizer which has found wide acceptance among serious archers.

"Unique features of the Hydraflight include an externally adjustable weight location feature, an improved hydraulic shock absorber, and aluminum and steel construction," Waller states.

The benefits to the archer using the Hydraflight are many, including a noticeable increase in shock absorption, reduced

muscle fatigue and joint stress, increased stamina and, last but not least, as proclaimed by Dave Stepp Jr., a professional 3-D archer and a big winner in money tournaments, "With Hydraflight's weight location feature, I can balance any bow perfectly, any time, any place."

That's quite a statement, but one has to look at the fact that there are adjustable stabilizers and there are hydraulic stabilizers. Until introduction of the Hydraflight, there never has been a bow stabilizer that is both adjustable and hydraulic. Incidentally, a patent now is pending on this Eason & Waller development.

The device itself consists of an outer tube that carries internal threads, while an inner tube carries the unit's weight and shock-reduction assembly. The assembly is threaded on its exterior surface to match the threading in the outer tube. Actually, it is more simple than it may sound.

The inner tube, filled with hydraulic fluid, is sealed at both ends, its threads matching those of the outer tube. Thus inserted, it can be screwed in or out to change the balance of the tube. A locking nut holds the inner tube assembly in position once the individual archer has established what he considers to be optimal location.

A $3/16$-inch Allen wrench, carrying a $4^3/4$-inch shaft, is furnished with the stabilizer. This tool loosens and removes an outer cap screw that resides in the forward end cap. The shaft that is affixed to the Allen wrench then can be inserted into the cap hole and manuevered until it aligns and drops into the internal locking nut situated on the end of the shock assembly. This internal locking nut may be snugged down tight and requires some force to loosen. The nut is unlocked by turning it counter-clockwise. According to Charles Waller, the nut should be rotated one full turn before going to the next step.

With the locking nut loose and rotated as described, the long shaft on the Allen wrench is maneuvered farther into the stabilizer's innards until it makes contact with a second socket engineered into the weight/shock assembly. We found it necessary to turn the wrench slightly, searching blind so to speak, until the end of the shaft drops home.

With the Allen wrench's shaft in proper position, the shock assembly can be moved in either direction simply by turning the tool. A clockwise twist will move the assembly in the direction of the bow's riser; turning it counter-clockwise tends to move weight away from the riser. This is all accomplished, of course, by the inner tube being moved along the matching threads of the outer tube.

According to Eason & Waller engineers, the Hydraflight stabilizer is designed to operate on what amounts to two levels; the hydraulic action helps to absorb some of the shock resulting from arrow release, and, at the same time, the actual weight of the device will aid in positioning the proper balance of the bow.

We found that determining the optimum positioning for the internal weight requires a bit of diligent experimentation. The

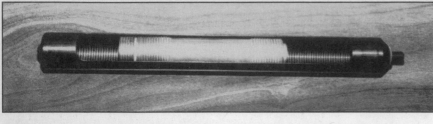

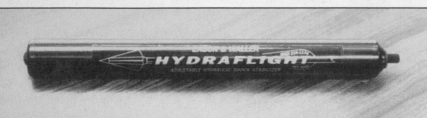

This cutaway version of the Hydraflight stabilizer shows the inner components. The internal surface of the tubing is threaded to accept the male-threaded hydraulic piston that moves as it is turned.

Bowhunters may prefer the 9- or 12-inch versions of the stabilizer. Each is available in two weight choices.

best system for proper adjustment, it seems, is for the archer to install the stabilizer and, without disturbing the factory-determined settings, shoot a few arrows to get the feel of the unit and to note any changes that should be made in balance.

Then, one should unlock the weight assembly, using the Allen wrench, move the assembly either backward or forward, cinch it down once more, then shoot a few more arrows. It may be that, on the first try, you moved the unit in the wrong direction. However, this move-and-shoot routine should be continued until the balance and pivot of the bow in the hand reach their ultimate comfort.

As indicated, the weight/shock assembly is locked in place by tightening the internal locking nut down snuggly onto the assembly. Care should be taken, according to Charles Waller, not to lock the nut too tightly. We made that mistake and found it required considerable force to loosen it again.

The final step is to replace the button-head screw in the forward end cap. It should be fairly tight so that it will not vibrate loose in the field or on the target range and be lost. The unit will act as advertised without the screw, but there is a danger of dirt, grit and moisture getting into the internal screw heads. The severity of that problem probably doesn't need further discussion!

As for current production, the Hydraflight is being manufactured in several combinations of weight and length. Among the buyer's options are a 12-inch stabilizer weighing 19 ounces, another 12-incher with a weight of 21 ounces, a 9-inch unit weighing 15 ounces and another of the same length that weighs

17 ounces. Longer stabilizers for target shooters are also in production, as of early 1995.

According to Waller, an additional weight plate can be screwed into the cap screw hole, if desired. In fact, a longer standard stabilizer can be threaded into this hole for use in target shooting.

A Browning bow was used to test the new stabilizer, and there was considerable reduction in felt recoil. Others apparently feel the same way. Steve Lewellan, a recognized Pope & Young trophy elk hunter, says, "Bowhunters need every advantage we can get. The stabilizing effect of the Hydraflight outdistances all the others, and you have the added bonus of increased shock absorption."

Stewart Bowman, a high-ranked professional archer and the maker of Accu-Riser custom bows, is another who has tried the unit and opines, "The unique adjustment feature allows individual fine tuning for optimum performance. The improved design increases shock absorption noticeably."

Professional archer Frank Pearson is another target shooter who is high on the Hydraflight. During his two-day shooting school in Arizona, he demonstrates its use and recommends it to all his students. The best recommendation is seeing Pearson win all those tournaments while using the stabilizer on his Browning bows.

Those are some pretty impressive endorsements by archers who know what works and what doesn't. At this writing, however, the Hydraflight stabilizer is still finding its way into the nation's archery shops.

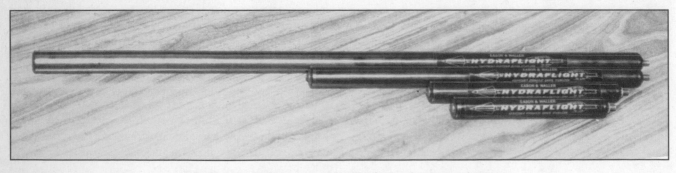

Hydraflight is made in several lengths for bowhunters and target shooters. The longest is 35 inches, weighing 26 ounces and featuring additional sets of optional weights.

Indian Archery

The reflex design on Xi's new Millennium bow is made of aluminum, said to be 30 percent stronger than cast magnesium. Xi claims 280 feet per second from the bow, which has epoxy fiberglass limbs, Wide Tac Cam system and eighteen-strand string.

IT HAS BEEN a long trip in time since 1927, when one H.M. Bradley gathered together several investors and rented a small room in downtown Evansville, Indiana, to start Indian Archery. It was a big gamble, for archery was not a major sport and bowhunting was virtually unheard of.

However, it was not long before the work force had grown to more than twenty and Indian archery equipment was being exported to five overseas markets as well as throughout the U.S. Those early bows were handmade from lemonwood, hickory and Osage orange. Arrows were fletched with turkey feathers.

In 1937, the fiberglass bow was introduced, and the work force eventually grew to more than 250 employees. With the sudden growth of interest in target archery and, perhaps more importantly, bowhunting, competition began to grow. With the increase in the number of bowhunters across the nation and in Canada as well, there was an expansion of archery shops and sporting goods stores.

Viewing this, Indian Archery realized that modern technology had become a necessity. The compound bow had been introduced and lent itself to such production. The beginning of what the company calls Xi was just around the corner.

In 1984, Al Rinehart signed on as national sales manager, a position he still holds. This was a good choice, for he was well known in target archery circles and had been a bowhunter hunter for twenty-five years.

Within a short time, Indian had introduced their pro shop line—Xi. This equipment found quick acceptance, but Jon Ruthenburg, now the company president, realized the company needed "someone who had integrity and had not been footballed around from one company to another."

Myles Keller of Clairmont, Minnesota, ultimately was signed on as senior bowhunting staff director. Keller was well known in bowhunting circles, having taken several Pope & Young record deer. He didn't want to be simply an endorser of Xi equipment, but wanted to contribute to design and use.

"Although, he has taken thirty-nine bucks that have made it into the record books, he is not an ego-booster for himself," Ruthenburg verifies. "This is another quality Xi wanted in an endorser." By 1987, the Xi Pro Shop line included three Signature Series bows, Myles Keller's signature appearing on the limb of each.

Xi continued to grow and introduced broadheads, hunting sights, quivers and other accessories to back up their bows. Distributors across the nation had joined in the growth of the line, and Monsena, Canada's largest distributor of hunting equipment, was handling the line in that country.

There doesn't seem to be any doubt that Xi is here to stay as a power in the archery industry, but what does the future hold?

"Our goal is to capture a large percentage of the fragmented market share and continue to promote and support the sport of archery and bowhunting," declares Al Rinehart.

Xi utilizes a glass-enclosed dry-fire testing machine to determine the endurance of bow designs, giving them more abuse than any archer might give. This bow has undergone 1,079 unloaded string releases without breakage.

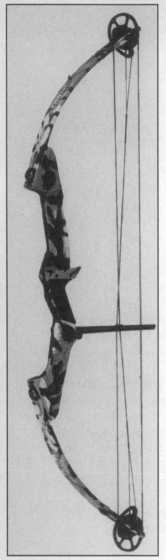

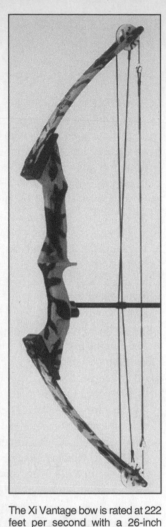

The Xi Vantage bow is rated at 222 feet per second with a 26-inch draw length and 50 pounds of draw weight. Draw length adjusts within a 3-inch range to match developing young archers' abilities.

New Xi Paragon bows feature built-in overdraw shelf handguards. The riser is made of cast aluminum, and the string is eighteen strands of Performa material for a long string life.

This procedure is conducted in a specially constructed chamber that dry-fires the bows and simulates live shooting conditions. The machine allows single shot testing or continual cycling with an adjustable recycle time of three to nine seconds. The continual cycle is controlled by a variable-speed master control. Draw length, draw weight and arrow weight all can be adjusted to accommodate different shooting scenarios.

"Safety of the engineers and spectators was of utmost importance in designing the machine," according to Al Rinehart. "The chamber is encased in clear Tufflax, which is stronger and more shock resistant than Plexiglass. Also, the door is key-locked and equipped with a safety switch that stops the mechanical arm instantly at any time during the cycle, if the door is opened. The riser is clamped into a bow nest manufactured of T6-6061 aircraft aluminum, and the table base is 1 inch of solid steel. The entire testing chamber weighs about 1,500 pounds."

Recent dry-fire testing of an Xi Ultima bow was stopped at 1,860 cycles to be replaced by another bow model. However, according to Rinehart, the Ultima bow was still intact.

At this writing, Xi is marketing nearly twenty different models, but the Ultima is the bow being built on the new Power Deflex riser that is meant to combine great speed with a forgiving feel.

The bow incorporates Fusion Force limbs, a product of composite technology which calls for fusing up to forty layers of composite fabric under intense heat and pressure. According to Al Rinehart, "This state-of-the-art technology eliminates limb torque and removes the need for limb fork buttons."

Another bow introduced early in 1995 is the Paragon, which is designed to combine speed with performance. The bow is built on Xi's new cast aluminum riser, which the company claims is stronger than either a magnesium or machined-aluminum riser.

Xi's newest high-speed bow is called the Millennium and is reported to deliver an arrow to its target at 280 feet per second. According to company engineers, the stored energy in the bow's Epoxy Glass Flex limbs is coupled with new a system of Wide Tac Cam eccentrics, producing the high velocity.

The Millennium weighs only 4³/₄ pounds and measures 40 inches, axle-to-axle, delivering 60 percent actual let-off, according to Rinehart.

As a move in that direction, the national sales manager has worked hard at developing a sales network. A few years ago, the company had sales representatives across the country who knew little about the sport of archery or the equipment needed.

"Today, we have one of the best and most knowledgeable sales forces in the archery business," Rinehart insists. "These are individuals who bring instant credibility among the dealers with whom they are involved."

Originally, Indian Archery concentrated on bows and arrows for beginning archers. Time has required that changes be made in order to compete. Today, Xi compound bows and accessories easily compete with top-of-the-line items from other makers.

Much of this forward marching is the result of new techniques and materials. Xi's new fusion force composite limbs have undergone the most abusive punishment possible—repeated dry-firing.

Jennings Compound Bows

(Left) Ever the tinkerer, Tom Jennings has one of his designs in a bow presss while he adjusts the draw length for a shooter.

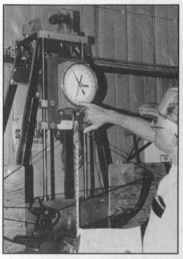

(Right) Jennings demonstrates the draw weight and let-off percentage of the Jennings Unistar bow.

LIKE MANY YOUNGSTERS brought up in the pre-Space Age era, Tom Jennings devoted some of his adolescence to playing Indian with the bows he made from green tree limbs and a bowstring made of ordinary string. However, by the time he was eleven, he was truly hooked on archery.

A friend, Billy Rumer, arrived one day in the Jennings backyard in Van Nuys, California, with a handmade bow that had been fashioned from hickory and finished with a coat or two of spar varnish.

"It was a little over five feet in length—longer than I was tall—and it had a leather grip, an arrow plate that was made of abalone shell and a twisted linen bowstring," Tom Jennings still recalls today. "I thought it was the most beautiful thing I had ever seen!"

His young friend had built the bow under the guidance of Creed Kelly, a Boy Scout counselor. Young Tom enlisted Kelly's help and built his own bow—after he was able to save 75 cents for the hickory bow stave that was the prime necessity.

With the success of that first effort, Jennings was hooked and immediately made a longbow from a lemonwood stave that had been imported from Cuba. This one turned out well enough that he soon was making bows for his friends, who were quick to accompany him on neighborhood bowhunting safaris for small game such as rabbits.

Graduating from Van Nuys High School in 1942 after attending classes with future film stars Jane Russell and Marilyn Monroe, Jennings went to work at Lockheed Aircraft in nearby Burbank. Pearl Harbor had been bombed only months before his graduation, and World War II was in full swing. After spending eight months building military aircraft, Jennings enlisted in the U.S. Army Air Corps and was trained as an airframe mechanic, serving in North Africa, India and Burma.

With the end of the war, Tom Jennings came home to Southern California and took up archery and bowhunting once again. He shot his first deer with a bow in 1946, but he did it with a Bear recurve. He had tried his old, handmade bow that had been in storage during the war, and it shattered on the first draw.

At that time, Tom Jennings didn't even dream of a career in archery; it was his hobby. He made a livelihood in the heating and air-conditioning business, but became active in the National Field Archery Association and joined every archery club in the area. On almost every weekend, he took part in some sort of archery competition—when he was not experimenting with designs for his own bows.

A fateful year for Tom Jennings was 1950, when he met M.R. Smithwick, another backyard bowyer, during an indoor shoot. The two soon found they had many things in common, but their relationship was interrupted temporarily when Jennings signed on to work as a sheet metal fabricator on two military projects in Greenland.

Upon his return, however, Jennings had enough capital that he was able to join Smithwick in forming S&J Archery Sales in North Hollywood. That was in April, 1953. The pair sold Bear and Damon Howatt production models, as well as building and selling their own line of Smithwick bows.

Three years later, Jennings bought out his partner and, with five employees, upped production. The Smithwick bow was renamed the Citation, after the first race horse to win more than $1,000,000 in prize money. During the decade that followed, Jennings and his crew turned out more than 25,000 recurve bows, pioneering such innovations as exotic hardwood handle risers and innovative grip designs. He also was a pioneer in measuring the traveling speed of arrows.

In the mid-'60s, Jennings became aware of the compound

lowed, Jennings doubled production every six months, necessarily expanding to three locations. The North Hollywood shop finally was replaced by a 43,500-square-foot facility in Valencia, California

By the early '80s, twenty-five other companies were making and marketing various versions of the compound bow. New facets of design were incorporated almost daily, and Jennings and his crew of some 180 workers produced as many as 75,000 compounds which were sold exclusively through archery pro shops.

In December, 1982, disaster struck! A ruling in a federal court on a patent case left Jennings and his company without a license to produce compound bows. There was nothing left to do but close the doors!

In April, 1983, Bear Archery acquired the assets of Jennings Compound Bow and the services of Tom Jennings as a consultant. Today, the Jennings designs are being built in the Bear Archery plant in Gainesville, Florida.

Tom Jennings now resides in the small town of Stover, Missouri, spending most of his days in his workshop where he continues as a product designer for Bear Archery. He is heavily involved in the public relations aspects of promoting Jennings compounds, making numerous appearances at sporting goods trade shows and archery events. However, the greater part the old pro's waking hours still are devoted to doing what he loves most—designing and building bows that will find their way to dealers' racks and, ultimately, into the hands of archers across the nation.

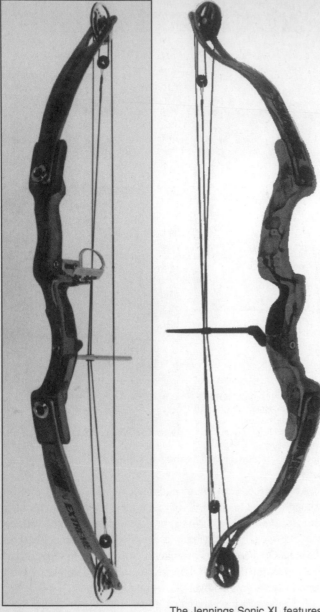

One of the newer Jennings designs is the Carbon Extreme, proven popular with bowhunters and target shooters.

The Jennings Sonic XL features recurve limbs, pushing out fast arrows.

No longer built, the Jennings Unistar bow utilized several principles leading to a single cam bow design. The compounding action was in the center of the bow.

For many years, the Forked Lightning was one of the most popular Jennings sellers.

bow and, after considerable study, began to produce his own version of the innovative arrow launcher. In 1966, he changed the name of his company to Jennings Compound Bows.

By his own admission, Jennings' early compounds looked more like an assembly from a youngster's Erector Set than a working bow, but he also was aware that archers—and bowhunters in particular—were looking for bows that were faster, more powerful and stronger than the recurve. In fact, in 1967, Jennings quit making recurves entirely.

Frank Katchum won the 1970 national championship of the National Field Archery Association with a Jennings compound, and the company suddenly found itself eighteen months behind in production. During the five years that fol-

Kwikee Kwiver

The Torque-Snuffer is the latest product from Kwikee Kwiver. When mounted, it moves the bow quiver forward and to the middle of the bow riser.

Kwikee Kwiver's Torque-Snuffer has a patent pending.

Bob Stinson heads up Kwikee Kwiver, the outfit that has made more bow quivers than any other manufacturer.

YOU PROBABLY have used a Kwikee Kwiver for years, although you might not know that is what you were using. The Kwikee Kwiver has been around for nearly forty years and is still going strong. Quivers are still the primary products, but the company is branching out into other related areas, too.

Bob Stinson heads up Kwikee Kwiver, which still is headquartered at its primary location of Acme, Michigan. This is a short distance from Traverse City, along the eastern shore of Grand Traverse Bay, Lake Michigan. All this is to say that the location is unobtrusive and somewhat surprising to encounter amid the summer homes and resorts of that northern part of the state.

Stinson's background includes the manufacture of moulded plastic components for the automobile industry. As it turns out, the techniques for manufacturing moulded plastic bow quivers and similar accessories is not unlike those for certain auto parts. A visitor to the production facility might see Kwikee Kwiver components being turned out in one end of the factory, while

such items as engine covers, bumper members and interior components for nearby automobile assembly plants are produced at the same time in another area of the plant.

The quiver parts are stamped out, packaged and transported to the Acme location for final assembly, inventory and shipment to customers.

Kwikee Kwiver has been in operation since 1957, turning out the bow quivers we all have used. Many bow manufacturers rely on Kwikee to produce their quivers as original equipment. The broadhead protection hood can be made in black or olive drab, or in any of several camouflage patterns and colors such as Realtree, Bottomland Mossy Oak, Tree Stand Mossy Oak and Gray Mossy Oak. There is no reason that the hood cannot be ordered in some other color or pattern, as well. The camo patterns are applied hydroscopically with a clear finish and a flat epoxy top coat that should protect the colors for many years.

Over the years, the Kwikee Kwiver design has seen several improvements, thus adding to its popularity. Among the latest innovations are such features as an Ultra-Lock double-locking bracket system that prevents any chance of noise or accidental knock-off while hunting. The back-up knob tightens or releases in $1\frac{1}{2}$ turns, and the quiver does not loosen.

Another new model is the Artic-2 holder that is made of a material that will remain pliable even in below-zero weather. The Artic-2 provides a tight grip on the arrow shaft in any temperature and is easily put on or taken off in any weather. An optional holder is available for carbon arrows in hunting sizes, too.

Some broadheads have cutting diameters of up to $1\frac{1}{2}$ inches, and the new quiver has a thickened shield that will accept six arrows so equipped. Inside the shield, built into the liner, is an enlarged scent pad made of open cell foam. Kwikee Kwivers are made of polycarbonate plastic material, which is said to offer the maximum strength with the maximum resistance to the effects of ultraviolet rays and ozone.

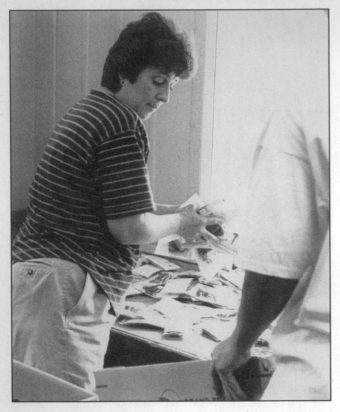
As products are assembled, counted and packaged, they are ready for shipment to dealers everywhere.

One of the latest new products from the mind of Bob Stinson is an item he calls the Torque-Snuffer. This is an aluminum alloy plate or bracket that places a bow quiver more toward the rear of the bow, rather than at the side. The idea is to reduce the amount of weight transferred to one side of the bow with all of the arrows in the quiver, improving the balance and reducing the amount of torque caused by weight of the quiver. When the patent-pending Torque-Snuffer is mounted on the bow, the quiver then is mounted on the plate the same as it would be on the bow.

One of the more popular products in recent years has been the Kwik-2 two-arrow bow quiver. This small, lightweight quiver folds down into a package small enough to fit into the bowhunter's pocket or pack. It unfolds to a full-length quiver that will hold two arrows. Some hunters will put the little Kwik-2 on the bow and carry a normal supply of arrows in a back or belt quiver.

The two arrows on the bow would be useful for those stalking game or when walking to a tree stand location, ready for the unexpected deer to show up on the trail. Many bowhunters are in the habit of hanging their regular bow quiver on a branch or on the tree stand as they wait out a whitetail deer. The little Kwik-2 might be mounted on the bow while on stand and carried back to camp with the arrows removed and the regular quiver re-mounted on the bow.

Stinson is working on the Kwik-3 quiver. As the name implies, it is another small, lightweight quiver that holds three arrows instead of two. It, too, folds down into a small package when not in use.

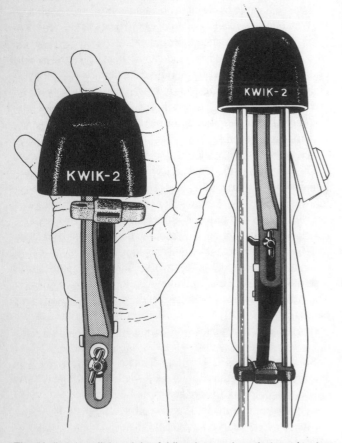
The Kwik-2 is a lightweight, folding bow quiver that carries two arrows. It telescopes down to hand size.

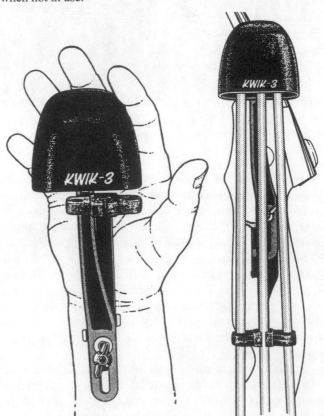
The Kwik-3 holds three arrows, weighing only 3½ ounces. It holds aluminum or carbon-fiber arrows.

14 *Martin Archery*

Company founder, Gail Martin, checks out the packaging of some Martin Archery products before shipping.

IT WAS IN 1948 that Gail Martin bought his first bow. The following year, he began fletching his own arrows, then doing it for others. It also was in 1949 that he designed and built a machine for making bowstrings. The work of this mechanism never has been bettered, and from his shop in Walla Walla, Washington, he began supplying strings to archery shops.

In 1950, Martin hired his first employee and, for all practical purposes, Martin Archery was born, although the company was not incorporated until 1973 as a family-held corporation. In spite of that delay in corporate formalizations, by 1959, Gail Martin had become the nation's largest supplier of bowstring, even furnishing his product to major bow manufacturers.

In the 1960s, two sons, Terry and Dan Martin, joined the business, as the first Martin bows were being produced. The first bow to come out of the infant factory was a strange-looking mechanism with recurve limbs and early eccentric cams mounted on added straight limbs. This was patented as the KAM ACT bow.

Bowyer Damon Howatt had been making commercial retail bows in Yakima, Washington, since 1944. In 1976, Martin purchased Damon Howatt Archery and, today, continues to produce many of the traditional bow designs crafted originally at the Yakima facility. In spite of the popularity of the compound bow, there still is great call for recurves as evidenced by the fact that Martin still sells more of them each year than was done in peak years by Damon Howatt Archery.

With bow sales continuing to increase annually, Martin Archery had to add a new manufacturing building to its Walla Walla facility in 1993. This structure has improved the company's inventory and warehousing performance, according to Dan Martin.

Like all of the Pacific Northwest, the Walla Walla area has grown considerably in recent years with residents and businesses moving in as people seek more open space. However, the Martin Archery facility is located in a rural area, and not far away are such game animals as deer, elk and black bear that make this prime bowhunting country.

Recurves and longbows are not the only bows made there. The annual catalog lists more than a dozen compound models. The company holds dozens of patents, with dozens more pending on developed products. The catalog also lists what seems to be an endless number of tools, accessories and other archery-oriented items. Considering all possible combinations of finishes, colors, draw lengths, draw weights, camouflage patterns, styles, sizes and product variations, the number pushes 750,000 inventoried merchandise items, according to company computations.

For example, each compound bow usually is available in two or three camo patterns, as many as a dozen brighter tournament colors, and have two or three different limb styles. Other variations for this particular bow probably include three or four different wheel designs, grips, different wood combinations and riser materials.

According to Dan Martin, new products are being added almost daily, the result of a hard-working research and development team. As a result, keeping track of the inventory is a formidable job. However, this is accomplished by an ingenious system of labeling and computer tracking.

An adjunct to this system is Bownet, which allows dealer access to all of the bows and accessories in stock. A Martin Archery dealer with a computer and modem can access the Bownet system around the clock, 365 days a

In the foreground, pre-assembled bow cables and strings await the appropriate bow with draw length and weight to match the rigging. Although automated, bows still require plenty of hand work.

After assembly, each Martin bow is checked for function and draw weight as specified by the customer.

year, to determine what equipment is in stock for immediate shipment.

Gail Martin is president of the corporation and takes an active role in the daily operations. His wife, Eva, is secretary-treasurer, while sons Terry and Dan are vice presidents. Terry Martin is sales manager and also is in charge of research and development. Dan Martin is charged with purchasing and inventory control for the corporation.

The business system that this family team has developed is unique to the archery business. For example, when an order for a compound bow is received at the Walla Walla installation, an order/shipping tag is made up immediately. On this tag are listed the type of bow being ordered, with information on the riser, wheels, string, type of grip, draw weight, draw length, colors and whatever additional specifications are involved.

A bow assembler is given this tag and uses the included information as a guide. He or she uses the exact specifications on the tag to gather the correct components and assemble the bow that the customer wants. The tag stays with the bow until it is shipped from the plant to the ordering dealer. According to Gail Martin, an experienced assembler can put together several hundred bows each day, each of them assembled with that specific list of components.

Once the bows are assembled, they are checked against the order, then tested for draw weight, draw length, the percentage of let-off and other requested specifications. The finished bows are examined minutely, then packed and labeled for shipment to the dealer.

There has been one downturn in the Martin operation, however. Gail Martin started the business by fletching arrows for others. There was a time, also, when Martin Archery turned out thousands upon thousands of dozens of fletched cedar arrows a year. In later years, however, Port Orford cedar, the ultimate

A couple of decades ago, feather-fletched wooden arrows were a large part of Martin's business. Today, most arrows sold are aluminum with plastic vane fletching.

wood arrow material, became virtually unobtainable. However, Martin rode over that hurdle and had dozens of multiple arrow-fletching tools filled with production aluminum arrows.

Today, however, only a couple of carousels satisfy the need for arrow manufacture. According to a company spokesman, most arrows today are built for customers by local dealers and pro shops.

"Actually, the arrow business was a start for this company. We probably don't make any money with the few we make up today. It's sort of a nostalgia thing, I guess. A way of remembering our roots," this individual stated.

As it is, Martin Archery has a tradition that extends back over nearly half a century. With expanding capacity, new product development, tight quality control, aggressive marketing and a roster of loyal employees, the company appears to be ready for the second half of its century of existence.

Andy Simo—inventor, manufacturer, engineer, bowhunter—is the man (center) who heads up New Archery Products with its long line of accessories.

ANDY SIMO IS another manufacturer of archery products who was a bowhunter before he became a maker. He has been a bowhunter for more than thirty years and, while living in Seattle, bowhunted with Glenn St. Charles and Mel Malinowski, founders of the Pope & Young Club, the organization responsible for bowhunting records. Today, Simo heads up New Archery Products, an Illinois firm catering specifically to the needs of archers.

Born in Czechoslovakia, Simo remembers playing with his bow and arrows in the mountains surrounding his village during World War II. The mountain sojourns, he recalls, were a way of getting away from the German occupation, at least for a short time. Simo's family moved to the United States in 1948. His father and grandfather both were watchmakers, but young Andy was more interested in airplanes. He eventually entered Purdue University's school of aeronautical engineering.

Following a 1961 graduation, Simo moved to Washington for a job with Boeing Aircraft. It was there that he began bowhunting. Later, his aviation career took him to such far-flung places as Huntsville, Alabama; New Orleans, Louisiana; Marietta, Georgia; and, ultimately, Chicago, Illinois.

Today, New Archery Products is headquartered in Forest Park, Illinois, a Chicago suburb. Simo now is the holder of eighteen patents and is the designer of the Razorbak and Thunderhead broadheads, as well as the Centerest Flipper arrow rest. This engineer's first successful archery product was the Flipper rest, which was designed in his basement, while he was employed by Lockheed-Marietta working on the C-5A aircraft project. It was in Georgia that New Archery Products was founded.

In 1973, Simo moved the business and his family to Illinois, operating in the Chicago area for some two decades. In 1993, he had to accept the fact that the design and production facilities he was occupying had simply become too small. A new structure, one designed specifically for his business needs, was built in nearby Forest Park. The building, covering some 20,000 square feet, was occupied in June, 1993.

The new home of New Archery Products is light, airy and functional, and the walls of Simo's office have been modified and strengthened specifically to carry the weight of his mounted bowhunting trophies. The facility houses what appears to be a maze of modern machinery and electronics, all necessary for the design and production of New Archery Products.

Simo's engineering background makes him something of a fanatic in insisting that each part of his products be held to extremely tight tolerances. Thus, parts are tested constantly for design compliance during and after final assembly.

In touring the plant, we noted that most of the company's products appear deceivingly simple in design. After all, how complicated can be the design and production of a new broadhead or arrow rest? As an example, the company recently introduced the PlungerRest. Officially cataloged as the PlungerRest/Arrowrest/Cushion Plunger System, this device is simple to install and use, due to the thought and engineering that went into it from the beginning. This accessory combines a high-performance arrow rest and an adjustable cushion plunger into a single compact unit. It is manufactured of heat-treated stainless steel and brass, with low-friction Delran also used to eliminate any bow scratching potential. According to Andy Simo, every part of the precision-made unit is tested extensively prior to assembly.

Incidentally, installation of the PlungerRest requires no tools, which was part of the original concept. It is adjustable for centershot shooting if that is what the archer prefers. In installation,

Many of New Archery Products' production personnel are long-time employees loyal to the firm and to Simo.

one need only hand-tighten a large knurled lock nut that sets the rest for shooting and further adjustment.

When all of the adjustments have been made to the individual archer's needs, a small set screw on the lock nut is tightened. Once adjusted and set, it can be removed, then reinstalled in the hunting field without the need of tools. Of course, the setting will be the same as when it was removed from the bow.

Andy Simo shows obvious pride in what he says is another unique feature of his PlungerRest. The unit provides for vertical rotation which virtually eliminates porpoising, or the up and down travel of an arrow. Simo's PlungerRest has incorporated the same flipper arm used by a great many archers. The arm folds in action so the arrow's fletching will clear it as the shaft is released. Folded back, it is less likely to catch in brush or branches in the hunting field. When needed, the archer has only to flip the arm into shooting position.

As with all of New Archery Products' items, the PlungerRest is made in both right- and left-hand models. Several other types of rests also have been developed and marketed by the Midwestern company.

Andy Simo also is proud of his broadhead lines, which he designed. The Razorbak broadhead system includes heads of 125 and 142 grains, each equipped with non-vented stainless steel blades. The three-blade Razorbak 3 has hollow-ground blades for a cutting radius of $1^1/_8$ inches. A patented rotating blade cartridge allows the arrow to continue to spin after impact. Simo explains that this action tends to minimize vibration while maximizing the forward penetrating energy. Incorporated in the rotating cartridge is a special lubricant that serves to maximize rotation and further enhance penetration. Practice heads, identical in weight

and shape to the actual hunting cartridge version, also are available.

The Razorbak 4 and Razorbak 5 styles have features similar to those of the Razorbak 3, but each of the former weighs 142 grains. Both have hollow-ground stainless steel blades and the rotating blade cartridge, but according to Andy Simo, "We perform an additional stropping operation the these blades, making them the sharpest broadheads available today."

That is quite a claim, of course, but it goes unchallenged in the archery community. Nonetheless, Simo has not rested his manufacturing laurels on the Razorbak and has gone on to develop another family of broadheads which he calls the Thunderheads. This array of death-dealers includes broadheads weighing 100, 125, 150 and 160 grains. The 100-grain head has three stainless steel blades measuring .027-inch in thickness, as well as anodized ferrules that have been scooped out on the sides to reduce drag. Included with each broadhead is an O-ring washer that, with the patented seating design, assures perfect alignment when the head is tightened on the shaft. According to Simo, the washer also acts as a shock absorber, resulting in reduced blade breakage.

The Thunderhead 125-grainer has three stainless blades offering a cutting diameter of $1^3/_{16}$ inches. The Thunderhead 150 features only two blades for those who prefer the style. This head is designed for animals with heavy bone or fur and has a cutting diameter of $1^3/_8$ inches. The Thunderhead 160 style has three blades with the same cutting diameter as the 150-grainer. According to Simo, this heaviest broadhead is meant to be used with bows having draw weights of 55 pounds and over.

The increasing popularity of carbon-fiber shafts has prompted New Archery Products to design and market new glue-on broadheads that require no outserts for mounting. These heads weigh 130 grains.

"For those using carbon-fiber shafts, we wanted to offer a superior broadhead," Andy Simo explains. "By virtue of its design, the Razorbak series was ideal for modification to a glue-on type head.

"By eliminating the outserts, we were able to design additional strength into the broadheads. In doing this, of course, we had to be certain that the balance point, plus the effect on the spine, were minimized." The resulting heads are listed as the RB4 and RB5, and are available with replacement blades.

Meantime, Andy Simo is continuing to put more "new" in the name of his company, developing new products that will see dealers shelves in the coming months.

The new headquarters and manufacturing facility for New Archery Products is located near Chicago.

Oneida Labs, Inc.

IN 1975, JOHN ISLAS was granted a patent for a compound bow he had invented, with the belief it would revolutionize the archery industry. Although Islas sold the patent to a major archery company, he retained a license to produce the bow himself, as well. He established Oneida Labs, Inc., in 1980, manufacturing the Eagle bow until 1982. However, production was limited due to lack of available capital.

Peter Coyne became familiar with the Oneida Eagle bow and was impressed by its potential. In 1983, believing his manufacturing experience could bring this potential to fruition, Coyne acquired controlling interest in Oneida Labs. Under his leadership, the growth of the company has been substantial.

In 1984, Oneida Labs purchased the patent back from the earlier buyer. At that time, the work force at Oneida Labs consisted of eight people who doubled as salesmen and production staff. The company had approximately 170 active dealers.

The performance of the Oneida bows started drawing attention to these radically designed compounds. After testing the bows, Norb Mullaney, Emery Loiselle and other experts in the archery field added that extra boost needed to get Oneida Labs off the ground, and demand for the bows steadily increased. In 1985, with a growing dealer network, demand for Oneida bows took an astounding leap forward. This led to the automation of the accounting system and the purchase of a multi-use computer system.

Oneida Labs also entered into a sales agreement with Masten Wright, Inc., an export firm located in Connecticut. Masten Wright now represents Oneida Labs throughout Europe, Asia, Africa, Australia and South America.

Employment steadily increased in 1986, and sales surpassed any previous year. In addition to advertisements already running in top archery-related magazines, Oneida Labs, along with Remington Arms and Ranger Boats, became a major sponsor of the nationally televised program, *The Great American Outdoors*. This program sparked a great amount of interest with the outdoor audience, as they were able to actually see the performance of Eagle bows.

The newest bow model from Oneida is the Aero-Force MR-80, available in camouflage dress or in bright colors for the tournament shooter. The Oneida line is the most unusual design currently on the market.

Completed bows are protected, carefully packaged and boxed before being shipped to customers.

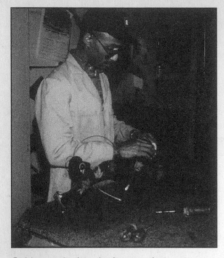

Cables and other rigging are the most complicated and critical components of the Oneida bows.

Plenty of hand work as well as factory production line methods are part of the construction procedure at Oneida Labs.

In 1987, the company's new Screaming Eagle bow was introduced. It was the industry's first compound bow to come equipped with a Fast Flight (non-stretch) string. Other compound bow manufacturers were unable to use this type of string on their bows at that time. The Oneida Eagle was strong enough to incorporate the new string without modification. The geometry of the bow was modified, and the new configuration developed more energy, but maintained its mild draw and recoil-free shooting—trademarks of all Oneida bows.

A banner year found Oneida Labs' innovative bows taking the archery world by storm, and sales again surpassed the previous years. In early 1989, Oneida's research and development branch was focusing on a completely new line of archery bows. However, sales had slowed and competition was fierce among archery manufacturers. Oneida Labs management realized the company had to come out with an interim bow that would compete with other manufacturers and increase sales, until the introduction of the 1990 line.

Modifications were made to the Screaming Eagle and the result was the new LXV model, which made its debut in June, 1989. Sales of the LXV accounted for 70 percent of the Oneida bows sold that year.

In 1990, Oneida Labs introduced three "New Breed" bows. The Tomcat, Phantom and Strike Eagle bows were redesigned to incorporate the changing needs of the modern-day archer. These bows provided the archer with multiple draw length and let-off capability, yet still maintained all the characteristics that have made the Eagle models among the most popular bows on what amounts to a worldwide scale.

With 1992 came introduction of the new Aero-Force and "K" Cam system. This totally redesigned alloy cam system was called the most significant breakthrough in speed enhancement technology in years. The "K" Cam and the new outboard limb configuration contributed to the phenomenal 240 feet per second (AMO standard) velocity rating of the 1992 Aero-Force, thus making this one of the most sought-after bows on the market.

Then in 1993, Oneida introduced many new developments and improvements with the unveiling of the Silver Eagle and the Tomcat II EXP bows. Due to the overwhelming success of

the Aero-Force, a 3-D target version called the Silver Eagle was introduced. Innovations such as torture-tested Armor-flex power limbs, a positive timing lock system and heavy-duty yoke cables were all standard equipment on this model.

The Tomcat II EXP was engineered with the youth market in mind, covering draw lengths of 22 to 28 inches and draw weights ranging from 25 to 70 pounds. The EXP kit, also ideal for small-frame adults, could be purchased for any Oneida bow model.

Sales for 1993 remained consistent with those of 1992 due to the general economic climate in the U.S., though the bow industry, as a whole, was down. Oneida Labs, with a strong dealer base, improved their standing among competitors by capturing a larger market share.

In 1994 came the introduction of 80-percent let-off and the new X80 line of Oneida bows, as well as a custom bow shop. Oneida claims to be the first to achieve true 80-percent let-off and incorporated this feature on the new X80 Series—the Tomcat X80, Phantom X80 and Aero-Force X80. The X80 bows still maintain Oneida's smooth draw curve without any harsh letdown, company engineers contend.

"Another way Oneida is striving to meet the needs of its customers and maintain its standing as the pioneering leader in archery technology is the development of the innovative Oneida custom shop," according to Oneida president Peter Coyne. The custom shop will handle any special request—an exotic camo finish, color-anodized metal fittings, exacting draw length, 80- to 100-pound draw weight range and high-gloss target finishes!

"Oneida Labs, Inc., is the only archery manufacturer that can fulfill the most extraordinary needs of its customers," Coyne states.

The future looks bright for Oneida Labs, Inc. The Aero-Force X80 is the most popular Oneida bow built to date, with features consumers are looking for these days—speed, smooth draw, quiet shooting and adjustability.

In 1995, Oneida's new Aero-Force MR-80 is being introduced to keep up with the demand for machined aluminum bows, according to Coyne.

Ben Pearson Archery

The Striker compound bow, complete with overdraw shelf, bow sight and stabilizer, is one of the modern, popular products from Pearson Archery in 1994.

Modern machines and manufacturing techniques set the tone for bow production at the Pearson plant in Pine Bluff, Arkansas.

THE INTRODUCTION TO this chapter explains how the late Ben Pearson developed an interest in archery and moved to Pine Bluff, Arkansas, where there were a number of enthusiastic and dedicated archers. He became a part-time bowyer, supplying archery enthusiasts with the needs of their sport, while working for Arkansas Power & Light.

When Pearson lost his job during the Depression, he began making bows on a full-time basis, forming Ben Pearson, Inc., in 1939, with the backing of an Oklahoma oilman, Carl Haun. The company was headquartered in an old sorghum mill on the outskirts of Pine Bluff. Rent, according to Pearson's later recollections, was $50 a month!

Before the first year of operation had ended, Pearson had thirty employees and had printed a small catalog. A sign reading "World's Largest Manufacturer Of Bows And Arrows Of Excellence" hung above the entrance to the factory. Pearson, himself, engineered, designed and made most of the machinery with which he and his staff began to turn out archery equipment on a mass-production basis.

The advent of World War II, however, brought some major complications. With much of America's youth in uniform and dispatched to foreign shores, the archery industry slowed. Steel was needed for guns and tanks, and thus was not available for arrow points. Ben Pearson managed to solve this problem by developing an arrow head of plastic. Nor did he allow these setbacks to affect his patriotism. He sent hundreds of bows and arrows to the Red Cross to be distributed to military units for recreational use.

However, the archery business continued to drop during the war and descended still further after hostilities had ended. Ben Pearson began to look around for other products that could be manufactured with the machinery he already owned. There was quite a procession, according to those who worked with Pearson at the time. In 1948, the company was manufacturing wooden boats; in 1950-51, the workers were building portable corn cribs and, in later years, made children's toys, garden equipment and even a dry ice-powered boat trailer! It was Ben Pearson and his people who designed and manufactured the first mechanical cotton pickers in the 1950s.

By 1958, the cotton business was prospering, and there was a growing demand for Pearson's cotton-picking equipment. The company had grown into a new factory with 200,000 square feet of floor space. However, while his company was growing by leaps and bounds, turning out cotton planting and picking machinery, Pearson never gave up his greatest enjoyment—archery. And when the sport began to regain some of its former stature and popularity, it was not long before Ben Pearson, Inc., was back in the archery business, producing as many as 4,000 hickory bows and 3,000 dozen arrows each day!

Ben Pearson, himself, began designing archery tackle again and developed what came to be marketed as the Deadhead broadhead. This particular hunting point sold by the

The Ben Pearson FPS-2000 compound bow, with its machined alloy riser, is typical of the modern high-tech bows from this old-line company.

With all the modern machinery and equipment available to bow manufacturers, there is still the requirement for plenty of hand operations during production.

thousands and still is sought and used by countless bowhunters today.

In the 1960s, Ben Pearson and his staff developed automatic archery lanes. These were indoor installations set up much like bowling alleys, featuring electronically controlled targets for retrieving arrows and returning them to the shooter. One also could use the electronics to move the targets to varying distances at the press of a button.

There was a rush to get into the automated lanes by archery promoters across the country, but there was a problem. Many of the lane operators had little business experience, and poor management led to the downfall of many of the installations. Today, there still are a number of these operations in business across the nation. Where promotion and business practices have been good, the concept does still flourish.

By 1965, Ben Pearson, Inc., was once again the largest archery manufacturer in the world. It was during that period of success the pioneer decided it was time to retire. He sold the archery segment of the business to a conglomerate that seemed to be attempting to buy up all sorts of successful

recreation-oriented companies. Proper management of this conglomerate was lacking, according to some observers of the time, with the companies involved being milked without any great deal of money being put back into research and development or promotion.

Throughout the years that Ben Pearson had owned the company, he had served as the figurehead, featuring his own bowhunts in corporate promotions. However, he was well into his sixties when he sold the company. Age had slowed Ben Pearson, and he no longer wanted to climb the mountains or invade the swamps in search of game. The search was on for a new personality who could be used in advertising and publicity promotions.

Jim Dougherty, a young California bowhunter, was selected as the new figurehead, making safaris in Africa and other far corners of the world to promote the Pearson line. During this period, headquarters for the company were moved to Tulsa, and when the conglomerate later fell on hard times, Dougherty remained in the Oklahoma city, starting his own archery company. Meanwhile, Ben Pearson died in 1971 at the age of seventy-three.

Ben Pearson, Inc., underwent several changes in ownership and management, including one in which former Arkansas employees purchased the company and returned its headquarters and operations to Pine Bluff.

Then in 1982, the Sierra Corporation, a ninety-year-old manufacturer of sporting goods; home, recreational and casual furniture; as well as lawn, garden, institutional and educational products, purchased the archery company. The parent company is headquartered in Fort Smith, not far from Pine Bluff, and management was perfectly content to leave Ben Pearson, Inc., in its original surroundings.

Ben Pearson's spirit of innovation seemingly was revived in 1994, with the introduction of a whole new line of Pearson bows. Designed to offer archers the high-performance equipment they demand, Pearson's new 440 MAG and FPS-2000 hit the market.

Featuring machined aluminum risers, these bows quickly proved themselves to be exceptional when they were used in winning both national and world championships of the International Bowhunting Organization. Two-time national champion Bryce Pennington was shooting with the FPS-2000, while the new world champion, Bryan Marcum, was equipped with the 440 MAG.

Rodger Austin, director of marketing for what is now incorporated as Ben Pearson Archery, was elated, but not necessarily surprised at these titles being taken with Pearson bows.

"We believe that Pearson is producing the best product at the best possible price to give the archer what he wants and what he needs," Austin declared.

The current owners declare that Ben Pearson Archery is dedicated to the legacy of what they call "the founder of modern archery"—Ben Pearson.

"The same craftsmanship, quality and dedication to the sport of archery that inspired Ben Pearson to build that first bow is present still at Ben Pearson Archery," Austin contends.

Pro Line Company

The new Pro Line headquarters and production facility is located in Hastings, Michigan. It is larger and newer than the previous location, not many miles distant.

The Pro Line factory interior is clean and neat, with plenty of excellent lighting, important in the order checking department.

THE PRO LINE Company moved into newer, larger quarters in 1993. With the move, the firm began a more aggressive attitude toward research, development and marketing of their new high-tech equipment. The building, in the central Michigan town of Hastings, is considerably larger than the previous location in Gun Lake, Michigan, permitting the installation of new manufacturing machines and production processes that speed and streamline Pro Line's output.

A visitor to the new installation will be impressed with the modern concrete exterior of the building and its close proximity to rail, highway and air transportation. The building was not built exclusively for Pro Line, but it obviously has been cared for with consideration by its previous tenants. The structure now is serving the archery company well as a manufacturing, administrative and shipping facility.

The structure's interior is no less well maintained. The manufacturing portion is clean, with plenty of room for machines, and has dust and noise suppressors installed for the protection of employees and visitors. In many production areas, eye protection is required for all persons working or entering the facility. The building interior is well lighted and appears to be a reasonably comfortable and safe place to work. It quickly becomes clear that both management and the labor force are proud of the new location.

As do many of its competitors, Pro Line is manufacturing its risers in its own factory to better control the availability and quality of the bows. Pro Line is producing machined aluminum risers at the Hastings factory, with all the latest features that modern archers demand. For instance, one of the newest bows in the line is called the Center Fire. It has the aluminum riser with an in-line power stroke design and plunger hole in the center of the handle to produce a true centershot bow.

The Center Fire's carbon-reinforced recurve limbs are connected to the riser with a new CNC-machined pivoting limb pocket design. The bow's modular Flight Cams are also CNC-machined at the plant. The bow also features a split-cable system to equalize stress, protect the limb forks and prevent wheel lean. The feature permits a bow string change anywhere, without the necessity of a bow press.

While much of the production at the new factory is automated and computer-controlled, there is still the need for plenty of human hands and interaction with the machines. Each step in the production line of bows, components and accessories is carefully inspected. Each assembly is tested and examined as it is installed on the bow. With all the computers and machines, there is still considerable hand work required in the painting and finishing of each bow. A majority of the camouflage painting is done by the most experienced personnel. The spray paint is cured in automated ovens and drying rooms, but the application of the camo colors is done mostly by hand.

Pro Line has developed its own camouflage colors and patterns, and the employees take pride in the final appearance of

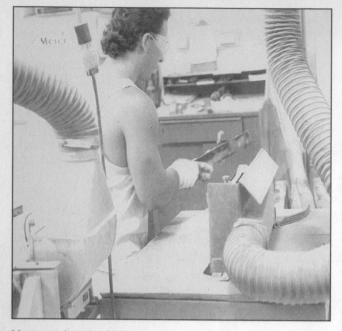

Most manufacturing facilities have to contend with dust. Pro Line has included dust-reduction and disposal provisions in its factory.

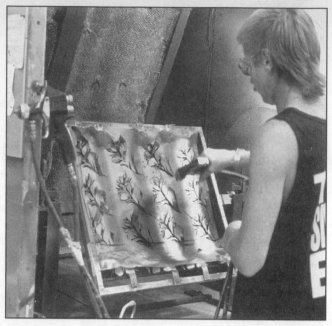

Much of the camouflage application procedures are done by hand at the Pro Line Archery production facility.

Order packaging and shipping must keep up with production. Everything is checked before final steps of shipping.

each bow and accessory. Pro Line has a custom paint-coloring room that can invent or duplicate any color. A number of custom colors are popular on some of the target bows from the company. In fact, a customer can design his or her own special color that, upon order, Pro Line will reproduce for that customer only. Each archer or team can have a custom-colored bow and/or accessories, if desired.

Each step of the production process is monitored by computer-driven and human inspections. The correct riser and riser color must be matched with the specified limbs, draw length, draw weight, string material and length, type of wheel, optional wood grip or not, plus all other accessories and options. The order date and completion dates must be determined and observed, and even the shipping labels are monitored before the packaged products are shipped. Nothing is left to chance or to the human memory. Checks and double-checks insure that each bow and the various Pro Line accessories are built and shipped exactly as ordered.

The design and construction of bows and equipment requires many small parts and components to be on hand when and where needed. Pro Line's production line lacks none of these essentials, but there is order and neatness to the operation. These speak well to the pride of workmanship and dedication of the employees.

In addition to the United States and Canada, Pro Line enjoys popularity in Europe, especially as field archery grows outside of North America. Terry Ploot, the company's sales manager, was born in Norway and has an international outlook. Ploot is a great believer in the importance of ensuring that youngsters and women are continually introduced to the sport. New shooters, he says, are the only way to guarantee that archery will have plenty of participation in the future. Pro Line offers plenty of support for archery youth programs where and when it will be beneficial.

14 ▸ Precision Shooting Equipment

Pete Shepley, founder and president of Precision Shooting Equipment. Shepley is also an avid bowhunter, testing out much of his new equipment on the hunt.

BACK IN 1970, Pete Shepley used to be the victim of a great deal of good-natured ribbing from his fellow product engineers at the Magnavox Corporation in Champaign, Illinois. The ribbing invariably concerned Shepley's preoccupation with designing new archery equipment during company lunch hours.

Today, Pete Shepley is the one who is laughing. What was his hobby has become what he contends is the largest archery equipment manufacturing company in the world. And now he spends all his time developing the most technologically advanced compound bows and related equipment ever produced.

In the early '70s, Shepley was experimenting with innovative designs for bow release aids, and later he developed a plastic flexible arrow vane to replace feathers for longer life and weather resistance. His vanes became known as Pro-Fletch, and today, this material is considered among many hunters and target archers as the finest fletching available.

During this same time frame, Shepley turned his design energy to the perfection of his first compound bow. He introduced his prototype to archers at an Indiana tournament, and within a week, he received orders for some 200 just like it. The following two weeks brought an additional 700-plus requests from across the country, the result simply of word-of-mouth advertising following exposure of the bow at the tournament.

Thus, Precision Shooting Equipment—initialized by the archery trade simply as PSE—was born. In the early stages, Shepley and a few friends built bows in a barn on his rural Illinois property. Soon afterwards, PSE had a "real" home—a humble, 700-square-foot building in Mahomet, Illinois.

In 1982, PSE moved its entire operation—employees and all—to Tucson, Arizona, incorporating the manufacturing production in one location. Within six years, PSE had outgrown its several buildings totalling 75,000 square feet, and in early 1989 the move was completed to its present location—a 143,000-square-foot facility located on nearly 27 acres in Tucson. Now, PSE's entire manufacturing, warehouse and office operations are located under one roof.

Pete Shepley takes great pride in the fact that PSE is primarily "self-sufficient," with all corporate, sales, manufacturing, and promotional and marketing functions taking place in one location. Unlike other manufacturers whose practice it is to contract-out different manufacturing, advertising or public relations duties, at PSE it all happens in one place. According to Shepley, not only does this provide for greater quality control, but adds to a strong feeling of teamwork by employees—making for a dependable, popular product.

As part of the operation, PSE owns Precision Plating, also

The PSE headquarters and manufacturing facility is located within a large building in Tucson, Arizona.

One of PSE's marketing efforts has been the Promotion Express, a complete mobile repair and display unit that travels around the country, appearing at dealers' stores, hunting shows and large archery tournaments.

located in Tucson, where anodizing of parts and accessories takes place. Another subsidiary, King Products, produces leather and fabric quivers, arm guards, backpacks, bags and bowhunting items. PSE produces its own catalogs and print advertising through its in-house advertising offices—something few other bow companies can boast.

Also "under the same roof" is PSE's Adventures in Video department. PSE has produced more than a dozen hunting and instruction videotapes as well as marketing and distributing near-

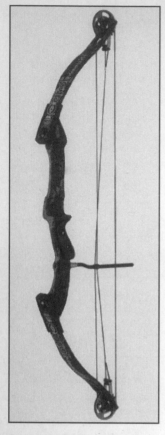
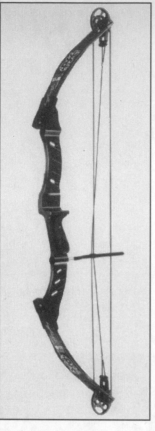
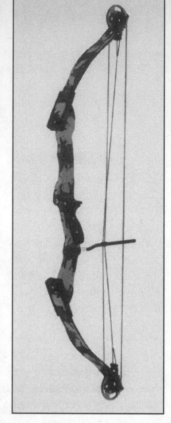

For 1995, PSE is offering the Carroll Marauder II compound bow for hunters.

The target shooter may prefer the PSE Infinity XLR-900 compound bow with its bright colors and machined riser.

Another new PSE bow for the 1995 season is the Gamesport Fire Flite Hunter.

The PSE Buckmasters bow is fast and powerful, intended for the 3-D target shooter who wants to take the same bow hunting.

ly 200 other titles to PSE's dealer network. Also unique to the industry is PSE's *Today's Bowhunter*, a quarterly video magazine promoting bowhunting as well as serving as an important marketing tool for the company.

Considered by many as one of the country's premier bowhunters, Pete Shepley is fortunate to be able to spend a lot of time in the forests and mountains, directing and producing hunting videos as well as testing PSE prototype equipment. In the past few years, he has taken grizzly, moose, barren ground caribou, black bear, elk, whitetail, mule deer, antelope, cougar, stone sheep, desert bighorn, two species of wild turkey, javelina and wild boar. Many of these animals have been difficult to stalk and take, meaning that the corporation head has to take time out of his working schedule to keep in shape for such outings. However, even with all of his hunting, Shepley continues to be the guiding force behind the innovative PSE engineering and product design department.

With the move to its spacious new facilities, PSE began a pair of premier industry programs—the PSE Dealer School and PSE Shooter's School. Both programs are directed by George Chapman, who has worked with Shepley since those first days back in Illinois.

The Dealer School is offered at no cost to authorized PSE dealers and is an intensive, five-day course designed to enhance sales ability, bow knowledge and business management. Since it was started in 1989, more than 1,000 archery dealers have

become factory-trained PSE dealers. The Shooter's School is offered as a two-day course and is centered on each individual's shooting desires and goals.

PSE continues to be one of the top award winners in archery, both off and on the field. Four of the top five Pope & Young Club-recognized Yellowstone elk were harvested with PSE bows, and PSE bowhunters annually take many record book animals. Likewise, Shepley's belief in high-tech design reportedly has led to more awards in its field than any other archery manufacturer from the National Association of Federally Licensed Firearms Dealers and *American Firearms Industry* magazine. On the tournament circuit, some of the nation's top archers shoot and promote PSE bows, including world champion shooters Terry and Michelle Ragsdale.

PSE also hosts its own annual tournament, the Pete Shepley Team Archery, big-money Shootout Series, each April in Tucson. It annually attracts hundreds of professional shooters and industry leaders from across the country.

As chief executive officer of the company he founded, Pete Shepley is active in management of all areas of the company, with particular emphasis on product design, engineering and marketing. Now in his early fifties, Shepley was educated at Southern Illinois University. Prior to founding PSE in 1972, he was an engineer with the Magnavox Corporation. Prior to that, he had been an engineer with the U.S. Steel Corporation and Olin Chemical Corporation.

14 Saunders Archery Company

Chuck Saunders is the man who began the company more than fifty years ago. One of the living pioneers of modern archery equipment and supplies, he is still active in the business, here giving a volunteerism award to Kletis Wheatley in 1993.

"MAYBE THE HISTORY of the Saunders Archery Company should start with my first hickory bow and how I used it to shoot my first game—a pigeon," suggests Chuck Saunders, founder and president of the Nebraska-based firm. "Or perhaps it started when I attempted to make an Indian arrowhead out of flint. That project was unsuccessful.

"Or maybe the real beginning was when I made my first stacked bow and took it down to a public park in Chicago to flight-shoot arrows in order to check the cast of the bow. Somewhere during that period, archery captured me in a relationship that has gone on for close to sixty years!"

After making some experimental bows in the 1930s—the era of the Great Depression—then expending his time in a somewhat half-hearted attempt to design and build a machine that would grind turkey feathers into proper fletching material, ready to glue to the Port Orford cedar arrow shafts that were favored in that era, Chuck Saunders found what he considers his niche. He developed the Saunders Indian Cord Fiber Matt for target shooting.

Until May, 1941, all of these matts were constructed by hand. "Making a straw matt by hand was a hot, dirty job. That had to be the big reason why Ben Pearson and I both got the idea of designing a machine that would do the job."

Both archery pioneers—Saunders and Pearson—started the design for a matt-making mechanism in 1939, but it was nearly two years before either succeeded. Pearson put his machine into operation in May, 1941; Saunders' first production by machine started a month later.

"Of course, neither of us knew of the work of the other and we were surprised—even upset—by the coincidence," Chuck Saunders recalls today. They two continued to be friendly competitors until the late 1960s, when Pearson went out of the target business to concentrate on building bows and accessories.

As one might assume, from target matts to stands to hold the big straw discs was a logical step. From that, Saunders progressed to producing target faces and other accessories.

"At that time, there wasn't much in the way of big game to hunt in our section of the Midwest," the company president recalls. "As hunters, we tended to focus our efforts on small game such as squirrels and rabbits."

Saunders felt that the blunt arrowheads used for small game were less than adequate, and some others agreed. One hunter of that period described the head as "a club on the end of an arrow shaft." Out of this thinking, Chuck Saunders developed the Bludgeon, a small-game blunt that still is popular today for small game hunting.

"Shooting in freezing weather, I found that my hands would get cold while trying to hold the arrow on the rest," he says, "so I developed the Kwik Lok. Also, I had found it a really slow job to serve a nocking point on a bowstring, and this serving was impossible to move if it turned out to be positioned incorrectly. That's why I developed the Nok Set."

With the growth of bowhunting across the nation and the increased number of game animals in most states, there also developed an ever-increasing market for accessories designed to make the hunt more comfortable and successful. In addition to the Kwik Lok, another item aimed at making the archer more comfortable has been the Trophy Tracker, a device for following game that has been shot with an arrow.

The Saunders Combo Point arrow head is designed to be shot into 3-D archery foam targets with less damage to the targets. The points are available in 85, 125 and 145 grains.

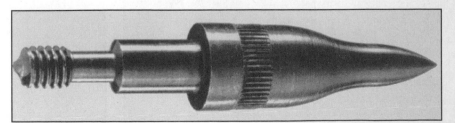

Designed specifically to increase the accuracy of an arrow is a device called the Torque Tamer, while the Saunders Kwik Slide is designed to silence the sounds created by the bow when the arrow is launched. Designed to improve arrow flight are the Gold Star arrow rest and another called the Kwik Flite.

"Our goal has been to produce archery equipment for both the target archer and the bowhunter that saves time, improves accuracy and arrow penetration, but primarily, we want shooters to have more fun," Saunders explains.

Will improvements by Saunders and others end eventually?

"It must seem to some that changes in archery have about run their course," Saunders concedes, then adds: "I don't know about other archery-oriented companies, but our tool and die department is behind in getting the dies ready to make products we now have on the drawing board. And there are areas we have hardly explored.

"I think we still have problems to solve and work to do before we can call it quits," this archery pioneer is quick to announce.

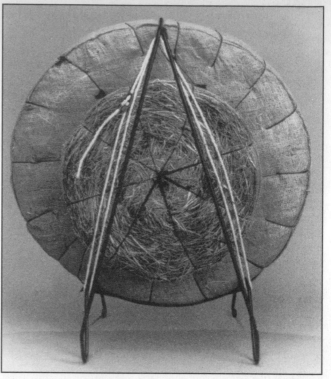

Saunders' Lifetime target matt is designed to stop thousands of fast arrows without undue damage to the front. The matt is made of spiral-wound cord grass, long a favorite of archers around the world. The front matt is 30 inches across; the rear, backup matt measures 20 inches.

The Hell Diver fish head is Saunders' newest for bowfishing. Once in the fish, the barbs fold out to hold the fish to the line and will fold forward to remove the fish from the head.

A new blunt Bludgeon arrow head from Saunders is said to be more lethal on small game such as wild turkeys. The head is 7/8-inch in diameter and is available in 100-grain slip-on or 145-grain screw-on versions.

Saunders' Clear View string peep aperture is designed to permit the minimum amount of restricted vision when mounted on the bowstring.

14 Timberline Archery Products

Lewiston, Idaho, is the home of Timberline Archery Products. Accessories were developed out of hunting frustration by Jim Sherman.

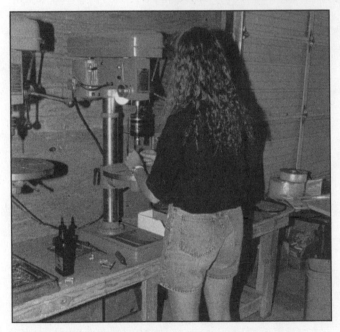

The small, efficient shop is equipped with modern power tools.

THE YEAR WAS 1988, and a gent named Jim Sherman was seated in a tree stand positioned over bear bait that had been set in a deep Idaho canyon. Sherman had spent three weeks on the trail of a huge cinnamon bear and held his breath as the animal came cautiously out of the forest and approached the bait with a wariness born of experience.

"It was fairly dark in the deep canyon," Jim Sherman recalls, "so I tried to turn on my electric sight pin for the shot. Nothing happened. It wouldn't come on!"

He didn't realize until close inspection much later that the battery was dead, but he brought his bow to full draw in the growing darkness for a shot. Even as he did so, he knew it was not going to happen. He couldn't see the sight pin well enough, and he certainly didn't want to merely wound his quarry.

In frustration, Sherman carefully eased the tension on the bowstring and laid his head back against the trunk of the tree where he had stationed himself. He was looking straight upward to where the sky still was relatively bright.

"If I could somehow capture that light in a sight pin, I'd never have to worry about not being able to see my sight pin again!"

Those were the frustrated bowhunter's thoughts in that moment nearly two decades ago. That also was the moment in which the concept for Sherman's Natural Light Site was born and, for all practical purposes, was the first step in founding Timberline Archery Products.

The corporation was formed the next year, in 1989, for the express purpose of building and marketing Sherman's sight, which was designed to gather light from the sky by means of fiber optics, then direct that light to the sight pin on a bow.

"This was in the same period during which the Pope & Young Club banned from its record books any bowhunting trophy for which an electric sight was used in the taking," Sherman reports. "Several states followed the equipment guidelines established by the Pope & Young people, and this opened up an immediate market for sight pins that were lit by means of natural light."

Timberline Archery Products' beginnings were modest, indeed, but in the years since the company's formation, this Idaho-based firm has gone on to become the world's largest manufacturer of light-gathering sights and sight pins. Sherman, the sole owner and president, holds five patents covering the concept and design of these sights.

According to Jim Sherman, the sights and pins all use a special material that gathers existing light, amplifies it, then transfers it to the aiming point.

"We have found, through use and testing, that all of our natural-light sights are visible throughout the legal hunting hours. As a result, Timberline Natural Light Sites are legal in every state.

Bow sights are small, requiring plenty of hand assembly to complete.

At Timberline, order forms are inspected and compared before products are boxed and labeled for shipment to customers.

One of Timberline's newer models of light-gathering bow sights features highly visible crosshairs in its solid body.

"Also, because the aiming points are bright and easy to see, we now are making them smaller than we did in the beginning. We have found that this smaller pin provides improved accuracy for the bowhunter."

The Natural Light sight pins and an aperture pin are sold individually so the bowhunter can install one of them on an existing sight on his bow. However, the units also are sold as parts of complete bow sights that range from super-strong bracket styles to sights that feature a double-bar dovetail.

"At Timberline, we are trying constantly to develop new technologies that not only will improve existing products in our line, but also will be of help in developing new ones," Sherman states.

To emphasize that statement, he points out that his Natural Light Site has been upgraded on three different occasions to date. Somewhat proudly, Jim Sherman explains that the sight's latest model uses special light collectors to gather and amplify available light, then transfer it to the fiber optic sight pins.

According to Sherman, this latest model is the Natural Light Crosshair Site. "The crosshairs are not hairs at all, but a thin, light-gathering material," he says. "They are only .012-inch in thickness, yet are easy to see due to their brightness."

This compact sight's design and construction support the crosshairs on both sides, so they stay parallel and don't sag. Introduced in 1994, it has been Timberline's best seller since hitting dealers' shelves.

Jim Sherman firmly feels that Timberline Archery's experience in continually working with light-gathering materials is the chief reason they are able to stay ahead of their competitors.

"We now are working on a new material and manufacturing process that should enable us to develop a new line of sights and sight pins," Sherman confides. "Timberline Archery Products intends to remain the leader in light-gathering sights. However, we fully intend to branch out into other areas of archery with new products and the technology to produce them well and at a competitive price."

With the manufacturing facilities situated in what is considered prime hunting country for such big game animals as elk, deer, bear and even an occasional moose, the countryside is ideal for Sherman and members of his staff to conduct practical, in-the-field tests of the sights that the production department turns out.

"Golfers insist that the worst day at their particular sport is an improvement over the best of any other outdoor activity," Sherman states, "but a lot of the folks at Timberline Archery feel the same way about bowhunting. Just being able to get out into the hills and pull a bow on a big buck deer or a bull elk makes the work more than worthwhile!"

Hidden away as it is in the Idaho hills, the Timberline factory is not overly impressive from outward appearance. Actually, it somewhat resembles a carriage house of the last century. However, it is filled with intricate equipment and local residents who know how to use it. Living primarily in the community of Lewiston, Idaho, not far from the Washington state line, the work force shows little turnover, their collective experience resulting in a continuing expertise.

Trueflight Manufacturing Company, Inc.

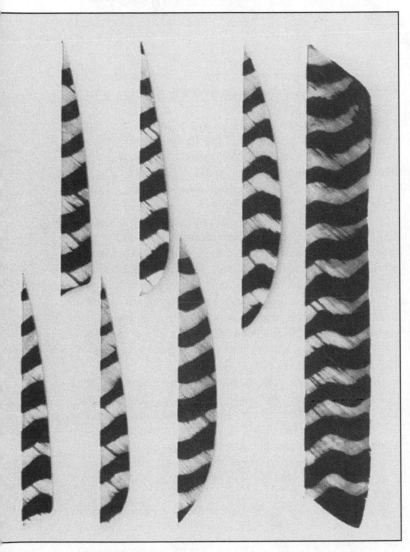

Trueflight's barred feather fletching is available in several cut patterns and colors.

A WISCONSIN BOWHUNTER who made and used his own bowhunting tackle, B.C. Roemer founded Trueflight Feathers—the forerunner of today's Trueflight Manufacturing Company, Inc.—shortly after the end of World War II.

In those post-war days of the late '40s, Roemer was having real difficulty purchasing good feather fletching, so he began to gather and process his own from surrounding turkey farms and other sources. In a few years, the Wisconsin bowhunter had grown tired of processing the fletching by hand, so he began experimenting and ultimately perfected a machine that would grind the base of the turkey feathers to the proper proportions.

Word began to spread among other bowhunters and even target archers regarding the quality of the fletching being turned out by Roemer and his machine.

"It wasn't long before he found himself in the feather business, and over the years, the business has grown," reports Peter P. Roemer, who now runs the company.

B.C. Roemer led his young company in the development of further improvements in feather fletching. This included offering to the archery community feathers that have been die-cut in a wide variety of styles, sizes and even colors. These feathers were ready to fletch as they came from the package and proved to be a big hit.

Along the way, the Wisconsin archer also patented what he called Brush Buttons. These were devices that attach to bows to deflect brush and help preserve one's archery tackle. The Brush Button, history shows, was one of the earliest commercially made bow accessories. Roemer also invented, patented and sometimes licensed other outdoor-oriented items, including one called the Pop-Up that was used in ice fishing.

Today, Trueflight Manufacturing still is based in Manitowish Waters, Wisconsin, a small town in the deep woods of the northern part of this state. However, the company has developed what amounts to a worldwide reputation as the leading supplier of quality feather fletching.

"Archers and bowhunters in Europe, Asia, Africa, Australia, South America, even on the islands of the Pacific, all use Trueflight feathers in their personal arrow fletching," declares Peter P. Roemer, who is the company's vice president in charge of engineering. When he makes this claim, his attitude is matter of fact, as if that's the way it should be. Roemer, incidentally, works closely with Bob Link, who is vice president and general manager of Trueflight.

Today, Trueflight feathers are sold in die-cut sizes that range from 2 inches to 5³/₄ inches in length. They are marketed by the Wisconsin company in shield back or round back shapes, or in their full natural length but with ground bases. Also, a wide range of colors—including the super-bright fluorescent shades—now are available.

"Trueflight feathers also are sold in what we call Trueflight Barred configuration," Peter Roemer says. As we understand it, most of the turkey feathers available today come from domestic

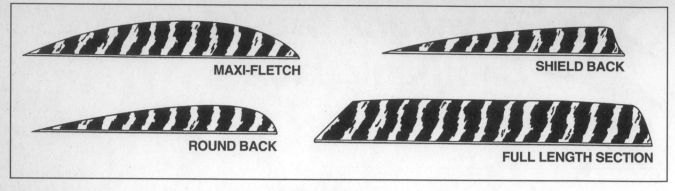

Trueflight barred shapes.

white birds. The imitation barred pattern of the wild turkey is added for what is meant to be a "traditional look."

According to Roemer, "After more than forty-five years, Trueflight feathers are more popular than ever. With the emphasis on high performance and ever higher arrow speeds due to new bow and arrow shaft designs and materials, the light weight and excellent guidance qualities of feathers are even more important today than in the past."

The question of whether feather-fletched arrows are faster in flight than shafts equipped with vanes has been bandied about on both sides for years. However, Easton Aluminum, which makes arrow shafts, conducted exhaustive tests on arrow flight early in this decade. These tests showed that arrows fletched with feathers traveled faster downrange during the first 41 feet of flight. From that distance to 61 feet—the range limit of the test range—feathers and identical plastic-fletched arrows were flying at virtually the same rate of speed.

Pete Roemer also claims that feather fletching gives your arrow better guidance.

"The surface of a feather has a slight roughness which helps 'grip' the air flow," he explains. "When the arrow yaws, this added grip helps to realign it quickly and efficiently.

"The huge weight savings with feathers also helps arrow stability. Any weight added to the rear of the arrow (like plastic vanes) makes the arrow less stable. Add too much weight to the rear and the arrow will attempt to swap ends!"

According to the engineer, "As the fletching crosses the arrow rest upon release, feathers simply fold down out of the way, then pop back up. Plastic vanes bounce the rear of the

arrow far out of alignment. This large deflection causes a substantial arrow 'swing' which is aggravated by the plastic vane's weight and lack of grip."

Roemer also insists that bow tuning is easier if the archer shoots feather-fletched arrows. "The feather's ability to fold down eliminates that large initial swing," he states. "The light weight of feathers inherently adds to the stability of the arrow. The grip of feathers adds further to clean, straight flight.

"The combination of all these advantages means that good, consistent arrow flight is built into the arrow. Because of this, the arrow will tolerate a wide range of bow variables. As a result, arrow rests, pressure buttons, release aids and even shaft spines are less critical, which means minimum required tuning."

An invariable question comes from the archer who shoots a high-tech cam bow with carbon shafts, overdraw and all the speed-up accessories he can load on his bow. Thus, being somewhat plastic-oriented, he wonders about the advantages of feather fletching with his setup.

"Feathers become even more important," Roemer insists. "High-performance setups mean more energy, higher forces and lower flight times. Thus, stability and solid guidance become even more important. Any errors or imperfections in either equipment or shooting form are magnified. Less time is available for your guidance system to do its job. Some 98 percent of the feathers we sell are used with modern archery equipment."

Pete Roemer and Bob Link have written extensively on their favorite subject—feathers. A brochure called "Feather Facts" is available at cost upon request.

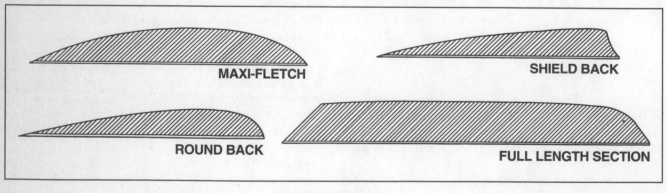

Trueflight feather fletch.

York Archery

As with any mass-production operation, York must deal with industrial air standards by having plenty of ventilation in its modern plant.

York Archery produces and markets thousands of arrows for beginners and advanced shooters.

The camouflaged and bright tournament bow limbs are silk-screened by hand at York.

THE INNOVATIVE TRADITION associated with York Archery had its beginnings in 1922 in a barn in Independence, Missouri. It was there that brothers and proprietors of Woodcraft Equipment Company, Orval and Alvin Swenson, specialized in the manufacture of fire-by-friction kits for the Boy Scouts of America. This was a successful enterprise with a continuing and relatively stable market, but the brothers operated on the theory that, in business, "to stay in one place is to move backward."

With this thought in mind, by 1927, the Swenson brothers had expanded their Woodcraft Equipment Company to include production of both finished and unfinished longbows that were made from a variety of woods, including Osage orange, lemonwood, yew and hickory.

It was not long before leather goods, finished arrows and archery accessories also were being made and marketed by the company. By 1928, the company had outgrown the old barn. It was that same year that Ken Smith, Sr., bought the expanding company and moved it to an established factory site. Thus, York Archery became a name to reckon with, and the first York Archery Tackle catalog was published in 1930.

This was the beginning of the Great Depression, and recreation dollars assuredly were in short supply. However, archery was not an expensive sport at that time and, unlike bullets, for example, arrows could be reused after being launched from the bow. The politically correct term today probably would be to list archery as a "recycling sport."

York Archery remained a division of the Woodcraft Equipment Company, and the seventy-two-year-old parent company has not stood on its laurels of success as has happened with some other firms. Instead, there has been a constant and continuing effort to stay ahead of the curve in updating production equipment and manufacturing techniques. Thus, as archery has flourished as a growing sport over the past seven-plus decades, the product base for York Archery has grown, improved and been diversified. Rodger Austin, York's director of marketing, declares, "With each introduction of our technologically advanced bows, York virtually changed the world of archery!"

That, in itself, is a pretty expansive declaration, but there is no denying that York Archery's introduction of the speed cam led to an improvement in the performance of compound bows. The theory was that this improved cam would allow bowhunters to launch their broadheaded arrows at greater speed because of the accelerated draw force curve.

Bowhunters had hardly gotten used to that idea when York engineers developed what came to be called "crossover rigging." This meant archers could place the bow string on the centerline of the riser and the limbs. This, in turn, helped to eliminate the side-to-side push of the arrow and created increased accuracy.

As another first in the manufacturing end of the archery industry, York created the first bow featuring a machined riser. That was in 1987, when the company invested in computer numerical control equipment (CNC) to machine the aluminum bar stock. For those not familiar with the technique, the CNC process computer-generates a precision-machined riser that is solid, exact and has no variations or compromise in its design. The resulting aluminum riser is both light in weight and superior in strength to wood.

Another York-pioneered innovation has been the STO. That acronym translates to "shoot-through-overdraw" and is a revolutionary concept that enables either the bowhunter or target archer to shoot their arrows through the center of the bow for what is purported to be better accuracy.

The latest from York's think tank and production facilities is the Wind Hawk family of bows. This concept was introduced in 1994 and, according to Rodger Austin, "was designed for the accuracy that is demanded by today's archers."

The Wind Hawk bow features a built-in overdraw on a riser of machined 6061-T6 aluminum. The bow also features York's Precision Adjust Tri-Draw wheels and the Precision Tune yoke system—concepts that were developed by the company's engineers.

Now, more than seventy years down the stream of time from the Missouri barn, Woodcraft Equipment and York Archery are part of The Sierra Corporation, a ninety-year-old conglomerate that makes and markets a wide range of products. In a corporate centralization move, operations of York have been transferred to Fort Smith, Arkansas, headquarters of the parent company.

"York is no longer a small family company," explains Rodger Austin. "Today, we comprise a team made up of seasoned engineers, bowhunters and craftsmen, and it is this team that is responsible for the innovative concepts we are taking to the marketplace. York's business is to provide the archer with the technology and equipment that helps him—or her—succeed."

Under the latest ownership, York is getting into some promotional ideas that had not been tried previously by this company. For example, a Hunting On The Wild Side adventure contest has been introduced for 1995. The winner will be awarded a guided combination elk/mule deer bowhunt in New Mexico. The lucky bowhunter also will have delivered to him a head mount of the trophy taken on the hunt. Second prize will be a custom-made Wind Hawk Hunter bow, plus a head mount of a 1995 harvested trophy. Other prizes also will be offered. If successful as a promotion, this could become an annual event.

York Gold is still another new program aimed at making the manufacturer's name more familiar among archers. This particular effort provides York the opportunity to help local tournaments provide prize money to tournament shooters. By registering the tournament as a York Gold event, tournament shooters can qualify for prize money. Bonus money also is available for the division with the most shooters and the highest scores. This concept would seem to be in keeping with York's contention that it makes "the bows that take the trophies."

"We see continued growth and enthusiasm in bowhunting and target archery," says Rodger Austin. "We are planning on continuing our leadership in the industry by growing and improving into the next seventy years!"

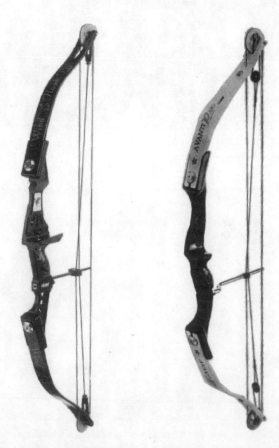

The York Wind Hawk Pro Signature Edition is a modern, machined-riser bow with the latest innovations favored by many archers.

The York Avanti Pro Competition bow is clearly a high-tech bow for competitive target shooters.

15

Make Your Own Bow

Basic Construction From A Commercial Kit Can Become A Labor of Love As Well As Frustration

SOONER OR LATER, most of us have to try making our own bow from the basic components. We can buy any of countless excellent bows that are on the market, so why go to the trouble of making one and shouldering all the problems involved? This is somewhat comparable to the challenge of climbing a mountain because it is there.

First, you must determine whether you want a single-unit recurve, a three-piece takedown recurve or a much-simpler-to-make longbow. Kits are easier to assemble, and there is less chance of problems when finishing the bow. You can find a basic bow-building kit advertised in any of the archery magazines. Several companies offer a bow kit with the basic components. A few companies offer a bow already made-up and ready to be finished by sanding and follow-up operations. You do have a choice.

The longbow selected for this project is a 50-pound draw weight bow that, when finished, most of us can pull without getting a hernia. There are those who believe you need a 100-pound longbow, but few of us can realistically draw and shoot those monster weights. Buy a kit bow with a draw weight you comfortably can control.

When the kit boxes arrive, you probably will receive the long laminates in one skinny, long package and all the other components, including illustrated instructions, in a smaller box. You should first go through the list of components to be certain you have all the required parts. There should be two-solution epoxy, a wide section of wood for the riser and two or more instruction sheets. One sheet will be for construction of the bow; the other for the hot box needed for correctly curing the epoxy so your bow will not come apart.

The long container may have two strips of black Bo-Tuf for the fiberglass face and back, several long sheets of thin hard-rock maple for the inner core and the templates needed for assembly. They also might include some strips of metal for maintaining constant pressure on the laminates while curing. All of this is explained in the instructions, so identify the various items, then lay them aside.

The thickness of the fiberglass facing and backing is something over which you have no control. If the kit maker has

Items supplied in the kit should include the riser material, two large blocks of hardwood, the laminates and the epoxy.

The riser in approximate position with laminate in the middle and glass and hardwood sections top and bottom. The makeup will be different, but this gives you an idea what it will look like.

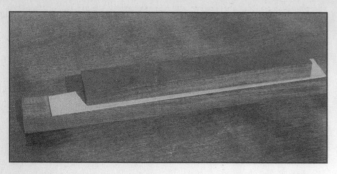

The first job of the kit is to laminate the two riser sections with the white spacer in the middle. These are covered with epoxy, clamped, cured, then sanded to shape.

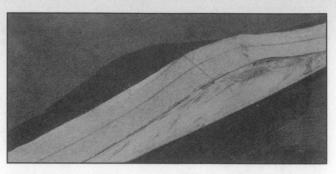

The kit bow as it appears when cleaned up after curing. The sides are usually covered with excess epoxy, but here have been cleaned up. The masking tape on top of the belly is marked for cutting, and the midline has been marked to give reference points for other layouts in the job.

shipped the correct thickness of each, you probably will be within a few pounds of hitting the draw weight you prefer. If they ship the wrong laminates, you won't know it until you have finished the bow and attempt to draw it. However, those who produce these kits are bowyers who know the correct items, thickness and other materials. They seldom make mistakes.

Before starting, you must make a curing box. This is simple enough, but will take some time. Actual size of the box will depend on the length of bow being made. For a three-piece takedown bow, you need a short box; to make the longbow, you need one at least 7 feet in length, and tall and wide enough to hold the completed bow for curing. The instructions will cover length, width, height and so forth.

The end product will house a pressure block 2 by 8 inches by almost 7 feet. The heat is produced by wiring four electric light sockets in series to provide constant temperature for at least four hours at 180 degrees Fahrenheit. It would not hurt to give it a trial run to see how hot it gets and how well it holds temperature. This can be regulated by changing to lower-wattage bulbs if it is too hot, hooking up a rheostat to the system for total control or something similar.

With the box done, you are ready to go to work on the bow. You need a belt sander for working on the riser section. It helps to have access to a good band saw to cut the long section on the limb. The fiberglass face and back will be hard on your saw blade. This is tough, mean stuff, so if you have an old blade or two, use them, since they will be shot when you finish cutting the fiberglass.

Place your laminates on a long work table in the order in which you will put them together. One piece of fiberglass goes shiny side down on the table; this will be the back of the bow. Next are two sheets of wood laminate for strength. The riser, still not shaped, is added to the stack. One sheet of wood laminate goes on, and finally the other sheet of fiberglass with shiny side up—this will be the belly of the bow. About all you can do at this point is to ensure that all parts are there in good condition.

The first gluing will be on the riser section. Before doing any gluing in this project, it helps keep the mess under control by laying out some waxed paper or similar household material. Plastic wraps sold at most supermarkets are good for this.

Mix a batch of the two-solution epoxy supplied and cover the upper side of the longer block. Place the wood laminate on top

of this, working it around to ensure all parts are covered. Spread epoxy on the top of this laminate, then apply the shorter block. With large C-clamps, tightly hold this section together and set it aside to cure.

When the handle is cured, you are ready for your first woodworking. Check the blueprint or instruction pattern and you should find a template for shaping the riser. Usually a flat top and bottom shape are formed now. Trace the pattern on the wood or, if you plan to make only one bow, cut and paste it directly on the riser wood.

Using a coarse, fast-cutting paper on the sanding belt, follow the pattern until you get close to the lines. Switch to a finer grit to make the last cuts; you want it rough enough for the glue to adhere, but not so coarse that you can't effect a smooth blending of glue to wood.

When you reach the outer edges of the riser, sand out to a fine, feather edge that will allow the laminates to be added later. A smooth transition is needed at the edge of the riser with no bumps or ridges. Take it easy and do it right.

With the riser shaped, you are ready to apply the laminates to create the rough shape of a longbow. Mix more two-solution epoxy in a batch big enough to do the entire laminating process; this is a one-time situation. Position wax paper on the table, then the black fiberglass—shiny side down—on the paper. Spread epoxy liberally on the back side of the glass, which has a rough texture. Make certain all parts of the glass are covered so you won't have the bad laminates termed dry spots, which allow a bow to blow up. This happens if the epoxy is spread too thin on the laminates.

Position the first wood laminate on the glued glass. Some home craftsmen use a disposable roller to roll the two sections, getting them as tightly together as possible at this beginning point. Place more epoxy on top of the wood and position another wood section on it. Press or roll for adhesion.

At the center section, position the riser with the long side on top of the wood laminate, the shorter handle side up. Press this down, and you now have one piece of glass, two wood laminates and epoxy under the riser.

Spread epoxy on the top of the riser—the laminates still have epoxy spread on them—and check the marking on the table to center the riser where it belongs. Place the last wood strip on top, starting on one end, forming it over the top of the riser and down the opposite side, smoothing it to the far tip.

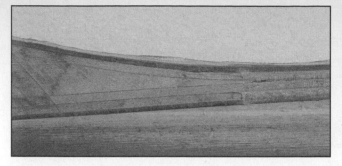

The riser section feathers into the multilaminates of the limbs as is shown here. You want a clean, smooth flow to the riser so no ridges appear on the feathering section. The rough edges are from bandsawing.

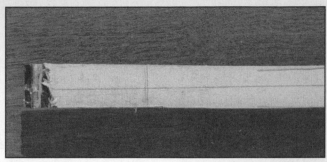

The limb tips are still round. The raw edges are shown as they came from the curing oven, but will be cut and shaped later. The crossline shown is the point you will cut your limb tip nocks for the bowstring.

The riser has a fine, feathered tip on each end, so the laminate will fit with hardly any seam showing if you did it right. This part is touchy, since the wood actually must bend over the riser at this point.

When satisfied with the setup, spread epoxy on the rough side of the last fiberglass section and lay it in place. This will complete the laminating process. It takes longer to describe than actually do, but at this point you will understand why

Using a 1/8-inch rat-tail file, you cut the nocks into the limb tip on both sides at least as deep as the bowstring shown in place here.

This tillering tube is a plastic pipe rather than a board, but works just as well. You sight down the string to see if the limb has any twist in it. The string is your center line, and as you see, there is no twist in the limb.

you need the wax paper on the table. There will be a lot of excess epoxy squeezed out, and the paper will catch all the run-off.

You now have what looks like a no-handle longbow. It is long, it has a bow shape, but the riser still is just a lump of wood in the midsection.

You might have a kit that allows you to make the wood laminate on the belly of the bow above the riser in two pieces. One piece comes from the one end to the feathered riser, sweeps up and ends just above the flat top section. The other end does the same with no laminates on the belly of the riser. This is another variation that also works well.

Another item you should have made prior to the lay-up procedure is the form or press unit. One uses a large block that has pegs or nails protruding from the sides about 3 inches down from the top. It's simple to make by cutting a 2x8-foot piece of soft wood, then marking off and putting in the pegs or large nails.

The form is used to put pressure on the laminated bow, allowing it to cure properly, not retaining any air gaps during the curing process. To accomplish this, place a section of plastic wrap material on the form, then place the epoxy-covered laminated mess we are calling a bow on top of the plastic. Place more plastic on top of the bow and you are ready to apply the pressure.

With this system, use rubber bands or something similar for the pressure. If you can find an old inner tube, cut equal-width bands to place on the form and thus generate lots of pressure. If you can't find an inner tube, use surgical tubing, but use several short lengths on the pegs. If you use one piece and it breaks, you will have lost all your pressure.

The limb tip has been shaped and sanded almost to final shape. Be certain to not sand too much and change the depth of the string nock. It helps if you leave the bow braced.

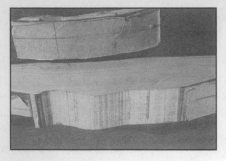

The handle grip area and the sight window have been rough cut to give location.

The sight window/shelf area shows the rough cut from the band saw. It is best to cut the shelf with a straight, flat cut, then shape it later.

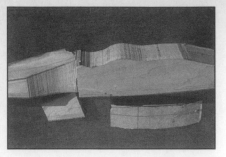

The rough cut window and shelf will need further work.

Place the bands on one side, pull up, cross over the bow and down the other side to the opposite pegs. You can go directly across or use a diagonal system. When you have banded one side, go back and cross over those bands, and you will have a series of X bands crossing over the top of the bow. This puts needed pressure on the bow while it cures.

Wipe up some of the excess epoxy that will ooze from the bow on top of the form and place the form in the hot box. After a final check, close the lid and turn on the lights to create the heat needed for proper curing. Check the time in your instructions; it should be around four hours at the 180-degree temperature. This is one phase you shouldn't rush. If it goes a bit over that time, it won't hurt, but if you pull it too soon, you may not have allowed the epoxy to cure properly.

After the bow has cured in the form, remove it from the box. Take off all the rubber bands and remove the bow from the form. If you want to save the form, you can clean it up later. Use a hand rasp or a sanding belt system to clean up the edges. Don't cut into the bow edges, just remove the epoxy.

Using the template supplied with the instructions, trace the upper and lower limb shape onto the bow. This usually is done on the back of the bow—the side without the riser bump—since it is flat and will work easier.

A section of masking tape running down the full length of the bow back makes a good pattern tracer. Trace your pattern on the bow, using a ball point pen so as not to cut the pattern. This will leave a tracing on the masking tape. When you remove the pattern, you can darken the tracing with a pencil. Go slowly, since this is the heart of your bow system.

You are now ready to start cutting or sanding the bow to final shape. If you don't have a band saw, you can use a sanding drum to fit the shape to the pattern. This creates a lot of wood dust, so keep this in mind when you choose a place for the sanding and cutting.

Common sense and patience can prevent accidents. When you start sanding and cutting hardwood and fiberglass, you should take a few precautions. It helps to wear an apron, eye protection and face mask. Sawdust is a problem, but you now are grinding and cutting fiberglass. This is mean stuff. The dust, combined with the hardwood, can cause a very uncomfortable rash that is hard to get rid of. You also might consider wearing old clothes for this last phase, then throwing them away. Should you wash these clothes with other clothing, this could spread these fine fiberglass particles into everything in the wash.

In addition to the other safety items, a pair of leather gloves can prevent fiber slivers from getting into your hands while sanding and shaping. These slivers are extremely fine, tough and sharp. If lucky, you can remove the filament with tweezers, but the strands usually break, and you either must dig them out or wait for them to work themselves out of your hide. Wear gloves!

Shaping is the first phase. All you want to do is make the limb shapes and basic shape of the riser. A bandsaw works best for this; final shaping comes later. Take your time and follow the outside edge of the pattern on the limbs and riser. If you want to modify your riser for a grip section, you can.

Try not to cut through the fiberglass on the back of the bow. You need this for strength, depending upon desired draw weight. You will probably follow the pattern on the limbs, but may vary it for the riser as you sand to fit your hand.

When the rough shaping is done, you're ready to move to final shaping and sanding. The first phase is to round off the edges of the limbs to remove any fiber splinters on those sharp edges. Sand from the riser down to the tip. Move the sandpaper or fine rasp from the handle downward. Work from the inner section, sanding outward. This will round off and clean up the edges without picking up the strands of fiberglass you would have if you had started from the bottom. If a fiber does come up, don't try to remove it by pulling. This could result in the fiber pulling the full length of the edge or moving into another area of the limb, creating a bad problem. The simplest method is to sand down toward it from above. It should fall right off.

When you have the rough edges removed, it might not be a bad idea to fold a piece of 120-grit sandpaper around the edge of the limb and sand moving from riser to tip. This will afford a finer finish to the edges, remove any glass fibers and roughen the shiny glass on the bow limbs. As you sand, also use this grit to roughen up the surface, so the finish will adhere to the fiberglass.

You now can shape the sight section, window and arrow shelf on the riser. Check the template, mark the bow and cut the shelf. This shouldn't be full centershot, since most traditional shooting groups want it farther out from center—$1/8$-inch at least. These can be cut with the bandsaw, following the pattern. There isn't much of a sight window. You can make it any way you prefer, but don't cut too deeply or the riser will break when braced.

Some of the small tools needed include a flat sandpaper block (left), flat/half-round rasp (middle), rat-tail file, long ruler and a caliper.

The bow is almost finished at this point. The sanding is completed; the shaping is done; and the nocks and tips cleaned up. Now for the spray finish.

Shape the handle by taking time—and sandpaper—to transform the square-edged riser to a rounded broomhandle-type or a more modern-shaped grip area. Remember, the closer the hand is to the arrow on the shelf, the better it will be for instinctive shooting. It's your bow, but these are points to consider. Rasp and sand until the handle fits the way you want it. Clean up the cut marks on the window and shelf, and you are ready to cut the bow tip nocks.

Some bow-building kits come with endless strings for the bow; while others use a Flemish or hand-laid string. It really doesn't matter, but the tip nocks should be cut as marked on the pattern. This is about 1 inch in from the bow end. There usually is a mark on the pattern for cutting the nocks. Use a 1/8-inch rat-tail rasp and cut in the depth of the rasp—1/8-inch. This is done on both sides of the limb, on both ends.

Check your bowstring for any problems. Your nock ends are still rough and the edges sharp, so if you have a string the right length, you might want to use it for the next phase and save the string supplied for shooting. Place the loop on the lower limb, making certain the string is deep in the nock, then pull the string tight. Now you can brace the bow by bending it, using a string bracer unit.

Do not try to push-pull brace at this point. This is a highly dangerous practice and shouldn't be used. If you try the old behind-the-leg, over-the-foot method of bracing, you could twist a limb before you get the bow finished. Using a tip-to-tip stringer works well, as do a number of safe stringing methods. Keep the back of the bow facing away from you. Thus, if anything lets loose, it will work away from you, not into you.

Hold the bow in the riser section, and face the limb with the back held away from you to check that the nocks are set right. All nock cuts should engage with the string loop fully. Now you can pull the bow for the first time and see how it feels. This is a moment of pure joy!

There are some things to check and possibly remedy before the final finish is applied. First, check the tiller. (This is a term used to describe the comparison between the bend of the upper limb and the bend of the lower limb.)

Place a ruler on the belly of the bow where the feathering of the riser fades into the laminates. Let's say it measures 7 3/4 inches on the lower limb. Set the ruler on the same position of the upper limb. It measures 8 inches. Does this mean it is out of tiller? No, that is normal, since most laminated bows are made to shoot with fingers, and the lower limb is made stiffer to allow for the two-finger hold under the arrow to draw.

Pressing an 18-inch piece of wood or pipe on the riser, draw the string and place it on the top of the pipe to check for limb twist. Look down the bow from the tip to the middle. If the limb twists, you will see it right away. If it twists right, mark that side, remove the tiller stick—or tube—and take the string off the bow. Cut the string nock a bit deeper on the side that is twisted. Restring the bow, place the tiller stick back in place and check it again.

This can be a deadly game. If you take too much off one side, you'll find it twists worse now the other way. Then you remove some from that side and...you get the picture. Remove just a touch of wood from the string nock at a time. It is better to keep bracing the bow rather than getting into that deadly see-saw problem.

Fortunately, this bow had no tiller problem when checked, and there were no twists in the limb. We must have done something right!

If the bow checks out, it is ready for final finishing. The string is removed and set aside. Final sanding can be done using 120-grit on the riser and limbs. You now should taper and shape the limb tips. A few passes with the sandpaper and things really start looking good. When you pronounce it done, you're ready to put on the spray finish.

Polyurethane sprays work well. If you plan to use several coats of finish, allow enough time for each layer to dry properly before spraying again.

This treatment will provide a clear, shiny finish on your bow. If you want it less shiny, rough it up with some fine steel wool. If you plan for this to be a hunter, you can spray it flat black— always a good choice—and you can add camo blotches at any time.

All that is left after the finish dries is the side plate for the arrow shelf and window. You can make it from one folded piece of soft leather like deerskin, some hair-on calfskin or some similar material to keep your arrow quiet on the bow when you draw and release the arrow.

The bow is now finished. If you know someone who has a chronograph, you could clock your arrow speed. If you find your grip on the riser isn't quite right, you could take some sandpaper and achieve the fit you want. After all, what's a riser change but a few seconds of sanding and retouching to get what you really want.

16 *Tree Stands*

Tree Stands Can Improve Hunting Scores, But Safety Must Be The Prime Consideration For The Hunter

TREE STAND USE by bowhunters has increased dramatically in the past couple of decades. So has the success ratio, especially for those hunting whitetail deer in the Midwest, Southeast and Northeast. In the West, where tree stand use has shown a steady increase for hunting mule deer, antelope, elk and bear everywhere, the most common usage is by those seeking to fill a whitetail deer tag.

Bowhunters learned long ago that deer, in general, seldom look upward for danger. Furthermore, the human scent so alarming to deer tends to dissipate into the air above the deer's noses when the hunter is 10, 12 or more feet up a tree. Consideration and understanding of both factors has put a lot of bowhunters up trees.

Technical improvements in materials, manufacturing methods and designs have increased the availability and lowered the price of tree stands to the point that many bowhunters employ two, three, even up to a dozen tree stands, rather than one stand for one season. The typical pickup truck seen traveling the rural roads of the South no longer has a rifle or shotgun hung in the rear window, but rather a bow or two. Several tree stands ride in the truck bed before and after deer season.

It all began as bowhunters, in an effort to ambush a deer, climbed handy trees to sit on a big pre-selected branch. Trees difficult to scale soon had spikes or large bolt steps projecting from their trunks or wooden ladder rungs nailed to them. In many locations, this was illegal and nailed-on steps never were safe.

Elaborate wooden tree stands with stairs leading to a platform are still found on private hunting leases or property, especially where rifles and shotguns are in season. However, after a couple of rough winters, wood rots and nails rust, making constant maintenance a necessity. In addition, platforms and stands are too visible and hold too much human scent to be of much help to bowhunters.

The simplest stand was and is a board that might be wedged in the crotch of a tree. In time, notches were cut on each end of the board, enabling the seat to be wedged tighter and with less tendency to rock or move when a hunter stood on it. These simple stands are still used in some locations

There are those bowhunters who believe the most important contribution to successful deer hunting, after the compound bow, is the use of tree stands. The stick ladder is lightweight and can get the hunter plenty high.

where conditions are right. They are light in weight, simple and cheap to make and, if lost or stolen, do not constitute a great loss.

Some crotch stands have become a bit more sophisticated, being constructed of lightweight metal with locking straps to keep them in position. They are the easiest of any to carry into the woods, and putting up several in potentially productive trees can be done in a day. Their only drawback is the required tree with a crotch in the right location and at the correct height.

Today's tree stands are made of steel, aluminum and/or plastic. Only non-bearing parts are plastic, however, as manufacturers learned some time ago that even the strongest hard plastics will split and crack under stress with disastrous results. The best tree stands are lightweight, strong, compact and safe when used in accordance with the maker's instructions.

There are several safety rules every bowhunter should always follow, no matter how experienced, how high or near to the ground the stand is, or what type of stand it may be. The first rule concerns wearing a safety belt at all times. There are any number of horror stories about hunters who have slipped while climbing a tree or when moving around on the stand, falling to their deaths or suffering serious, crippling injuries. Any stand or tree step can be slippery when wet or frost-covered, especially if the hunter is wearing rubber-soled boots. Tree limbs, when ice-coated, frosted or wet, can cause a slip or break under a human's weight, sending the safety-beltless hunter to the ground, injuries almost guaranteed. After several hours in the stand, along about mid-morning, thousands of bowhunters have experienced drowsiness or have even gone to sleep. Without a safety belt, an archer can tumble to the ground below, perhaps with an arrow nocked on the string.

The second safety rule every bowhunter will want to follow is to never climb up or down a ladder or tree while carrying bow and arrows in the hands. The accepted method is to tie a light rope or line to the bow and quiver, climb up into the stand, make sure the safety belt is on correctly, then haul the equipment up to the stand. Use the same method in reverse when climbing down from the tree stand. Several equipment makers offer a lightweight haul line and reel device that clips on the belt or fits in a small pack, ideal for the purpose.

The ideal height for a tree stand is a subject of debate among bowhunters. Personal preference also plays a role. There are those who say the higher, the better. Get up at least 25 feet and all human scent will dissipate far above any deer's nose. Others believe climbing above 15 or 20 is self-defeating. At that higher angle, the animal's exposed vital area is reduced and a lethal shot is more difficult to make. Unless the tree is on a steep hillside, they say, climb no higher than 12 to 15 feet. Not every hunter is comfortable high up in a swaying tree; others are fearless. Each individual must make his or her own decision about the height of the stand.

There are dozens of tree stand manufacturers and hundreds of different stand models from which to choose. Some are more expensive than others, but the hunter should not let a low initial cost be the influencing factor. Safety and comfort are more important. Types include climbers, portables, ladder stands and various combinations of these. Each fits a specific need, and an active bowhunter might use one or more of each type, depending on the situation and terrain.

A **climbing stand** is usually lightweight and portable. Most have backpack-type shoulder straps to help carry the stand far into the woods and to make it easier to change trees quickly should the need arise. There are several types available, but generally speaking, a climbing stand uses the hunter's arms and legs to lever the stand up the tree, little by little. One type has foot straps on the top of the stand and some sort of metal angle iron with teeth that grip the tree trunk. A separate hand or arm device allows the hunter to hang onto the tree as the feet raise the stand base up several inches. Then the base, with its metal teeth, is levered up, then down onto the tree trunk as the arm device is moved up to a comfortable height. This is repeated until the chosen elevation is reached. On some climbing stands, the arm component becomes the stand seat after it is locked in place.

Other models rely more on the climber's leg strength to climb the tree. Called climb-up, set-down stands, the upper seat portion is locked onto the trunk, the lower part is raised by the foot straps, and the hunter stands up, carrying the upper portion along. Then he or she sits down on the upper part and repeats the operation. Most of us have stronger legs and lower bodies than arms and upper bodies, and these stands are popular for those who like to climb higher.

Safety must not be forgotten during climbing. As weight is placed on the arm or hand assisting mechanism, the climber must make certain it is locked securely in place on the tree trunk before beginning to lift the foot platform.

The archer should not attempt to take too large a "step" up the tree in an effort to move fast. Taking smaller increments will be safer and quieter. Move at a pace that is not too tiring or stressful. Once the archer's weight is on the hands and arms, the foot platform may be lifted, heel first, from the tree and upward as far as the knees can be bent. Then, the angled teeth of the climbing platform are placed firmly against the tree trunk as the heels are lowered to keep the teeth biting the trunk. The platform must be level as weight is gradually applied by the feet. A little practice will tell the climber when the platform teeth are correctly biting into the trunk and it is safe to stand on the platform.

If the chosen tree is too small, not enough of the teeth will reach the trunk to be safe. Furthermore, too small a tree will tend to sway too much for comfort when the wind blows. A tree that is too large also will prevent enough of the angled teeth from biting into the trunk and the platform may slip, especially early in the climb.

The **portable climbing tree stand** is ideal for the hunter who is fully familiar with his hunting area and may change tree locations two or three times a day.

Changing wind directions, weather conditions and domestic agricultural practices may dictate moving stand locations sooner than planned when the hunt was begun. Or other hunters may stray into the area and spook the deer. Most bowhunters feel there is nothing to be gained by staying in a non-productive location after the deer have been frightened

Some portable stands are small, but the API Grandstand II is large enough to steady the nerves of the hunter who has reservations about being up too high. The stand folds flat and weighs 14 pounds.

The Alum-I-Lok Magnum is a fixed-position stand that weighs 10 pounds, is made of all-aluminum, welded construction. The folding seat is cushioned for comfort on long hunts.

Another lightweight approach to climbing high into trees is the Stackin' Stik by API. Other manufacturers have similar products. Sections of the single pole ladder are added as the archer climbs higher.

away by changing conditions. The answer is to bring the stand down, scout another location and put it up in another tree. With practice, this operation can be accomplished in fifteen minutes or less.

Another aspect to consider is the number and placement of branches on the tree. If the selected tree is scouted early enough in the pre-season, several branches may be pruned or sawed off without disturbing game during the hunt. The rut is no time to be sawing away on large tree branches. Try for a tree void of lower limbs, 12 to 30 inches in diameter and with room enough to climb up at least 8 to 10 feet, depending on the weather and terrain.

Any tree stand will be useless in mountains above the treeline and in several parts of the Southwest that have no suitable trees. There, other techniques must be studied by the successful bowhunter.

The **ladder stand** is a popular portable where nails or screws in trees are prohibited, or for those bowhunters not able to use the climbing stand.

Ladder stands are practical where the hunting area and selected trees are within easy distance from a road or trail. However, most ladder stands are too heavy and bulky to be carried by the average backpacking bowhunter. The larger models may weigh from 20 to 30 pounds. Although most have backpack straps, the extra weight becomes excessive after too many miles or on steep and rocky terrain. But the ladder can reach up to 10, 12 or 14 feet, and climbing one is far easier for an older bowhunter. It also works where suitable climbing trees are unavailable.

Most ladder stands have large, comfortable platforms on which to stand and move around; many have built-in folding seats. Some models feature 6- or 8-foot extensions for those who want to get higher. They may be rather heavy and ungainly, but their construction beats wooden ladders and steps for safety and portability.

Ladder stands are difficult to hide or lock to a tree with chains and are subject to theft on public land. For the most part, they should not be left unattended in public access areas, but they are ideal on private, patrolled lands with limited access.

A couple of variations to the ladder stand include the climbing ladder, made of tubular steel or aluminum, and what has become to be known as the **climbing stick**. Both of these devices are used to climb high without the use of screw-in steps or spikes for those areas that prohibit anything that may injure a tree. Another situation ideal for the lightweight climbing ladder is a section of private forest where several stands might be left in place throughout the hunting season. If the stands can be placed at about the same height, a single portable ladder or climbing stick will enable the hunter to climb the tree most likely to fill his game tag. If unauthorized persons have access to the property, the lack of spikes or steps might deter them to some extent.

Climbing sticks are a relatively new development for tree stand hunters. These sticks are a folding or accordian-like center pole or rod with steps protruding out each side. Typically, they are lighter in weight than a ladder and, when folded, are compact enough to be carried easily far into the woods without undue strain.

Straps keep the folded stick compact while it is transported. When a likely tree is encountered, the straps are removed and the climbing stick extended at the base of the tree. The bottom is placed against the tree, and the stick is levered up against the tree trunk. The lower step may be raised to a height that can be comfortably reached by the hunter, and the device is secured to the tree by straps, ropes or safety chains. At least one such climber, Loc-On, has a levering device on the top to lock the stick to a tree while the hunter is still on the ground. With care, the hunter will fasten two or three safety straps on the climber at the bottom, middle and top of the ladder. Climbing sticks hug the tree and provide a firm, safe-feeling method for getting to the stand above.

Tree steps are another portable alternative. Realizing that screwed-in bolts or pounded-in large nails are not always safe or strong enough, several manufacturers have come up with tree steps. These may be bolted to a tree temporarily to let the hunter gain the height needed to place a stand. On some models, the non-slip step folds up against the tree when not in use. Others are shaped like the letter "Z," with the top part being the threaded screw and the lower portion of the step a crank to turn the screw into the tree trunk. Some of these have folding step options, also.

For areas where any type of tree penetration is prohibited, strap-on steps are available. Instead of a bolt hole in the L-shaped step, a slot accepts a nylon strap long enough to fit around medium-sized trees without causing any damage. The strap-ons are removed easily as the hunter climbs down from the stand, which protects it somewhat from theft.

The third type of tree stand commonly used by bowhunters is the **portable stand** that locks onto the trunk with ropes, straps or chains. Some stands utilize a pin mount to hold them to the tree. A vertical pin may be bolted or strapped to the tree trunk and the stand slipped over the pin to mount it. Extra straps or chains lock it in place. This type has the advantage of affording quick changes of location, as conditions dictate, if extra pin mounts are in place on other stand trees. The portable stand is lighter in weight, as it does not have the hardware a climbing stand must have. It may or may not have an attached or auxiliary seat with it. Most models have backpack straps to make transport easier, and they may be made of steel or aluminum, coated with non-reflective camouflage paint. The top side of the stand should have a non-slip surface of metal or carpeting material.

Safety and strength are of vital importance to tree stand hunters. Each weld or bolted joint must be flawless and treated to prevent corrosion. Every piece of hardware, bolt, screw, washer, turnbolt and strap must be examined before each use. Nothing must be loose or weak from rust or corrosion. Aluminum will not rust, of course, but welds can crack and weaken the stand. A stand never should be used if it is not as good as new. The bowhunter must not take unnecessary chances on faulty equipment.

When considering the purchase of a new tree stand, the hunter first should consider the type of stand best suited to the habitat to be hunted. Then a decision must be made as to type of construction and materials used. There are a few tree stand manufacturers that have been in business for twenty or more years. New firms start up every year, but some do not survive for more than a couple of seasons. One of the greatest threats to any tree stand manufacturer is the possibility of an injury liability law suit. A number of tree stand companies have been sued out of existence by persons injured while using their products.

Bowhunters should realize there are two types of safety belts useful when hanging or moving tree stands. A safety harness, similar to the type used by utility pole climbers, is useful when putting up or taking down a stand. The harness is designed to be used while the hunter is facing the tree. It is easy to move up or down the tree as necessary. It can leave both hands free to handle the tree stand or to attach climbing steps on the way up. They may not be safe to use while facing away from the tree when in the stand.

After the stand is in place and equipment hauled up, the bowhunter should be wearing a hunting safety belt that allows more movement when one is sitting or standing on the platform. The hunting belt usually has some sort of sliding loop or ring on the waist portion so the hunter can turn at least 300 degrees with his back to the tree. The rest of the belt leads from the ring and around the tree. It should be adjustable for waist size and for girth of the tree trunk, yet be able to hold the hunter in a safe position should he slip or fall off the platform. The amount of slack is adjustable to meet the needs of the hunter.

The belt should be worn at all times while in the stand and when climbing up or down the tree. Every year, hunters are seriously injured or killed because they were not wearing safety belts. Safety must not be taken for granted. A fall from even a few feet can be lethal.

A well-made tree stand will have some sort of non-slip surface added to its steps and platforms as added safety measures. The upper surfaces of the steps may have sandpaper-like patches glued on. These should be carefully examined to make sure they will not peel off with the first rain or after a few climbs. The platform may be open grill work with protrusions to grip boots. However, when wet or frosty, the metal may become quite slippery. Many bowhunters will want to cement a piece of old indoor/outdoor carpeting on the platform. This inexpensive carpeting can be replaced when it wears out.

None of these safety features, including the belts, should be relied upon completely while the hunter is up a tree. Anything mechanical is subject to failure at any time. A tree stand is a dangerous place, no matter how experienced the hunter is nor what quality the equipment may be. Common sense is the best safety device yet invented.

Some things, such as electronic gadgets, continue to come down in price every year. Tree stands are improved from year to year and constitute better bargains all the time. Generally, a satisfactory tree stand may be purchased from about $80 to as much as $350, depending upon the extras and options. Tree stands also are built for the firearms hunter, but these are usually much heavier and more bulky than those designed for bowhunters. A gun stand may have railings and rifle rests in front and on the sides that would interfere with a bowhunter standing, drawing and shooting arrows. All sorts of additions are possible, including soft carpeting on the platform, extra padding for the seat, hangers for the bow and arrows, umbrellas and foot warmers. Each small item, however, adds weight to the stand, and most bowhunters will disdain too many amenities. Becoming too comfortable may lull one to sleep on the stand.

The buyer should talk to other hunters and outfitters, then visit several shops and read all the catalogs before deciding on which tree stand or stands to buy. Do not let the decision be based on a low price alone, but get the stand that will best serve the time and place to be hunted.

17 *Camo Clothing*

Modern Camouflage Dates From WWII—Today, There Are Dozens Of Colors And Patterns To Hide Behind

MODERN CAMOUFLAGE CLOTHING dates back to post-WWII military surplus clothing sold in outlets all over the country. As early as the '50s, some bowhunters were using the so-called woodland pattern camouflage, but the concept of complete camo for better hunting did not catch on until about twenty years later.

The early pioneers of modern bowhunting—Saxton Pope, Arthur Young, Fred Bear, Howard Hill and many others who followed close behind—did not wear camouflage, camo paint or face nets. Most settled for dull plaid or tan or green wool shirts to help them blend with the background.

All successful bowhunters know what those early modern bowhunters learned: There is no substitute for being completely motionless while on stand. Movement, when necessary, must be slow, unobtrusive and hidden from the game whenever possible. The best camouflage in the world will not hide a hunter's unnecessary movements. And just as important is camouflaging the hunter's human scent.

Many bowhunters today dismiss the importance of camouflage clothing, still managing to fill their game tags each season. However, most others realize they need all the help they can get when stalking a mule deer in the mountains of the West or waiting patiently in a Pennsylvania tree stand. They choose and wear appropriate camouflage.

Thousands of years ago, early hunters might have used animal skins, grass, shrubs, mud, leaves or anything else at hand in an attempt to get within arrow range of game animals. Camouflage uniforms were developed during World War II, their colors and patterns evolving throughout the Korean and Vietnam wars, continuing on through Desert Storm, when the predominantly brown desert camo was seen on television every night. Your local Army-Navy surplus outlet probably has examples of these and others from around the world.

Military pattern camo has its uses on the battlefield and serves a different purpose than that for the hunter. The pattern and colors must be universal for the general environment where the fighting takes place, be it jungles, hills, mountains, deserts or urban warfare. Most combat infantrymen do a lot of moving

The All-Season All-Terrain (ASAT) camouflage pattern features shades of brown, black and tan in contrasting colors. Full sets of hunting clothing in all-cotton are available.

and shooting. They hope to spot their enemy before he spots them.

The U.S. Army Natick Research, Development and Engineering Center at Natick, Massachusetts, has been developing a new camouflage fabric called reversible textile camouflage. It should allow troops to carry a single uniform that incorporates appropriate modern surveillance countermeasures for both desert and woodland environments. That would negate the need to carry or issue two different camo uniforms to the troops.

Multiple colors are printed on two sides of the new fabric, resulting in a reversible camouflage garment. Using two printing techniques, one side of standard military uniform cloth is printed with the woodland camo pattern, the reverse side with the three-color desert camo pattern.

Developers say the new techniques and fabrics will eventually be available to the civilian market, particularly to hunters. The reversible clothing might satisfy the needs of those bowhunters who hunt in a green environment in the fall and spring and in mostly brown habitat at other times. At this writing, the concept is still in the development stages and is not available to the general public. However, there are an almost unlimited selection of colors, fabrics and patterns for today's bowhunter that meet the requirements of almost any location, weather, terrain, season or altitude, no matter what the game. Camouflage clothing manufacturers introduce new colors, fabrics and patterns every year, some real departures from what has been available, others only slight variations of what is already available.

Camouflage patterns are printed on lightweight summer fabric, completely waterproof garments, heavyweight fleece or wool, all-cotton cloth, a combination of cotton and nylon, brushed cotton, rain gear, hats, gloves, face masks and boots. Even camouflage undergarments are available, with patterns to mix or match with bows, arrows, tents and other gear. All are designed to help the hunter disappear against virtually any environment in the world.

Not every manufacturer or hunter agrees on what constitutes a good camouflage pattern. One school of thought believes the colors and patterns should approximate the habitat being hunted. Variations include patterns that look like tree bark, others that resemble the forest floor and still others that blend with a tree's leaves and branches.

The trouble with that theory is there are dozens of different hunting habitats. The trees, bushes and undergrowth in each look different, depending upon the locale and season. Deer seasons open as early as July in California, and don't close in some states or provinces until the following January. The season stretches from mid-summer to mid-winter—with all the weather and environmental changes in between.

Many camo clothing manufacturers offer the same basic pattern in several color choices, attempting to match the season. This means the bowhunter who hunts in several locations or who lives where the seasons are extended might have to purchase more than one set of cammies. On the other hand, the hunter who hunts the same area year after year—perhaps from the same tree stand—will know what the onset of cold weather does to his favorite habitat. Tree bark is unlikely to change color with the changing weather, so one set of appropriately patterned camo hunting togs might be enough.

Many of these natural-looking patterns are developed directly from photographs of the leaf- and branch-covered ground or of tree trunks. The color photo images are transferred directly to cloth-printing screens and the colors are matched to produce the fabric. Some patterns are universal across a wide geographical area, such as the South where the flora is much the same throughout the hunting season.

ASAT Camouflage

A different philosophy is followed by other pattern developers, such as All-Season All-Terrain (ASAT). The design is predominantly shades of brown and black in large contrasting patterns. It is intended to provide any hunter, particularly bowhunters, with a pattern that is appropriate to any part of the country, during any season.

The concept does not rely on duplicating the patterns and colors of the area being hunted, but, rather, reflecting any environment in color, tone and light intensity. Tests have shown the ASAT pattern to look green in spring woods or dark timber and appear gray in shadow, rocks or low-light situations. The mild to moderate curvature of the earth tones of brown and black shapes blends into the surroundings.

The ASAT pattern was developed several years ago by hunting partners Jim Barnhart and Stan Starr, both experienced bowhunters. They set out to develop a single pattern appropriate for deer season in all hunting habitats and seasons, not just certain geographical areas. Their goal was to develop something appropriate for snowy winters, as well as early-season spring, Western high country and Eastern hardwoods.

Barnhart and Starr spent more than 15,000 hours testing the pattern in field conditions all around the country, studying game behavior and reactions to the pattern. They learned the characteristics that make a camo pattern work under all conditions.

One of the selling points of the ASAT pattern is that it retains its integrity at long and short distances, and does not tend to join together visually to form a dark, human form that will alert game animals. The pattern's overall light color and tone is said to be effective because it uses natural light reflection to blend into the terrain.

Hunting clothing with the ASAT pattern is marketed primarily though the mail-order firm of Brigade Quartermasters. It is produced with no optical brighteners, so the ultra-violet light reflections, which research has shown to aid animals in seeing humans, are minimized. The fabric is a brushed cotton and retains its contrasting colors if washing instructions are followed. Clothing for both warm- and cold-weather hunting, insulated and uninsulated, is available as well as hats, caps, gloves and face masks. The ASAT trousers and coat are patterned after a military uniform with plenty of pockets for the bowhunter to carry spare items on the hunt without a backpack. All closures are with buttons rather than zippers. Trouser cuffs have drawstring ties, and the waist has a 2-inch size adjustment to permit long underwear or other warm garments to be worn underneath.

The ASAT Ultimate Suit is popular with many bowhunters and turkey hunters.

The ASAT pattern is broken up by black strokes.

Military developments in camo uniforms may see a reversible forest and desert cloth. It may eventually become available to hunters.

Bushlan

Bushlan Camouflage was developed by a team of wildlife biologists, plant specialists and hunters to provide consumers with realistic, shape-disruptive camo patterns. The original Green Bushlan uses natural designs, including leaves, stems and open areas to provide a three-dimensional appearance. The developers say the light and dark areas of the pattern are the right mixture to break up the form of the hunter. Overlapping shapes and colors provide the pattern with a blending effect.

As Green Bushlan met with success, there seemed to be a demand for patterns and colors to match the more dormant winter habitat. Brown Bushlan followed with a predominantly brown pattern to blend with winter terrain and trees.

Bushlan includes a line of casual wear, such as jackets, vests and shirts. The ladies have not been ignored; women's styles include a jumpsuit and long-sleeve shirt. Headnets, bandanas, gloves, hats and caps of various materials are included in the Bushlan offering.

Full Contact Nature Company

The Full Contact Nature Company has approached the problem from a slightly different direction. Their camo system is patent-pending with one camouflage pattern printed on three-dimensional fabric. The pattern is called Mirror Image. Sunlight falling on the cloth casts shadows on it that tend to change with the angle of the sun. Mirror Image fabric is snag-proof and is said to glide easily through brushy areas, despite its three-dimensional quality. Little natural light reflects off the clothing, and the natural shadows increase the different dark and light shades in the printed camo pattern.

Kelly Cooper

The Tru-Leaf camo pattern, a product of the Kelly Cooper company, was introduced after seven years of research and development. The pattern is a three-dimensional leaf pattern intended to represent most of North America's common leaves such as oak, maple and beech.

The pattern is a non-directional design duplicating the arrangment of leaves over a typical forest floor. Light, overlapping leaf tones are on deep, multi-hued backgrounds intended to hide and break up the human form. The three-dimensional pattern combines eight fundamental earth-tone colors in a patented rotary screen-printing process and an over-dye treatment. Soft, muted tones above a shadowy background are the result. The over-dying and finishing treatments help reduce ultra-violet emissions.

Their Tru-Leaf pattern is printed in five season variations, including Spring Green, Fall Brown, Universal Green, Orange Leaf and Snow Leaf to match the seasons and geography for the bowhunter. Kelly Cooper manufactures garments in natural cotton, as well as blends of twill, chamois, acrylic knit and fleece.

Kool Dri

A company that does not produce any camo pattern of its own, but offers waterproof rainwear, is Kool Dri. It manufactures rain suits, parkas and jackets using such patterns as Realtree, Mossy Oak and military brown camo patterns.

The Kool Dri garments allow air to circulate through the rainwear, while remaining flexible and cool. The company claims long wear characteristics without snags, tears or frays.

Haas Outdoors

The numerous shades and variations of Mossy Oak camo have proven popular with turkey hunters and bowhunters, especially in the South. The inventor of the pattern is bowhunter Toxey Haas, who has hunted wild turkeys for years.

"I had turkeys in mind when I began work on the original

Mossy Oak pattern," he says, "because I knew if I could develop camouflage that was undetectable to turkeys, I would easily be hidden to deer and other game."

The first Mossy Oak pattern, known as Bottomland, has vertical and elliptical shapes in earth-tone colors to blend into the surroundings. Haas Outdoors has introduced other patterns beyond Bottomland. Greenleaf uses an overlay of sapling leaf images for a more three-dimensional look. The next variation, Treestand, which has become popular with bowhunters, utilizes the original Bottomland background and combines it with an overlay of limbs to break up the hunter's outline.

Next on the planning board were Full Foliage and Winter Treestand. Full Foliage adds predominant greens of large and small leaves to the Treestand pattern, ideal for spring and fall hunting. For late-season hunting, the Winter Treestand features an overlay of limbs on a snow background for a three-dimensional effect.

The Mossy Oak clothing is available in various fabrics and weights for men, women and youngsters. Several other clothing manufacturers also are producing garments, bows and accessories with the Mossy Oak camo pattern.

Skyline

George Haskell conceived the Skyline camouflage pattern based on the needs of a late-season tree stand hunter. It is useful after the leaves have fallen or if one is hunting in snowy terrain. Twenty years ago, says Haskell, no other company had a such a pattern. The next step for Haskell was the Skyline Treeline camo, using tree branches predominantly. Skyline has a mottled sky background with branch overlays. Treeline is a brown and tan background pattern with abstract branch overlays.

Haskell says that, in 1990, he began development of a new pattern. "After approximately two years of layout, drawings, hundreds of color schemes, thousands of photographs and hundreds of hours of field-testing, the Ultimate camo pattern was introduced. Ultimate was so widely accepted that the sales doubled in 1993. We ran out of inventory by September of that year."

The Ultimate camo pattern was designed to fit into almost any terrain, while breaking up the human outline. Ultimate has nine colors to represent treetops, branches, leaves, grasses, bark, rocks and patches of earth as seen from 5 feet to 100 yards. The small details are effective at close range, and the larger overall contrasting patches tend to break up the human shape at longer distances, according to the developer.

"We often have been asked to develop a green leaf pattern," says Haskell. "We wanted to make our leaves appear to be apart from our pattern and seem actually to be hanging out in front. We then needed to have a good mix of colors to fit the different terrains and weather conditions from cloudy to sunny. So we came up with three separate colors for the leaves to show shading and depth. We took hundreds of photos of shapes and colors to get the scheme just right.

"The end result is a green leaf pattern on our original Ultimate pattern with twelve colors. Our patterns are available in 50/50 cotton/poly, chamois, wool, hunt cloth, saddle cloth,

nylon, netting, fleece and several other proprietary materials. They are produced for insulated and uninsulated garments from gloves to parkas."

Spartan-Realtree

When he founded the Spartan Archery Sportswear Products company in 1982, Bill Jordan began by questioning the effectiveness of existing camouflage patterns, concluding most were variations of old military camo patterns. He soon came up with the Realtree pattern, a blend of vertical colors to match tree barks, marshlands and cornfields.

Jordan renamed the company Spartan-Realtree in 1985. New Snow and Brown-Leaf patterns were added to the original Grey-Leaf. He also was licensing several clothing and outdoor gear manufacturers to use the Realtree pattern on their products. Realtree All-Purpose camo was added in 1992, with many different looks in one pattern and six bark and earth tones. The All-Purpose pattern is different from the original Grey-Leaf, but the two can be used together, Jordan tells us.

All-Purpose Grey, a variation on the original pattern, was introduced in 1994. The original's name was changed to All-Purpose Brown since no green is seen in the pattern variation.

The Original Grey-Leaf has greens, grays and blacks. It is effective when used against a background of light-colored oak tree trunks or among limbs of scrubby brush and around gray rocks.

Realtree Snow is for those who hunt where snow is on the ground, as well as the desert areas with plenty of light colored sand. The pattern incorporates a number of leaves crossing the vertical lines of the pattern in a horizontal fashion.

All-Purpose Orange follows the standard pattern, but without most of the bark and leaves. The blaze orange pattern is intended for deer hunters in areas where they are required to wear hunter orange, even while bowhunting. The pattern is intended to conceal the hunter from game, but reveal him to other humans.

Sticks N' Limbs

Robert Hoague's Camo Clan was begun in 1977, as a pattern intended for bowhunters. Snow Camo was introduced in 1978, and a vertical print called Tree Stand was released in 1979. Unfortunately, in 1987, Camo Clan's fabric supplier had a four-month strike at the busiest time of the year, and Hoague's company went out of business.

Hoague continued with new ideas and moved to the town of Pancake, Texas, where he began his new company called Sticks N' Limbs. The company markets the Sticks N' Limbs pattern and licenses Jest Textiles of New Jersey to manufacture all-cotton, cotton/poly, nylon, Cordura and printed woollen fabrics. Menra Mills does the fleeces, and Winona Mills is the licensee for sweaters and other knit garments.

Hoague says, "I set my tree stands low, usually 4 to 8 feet off the ground. The average distance at which I take deer is 6 to 12 yards. When you draw a bow on a whitetail at that distance or from a stand that low, the camo has to work."

A veteran bowhunter for four decades, Hoague hunts white-tails ninety to a hundred days every year. He has bagged more than a hundred deer. "My camo prints are developed from the rules of visual perception. I avoid complex detail, because animals' eyes cannot see it from beyond 5 yards. I use big prints so they do not become big solids at a distance. I want my camo to work as well from far away as it does close. My designs are actually visual tricks that avert the animals' attention from the human form; it makes the hunter disappear.

"I have done extensive color research on deer, too. I can make a human being disappear with colors alone—the design does not matter. That is the direction my next pattern will take."

Timber Ghost

Kevin Carlile has developed his Timber Ghost pattern directly from photographs. "From the beginning, I wanted to produce a camouflage made specifically for the hardwood hunters of North America. Many designers will tell you their patterns will work against any background. Timber Ghost camouflage works in the hardwood forest. That is what it was designed to do, and that's what it does."

The secret, says Carlile, was in creating the design from photos. "Mother Nature was our designer. An artist never touched the Timber Ghost design. I photographed it and printed it on a quiet, brushed-cotton blend cloth. Nature did the rest."

Trebark Universal

Jim Crumley is the developer of one of the best-known modern camouflage patterns. In the 1970s, he noted that most hunters were using military camo patterns and time-proven plain shirts. While those patterns had served thousands of hunters for decades, Crumley noted that they were not the best for going unnoticed in the woods.

Crumley realized that most of his hunting was from tree stands. With that in mind, he began to design a special bark pattern. The development was named Trebark, the first camo designed especially for hunters and the first to feature a bark pattern. The design proved immediately popular with thousands of hunters.

Jim Crumley's original Trebark camo is the largest-selling hunting camo now available. It is licensed to more than 200 manufacturers worldwide and is found on every conceivable product and on a wide variety of materials, not just hunting clothes.

Since the first design, Trebark has added a leaf pattern and several color variations to accommodate special requirements. Trebark II is a blend of lighter colors and less greens for hunters in Western states or late-season areas with a predominance of brown backgrounds. Trebark Universal is a multi-tree pattern with seven earth-tone colors designed for use in a heavily forested area with plenty of large and small trees.

Trevanish

Brothers Terry and Ken Deaton created Trevanish in 1989. After a year of extensive research, they realized that most bowhunters shoot their game from 15 to 25 yards away. Con-cluding that their camo pattern must possess plenty of contrast to be effective, they conducted light reflectology work and determined that the optimum color for neutralizing natural light is gray.

The process of developing a camo pattern starts with combining exact colorations of black, brown and green over a gray base color. Variations of horizontal and vertical broken lines are added to the basic pattern with a vertical look to match the hardwood forests.

The Deatons soon learned that a fabric with a blend of brushed cotton and polyester does not shrink, absorbs less moisture than pure cotton cloth, and is strong and quiet. They worked with Jest Textile to develop a 7.5-ounce cotton/poly material for the Trevanish clothing. Licensing agreements will see the manufacture of more and different fabrics with the Trevanish pattern.

Woolrich

Among the licensees that utilize various camouflage patterns for their products is the well-known Woolrich Company. Woolrich is producing several clothing items using a blend of 65 percent wool and 35 percent Cordura nylon. The fabric, says Woolrich, has the softness and warming ability of wool, but adds the wearability of nylon.

Another product is called CamWoolflage, made of 100 percent wool. It uses the Realtree All-Purpose camo pattern with garments designed specially for bowhunters. The wool remains warm, even in wet weather, and is quiet in the woods. Many hunters swear by all-wool clothing in any kind of weather.

Among the clothing in CamWoolflage is the Woolrich Blanchard hunt parka and trousers. For cooler weather, the same pattern is available on the CamWoolflage Hunt Coat made of a heavier wool fabric with Thinsulate insulation.

The Realtree All-Purpose pattern on the same wool fabric is available in an archer shirt, trousers and bib overalls, as well as a matching sweater of all-wool. A wool field cap completes the outfit.

Each year manufacturers introduce more new camouflage patterns and color variations. New fabrics are utilized and new weatherproofing processes offered. Each year bowhunters are almost guaranteed several new companies with new approaches to the problem of disappearing in the woods.

There is no agreement among manufacturers nor among hunters as to which of the patterns, colors or fabrics is the ultimate answer. More research needs to be done on how deer and other game animals see colors and objects, stationary or moving. Most research has been based on how humans may perceive hunters wearing different camouflage patterns against different types of terrain and backgrounds.

No matter what type of camo is worn, there is no substitute for the careful bowhunter who moves little or not at all and who maintains control of his human scent. The best camouflage outfit in the world will not compensate for careless hunting practices.

On the other hand, most bowhunters will not venture afield without a full set of good camouflage clothing.

18 Hunting With A Bow

BOWHUNTING has been growing in popularity and economic impact for the past half-century. In several states, the number of bowhunting deer licenses sold exceeds 250,000 per year. Some states do not record separate archery tags during their hunting seasons, so the total number of bowhunters in North America is based on estimates, not on verifiable counts. The best estimates put the bowhunting population somewhere between two and three million. Those numbers include the avid, dedicated archers who are in the woods more than sixty days per year as well as those who pick up their bow and arrows only a couple of days a year after the season opens.

There is no question as to the favorite big game animal archers seek; it is the deer. In North America, two primary types of native deer are hunted—the whitetail and the mule deer. The whitetail is found in the Midwest and the East, while the mule deer most commonly lives in the West. Whitetail far outnumber muleys, and the bowhunting community follows those numbers.

There are several subspecies, according to game biologists. The tiny Coues deer of the Southwest is related to the whitetail, but is considered by game record keepers as a separate species. The same may be said for blacktail, found on the northern West Coast of North America. Blacktails are more closely related to mule deer, but tend to behave like whitetails. Due to the weather and terrain in which they exist, they present their own problems for hunters. Blacktail deer are broken down further into two different scoring categories, based on geography. Game biologists may break whitetail down into a dozen or more subspecies, but record books do not.

Target Archery Is Growing, But Bowhunting Continues To Dominate The Field

Technically, the wapiti (or elk), moose and several species of caribou are also in the deer family. They resemble one another in certain physical aspects, but are considered separate animals by hunters as well as by fish and game officials who establish seasons and issue hunting permits for the animals.

Antelope have enjoyed a huge population growth in some central plains and mountain states, particularly Wyoming. Antelope can be difficult game for bowhunters, but that is part of the challenge of the sport.

Black bear populations are growing in many states and provinces, and consequently the number of bowhunters who pursue them also is increasing. Black bear are by far the most common game. Brown bear—grizzlies are a part of the family—and polar bear are not for the faint-hearted and the financially challenged. The record books have categories, but only a tiny number of bowhunters ever draw a tag or can afford the cost.

Caribou have become popular with archers in recent years. In some parts of Canada and Alaska, caribou populations are rising and limits are generous. Outfitting and guiding hunters from the United States and Europe has become a large business for many in the Far North.

Huntable elk populations are to be found in several states and provinces. Generally, elk are found at high elevations of the West, usually in remote locations. It is not a spur-of-the-moment, weekend hunting proposition. Hunting elk takes ample planning and preparation. The successful elk hunter must be in good physical condition and be well practiced with his equipment.

There are many other animals that are legal game in most parts of North America, including all sorts of small game, birds and varmints. While their pursuit may be exciting and challenging, most hunters view these others as merely warm-ups and practice for their primary game—deer.

The pages that follow should provide insight into what the sport of bowhunting is all about.

Mule Deer

Even a small, but legal, mule deer is a challenge to hunt and kill. Habitat may be dry and hot during early seasons.

HUNTING MULE DEER is primarily an exercise in stealth. The hunter does not usually wait in ambush at a location where there is an expectation that a deer will pass. Mule deer are not the creatures of habit that whitetails are supposed to be. Muleys inhabit specific areas of their choice, but are not known to follow familiar and predictable patterns of behavior that will allow the hunter to hunker down with an expectation of filling a deer license tag at any specific spot.

Most bowhunters will agree that hunting mule deer is a lot of work. Much of mule deer habitat is public land, national or state forest lands, BLM or other local or federal property. That means access is open to anyone who can get to it. Often, that means driving many miles of narrow dirt roads to a trail head, then transferring to pack horses or moving higher on foot. There are plenty of outfitters and guides who have access to some of the better deer habitat in the West, but there also is plenty of area open to anyone with the strength, stamina and conditioning to make the trek.

Many mule deer herds are migrational, traveling from the high country in the winter as the snows begin to pile up down the mountains to winter feed areas. This permits game officials the luxury of counting the herds and observing their general health.

In many areas of the West, particularly in California, the earliest bowhunting seasons open in July and August. Those with a mule deer hunting tag have to battle the dry heat as

well as the altitude while chasing their game. Another hurdle is the possibility, in some years the probability, of forest fire closures in the area and during the season when the license is valid.

In many areas of the West, mule deer habitat is desert—high or low. Water availability is an advantage as well as an obstacle for the bowhunter. The hunter must be prepared for a lack of potable water at the base camp or hunting area ahead. When traveling by horse, enough water and purifiers are carried into the high camps, but when backpacking on foot, carrying enough water is a genuine problem. All water in the hunting area must be considered to be polluted and must be filtered, boiled or treated with chemicals to prevent serious illness to the human hunter. No matter how clean and pure a stream may appear, water from it should never be consumed untreated.

While a safe water supply is a problem for humans, that same shortage can work to the bowhunter's advantage. Deer must drink every day. Usually, deer sign may be found in the wet ground near streams, seeps or ponds, no matter how high up the mountains. Fresh green growth will clue the hunter in as to where water may be, and it will indicate where to begin looking for game, even without going near.

Good binoculars are essential to any mule deer hunter. Nobody on foot can cover all the ground necessary to locate the animals in their home habitat, and tramping around their daily drinking area will only serve to spread human scent and spook the deer away.

Mule deer are not traveling creatures, but they must drink, eat and rest each day. In the mountains, typical behavior might include bedding down for the night at the bottom of a valley,

Open terrain and low-growing brush make stalking a difficult task for any bowhunter.

draw or canyon, in thick brush and near a stream. Early, before real daylight, the deer begin to move upward, on the sunny side of the slope, browsing as they go.

The upward trip might take several hours until they reach another sheltered spot, not too hot, where the deer can lie down and observe possible dangers approaching from below. They will nap through the afternoon if not otherwise alerted to danger, awakening from time to time to smell and watch for predators. As the day begins to cool, the deer will awaken, stretch and begin to head back down the slope, or perhaps cross over the ridge to another canyon for water and another night down below.

Bowhunters will agree that spotting or finding mule deer is the easiest part of the hunt. Approaching to within shooting distance is the hard part. This is where your binoculars will come into use. If possible, the bowhunter will want to find a vantage point from which he can spot deer either in their afternoon resting place or along their travel route to and from water. Use good, light-gathering glasses to look under every tree, bush and shadowed area for a deer. In fact, the successful mule deer hunters will say not to look for a whole deer, but for portions—an ear, eye, the tip of a moving antler. Do your walking with binoculars and spend enough time to look into every hiding place before deciding there are no deer on that side of the valley.

Once a muley with a legal set of antlers is spotted, the real work begins. Most mule deer habitat is dry—full of loud and crunchy leaves, grass or loose rocks which create noise from carelessly placed boots.

Any deer must be approached with the wind blowing toward the hunter. In the mountains, the prevailing air currents tend to move downward in the mornings, as the air begins to heat up. Currents move upward in the late afternoon as warm air begins to rise from the canyon floor and the upper air cools. Approaching from above in the late afternoon just before the game begins to arise from its nap is good strategy.

The hunter might alert the deer and have to make a stalk several times in several days. Allow plenty of time for mule deer hunting. An unexpected change in wind direction will send the hunter's scent to the buck's nostrils and he will be gone in an instant. He may also spot movement, even though the wind is right and the hunter is above the site.

Most, but not all, mule deer hunting will be in habitat that is predominantly brown and gray in color, so camouflage clothing of mostly those colors will be most appropriate. Keep in mind that there are plenty of other areas of the West, and some years even in California and Nevada, with rainfall that will leave adequate moisture to turn things green in August and September. If an outfitter or local guide is used, he will be able to furnish information to the hunter if the hunt is in an unfamiliar area.

If an outfitter or guide is to be engaged for the hunt, he or she must be thoroughly checked out beforehand. Unless the individual(s) is known to the hunter or unless they have been utilized by someone near and dear, the hunter must investigate. Talk to previous customers and spend some time with the guide. Make sure the guide(s) and camp personnel are

In some high country, travel by horseback is the only way to get into mule deer country.

either bowhunters themselves or they really understand the needs of bowhunters. There are too many guides who just do not realize how close to the game the bowhunter must get before shooting.

On the subject of clothing, the weather is unpredictable all of the time in any high country. Snow, sleet, cold winds, thunderstorms, rain, dry weather and everything in between can be expected, and the hunter must be prepared for any eventuality. At high altitude, a summer rainstorm can quickly soak the hunter and the late afternoon can turn cold enough to make hypothermia a distinct possibility. Always carry an extra change of socks and some sort of rain gear when hunting anywhere in the West.

Buy and wear the best boots available within your budget. The terrain will be steep, loose and, possibly, wet. As every soldier knows, the feet must be protected at all times. There is no way to hunt mule deer without plenty of walking, whether on the flats or in the mountains. It has been said before, but do not expect to buy a new pair of boots just before the hunt and break them in while hunting. There is no sense in ruining a great hunt with sore feet.

The bowhunter should get in plenty of practice before the season opens. If there is room at home, set up a 3-D mule deer target in the backyard and shoot every day. Shoot from several different distances and from various angles. Do plenty of unknown-distance shooting, as that is the way the hunt will go. Often there is time for a reading with a rangefinder if the spotted buck is asleep as he is approached, but the hunter cannot count on it.

Shots are likely to be on the long side, rather than close. The Eastern whitetail hunter may shoot at a deer less than 20 yards from the tree stand, but the hunter is unlikely to get that close to a muley. The hunter must know his or her comfortable maximum accurate range and must not exceed it under any circumstances. Plenty of shots are downhill or across a deep ravine,

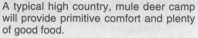
A typical high country, mule deer camp will provide primitive comfort and plenty of good food.

Water is usually in short supply in much of mule deer habitat. The hunter must be supplied with plenty of his own drinkable water.

rather than through a small opening in the trees. The bowhunter should practice until these and other difficult shots become automatic.

A fast-shooting, flat-trajectory bow and arrow combination will serve well. Take plenty of arrows and broadheads on the hunt. Mule deer habitat is generally as tough on bows and arrows as it is on hunters. Have a supply of spare parts, including an extra bowstring in the bow case. A good skinning or field knife is essential, unless the guiding personnel are going to handle that chore.

If possible, study the area to be hunted in advance. Pre-season scouting will at least familiarize the bowhunter with the terrain. In most areas, the size of the country is huge. Several days to a week are the minimum to scout unless the hunter, a friend or a guide is familiar with the zone. For many Western deer hunters, it may require several seasons in the same zone to learn the area well enough to be successful. An experienced guide can do the scouting ahead of time and will know where deer are likely to be moving.

During these early archery seasons, the deer are not likely to be in rut. In many Western states, the rut does not occur until November or later. The hunter can expect no help on that score. Using scent lures and antler rattling are usually fruitless. However, the hunter should do everything possible to cover up human scent and to remember wind direction at all times.

Trudging up a steep mountain trail can be hot, sweaty work, no matter what sort of physical condition the hunter is in. Drink plenty of safe water, rest frequently and move slowly. Some successful mule deer hunters recommend moving a few slow steps, then stopping, listening and scanning the area again with binoculars. Walking along at a relaxed, jaunty pace is not hunting, they say. A deer may be around the next bend or over the next ridge.

When traveling on foot or horseback, remember to check the back trail from time to time. Mule deer will circle about behind the hunter. It is common to travel up a trail in the morning, only to see plenty of deer tracks covering your boot prints on the way back down the same trail in the evening.

There is always a certain element of danger when hunting in the high country. The weather is one factor. In the mountains,

snow, thunderstorms, rain or mild weather may be expected in any month, even during the early archery season. Loose rocks, steep cliffs, swift-flowing mountain streams and rivers can prove dangerous at any time. Horseback transportation offers its own challenges. One must use care at all times when in mule deer country.

Unlike whitetail hunting, where the woods may be crowded with hunters, mule deer territory is open and lonely. If a guide is not employed, the bowhunter would be ill-advised to hunt alone. Always hunt with a buddy or two, and let someone else know where you are going and when you expect to return.

The mule deer hunter will seek to climb above game resting areas for a vantage point. Good camouflage colors will include plenty of brown, tan and open neutral colors to match the surroundings. Author Combs wears the ASAT camouflage pattern in Nevada.

Whitetail Deer

Dr. Bob Sheppard (left) and instructor Ronnie Groom use a deer anatomy chart to illustrate correct arrow shot placement.

THERE IS NO besting southern hospitality, and it runs rampant in Alabama. But if the southern matriarch doe didn't hurry and move out from behind that water oak, John Sloan was in danger of being late for class. Finally, with less than ten minutes until dark, she moved and the bowhunter released a 2216 Easton arrow shaft that downed his second deer in two days. Then he hurried to catch a ride to class.

It had been some twenty-four years since Sloan spent any time in school, but he said he wouldn't have missed this one for the world. You are never too old to learn, and even after forty years of studying and hunting whitetail deer, there was enough to learn.

Westervelt Lodge is snuggled into 14,000 acres that undulates across the Tombigbee River bottom in southwestern Alabama. It is located just outside Aliceville, 60 miles from Tuscaloosa. If you fancy deer and turkey hunting, there is no doubt about it being the place to go. Each year, Westervelt plays host to a school on bowhunting whitetail deer. Most of the lessons would apply equally well for any hunter.

This is not your normal school—not some opportunity for a hunter to pay a fancy price and go listen to some "expert" tell war stories about how he killed 135 monster bucks. This is a school with daily exams you grade yourself, and the instructors are taking the tests right along with you.

The instructors are not celebrities or famous deer hunters. None calls himself an expert or a trophy hunter, although they certainly qualify. Dr. Bob Sheppard lives in Carrolton, Alabama, and makes his living as a cardiologist. He doesn't need to conduct deer hunting clinics to put groceries on the table. Ronnie Groom lives in Panama City, Florida, and owns a couple of archery shops. These two are joined by the staff of Westervelt, and the knowledge flows as freely as the ice tea at dinner time in the main lodge.

It began as the Fred Bear Bowhunting School some twenty years ago. Bob Sheppard and Ronnie Groom have been instructors for more than fifteen of those years.

"The success of the school is due to the fine cooperation between visiting instructors and the staff," said Charles Bedwell, lodge manager. "We work to make the school a learning experience, and the instructors, Bob and Ronnie, come prepared and ready to teach. They have been doing this a long time, and they know what works and what doesn't. They know what is important and what isn't. We have more than a 50-percent repeat booking for the school every year. Most of our attendees come from the Southeast, but each year we get hunters from all over the country. It is a terrific program for the lodge, because we increase our bookings through word of mouth."

John Roboski, Westervelt's business manager, clarified it: "Hunters come to the school and see what we have to offer. They realize this is a family affair. They come back with friends and family, and those friends and families spread the word and we continue to maintain near capacity all season.

"The lodge can accommodate twenty hunters at one time. We provide private rooms with two beds per room and a private bath.

"Westervelt is owned by the Gulf States Paper Corporation. It has been in existence for over forty years, but it has been operated as a public hunting lodge for only about twenty years. Prior to that, it was a corporate retreat and was used for corporate business only. We view this public hunting as another wise use of the resource. We have the land and the trees. That is the corporate business. But hunting not only helps defray the cost of operation, it provides a source of income to maintain wise land use and habitat preservation," continued Roboski.

"Westervelt is managed to provide for the welfare of both the land and the wildlife," he declared. "We have been under a quality deer management program for four years, and the results are beginning to show. Just about every hunter is going to see a trophy buck. He may not get a shot, but he should see one."

Ronnie Groom is a quiet, soft-spoken, no-nonsense guy with the courtly manners of a true Southern gentleman of the old school.

"Anybody can be a deer hunter," Groom said. "We are trying

Part of the instruction at Westervelt includes the use of tree stands. Dr. Sheppard demonstrates the use of a special bowhunting climbing sling.

Shooting from elevated platforms gives students a feel for hunting from tree stands. Here, a 3-D animal target is the game.

to make *successful* deer hunters out of deer hunters. Quite frankly, in my opinion, a successful deer hunter is one who kills deer or has the opportunity to kill deer on a regular basis. That is what we are trying to do: Teach hunters to think and act in a manner that gets them in the right place at the right time."

"We focus on the segments of deer hunting," said Dr. Sheppard. "We take the most important aspects of deer hunting and break them down into understandable pieces. It doesn't do a hunter any good to know that deer eat acorns if you don't show him what acorns in what order of preference and how to hunt around the tree that is dropping the acorns. There is more to hunting a food plot than climbing into a ladder stand that has been on that food plot for fifteen years.

"You can hunt a food plot or you can *effectively* hunt a food plot. It is all in where you place your stand. It deals with how a deer is going to get to that food plot and if you can hunt that travel access with the wind you have at that time.

"The first day, hunters arrive at mid-morning. Before bedtime, we will have talked about and discussed hunting a food plot and tree stand placement and safety. We also will have hunted a food plot or some type of food source and we will then discuss habitat management and basic hunting techniques that go with that habitat."

"This is not a school to come to and learn to shoot your bow," Ronnie Groom added. "If you have a problem, we'll try and help you, but we aren't here to sell anything or teach you how to shoot. You can learn that at home. We are going to teach you how to kill deer and get you to understand why deer do what they do."

Westervelt has three full time guides. During the peak times and during school, they bring in some extra help. The "help" is unique. They all are graduate biologists on the payroll of Gulf States. They act not only as guides for the hunters, but as instructors, and know what they are doing.

Do not be misled by the use of the term guide. The hunter will not be led by the hand to his or her stand, says Sloan. This is a learning hunt. Twice each day, morning and afternoon, the guest is given the opportunity to hunt. Each student is assigned an area, a sizable area. His or her guide explains the area and goes over a map of that particular area with the stu-

dent. The guide points out important characteristics and gives a little advice on how to hunt it. The rest is up to the hunter. The hunter picks out the stand location based on what he has just learned in the classroom. The guides are there to help, not give orders.

Thursday, under threatening skies, the students began to arrive. They came mainly from Florida and Tennessee, many having been to Westervelt before. After quick introductions to the instructors, the group moved outside for a quick lesson in tree stand placement and safety. That was followed by a grand lunch of fried chicken with all the trimmings. Then it was off to the woods for instruction on how to hunt a food plot.

At 2:30 p.m., with a head full of new knowledge and under a downpour, Sloan and his fellow students went to the whitetail woods. Lodge manager, Charles Bedwell, dropped Sloan and three others off at their assigned places. Sloan wormed his way through the dripping cypress and water oaks to the tree of his choice. The stand was in the middle of a dry slough, halfway between a pine plantation and a food plot of standing corn and green growth of oats and crimson clover. There were rubs, tracks and deer droppings in the area, Sloan recalls.

Bag limits at Westervelt are liberal: The hunter may take one doe a day and one buck a day, six-point antlers or better. For the school, they had relaxed the six-point rule. Sloan, however, makes it a policy not to shoot little bucks on other folks' land. By dusk, he was beginning to regret that decision. Despite sometimes torrential rains and rapidly dropping temperatures to make hunting miserable, Sloan counted twenty-eight deer by 6 p.m. He missed one when a cypress tree jumped in front of his

Students and instructors set out for a class on tree stand placement.

arrow. Around 6 p.m., five bucks and one doe moved into the dry slough. Sloan waited fifteen minutes with all six deer within 20 yards before the doe moved into the open. This time he didn't miss. She went less than 60 yards, and he had his first deer of the hunt. Surprisingly, that was the only deer killed that day, but everybody saw some deer.

After a sumptuous meal of steak, baked potatoes and trimmings, it was back to class for a lesson in percentages. The class was on habitat management and hunting techniques. It may have been one of the most informative of the school. Dr. Sheppard, using a computer model, illustrated a breakdown of the chances of success under various conditions. It was easily understood how hunting specific locations under improper conditions will result in almost a zero-percent chance of success. To the students, this was important material often overlooked. If the conditions aren't right, just stay out of that area. Not paying attention to the percentages may hurt your chances for success. The behavior of a hunter may ruin the area for the entire season. Bucks do not act or move through an area the same way as a doe.

The night did not last long, reports Sloan. Breakfast was just like all the meals at Westervelt—delicious and plenty of it. The morning was clear, cool and sparkling with sun through the remaining raindrops. The forest and swamp glittered. Sloan saw two deer, and this prompted him to quietly move a stand for the afternoon hunt. It was a great morning.

Ted Holtzman lives in Palm Harbor, Florida, and has been bowhunting for three years. This was his first time attending the school.

"In the first sessions, Ronnie Groom stressed shot placement and taking the proper shot," Holtzman said. "Before that session, I probably would have messed up.

"I saw six deer, and at 8:45 p.m., this doe came out. I had to wait for what seemed like an hour, but finally she gave me the right shot. It was what Ronnie called a high-percentage shot."

The patience Holtzman exhibited is the kind of thing that makes for successful whitetail hunters. Whitetails are usually plentiful in most Midwestern and Eastern states, and the technique is to wait for the optimum shot rather than take the first one that shows itself.

Holtzman's Hoyt bow, set at 60 pounds draw weight, did the job, and he had his first deer. At age thirty-three, Ted Holtzman is a lifetime convert to whitetail deer hunting.

Westervelt manages ninety food plots spread across the 14,000 acres of the property. Not only are deer abundant, so are turkeys. The class learned about dealing with the wind and placing a stand to reduce the risk of being detected by either type of game. After a huge lunch, the group went to the 3-D target course to look at arrow and body angle, and good shot placement. The only recommended shots are the high-percentage shots.

It was that afternoon that the doe at the beginning of Sloan's story was about to cause him to be late for class. He was treated to a display of eight turkeys with a deer feeding in the middle of the flock. The doe was the eleventh deer Sloan had seen and was the one he was looking for. At 120 pounds and 4^1/$_2$ years old, this old girl was a trophy.

But the afternoon belonged to a Largo, Florida, resident, Dwaine Lents. Lents is fifty-seven years young and a delightful guy to be around, says Sloan. He has been bowhunting three years and never had shot at a deer until that Friday afternoon.

"Three friends of mine came to the school for two consecutive years and recommended that I come," said Lents. "The course is very informative. I can attribute this deer I killed to what I learned right here. Bob Sheppard stressed that the deer were feeding on acorns and taught us how to set up to hunt an oak tree. I found this oak dropping acorns and I set up as he said.

"I saw a spike come out of the thicket and watched him for ninety minutes, waiting for the high percentage shot. He traveled less than 20 yards after I shot him at 18.

"This is a fantastic place. There is none better, and I see no need to go anywhere else. You can bet I'll be back. This is the first deer I have ever killed. It was a great experience, because I did it myself."

The staff at Westervelt—consisting of Charles Bedwell, Bill Baker, Jay Steen and Steven Carroll—is tops, declares Sloan. They know the area and the know the animals. They blood trail with the best of them. Between classes, Steen and Sloan went back to get his doe. Using the brightest light John Sloan had ever seen, Jay Steen walked the 300 yards to that deer like he was on a string.

Is the school worth it for any bowhunter? Sloan says he has been hunting deer for forty years. He describes himself as a stubborn, hard-headed, opinionated son of a gun. But he learned a lot. Every bowhunter needs Deer Hunting 101.

Blacktail Deer

A Loc-On climbing pole is attached to an Oregon pine tree located near an intersection of deer trails. The underbrush is plenty thick! Author Roger Combs wears ASAT camo.

COLUMBIAN BLACKTAIL DEER make their home along the Pacific Coast from the central part of California north into the British Columbia rain forests. A second subspecies, the Sitka, is found farther north in Canada and Alaska, along the coast and on some islands. The Sitkas are smaller in number, and hunting opportunities are restricted to only a few. The most famous blacktail bowhunting is the annual Oregon National Blacktail Hunt in November.

Blacktail deer seem to prefer habitat that is colder, wetter, more heavily overgrown than that of the mule deer, although they do share the same areas in some places—but rarely. In some states, a tag for mule deer will also serve for blacktail. During the November blacktail hunt in Oregon, the season is archery-only, and the specified areas are host only to blacktail deer. Other states and provinces have much earlier seasons for muleys or blacktail, but the dates vary from year to year. Hunters should check with their game departments annually to keep track of dates, fees and limits.

Blacktail deer generally live their lives within the same mile or two. They do not normally migrate as do many mule deer. A standard-size buck will weigh 90 to 120 pounds, and the largest trophies may reach 185 pounds. Blacktail deer are hunted by those familiar with the subspecies, using tree stands at trails and travel routes or by the spot-and-stalk method. When spooked, blacktail deer will run and hide, but they will watch for a pursuing hunter. It is a match of wits that usually finds the deer the winner.

November in Oregon is normally cold and damp, although some sunny breaks in the weather are not uncommon. The bowhunter in the area must be prepared for wet, cold weather to avoid being uncomfortable or to protect himself from the dangers of hypothermia. The hunter never leaves camp in blacktail country without a complete set of rainwear. Waterproof boots are needed, even during balmy days, as the ground and undergrowth may be soaked from previous rains.

Brown or green camouflage pattern clothing will blend into most blacktail habitat. Some hunters in this type of country prefer wool garments, because of the way they keep the body warm even while wet.

The terrain includes valley floors, surrounding foothills and the extremely rugged coastal mountains of the Cascades. In northern Oregon and into Washington, the undergrowth is generally thicker and tougher to pass through. Southern Oregon and the northern half of California will be drier and more open. Most hunting is done at elevations of 2,500 feet or less, but there are blacktails as high as 6,000 feet in all their habitat. The folks who host the National Blacktail Hunt in Oregon have found that most record-book animals have been found at the lower elevations.

Much of the Western states' hunting areas are on public

In typical blacktail terrain, the weather may be cold and wet.

Sunny patches are not unknown during a November blacktail hunt. Combs is wearing a Woolrich CamWoolflage waterproof hunting suit.

Binoculars are used to scan hillsides and valleys where blacktail deer may be bedding.

lands, open to anybody. The problem is, even though there are millions of huntable acres in blacktail habitat, a great deal of the land is designated wilderness, difficult to reach by foot and prohibited from vehicle use. In some areas, much of the land is owned by timber companies and is open to hunters at no charge. A big advantage to hunting in November during the National Blacktail Hunt is that the sponsoring organization, the Oregon Foundation for Blacktail Deer, will put the visiting bowhunter with members familiar with the area to be hunted. Detailed maps are also available for each hunter.

Oregon requires hunters to purchase licenses and deer tags by late August, even though the hunt there is in November. Other states have even earlier deadlines.

Hunting blacktail deer is a challenge. It requires extra care and preparation. Weather, habitat changes and local hunting pressures can frustrate the bowhunter, but there is a healthy population of blacktail deer where they range.

In recent years, logging restrictions have curtailed much of the timber industry from harvesting all the trees they would like, but there are plenty of recent clear-cut areas that provide ideal deer habitat. The timber cutters plant new trees on the cut-over hills to encourage new growth. Some of the best places to hunt these deer is in areas burned over two to a dozen years ago. The new growth in the burned areas is what deer prefer to eat. Later, when the trees have reached some height, they begin to shade the undergrowth, and the trees take over. In old-growth forests, most of the food deer seek is found in open pastures, along streams and ponds and near abandoned logging roads.

Since blacktail are creatures of habit, many hunters believe they can pattern their movements and behavior. When enough evidence is found to predict movement along a specific route, a portable tree stand may work well. A stand can be established above logging roads with plenty of tracks. Roads opening onto farmland are often preferred by deer sneaking down into the valleys for domestic animal pastures.

Most of the trees that might hold a tree stand are on timber company or public lands where spikes or screws in the trunks are prohibited. Climbing stands that do not cut into the bark or portable ladder stands are ideal for this type of hunting. Leaving any stand on trees in any public property is always a risk, another reason for using only lightweight portable stands under such circumstances.

Wind direction must always be considered when using tree stands. The prevailing wind in the afternoon may be from a different direction than what it was in the morning. The game trails may be on hillsides, so even if the stand is quite a distance up the tree, the hunter may still be no higher than the deer coming down the trail.

Old logging roads are also good places to provide vantage points from which to spot blacktail deer. If the hunter is afoot, the roads are much easier to negotiate than trying to climb up the hillsides. Walk the roads as quietly as possible, always keeping the wind direction in mind. Move slowly, stopping frequently to look and listen. Rainfall or recent precipitation will help cover or reduce the sounds of movement through the forest. If traveling by vehicle, the roads may be slippery and dangerous in rain or snow. The hunter must be cautious.

The hunter must be prepared for any weather in November, including sudden snow storms.

A technique that has worked for some hunters is to move slowly along the edge of a logging road, pausing often to use binoculars to glass the hillsides below the road. Even if the weather is not too clear, good light-gathering binoculars will help spot and identify deer that may be moving or bedded down below the road level. Hunters have reported spotting deer moving along on the logging roads above and below. However, deer will usually spot hunters long before they see the game.

If the weather has been dry, moving quietly will be all that much more difficult, especially on a stalk. Dry leaves and loose rocks are likely to provide the deer with plenty of early warning of a hunter in the area. Rain will soften the ground and brush, and may cover the sounds of movement. Snow will also be a help to the hunter if it is not too deep. The successful hunter will be prepared for any weather.

In most areas of the West, camping is permitted on any public lands, unless there are fire restrictions or dangers at the time. Backpacking into the higher mountains away from traveled roads is a pleasant way to locate more blacktail deer. As is the case when hunting mule deer, the hunter must be sure of a water supply before venturing into unknown country.

A supply of emergency equipment when hunting the mountains is always a good idea. Carry the appropriate maps, preferably detailed topographic maps, a compass, emergency space blanket and/or shelter, flashlight with fresh batteries, knife, extra gloves and socks, cover scents, emergency rations, a couple canteens of water and water purification materials, toilet paper and extra rain gear. Bowhunters will want to add a spare bowstring and trail marking paper, for which toilet paper is an ideal substitute.

Another benefit of hunting Oregon blacktail in November is the help at hand if a deer is downed. The hunter may or may not be near a road reachable by truck. It always seems that a deer will succumb at the bottom of the hill and have to be dragged up to the road, rather than at the top with a road below.

Blacktail hunters are a friendly bunch. Most can be relied upon to help another hunter locate deer. In some whitetail country where most of the hunting is on private land, some bowhunters zealously guard their secret hunt locations. Where most hunting is on public lands, accessible to all, there is little to be gained from not sharing as much information as possible with other hunters.

Some blacktail hunters have found success by mounting loose drives through areas known to hold deer. Small pockets of deer are common in valleys and natural pastures. One or two hunters may position themselves behind cover and facing the wind. Another one or two hunters will proceed to circle around the area where deer are known or suspected to be. The route should be wide and with the wind so as to not spook the deer away from the waiting hunters.

The drivers should proceed slowly and cautiously back toward the waiting hunters. They must take their time, moving with the wind, and not so fast that the deer take off running. The drivers also must try to prevent the deer from doubling back and circling around behind them again. The real trophy bucks will not be fooled by such tactics, but driving can push a couple of decent bucks or does past the waiting hunters.

In some circles, blacktails are called America's toughest game animals. By any measure, hunting them is a real challenge.

The blacktail deer hunter will study the terrain for sign of deer trails. Blacktails may not travel far from their home as they feed.

Joe Byers stalked the 6x5 satellite bull for an hour before finally bringing it down.

ORDINARILY, THE GUIDE doesn't challenge herd bulls, because they usually move their cows from the aggressor, rather than leave them unguarded to face a rival, reports Joe Byers. However, this one seemed so fired up that Alan Blair and Byers closed half the distance to the monarch while Clyde, their guide, mocked bugles and bashed brush, trying to bring the bull past their concealed locations.

Byers' plane had arrived in Alamosa, Colorado, at 10:30 p.m., the evening before. From there, George Taulman, president of United States Outfitters (USO), an old friend, drove two hours to the Chromo Mountain camp. Despite the 3:00 a.m. arrival, the many exploits and adventures from other hunters in camp kept the new arrivals alert. Taulman operates a large elk hunting operation and leases nearly a million acres of huntable habitat in New Mexico.

While Clyde did his best to bugle, cow-call and branch-break to provoke the herd bull, the monarch proved to be more in control of his destiny than his bugles implied. After half an hour, the hunters mustered to start Plan B.

All USO guides get ABA degrees from their boss, George Taulman. Although not hanging on any office wall, their Always-Be-Aggressive approach brings success for bow-

hunters. While Clyde kept the big bull occupied, Blair and Byers stalked his position.

The bull and cows were on the edge of a large park, the old boy just inside the timber. Blair tried to work through the park, taking advantage of sparse aspen, while Byers tried to circle downwind to get below the herd.

The dark timber was thick with underbrush, making the stalk difficult. The hunter tested the wind often and did his best to maintain his sanity. The bull was less than 100 yards away, and Byers expected to see him at any moment.

Suddenly, Byers heard cows calling just ahead. Slightly below the herd, Byers was in the perfect spot for the group to exit the park. He found a big tree to stand against and mentally began to select shooting lanes. He could hear footsteps pounding his way.

Minutes passed, but no elk appeared. The bull's next bugles seemed to be farther down the park. Taulman's advice about stalking elk: "Most hunters greatly underestimate how fast an elk can walk. Following elk is almost always fruitless. The best approach is to drop off and run as fast as you can to get in front of the herd."

Byers remembered the advice and dropped a hundred yards below the park and moved quickly to close ground. The 10,000-foot altitude was taking its toll. He could hear the bull bugle directly in front.

The next bugle was more distant, and Byers tried the circling strategy once again, this time covering twice as much ground as before. A period of anxious silence was shattered as a bugle exploded about 75 yards behind.

Byers climbed 15 yards to the level of the bull and nocked an arrow. A combination of altitude and excitement brought on slight dizziness. The hunter paused a few seconds to gather his composure, then sneaked over the ridge, searching for any movement in the dense conifers.

Tense minutes passed. Suddenly the bull bugled a hundred yards down another ridge. How had he gotten past? Elk can move with incredible stealth. Just then, Blair appeared along an old logging road and the pair discussed options. Blair had hunted this area before and predicted the herd would move onto a steep eastern slope, the direction of the last bugle. Blair is an experienced and enthusiastic bowhunter with five elk under his belt.

"One of us should try to get ahead of the herd, while the other stays close behind," Byers suggested.

Blair nodded in agreement and moved hastily down the canyon to get ahead of the bull. The herd master made things a little easier by bugling again, indicating he was in about the same location as before.

Blair had been out of sight for only minutes when Byers saw movement and tall antlers headed in his direction. Could the herd bull finally be coming his way? That question was answered as a screaming grunt emerged 50 yards behind the bull.

Byers assumed it was a satellite bull, a male that circles the fringe of a herd hoping to find an unguarded cow to breed while the herd bull is otherwise occupied. The bull was at about 40 yards, an impossible shot in the thick

Byers uses a Sceery cow call with full camouflage to lure bull elk into close range for a shot.

Even if the animal is down, it must be approached cautiously. You must be ready to shoot again.

conifers. Stalking was out of the question, but cow-calling had promise.

The physical conditioning the hunter had undergone the previous two months was paying off. Although Byers hadn't been able to overtake the herd bull, those multi-mile rapid walks back in Maryland built enough lung power to handle the thin air.

Byers' gear had been selected carefully. The bow-and-arrow setup would deliver maximum power at a moderate to low poundage. The extra brace height of the Golden Eagle 3-D bow, combined with Easton Ultra-Light 2212 shafts tipped with Satellite 90-grain broadheads, provided a hard-hitting arrow with excellent trajectory, despite the moderate 54-pound draw weight. Byers was totally camouflaged from gloves to face net in the Mossy Oak Treestand pattern.

Byers called a soft cow sound and the bull reacted. He turned from his uphill course and quartered toward the hunter's position. The elk had an unusual antler on one side of what appeared to be a six-by-five rack, numbers that computed into go, despite the early stage of the hunt, barely an hour old.

The bull walked through a small opening at an estimated 35 yards, but there were numerous sticks and branches potentially in the way.

"Be patient, wait for a good shot," Byers prompted myself.

The elk was not in any hurry. Several minutes passed before he took deliberate steps into thick brush, about to leave.

Confident that his camouflage would hold, Byers stood motionless in front of a small spruce as the bull searched the vicinity for the female he thought he heard. More minutes passed before the bull began moving slowly down the hill.

Calculating a range of 30 yards, Byers drew the bow. Once again, the animal paused and he was forced to relax his draw. The good thing about the low poundage was that he could hold a long time and not exhaust his muscles.

Once again, Byers turned his head and made two soft cow calls. The response was immediate. The bull rotated and began walking, angling slightly up hill. Byers came to full draw. Fortune shined as the elk entered a small window of spruce, exposing his shoulder and vitals.

The arrow released, sending the shaft deep into the ribcage. In a flash, the bull wheeled and ran out of the

Part of the lure of bowhunting is packing out the trophy antlers, as Byers is doing.

The Golden Eagle bow was set at a relatively light 54 pounds of draw. Byers used 90-grain Satellite broadheads for the hunt.

canyon, pausing about 75 yards away. He ran on, and in a moment, all was quiet.

The hunt had lasted an exciting ninety minutes.

There was little doubt about shot placement. Byers found the broken shaft and evidence that the arrow had penetrated about 20 inches, enough for a double lung hit and exactly the impact any bowhunter hopes for. A short bit of trailing and Byers found the animal lying in the open, 40 yards ahead. It traveled only 100 yards and succumbed in a matter of seconds.

Although there were many larger bulls on Chromo, this was a respectable animal. The hunters ate the tenderloin the next day, and the meat was delicious, Byers reports. The low poundage bow and fast arrow setup worked well. The point of the Satellite broadhead had broken the hide on the far side of the bull.

Chromo elk are typical of the excellent hunting available in New Mexico. The USO guides were competent and friendly. Walt, the cook, could qualify as a world-class chef, and accommodations were comfortable.

Physical conditioning is important to make the most of this hunt. Although some roads on the ranch make retrieving an elk easier, most hunting is done on foot.

New Mexico, Colorado, Arizona, Wyoming, Idaho, Oregon, Washington and Montana are among the top states for elk hunting in the U.S. Some have large elk populations, but not many giant bulls, while others have the real trophy animals, but in limited numbers. Many states have strict requirements and controls on the number of hunting permits issued per season. Many are based on a computer drawing and require applications from

Calling may be tried when hunting elk. The far northern part of New Mexico is a bowhunter's paradise.

bowhunters early in the year. Each state or province seems to be different, and seasons, dates and fees are always subject to change. Last year's rules are not this year's rules. As elk numbers improve and the popularity of elk hunting continues to increase, bowhunters can expect more restrictions. The wise bowhunter will inquire of the game department of the state to be hunted well in advance of the season.

Moose are large, usually found in limited numbers and in but a few locations. They are challenging archery targets.

Stan Chiras is an experienced bowhunter with more than thirty years experience seeking most North American big game. He knows some moose tags are hard to come by, and the opportunities to hunt these animals are quite limited. For some, it may be a decade of waiting to obtain a permit. Recently, though, Chiras had some good luck on Shiras moose.

TO PURSUE SHIRAS moose, you need more luck than the average lotto jackpot winner. They're hunted in limited numbers in Colorado, Montana, Idaho and Wyoming. Chiras' hunt was in southeastern British Columbia, in the famous Kootenay Mountain Range. Tags there are no easier to get than in the Shiras' U.S. range. An outfitter was allocated only one every three years!

A tag was available in Area 4-1, where Safari Club International and the Boone and Crockett record-keeping club has recognized the Shiras subspecies. This is due to the mutual research of British Columbia and Montana, in essence saying that the Shiras travels freely across their borders. It seems that radio-collared Montana Shiras moose have been showing up in southeastern British Columbia.

Stan Chiras jumped at the opportunity for a hunt, and did so regardless of the archery-record-keeping Pope & Young Club's failure to recognize this obvious extension of the Shiras' range. The moose weren't told about the U.S.-Canada border as they expanded their range in the early 1900s. Logging operations transformed the once moose-free mountains into suitable habitat due to the abundance of feed which grows in the many clearcuts left behind by the loggers.

Chiras met outfitter Bob Cutts at the Kalispell, Montana, airport and made the three-hour drive to Fernie, B.C. Chiras thought moose were lowland animals, frequenting swamps and bogs near lakes and rivers. Cutts told Chiras he would be hunting high, probably in the snow.

It was 6 a.m. when the guide, Kevin Rookes, knocked on Chiras' door. All Chiras wanted from Rookes was to be in the right area, get a little information on the terrain and some help in spotting. That meant stalking alone and depending on his own judgment once the game was spotted.

After no more than ten minutes of glassing, the guide spotted moose about a mile away in an old burn. Spotting game on the

An arrow with a Muzzy broadhead brought down the moose. He fell just inches from an icy cold river, making field-dressing chores easier for the hunter.

Downed bull moose are huge and must be approached with caution. If only wounded, an animal this large can run down and trample the hunter.

first morning was a good sign. A closer look with the spotting scope revealed a bull, although how good a bull had yet to be determined.

Shiras are a diminutive moose. They might compare with Cones whitetails, about half the size of an average Midwestern deer. Shiras are smaller in body and even smaller in the antler department. But that doesn't make them any less of a trophy. As a matter of fact, by virtue of the extremely limited permit opportunities—compounded by the rugged places in which these animals prefer to live—they are considered the most difficult trophy in the moose family.

Canada moose, found throughout most of Canada, are larger. The Alaska-Yukon moose, largest of all, is found where its name indicates. It is easy to get tags for both, and they live in

the watery environs usually associated with these black leviathans.

One interesting thing both Kevin Rookes and Bob Cutts had said was that Shiras moose often spend long periods going nowhere. They just feed and feed, then bed in the same spot for hours. It was a stalker's dream! British Columbia is trying to build up its moose herds and has seen to it that their short, ten-day hunting season takes place long after the rut is past. While it makes for harder hunting, more game is able to survive. They also severely limit the numbers of both resident and non-resident tags. As a result, the hunting is reportedly getting better.

Suddenly, the moose jerked up their heads. At first, Chiras thought they had seen or heard him. He soon noticed they were

Shiras moose may make their home in the higher elevations. Snow is always a possibility during hunting season.

looking over his shoulder, not at him. One by one, the moose lumbered up the steep mountain and disappeared over the ridge, obviously spooked. Chiras headed back to the truck. Then he saw them; three orange-clad nimrods practically running at the moose, rifles at the ready.

Unfortunately, B.C. has a short bow season—only nine days. Moose aren't in season during those nine days! Most hunters don't have opportunities like that on the first day of a hunt and most times don't expect to get another.

It was a scenic drive to base camp with Cutts through a high mountain pass that ended deep in snow country. The wind was howling and a foreboding storm was lurking on the horizon. Chiras was assured that this was Shiras moose country.

That night it snowed to the point the hunters gave consideration to leaving before they were covered up for the winter. But the storm abated somewhat by morning, and the hunter and guide spent the day alternately glassing in the dense snow flurries and hiking various mountain passes. Moose usually hole up during storms, and the hunter saw nothing.

The next morning was spent glassing the area. The guide spotted another small bull that night, but it was on the move. Perhaps a late rut was on.

The fifth day began with yet another snowstorm, which dashed the hunters' spirits. Chiras was inspecting a patch of willows about two miles away that seemed to have two dark spots lurking like shadows.

The guide suddenly described where he was looking and, lo and behold, a bull was found about 100 yards from where Chiras had been concentrating on the dark spots! The snow had started again, and a check with the spotting scope revealed nothing but two miles of compressed snowflakes! Nevertheless, Rookes was sure he had seen paddles, an animal with a huge chest and shoulders, indicative of a bull. The animal then bedded, right on the open hillside.

The two drove around and behind the ridge where they had last seen the moose. After moving back and forth, up and down, they concluded he just wasn't there. The experienced bowhunter decided to move in anyway, to find his track and see if he had spooked or simply moved off.

The snow was squeakier than ever. It was impossible to move quietly. As Chiras neared the spot where the moose was last spotted, he saw antlers no more than 25 yards away. He was there after all, too close for comfort. The antlers were pointing straight in the hunter's direction, indicating his radar was turned on. Chiras quickly drew an arrow from his quiver and jammed it on the rest.

Moments later, with absolutely no warning, the bull surged to his feet and whirled. Chiras came to full draw and grunted twice. The bull came to a screeching halt! He had managed to turn, offering the hunter a severe quartering-away shot through the smallest of openings. Chiras settled his 20-yard pin on the animal's ham, knowing full well how effective the shot is from ground level, and released. The arrow smacked home with a resounding thwack. It was a perfect femoral artery hit, one that virtually never fails. The hit was a good one, and the bull would soon be down.

Hunter and guide trailed the bull for almost a mile before coming upon him, just as he was running out of steam. Another arrow, skewering the bull literally from stem-to-stern, did the trick. He literally dropped on impact. The first arrow had done the job, and the second immediately finished the bull.

The local meat processing plant said the moose was the largest taken that season. British Columbia is a true hunter's paradise, with more species of big game than anywhere else in North America, including the hard-to-find Shiras moose.

18 ▶ Antelope

The American pronghorn antelope population has seen a dramatic comeback in this century after almost disappearing from the scene. Wyoming has the largest herds.

ANTELOPE HAVE a well-deserved reputation for running fast, possess excellent eyesight and are known as being difficult game for usually successful hunters. All these things are true, but this species can be taken by bowhunters who are willing to work hard and follow the rules of stealth on the prairies.

There was a time, earlier in the 20th century, when the American pronghorn antelope almost disappeared from its habitat. The numbers were way down, and they were unappreciated by hunters. However, thanks primarily to the game managers of Wyoming and surrounding states, the number of pronghorns running free today adds up to more than a million and growing. Wyoming remains the number one state for most hunters, but several other Western states have antelope seasons, including California, Nevada, Utah, Colorado, Montana and New Mexico.

The pronghorn antelope belongs to the goat family and actually is not a relative of the deer. When they have adequate water and food, and the space needed to roam, antelope will thrive. Their range is expanding, as are their numbers.

The former Dust Bowl area of northern New Mexico is ideal habitat for the speedy animals. This area is part of the high prairies, where altitudes are 5,000 feet and higher. In most years, the area gets plenty of winter rain and snow, resulting in the good growth of grasses and plenty of drinking water. A combination of drought and improper farming practices brought on the Dust Bowl in the 1930s, driving most of the farmers off the land. Today, the area is grazing land for cattle, sharing the pastures with thousands of antelope and a lesser population of deer. The government forbids any other use of the land. No plow or disc is allowed to break the ground, exposing the soil to the ravages of the nearly constant winds. Most, if not all, of the

small farms and homes, as well as some towns, have been abandoned for years, leaving only large land holdings and cattle grazing operations in the spring, summer and early fall.

Winter comes early to the area. Cattle are rounded up and moved to lower, warmer pastures before snows fall. During hunting season, though, they share water and food with wild game.

New Mexico schedules a special archery-only antelope season in early August. Most of it is on private property, and hunters must work through outfitters and guides who hold the hunting leases on property throughout that part of the state. Some utilize the abandoned buildings as hunting lodges. They have been cleverly rebuilt to make the hunters' stay comfortable. One does not have to rough-it to enjoy antelope hunting.

Basically, there are two techniques for hunting antelope, neither much different than hunting deer. One may spot and stalk the pronghorn antelope, or the hunter may choose to attempt an ambush from a blind. Hunting from a blind is most common in antelope country. The blind may be simply hiding behind some natural high grass or shrubs, or a pit dug in the prairie within arrow distance of a drinking spot. The high-prairie cattle ranches are spotted with windmills that pump water into drinking tanks. These attract not only cattle, but wild game, too. When water is scarce, the tanks are utilized at least daily by antelope. But if the high prairie has a wet summer, natural springs, ponds and streams will be well filled with water and antelope will be more scattered. Antelope browse rather than graze, and they cover a lot of ground in any given period of time.

In dry years, many watermills have hunters sitting in them, awaiting the daily visits by antelope. In hot weather, antelope

Texas bowhunter Charles Markwood found the trip to northeastern New Mexico worth the effort as he shows off his trophy.

A typical box blind on the high prairie is set in place before hunting season so antelope are used to it. It should be strong enough to withstand curious cattle.

usually drink once a day. If the bowhunter is sitting at a water tank when the animals come in to drink, a tree stand-type shot is possible.

Antelope are not only fast travelers, but have excellent eyesight. The slightest hunter movement will spook them, no matter how dry the season. The antelope will wait until after shooting hours, or they will travel elsewhere for a drink. The wait in a windmill can mean long hours of no movement by the hunter. Because of the game's eyesight, the hunter must be in the windmill tower before daylight or the antelope will spook from all the movement and noise of arrival and climbing.

A typical method in some areas of Wyoming and Colorado is to hunt from a pit blind. Often the blind is dug ahead of time by guides. First, the area must be scouted to locate a watering hole and to determine the direction of the prevailing winds and sunshine during typical hunting hours. The site must be downwind from the watering pond, but within arrow distance.

The pit should be surrounded by brush, sagebrush or other natural growth, possibly hauled in from nearby. The cover is arranged to shield the hunter from the back, as well as the front. With an open back, the slightest movement by the hunter while in the blind will alert the antelope when they spot the silhouette. The hunter must be careful to make only the slightest movements when antelope are within view. It is believed they can see human movement from at least as far away as we can see them.

The pit or hole in the ground should be deep enough that the hunter can sit with some comfort, perhaps able to shift his legs and torso out of sight below ground level. There should be room for a water bottle, perhaps a relief container, lunch and maybe a stool.

Arriving before daylight, the hunter will want to examine the pit with a flashlight to make sure no rattlesnakes have taken advantage of the new hole in the ground. A top or cover over the blind will protect the hunter from the fierce rays of the overhead sun. The extra shade from the top cover also will help conceal the hunter in the blind. On private land, permission to dig a pit always must be obtained first, and the hole should be filled in after hunting season. Check regulations on public land before

digging. Cattle are curious animals and can be injured by stumbling into a pit blind.

On private grazing areas where no brush is available, box blinds are typical. A pit is dug in the ground near places such as fence corners or other strategic locations. Then, green-painted plywood boxes are placed over the pits. The boxes have shooting ports in the direction the animals are expected to arrive and a shade top of wood or burlap for protection from sun and sudden thunderstorms. The blinds are sturdy enough that cattle cannot move them and fall into the pits. The shooting ports may be screened with strips of burlap to hide any hunter movement inside. Usually, the box blinds are set in place well before hunting season so the antelope have time to get used to their presence. They are removed and the holes filled in after hunting season.

Good locations for box blinds might include those within a few yards of crossing game trails, near water sources or where evidence indicates the antelope are crossing fences. Antelope are capable of high, long leaps, but often seem intimidated by barbed-wire fences they can clear easily. They are known to favor certain crossing points where the wire has sagged. There will be plenty of tracks leading to and from such locations.

Properly placed box or pit blinds will let the hunter see approaching antelope from a long distance. It is then that the bowhunter must use the utmost caution about movement inside the blind. Moving binoculars up to the eyes, nocking an arrow, drinking from the canteen or other movement can be spotted by the antelope. They will tantalize and frustrate the bowhunter from just outside archery range for hours at a time. Patience is the most important ingredient the bowhunter must have when hunting from a blind.

Antelope are commonly seen in herds, large or small, from a distance—usually a long distance. The spot-and-stalk hunting method is possible on antelope, and most hunters feel it is a lot more fun than sitting in a blind for hours at time. In some areas where antelope roam, stalking is more productive than blind-sitting. Most guides will have some idea of where the local herds are expected at certain times of the day and will be able to take the bowhunters to vantage points. Often, the antelope can be seen from pick-up trucks traveling the roads. The prairie may seem completely flat at first, but there are plenty of hills, draws, streambeds and canyons in most antelope country. These permit spotting from a long distance and provide approach routes for those who want to work at it.

Terrain may include plenty of sharp rocks, sand, holes and thorny plants as well as cattle feed. When a herd of antelope is spotted, they may be evaluated through binoculars to determine possible trophy value. Both bucks and does have horns—they are horns, not antlers that drop off each year—but the male antelope have thicker, heavier horns with the little fork or slight branch near the tip that leads to the name pronghorn. During the special New Mexico archery season, either does or bucks may be taken on a tag. In some parts of Wyoming, in some years, an over-abundance of animals will cause the game managers to issue extra doe-only tags to those who have already taken an earlier buck.

Creeping and crawling across the rough prairie floor can be tough work, especially if the distance is long—and most stalks are. The hunter must keep the wind in his face and not give into the temptation to take a peek over the next rise to verify the antelope's location. One wrong move and the stalk is over. The antelope will be gone or will play games and stay just out of bow range as the hunter tries to move closer.

When hunting with guides, an attempt that is sometimes successful has the hunter in place behind any natural cover after a herd is spotted some distance away. The guide or perhaps a

Using windmill stands overlooking water tanks is a typical antelope hunting technique. Animals must drink each day.

hunting partner may circle around behind the herd and, on foot, attempt a loose drive. The herd may be a mile away and can turn off from the direction of the hunter at any time. The driver's technique will be to walk slowly and casually in a zig-zag direction, generally in the known direction of the hunter. It can work, but a wind change or inadvertent movement from the hunter will spook the pronghorns. Again, patience is the key to success.

While overly long archery shots never are recommended, the antelope bowhunter must be prepared for arrow shots longer than the typical whitetail deer shot. The ranges will be more like mule deer hunting. The flatter the arrow trajectory at 20 to 40 yards, the better chance the bowhunter will have. There may or may not be time to use a manual rangefinder to determine the distance to the target, especially while stalking. Hunting from a blind, the distance to the anticipated target may be paced off in advance or the guide may already know the ranges from the hunter.

A fast, lightweight bow and the strongest broadheads possible are basic equipment. Antelope are not tough-skinned, but they are slightly smaller than they appear; misses are common. The rocks will destroy a lot of arrows.

Antelope country is always rough country. A good, solid pair of boots is a requirement for comfort and safety. In a pit blind, the hunter does almost no walking, but for stalking, high-top hunting boots with good soles will deliver protection to the feet and ankles. Thunderstorms are not uncommon during hunting season, and a pit blind can fill with water in minutes.

For most locations, some sort of lighter-colored camouflage pattern will be in order. The high desert and high prairie of antelope country are colored generally by shades of tan and brown, with plenty of dark shadows. The prairie may be green with grass, but brown predominates. The camo colors should match the terrain. Full camouflage cover, including face paint or head net and gloves, is necessary.

The bowhunter may anticipate hot weather while hunting antelope. Heavy woolen or fleece garments may not be in order in these parts at this time of year. The evenings may be chilly, especially after a thunderstorm, but the days are mostly hot and sunny. Early mornings at an altitude of 6,000-plus feet usually range from chilly to downright cold, but when the sun comes up, things will warm up rapidly. The prepared hunter will use the layering system, able to remove some outer clothing as heat builds during the day.

As mentioned, a pair of good binoculars is a must for locating and evaluating antelope. The hunter will want to have at least one canteen to carry into the blind or on the stalk. A small day pack or fanny pack will hold spare parts, flashlight and lunch for the day while the hunter is away from the base camp or hunting lodge. Some pit-blind hunters have been known to carry along a soft-cover book to help wile away the hours until antelope make their appearance at the water hole.

The number of antelope permits vary from state to state and from year to year, depending upon the previous year's conditions and hunter success. In most areas, the herd numbers are increasing and limits are becoming more liberal. Check state game regulations for details.

18 *Caribou*

Schefferville, Quebec, is well known to caribou hunters traveling to Canada. The sign says it all.

Minnesota hunter Gary Clancy took a caribou in Newfoundland with bow and arrow.

TO NATIVES OF the Far North, nothing from the caribou goes to waste. Every part—including the bones, hide, antlers, meat and everything else—has a use. This was true in the past, before the arrival of Europeans on the continent, and it is true in the late 20th century. Caribou still feed and clothe the Inuits and Indians who live that far into the wilderness. The animals have a special significance for those who are able to utilize them, and these days, this is true for the hunters from farther south who seek the caribou.

The Pope & Young Club recognizes geographical sub-species of caribou, across Alaska and Canada, from coast to coast. Perhaps the best known are the animals which make their home in northern Quebec. Stories of the migrations of these animals are legion and legend. The herd numbers vary from year to year, but is usually estimated to be more than half a million. If the hunter is in the right place at the right time, thousands of caribou will pass by the camp or blind over a period of a few days. All the hunter needs to do is sit and wait for what he guesses to be the largest set of antlers and shoot. On the other hand, the hunter may see no caribou at all during the week of his hunt.

Seasons in Quebec may vary slightly from year to year, as the province closely monitors the number and health of the caribou herd. Hunting is strictly controlled, but the opportunities for

Stateside hunters are terrific. The migration of the so-called George River caribou herd usually takes place from early August through the end of September. Most years, hunters are permitted to take two animals per license. Hunters may take an animal with a rifle—blackpowder or smokeless powder—or a bow, or he may take one with each arm. Many animals from the George River herd have found their way into both the firearm and archery record books.

The season is timed for when the migration is expected, but is always over by the end of September, because of the weather problems that far north. Most years, the lakes and rivers on which the bush planes must land and take off are frozen over by the end of September. The hunting camps, monitored by the province, are all closed for the season shortly thereafter, while the seaplanes can still ferry out the guides and outfitters.

Even as early as the first of August, hunters in the area can expect the worst and best weather, from rain, wind, sunshine or calm, to snowstorms and deep cold. Hunters must be prepared for everything, especially wet weather. All clothing, from boots to hat, must be waterproof, not water-repellent. Many wear hip boots or waders while hunting caribou. The hunter should not leave home without two pair of waterproof footwear. Wet feet can be a serious survival matter and should not be tolerated.

Speaking of twos, any visitor to this part of the world should have at least two sets of long underwear. They should be insulated with a modern material that will wick away moisture and sweat that is sure to be generated while walking. Wool is the choice of many hunters in this part of the world, including many of the locals. Wool will continue to keep the wearer warm, even when wet, an important point when hunting caribou in the rain.

Quebec requires all hunters, including those with bow and arrow, to wear bright orange. Most bowhunters choose a bright vest or jacket of some sort, plus perhaps a hat, and wear them even while also wearing camouflage clothing. The guides and outfitters all stress the rule, and it is observed by all. If the vest is one of the reversible types with insulating material in it, it will add another warm layer for the hunter and is sure to be appreciated sometime during the hunt.

Bowhunting equipment is the same as for deer. Caribou are not particularly thin-skinned. If the hunter is lucky and finds himself in the middle of the migration, the shot will be close—

perhaps as near as 10 yards. Plenty of arrows should be carried, and adequate spare equipment, too. Caribou country is really a long distance by bush plane from what might be considered civilization; archery shops or UPS deliveries are only in dreams. Extra broadheads and at least a spare bowstring are the minimums to be taken to Quebec. A pair of tough, waterproof binoculars is also essential to study the caribou as they swim the rivers and streams, if the goal is to take a trophy animal. Bulls and cows without calves are legal during the caribou season, and both carry antlers, although the cows' are considerably smaller.

Hunting camp accommodations may range from rather primitive to almost luxurious. On a recent hunt, some archers were treated to a camp with a modern building not unlike a mobile home. It was constructed of wood and transported to the site in sections during the short summer. The building, on the shores of the Leaf River, had five double bedrooms, indoor plumbing with two baths and showers, hot water, a modern kitchen with freezer and gas-operated refrigerator, lights, and plenty of cut wood for the fireplace. Picture windows overlooked the river for miles, and non-hunting family members could observe caribou swimming the river from the comfort of the lodge. At night, the *aurora borealis* was visible from the outside deck of the building. Hunting caribou is not a sport restricted to men only. There are an increasing number of women bowhunters in caribou country. The improved hunting camps may be a reaction to that fact.

From the lodge, hunters could move either direction along the river, using well-worn caribou trails covered with thick, spongy tundra and moss, and free of undergrowth or bushes because of the passage of thousands of animals annually. If the hunters lucked out on the migration, both game tags could be filled within sight of the lodge. Otherwise, considerably more work is required.

At the other end of the accomodations spectrum was a tent camp on the edge of a small lake. Here, two sleeping tents, a cook tent and a game storage tent—all with raised wood floors—were the accommodations. There was a short dock with two motorized canoes to be used by the hunters, and wood had to be cut nearby to feed the heating and cooking stoves. The camp, known as Camp Ritchie, was in terrain not as open as Camp Kuatasou. Visibility was restricted by more trees and undergrowth, although that far north, none of the

Good binoculars, waterproof and armored, are an asset during a caribou hunt in the Far North. The camo outfit is from Woolrich and has a Gore-Tex waterproof lining.

trees are really very tall—20 to 30 feet is an old, tall tree.

When the caribou are migrating, they will move through the hunting area, seemingly almost oblivious to humans. They move with purpose, as singles or as herds of hundreds at a time. Caribou are excellent swimmers, with wide, splayed feet that propel them through the cold water at surprising speeds. Their hollow, insulating hair, used to keep the natives warm, also keeps the animals warm as they swim.

A common hunting technique has hunters spotting the animals as they begin swimming from the far shore. They are spotted easily with good optics. During even the slow part of the migration, they may enter at any location and reach the opposite shore farther downstream. The hunter usually can predict the landing beach and reach the area after a fast walk along easy trails, staying out of sight of the caribou. The trick is to set up an ambush behind a large rock or above the river bank, where one thinks the caribou will come ashore.

It is not legal nor ethical to shoot swimming animals, and

The province of Quebec requires all hunters to wear blaze orange while hunting.

Caribou cows have smaller horns. Often, they may be approached more closely.

Not every caribou is a wall-hanging trophy, but all make good eating. The shores of Lake Ritchie have plenty of snow, even in early September.

they must be allowed to leave the water and reach solid ground before the hunter releases an arrow. If the hunter is waiting above the river bank, hidden by trees or shrubs, that will not be a problem, as the river bank may be 20 feet high or more.

If the hunter miscalculates the landing zone, some movement is acceptable. Most areas have enough plant growth to allow the hunter to shift positions several times during the caribou's swim before the herd hits the beach. However, if the hunter has established a spot behind a beach boulder to await the swimming caribou, movement must be held to the same minimum as for deer hunters.

At times, caribou can be approached closely as long as they do not catch the scent of the hunter. Migrating caribou have been known to pass within a few feet of humans without reacting, until they moved downwind.

The small, former mining boomtown of Schefferville, several hours north of Montreal, is the jumping-off place for all non-resident caribou hunters seeking the George River herd. Every hunter passes through the little town. It is only a few blocks square, and since the iron mines closed several years ago, its only industry is catering to fishermen in the summer and hunters in the fall.

However, thousands of hunters pass through during the short season, and most are treated and fed well, and make their connections on time. All the outfitters have headquarters in Schefferville, accommodating the hunters at either the small hotel in town or in one of the many government-built houses around town, unused otherwise. The hunters must buy their meals—at high prices, despite the value of the Canadian dollar—because of the town's isolation.

Some hunting camps require the hunters to bring in their own food and fix their own meals. Others are furnished with camp cooks and flown-in food. Of course, the successful caribou hunter will have a couple of meals of caribou meat, sweet and tender, while still in camp.

Perhaps the taste of caribou is one of the reasons for the increasing popularity of hunting these large animals. Another reason is the increased accessibility of the game. More and more outfitters and guides realize the interest from Americans, Canadians and Europeans. Some outfitters make it a point to attend outdoor shows in France, attempting to interest French

hunters in coming to Quebec for caribou. After all, they speak the same language. Many, if not most, Canadians living in Quebec are at least bilingual. Some Indians and Inuits speak at least three languages; many are conversant in more.

Bowhunters in the northern tier of the United States are not that far from Montreal and Schefferville. There are some who drive to the railhead and take a train to Schefferville. Most fly into Montreal to be met by their outfitters' representatives, remain overnight in Montreal enjoying the Quebec hospitality, and catch another Air Canada plane for the flight to Schefferville.

Air Canada employees understand the needs of hunters, going and coming. They cheerfully handle the antlers and boxes of meat, plus all the other hunting gear taken along. They have their rules about firearms and bows, but they do not hassle the hunters when checking through airports or onto airplanes. Furthermore, the service and schedules are excellent. The same may be said for hotel personnel in Montreal. They are used to dozens of hunters trying to check in and check out at a time, carrying all sorts of cases, bags, boxes and perhaps large caribou antlers. Hotel employees efficiently see that each traveler's boxes of caribou meat are stored in large freezers in the hotel kitchen, labeling them and having them ready for the hunter taking an early shuttle to the airport.

While the famous caribou migration can be an impressive sight, only the animals determine when and where it will occur. The hunter might miss the exact locations by a few miles or a few days, or he may be at the right place and right time. Weather conditions, predators and unknown conditions may increase or reduce the herd size. The numbers seem to run in cycles. Canadian outfitters will have the latest information on caribou numbers.

There are some special Canadian travel and hunting requirements the American hunter will encounter. Any outfitter will outline the license and hunt costs, as well as the special requirements to American hunters. The outfitter will also explain the equipment recommendations, the hunting dates and what to expect, as well as provide references that may be approached.

The cost is not much more than a long whitetail hunt, the equipment requirements are much the same—and the rewards are great!

Bear

The use of tracking hounds is still legal and useful when hunting bear in many areas. However, anti-hunting groups are attacking the practice.

Most bowhunters hunt bear from a tree stand over some bear bait.

BLACK BEAR POPULATIONS are large and growing. With a couple of exceptions, almost every state and province has archery seasons for bear. Through enlightened game management, most officials are increasing the opportunities for hunters to seek black bruins with archery tackle.

Brown, grizzly and polar bear hunting are special situations only in limited areas and at the most expensive costs. They will not be treated here except to say that those animals can be the most dangerous in North America. When hunting other game in those habitats, all hunters must give browns and polars the utmost respect and use caution when any are present.

The fact that most black bear populations are increasing does not mean they are easy game or that hunters are not faced with problems connected to them. Several states are faced with increasing restrictions on bear hunting from anti-hunting and animal-welfare groups. In some areas, hunting bear with bow and arrows has been banned for a time. In others, heavy restrictions on the use of trailing hounds or bear bait have been enacted, effectively banning or seriously restricting bear hunting. In some locations, these restrictions have been reversed by voters' actions, but in others, the battle may be lost.

Perhaps it is because young bear cubs look so cute in pictures that the anti-hunting groups are able to more easily and successfully attack some bear hunting. Savvy hunters understand that some restrictions ultimately lead to others. An attack on any part of hunting is an attack on all, particularly bowhunting.

Perhaps the most popular method of bowhunting bear is from a tree stand placed over some sort of bear bait. The technique is most common in Canada and many states. While the do-it-yourself hunter might find success with bait, the method is usually a task for outfitters and guides who set things up in advance of the season, ready for hunters.

Many outfitters will establish several, perhaps dozens, of bait locations. Each station must be checked and serviced daily, usually requiring plenty of hard work from several people. The locations must be set up before hunting season and maintained so that bear will continue to use them during the season.

Bear bait may be any of several things, depending upon local availability. Food may include bakery leftovers such as bread, donuts, sweet rolls and the like. It may be meat scraps, preferably old, rotten meat with plenty of scent to attract bear from afar. It may be supplemented with scent-enhancers—honey, syrup, animal scraps and anything else that can be found and used. It becomes obvious that with a dozen or more bait sites, maintenance becomes a genuine problem in logistics. If a bait station should run out of food for a couple of days, the bears will get out of the habit of visiting there and look elsewhere to eat. There goes a potential hunting spot.

The bait must be placed in strong, bear-proof containers of some sort. Many outfitters use 55-gallon drums chained and secured to large trees that bears cannot move. Some build log feeders with openings large enough that bears can stick their heads in and eat. The log feeders must be extremely rugged to withstand the power of a large bear determined to tear them down to get at all the food.

A tree stand must be placed downwind of the bait, high enough to be out of reach of a standing bear, but not so far away as to be out of range. Hunting over bait is further complicated by the conditions usually found at the site. Most bait stations are in heavily wooded areas and usually in shade most of the day. The area will be dark. Black bear, even those that go through a brown stage, are dark and hard to see in deep shadows or shortly before dark. If the bait container is placed the wrong way, the feeding bear may be facing the wrong way, not offering the hunter a shot. The preferred bear shot is directly from the side.

The bear vital area is somewhat smaller than on a whitetail deer and is protected by thick bone, muscle and heavy fur. The prospective bowhunter should study bear anatomy charts to thoroughly understand the location of the bear's vital organs. Trailing a wounded bear in the thick, dark woods is a task neither hunter nor guide will relish.

Some states and provinces have fall bear seasons, but most bear hunting takes place in the spring, shortly after hibernation has finished. Spring bear hunting is usually preferred. The bears are just out of their winter naps, are plenty hungry and have less fat on them. Because they are hungry, they will be out roaming around seeking food, and that is why they may be baited. For trophy hunters, spring bear should have a better coat, not rubbed or damaged from a summer of passing through the heavy forest.

In many locations, bears may be stalked as well as hunted from stands over bait. In areas where baiting and trailing hounds have been prohibited, stalking is the only way. Most bowhunters believe that the spot-and-stalk method of hunting bears is successful only in areas with large bear populations and where they are largely without contact with humans most of the time. Where could that be? Alaska, at least southern Alaska, is one place that fits that description.

The southern part of the forty-ninth state extends down along the coast of what otherwise would be British Columbia, Canada. Offshore are thousands of islands, large and small. Many are not inhabited by humans, but support large populations of black bear, deer and other game. On some of these islands, the bears have never seen humans, or if they have had encounters, they were not with hunters.

The coasts of the islands are mostly rocky cliffs, but here and there are sandy inlets with wide beaches. Otherwise, the interiors are tightly filled with trees, vines and undergrowth resulting from plenty of rain and rather mild temperatures. The only way to reach the islands is by boat, and only the relatively narrow beaches are passable to humans.

Alaska's southern black bear season opens in early May. It is a bear hunting season, not an archery season. Any legal arm may be used to hunt bear, once the required licenses and tags are obtained. The bowhunter may carry a sidearm while hunting, and many do, especially when hunting grizzlies or brown bear, but also when hunting other game in bear country.

Pennsylvania bowhunter Bob Foulkrod is a successful black bear hunter.

Non-resident bear hunters in Alaska must be accompanied by a state-licensed guide. As a practical matter, hiring a guide or outfitter to obtain boat transportation around the islands is the only possibility. The guide will have a boat large enough to serve as the base camp; sleeping and eating accommodations may be provided at a hunting lodge. The Alaska guide will also have one or two smaller motorboats to get to shore when bear are spotted. Most importantly, he or she will have knowledge of the surrounding waters, weather conditions and bear hunting grounds. An uninformed hunter might sail the inland waters for months and not reach the right island.

The hunting season opens soon after the black bears have awakened from their hibernation. They are hungry, seeking food along the beaches of their islands. They can be spotted from the motorboats patrolling around the island. Some beaches, especially at low tide, may be quite wide and deep. Inland, plenty of tender spring grass grows, drawing the bears to feast. Omnivorous, the bears will graze on the grass as well as scarf up any sea denizens left by the retreating tide.

Often on these beaches, a dozen or more bears may be observed grazing at once. With good light-gathering binoculars, the bowhunter may study the animals and decide on which one to put a stalk. The hunting party lands ashore downwind of the bears and can begin the stalk, even on the rocky shoreline, as long as the wind remains favorable. On some islands, bears seem unconcerned or perhaps unaware of the human hunters. As long as they do not catch wind of the humans, they will continue eating as the archers approach within arrow distance.

Bears have tough hides, plenty of thick fur and heavy bones, as well as smaller vital areas. The bowhunter must have a hard-hitting, fast-shooting bow-and-arrow combination with only the sharpest, strongest broadheads. Some bear hunters advocate

In Alaska, the bowhunters' lodge may be one of the small boats from an island off the southern coast.

Alaska guides will advise the hunter of correct trophy care until the hunting party reaches the dock.

using the more traditional two-blade broadheads, honed to a super edge. Others prefer three- and four-blade broadheads with their extra set of cutting edges. Spring bears do not have as much fat on them in May as they might by September, but they have more than the average deer. That means the wound will close, reducing the blood trail. All the long fur also helps absorb the blood on the outside, leaving little to trail.

Black bear will run when hit and must be watched closely to see where they disappear from sight. When hit on the beach, the bear is likely to head for the thick underbrush of the island interior. Trailing a wounded bear through thick, dark underbrush is not easy and is one reason most bowhunters also carry a large-caliber revolver. The underbrush will be wet, even if it is not raining at the time of the shot. However, the odds are that it will be raining; it usually is in that part of the world. The rain will wash away the meager blood trail, making the job even more difficult. An accurate shot is essential. If the hunter is not confident of his abilities to make one, the shot should be passed up. There are plenty of bears in that part of Alaska.

Most shots at bears will not be far, but a hard-hitting arrow is essential for success. A bow of at least 60 pounds draw should be considered the minimum. Get plenty of practice at a 3-D bear target, and study charts and drawings for an understanding of the vital area.

Camouflage clothing may be worn, but many bowhunters in Alaska don't bother. Plenty of waterproof and warm hunting garments are important, as are waterproof boots. Many Alaska hunters rely on rubber hip boots when hunting. Much of the undergrowth will be at least knee high, and it is always wet in the spring. A couple of sets of long underwear and several changes of wool socks will be welcome. Hypothermia is always a possibility in wet, windy weather, sure to be encoun-

tered in the Alaska springtime. The wet hunter will appreciate the boat/lodge for the warmth and hot food at the end of the day.

Unless you are a resident of one of the coastal island towns of southern Alaska, you will be flying into the place designated by the outfitter or guide with whom you have made arrangements. Most of the time, airplanes are the only mode of transportation practical in most of Alaska, but especially in the southern part. State licenses and game tags are available at specified retail outlets, or they may be purchased in advance from the state fish and game department in Juneau.

All those island cities where your outfitter is headquartered have game processing and taxidermist services. If you have not made advance arrangements, the outfitter can assist with that. If a bear rug for the den is in your plans, your guide will show you how to care for the bear skin on the shore or in the boat until you reach your taxidermist.

Bear meat is certainly edible, but must be treated with the same care as pork. Trichinosis will be present, and all meat must be cooked thoroughly before it is consumed. Follow the advice of your guide.

Alaska law forbids wasting any game food. Details of that important provision will be found in the current hunting regulations available where licenses are sold.

Manufacturers and Equipment Directory
For Archery and Bowhunting

A

A&R Outdoors, Inc., 1340 C.R. #6 West, Elkhart, IN 46514
A-Way Hunting Products, P.O. Box 492, Beaverton, MI 48612
Abel Mfg., 6915 N. Frontage Rd., Fairland, IN 46126
Accra 300, Mr Rick Gilley, 805 S. 11th St., Broke Arrow, OK 74012
Accu-Sights, P.O. Box 1256-X, Painstville, KY 41240
Accurest, Inc., P.O. Box 566, Wauconda, IL 60084
Adams Archery Systems, 41113 Southwind Dr., Canton, MI 48188
Advanced Bowsights, Box 279, Dominion Cir., Huntsville, AL 35811
Aerospace America, P.O. Box 189, Bay City, MI 48707
Alaska Bowhunting Supply, 14000 Golden View Dr., Anchorage, AK 99516
Alaska Frontier Archery, P.O. Box 92089, Anchorage, AK 99509
All-Rite Products, 5752 N. Silverstone Cir., Mtn. Green, UT 84050
Allen Products, 509 Gail Ave., Greer, SC 29651
Alpine Archery, P.O. Box 319, Lewiston, ID 83501
ALS Enterprises, Inc., 3365 Leon St., Muskegon, MI 49441
Altier Archery, Rt. 6, P.O. Box 286, Honesdale, PA 18431
Ambush, P.O. Box 337, Shakopee, MN 55379
Ambusher, 2007 W. 7th St., Texarkana, TX 75501
American Arrow Co., 615 N. Poplar, Orange, CA 92667
American Excelsior Co., 850 Ave. H East, Arlington, TX 76011
American Standard Co., P.O. Box 325, Southington, CT 06489
American Whitetail, Rt. 1, Box 244J, Ferdinand, IN 47532
Americase, Steve Buchanan, P.O. Box 271, Waxahachie, TX 75165
Ameristep, 4407 W Stanley Rd., Mt. Morris, MI 48458
Ames Industries, 3631 Interlake Ave. N, Seattle, WA 98103
Anchor Point Archery, 3746 Fairview, Downers Grove, IL 60515
Anderson Archery, P.O. Box 130, Grand Ledge, MI 48837
Antler King Trophy Deer, Mineral Rt. 1, Box 19, Black River Falls, WI 54615
API Outdoors, P.O. Box 1432, Tallulah, LA 71282-1432
Apple Archery Products, P.O. Box 111, Wellsville, PA 17365
Apro-Last, 1719 Monroe St., Shelton, WA 98584
APS Super Odor Eliminator, 353 Hwy. 46, Rockaway, NJ 07405
Archer's Choice Video, Prod., Inc., 6444 W. Cermak Rd., Berwyn, IL 60402
Archer's Edge, P.O. Box 935, Thompson Falls, MT 59873
Archer's Issue, Ty Brumfield, Rt. 6 Box 590, Sulphur Springs, TX 75482
Archers-Ammo, Inc., 4124 148th Ave. NE, Redmond, WA 98052
Archery Dynamics Archery, 2029 South Elms Rd., Swartz Creek, MI 48473
Archery Horizons, Inc., 159 Elkins Ave., Indiana, PA 15701
Archery Marketing, Inc., 2166 Lakeshore Dr., Sagle, ID 83860
Archery Pro. Dist., P.O. Box 1912, Bozeman, MT 59771
Archery Promotions, Cyde Hartsell, P.O. Box 1592, Lawrenceville, GA 30243
Archery Visions, P.O. Box 86, Pleasant Mount, PA 18453
Arizona Archery Enterprises, Tom Fisher, P.O. Box 25387, Prescott Valley, AZ 86312
Arizona Rim Country Product, 6401 W Chandler Blvd. #A, Chandler, AZ 85226
Arrow Manufacturing, 1365 Logan Ave., Costa Mesa, CA 92626
Arrowzona Products, Joseph Barraza, P.O. Box 1206, Gilbert, AZ 85299
Atsko/Sno-Seal, 2530 Russell SE, Orangeburg, SC 29115

B

B&R Game Calls, P.O. Box 104, Rudy, AR 72952
Ballistic Archery Prod., 446 South Rd., New Hartford, CT 06057
Barbour Tree Sights, 41 Oakwood Ln., Dadeville, AL 36853
Barramundi Corp., 6449 S. Tex Point, Homosassa, FL 34448
Barrie Archery, P.O. Box 482, Waseca, MN 56093
Basic Innovations, 1760 Hubert Rd., Midland, MI 48640
Basik Research, Inc., 1000 N. State St., Bldg. #10, Chicago, IL 60610
BBK, 119 Bobby Lou, San Antonio, TX 78218
BCY Fibers Division, P.O. Box 466, Old Lyme, CT 06376
Bear Archery, 4600 SW 41st Blvd., Gainesville, FL 32608-4999
Beman Archery Corp., 3682 Rennie School Rd., Traverse City, MI 49684
Bi-Delta Vanes, 25 Dempster, Buffalo, NY 14206
Big Buck Treestands, 855 W. Chicago Rd., Quincy, MI 49082
Big Bucks Archery Corp., P.O. Box 537, Saddlebrook, NJ 07662
Big Game Products Co., P.O. Box 197A, Windom, MN 56101
Big Man Tree Stands, Inc., P.O. Box 605, Harrisonburg, LA 71340
Bingham Projects, 5739 Monte Vernon Dr., Mountain Green, UT 84050
Black Swan Archery, 1895 Highway 61, Columbiana, AL 35051
Black Widow Custom Bows, P.O. Box 2100, Nixa, MO 65714
Blaze Mfg., P.O. Box 30, Marlow, NH 03456
Blue Mountain, P.O. Box 777, Milton-Freewater, OR 97862
Bob Kirschner, 550 Mamont Rd., Murrayville, PA 15668
Bodoodle, Inc., 3301 US Hwy. 84N, Coleman, TX 76834
Bohning, 7361 N. Seven Mile Rd., Lake City, MI 49651
Bow-Pro Archery, 1605 Treanor, Saginaw, MI 48601
Bowhunters Choice, 2518 Old Humble Mill Rd., #87, Asheboro, NC 27203
Bowmar Archery Products, Scott Bowmar, 1095 Goodrick Dr., Tehachapi, CA 93561
Bows By Groves, 116 Veranda NW, Albuquerque, NM 87107
BPE, Inc., 890 County Rd. 160, Emporia, KS 66801
Bracklynn Archery Products, 4700 Sandersferry Rd., Tuscaloosa, AL 35401
Brell Mar, 5701 Hwy. 80 West, Jackson, MS 39209
Brigade Quartermasters Ltd., 1025 Cobb International Blvd., Kennesaw, GA 30144-4300
Brown Mfg., P.O. Box 9219, Akron, OH 44305
Brownell & Co., P.O. Box 362, Moodus, CT 06469
Browning Archery, Rte. 1, Morgan, UT 84050

Brunton USA, 620 East Monroe, Riverton, WT 82501
Buck Knives, Inc., P.O. Box 1267, El Cajon, CA 92002
Buck Pole Archery, 20669 30th Ave., Marion, MI 49665
Buck Shot, P.O. Box 7127, Wilmington, NC 28406
Buck Stop Lure Co., 3600 Grow Rd. NW, Stanton, MI 48888
Buck Wing Products, 420 West Emaus Ave., Allentown, PA 18103
Buck's Bags, Inc., P.O. Box 7884, Boise, ID 83702
Bullet Archery, 509 Oakwood Ave., East Aurora, NY 14052
Bushlan Camouflage, 313 Mill Run, Kerrville, TX 78028
Butski's Game Calls, 453 79th St., Niagra Falls, NY 14304

C

C&T Performance Treestands, P.O. Box 11548, Montgomery, AL 36111-0548
C.S. Gibbs Corp., 12195 Rae Ann Rd., Roscoe, IL 61073
C.W. Erickson Mfg., P.O. Box 522, Buffalo, MN 55313-0522
Cabela's, 808 13th Ave., Sidney, NE 69160
Cardoza Creations, 2541 South 5th Ave., #E, Oroville, CA 95965
Carlton's Calls, Inc., P.O. Box 3248, Montrose, CO 81401
Carry Lite, 5203 West Clinton Ave., Milwaukee, WI 53223
Carter Enterprises, P.O. Box 19, St. Anthony, ID 83445
Cary Archery, P.O. Box 707, Milford, MI 48381
Cascade Release, 36945 S. Nowlens Br. Rd., Molalla, OR 97038
Cavalier Equipment, P.O. Box 753, Gilbert, AZ 85299
CB Manufacturing & Sales Co., P.O. Box 37, West Carrollton, OH 45449
CDM, Inc., P.O. Box 128, Geneva, IN 46740
Centaur Archery, 45 Hollinger Crest Unit 2, Kitchener, Ontario N2L 2Z1, Canada
Champion Game Calls, P.O. Box 388, Glenmont, OH 44628
Cheater Slings, 2400 E Chicago Rd., Jonesville, MI 49250
Chek-It Products, W7385 County Trunk ZN, Onalaska, WI 54650
Clark Vanes, P.O. Box 306, Wayne City, IL 62895
Clarkfield Enterprises, Inc., P.O. Box 457, Clarkfield, MN 56223
Clearwater Archery, 2980 Rudo Rd., Orofino, ID 83544
Climax Tree Stands, Inc., RR 1, Box 224Z, Franklinville, NC 27248
Cobra Mfg., P.O. Box 667, Bixby, OK 74008
Continental Archery, Inc., 210 Railroad Ave., Amber, PA 19002
Cosmos Archery Systems, Inc., 3314 Denton Hwy., Ft. Worth, TX 76117
Cougar Claw, 9559 Hickory St. S., Foley, AL 36535
Coulston's Duranon, P.O. Box 30, Easton, PA 18044
Cover Up Products, Rt. 1, Box 66, Hill City, KS 67624-9509
Coyote Unlimited, Inc., 2968 W. Ina Rd. #200, Tucson, AZ 85741
CRDC Laser Systems, 3972 Barranca Parkway J484, Irvine, CA 92714
Crooked Horn Outfitters, 26315 Trotter Dr., Tehachapi, CA 93561
Cross River, P.O. Box 37, Nekoosa, WI 54457
Custom Bow Equipment, 38 Hickory Dr., Dudley, MA 01571
Custom Classics Paint, 8944 Vann Rd., Newburgh, IA 47630
Custom Outdoor Products, Rt. 3, Box 1760, Bainbridge, GA 31717

D

D.A.T. Mountaineers, Rd. 1 Box 116 Rt. 68, Rochester, PA 15074
Dabyca Archery, 378 Principale East, Farnham, Quebec J2N 1L8, Canada
Damascus Glove, P.O. Box 543, Rutland, VT 05701
Dan Quillan's Archery, Traditions, 196 Alps Rd., Athens, GA 30606
Danner Shoe Mfg. Co., P.O. Box 30158, Portland, OR 97230
DART International, 7120 East Orchard Rd., #300, Englewood, CO 80111
Darton Archery, 3540 Darton Rd., Hale, MI 48739
Dave's Scent Dist. System, 8691 Wall Rd., Armstrong Creek, WI 54103
Deer Dust, 505 Main Ave. NW, Cullman, AL 35055
Deer Me Products Co., 1208 Park St., Box 34, Anoka, MN 55303
Deer Run Products, Inc., 261 Ridgeview Terrace, Goshen, NY 10924
Deer To Me Scents, P.O. Box 109, Pittsboro, IN 46167
Deerhunter Tree Stands, Rte. 8 Box 1397-D, Hickory, NC 28602
Delta Industries, 117 E. Kenwood, Reinbeck, IA 50669
Densmore Enterprises, Rt. 3, Box 1455CC, Morgantown, WV 26505
Dick Palmer Archery, P.O. Box 1632, Fayetteville, AR 72701
Dixie Outdoor Products, Rd. 2 Box 2186, Dawsonville, GA 30534
Doskocil, P.O. Box 1246, Arlington, TX 76007-1246
Douglas Targets, P.O. Box 70601, Knoxville, TN 37918

E

E.A.R., Inc., P.O. Box 21A6, Boulder, CO 80306
E.W. Bateman & Co., P.O. Box 751, Fisher, TX 78623
Eagle Enterprises, P.O. Box 958, Bristol, RI 02809
Eagle Timbershaft, Inc., 3255 Highway 135 NW, Corydon, IN 47112
Easton Aluminum, 5040 W. Harold Gatty Dr., Salt Lake City, UT 84116
Eddie Salter Calls, Inc., P.O. Box 327, Brewton, AL 36427
Elk Mountain Archery, P.O. Box 803, Aspen, CO 81612
Emerging Technologies, P.O. Box 3548, Little Rock, AR 72203
Encapsulated Products, 8691 Wall Rd., Armstrong Creek, WI 54103
Ever True Arrow Co., Rte. 4, P.O. Box 376, New Prague, MN 56071
Eze-Lap Diamond Prod., 15164 West State St., Westminster, CA 92683

F

Fail Safe Sports, 2744 S. Sheridan, Tulsa, OK 74115
Feather 'n Fletch, 90-25 Eldert Ln., Woodhaven, NY 11421
Feather Flex Decoys, 1655 Swan Lake Rd., Bossier City, LA 71111

Fieldline, 1919 Vineburn Ave., Los Angeles, CA 90032
Fine-Line, Inc., 11220 164th St. East, Puyallup, WA 98374
Finished Archery System Tech., 775 Rt. 82 N. Hopewell Plaza, Hopewell Junction, NY 12533
Fitzgerald Hunting Corp., P.O. Box 126, Tecumseh, MI 49286
5-X Archery Products, Marvin Patterson, 13208 Horseshoe Dr. W., Smithville, MO 64089
Flambeau Products Corp., 15981 Valplast Rd., Middlefield, OH 44062
Flex-Fletch Products, 1840 Chandler Ave, St. Paul, MN 55113
Flow-Rite Of Tennessee, Inc., P.O. Box 196, Bruceton, TN 38317
Foam Designs, P.O. Box 11184, Lexington, KY 40574
Foresite, 33203 Highway 1019, Denham Springs, LA 70726
Forge Flite, Inc., 2860 South 171st St., New Berlin, WI 53151
Foster Manufacturing, P.O. Box 779, Milford, OH 45150
Freeman's Targets, 5324 W. Washington St., Indianapolis, IN 46241

G

G&B Specialties, 6 Center St., Rome, GA 30165
G&L Timbershaft, Inc., P.O. Box 20272, Columbus, OH 43220
G-P Products, Inc., 15331 Holub's Pl., Bellevue, NE 68005
Game Country, 2403 Commerce Ln., Albany, GA 31708
Game Tracker, 3476 Eastman Dr., Flushing, MI 48433
Gamefinder, 1311 North Memorial Parkway, Suite 100, Huntsville, AL 35801
Gametamers, Inc., One West Austin St., Center, TX 75935
Gateway Feather, Hwy. 53 N., Box 165, Holmen, WI 54636
GLG Ent., 4009 33rd St. S., Fargo, ND 58104
Gold Tip Corporation, 4632 West Harbor St., Valley City, UT 84120
Golden Eagle/Satellite Archery, 1111 Corporate Dr., Farmington, NY 14424
Golden Key-Futura, P.O. Box 1446, Montrose, CO 81401
Grampa Specialty Co., 3304 Woodson Rd., St. Louis, MO 63114
Grampa's, Inc., 57 M-35, Negaunee, MI 49866
Gray Loon Marketing, 204 Main St., Evansville, IN 47708-1480
Grayling Outdoor Prods., P.O. Box 192, Grayling, MI 49738
Great Northern Longbow Co., 201 N. Main, Nashville, MI 49073
Great Plains Traditional Bow, P.O. Box 1212, Pampa, TX 79065
Gryphon Engr. Co., P.O. Box 367, Richmond, MI 48062-0367

H

H&M Archery Products, 1685 Victor Ave., Ypsilanti, MI 48198
Haas Outdoors/Mossy Oak, 200 E. Main, West Point, MS 39773
Hansell Sights, P.O. Box 851, Winona, MN 55987
Hawgs Limited, 5410 North 39 Rd., Manton, MI 49663
Hawkeye, 822 1st Ave. North, Escanaba, MI 49829
Hawkins Deer Scent Co., Rt. 3, Box 731, Poplar Bluff, MO 63901
Haydel's Game Calls, Inc., 5018 Hazel Jones Rd., Bossier City, LA 71111
Heat Factory, Inc., 23362-G Madero Rd., Mission Viejo, CA 92691
Heavy Waite Targets, P.O. Box 636, Shedial Bridge, NB E0A 3H0, Canada
Hesco, Inc., 2821 Greenville Rd., La Grange, GA 30240
HHA Sports, 6511 Crest Ridge Ct., Wisconsin Rapids, WI 54494
Hi-Tek Sports Products, P.O. Box 208, Gwynedd Valley, PA 19437
High Country Archery, P.O. Box 1269, Dunlap, TN 37327
High Country Outdoor Products, 19991 SE Foster Rd., Boring, OR 97009
Holden Treestands, P.O. Box 563, Marble Falls, TX 78654
Horizon Archery, P.O. Box 0888, Loveland, CO 80539
Hot Trails, P.O. Box 460221, San Antonio, TX 78247-0221
Hotronics USA, Inc., P.O. Box 3159, Burlington, VT 05401
Howard Hill Archery, 248 Canyon Creek Rd., Hamilton, MT 59840
Hoyt USA, 475 N. Neil Armstrong, Salt Lake City, UT 84116
Huey Outdoors, Inc., 702 Airport Rd., Jonesville, LA 71343
Hughes Products, P.O. Box 1066, Thomasville, NC 27360
Hunt-All Enterprises, 77 South End Plaza, New Milford, CT 06776
Hunter's Choice, P.O. Box 414, Westminster, MA 01473
Hunter's Specialites, Inc., 6000 Huntington Ct. NE, Cedar Rapids, IA 52402-1268
Hunting Adventures, 10901 Stinson Dr., Dallas, TX 75217
Hunting Innovations, 223 Linfield Trappe Rd., Royersford, PA, 19468
Hydraflight, 2010 North 22nd Ave., Phoenix, AZ 85009

I

I.A.D.C., 157 Bank St., Waukesha, WI 53188
Ideal Products, P.O. Box 1006, Du Bois, PA 15801
Impact Industries, 333 Plumer St., Wausau, WI 54403
Indian Archery Video, 101 West Railroad Ave., Ridgeland, MS 39157
Indian Archery, 817 Maxwell Ave., Evansville, IN 47711
Interactive Target Systems, 23830 SE Kent Kangley Rd., Maple Valley, WA 98038
Invader Hunting Products, P.O. Box 624, Como, MS 38619
Inventive Technology, P.O. Box 266, American Fork, UT 84003

J

J.K. Chastain, 490 S. Queen St., Lakewood, CO 80226
J.R. Nielsen & Sons, Inc., P.O. Box 132, South Windsor, CT 06074
Jackie's Deer Lures, Rt. 1, Box 306-B, Tollesboro, KY 41189
James Green Archery Products, Rte. 1 Box 895, North Wilkesboro, NC 28659
James Valley Scents, HCR 1, Box 47, Mellette, SD 57461
Jeffery Archery, P.O. Box 9625, Columbia, SC 29290
Jennings Compound Bows, 4600 SW 41st Blvd., Gainsville, FL 32608-4999
Jenny Vanes, P.O. Box 367, Osseo, WI 54758
Jerry Hill Longbow, 231 McGowan Rd., Wilsonville, AL 35186
Jim Dougherty Archery, 4418 S. Mingo Rd., Tulsa, OK 74146
Jim Fletcher Archery Aids, P.O. Box 218, Bodfish, CA 93205
Jo Jan Sportsequip Co., West Pointe Dr., Bldg. #3, Washington, PA 15301
Johnny Stewart Calls, P.O. Box 7594, Waco, TX 76714
Johnson Labs, Inc., P.O. Box 381, Troy, AL 36081
Journeyman Broadheads, P.O. Box 825, Erin, Ontario N0B 1T0, Canada

K

Kapul, P.O. Box 9018, Trenton, NJ 08650
Kathy Kelly Design, Rt. 1, Box 109A, Newburg, OR 97132
Keller Mfg., 5628 Wrightsboro Rd., Grovetown, GA 30813
Kelly Cooper, P.O. Box 49, Picture Rocks, PA 17762
Keowee Game Calls, 608 Hwy. 25 N., Travelers Rest, SC 29690
Kil-Dir, Inc., P.O. Box 82, Eau Claire, WI 54702
Kinetronics, 106 Mancil Rd., Media, PA 19063
King Of The Mountain, 2709 Eisenhower Blvd., Loveland, CO 80537
Knickerbocker Ent., 15199 S. Maplelane Rd., Oregon City, OR 97045
Knight & Hale Game Calls, P.O. Box 670, Cadix, KY 42211
Kodiak Products, Inc., P.O. Box 761, Greenville, MI 48838
Kolpin Manufacturing, P.O. Box 107, 205 Depot St., Fox Lake, WI 53933
Konifer Camo, 916 Westcott Square, Suite 201, Eagan, MN 55123
Kudlacek's Archery, 1235 Commerce Ave., Longvie, WA 98632
Kwik-Slik, Dana Products, 4321 Fireside, Irving, CA 92714
Kwikee Kwiver Co., Inc., P.O. Box 130, Acme, MI 49610

L

L&L Enterprises, P.O. Box 318, Leakesville, MS 39451
L&S Tool, 2850 Teresita Rd., Owenton, KY 40359
L.C. Whiffen, 923 S. 16th St., Milwaukee, WI 53204
Lacrosse Footwear, P.O. Box 1328, La Crosse, WI 54602
Lakewood Assoc., 2905 Silver Cedar Rd., Oconomowoc, WI 53066
Lakewood Products, P.O. Box 230, Berlin, WI 54923
Lee's Pure Deer Urine Co., 2125 Miller Dr., Niles, MI 49120
LEM Productions, P.O. Box 244, Miamitown, OH 45041
Lenartz, Inc., 5052 Mildred Ave., Kentwood, MI 49508
Lewis & Lewis, 1013 County Hwy. AA, Nekoosa, WI 54457
Lighthouse Dist., 9476 Braden, White Lake, MI 48418
Loc-On Co., 6903 International Dr., Greensboro, NC 27409
Loggy Bayou, 10397 La. Hwy. 1, Shreveport, LA 71115
Lohman Game Calls, 4500 Doniphan Dr., Neosho, MO 64850
Lone Wolf, Inc., 5615 S. Pennsylvania Ave., Cudahy, WI 53110
Longhorn Archery Systems, P.O. Box 5989, Kingwood, TX 77325
Ludwig Mfg., 4716 Perry Ave. N, Minneapolis, MN 55429

M

Magic Fix, Inc., 3231 Big Oak Lake Rd., Spring Hill, TN 37174
Magnus Archery, P.O. Box 1877, Great Bend, KS 67530
Mar-Den Co., P.O. Drawer "K", Wilcox, AZ 85643
Mark June Lures, 7198 Seymour Rd., P.O. Box 35, Swartz Creek, MI 48473
Martin Archery, Rt. 5 Box 127, Walla Walla, WA 99362
Master Hunter, P.O. Box 220, Gerald, MO 63037
Mathews Archery, RR 4, Box 12, Austin, MN 55912
McKenzie Natra-Look Targets, P.O. Box 480, Granite Quarry, NC 28072
McPherson Archery, Inc., P.O. Box 327, Hwy. 31, S. Brewton Ind. Park, Brewton, AL 36426
Mel Dutton Decoys, P.O. Box 113, Faith, SD 57626
Metal Assembly, Inc., P.O. Box 67, New Era, MI 49446
Methods, 1665 Precision Park Ln. F, San Ysidro, CA 92173
Miami Valley Outdoors, 800 South Downing, Piqua, OH 45356
Minnestoa Storm, 1532 University Ave., Suite 101, Box 125, Saint Paul, MN 55104
Mohawk Sports Equipment, P.O. Box 992, Elyria, OH 44036
Mohr's Widow Maker, P.O. Box 103, Bainbridge, PA 17502
Montana Black Gold, 1716 W. Main, Bozeman, MT 59715
Montaska Archery Co., P.O. Box 410, Spencer, NE 68777
Morrell Manufacturing, Inc., 1721 Highway 71 North, Alma, AR 72921
Mountain Ridge Sights, 25267 Baser Dr., P.O. Box 4456, Crestline, CA 92325
Mountaineer Archery, 1312 7th Ave., Huntington, WV 25701
Mrs. Doe Pee's Buck Lure, RR 4, Box 240, Mt. Pleasant, IA 52641
MTM Case-Gard, P.O. Box 14117, Dayton, OH 45413
Muzzy Products, 2100 Barrett Park Dr. #504, Kennesaw, GA 30144

N

Natgear, 1200 John Barrow Rd., Suite 303, Little Rock, AR 72205
Nature's Essence, 6950 Rawson Rd., Cuba, NY 14727
Nature's Reflections, 1904 9A Ave. NE, Calgary, Alberta T2E 0W5, Canada
Neet Prods, Rt. 2, Highway 269-B, Sedalia, MO 65301
New Archery Products, 7500 Industrial Dr., Forest Park, IL 60130
Northeast Archery, Inc., 335 West John St., Hicksville, NY 11801
Northern Whitetail, 1930 Ridgewood, White Bear Lake, MN 55110
Northwoods Archery, P.O. Box 175, Clio, MI 48240

O

Okaman, P.O. Box 239, Elysian, MN 56028
Okie Mfg., Ht. 1, Box 234, Hendrix, OK 74741
120x Scopes, Rte. 3, Box 580, Rogersville, TN 37857
120x Sighting Systems, Rte. 3, Box 237, Dobson, NC 27017
Oneida Labs, P.O. Box 68, Phoenix, NY 13135
Oregon Bow Co., 250 E. 10th Ave., Junction City, OR 97448
Original Brite-Site, 34 Kentwood Rd., Succasunna, NJ 07876
Outdoor Technologies, 23179 Bear Run Rd., Danville, OH 43014
Outdoor Trader, 185 W. Hamilton St., W. Milton, OH 45383
Outdoor Videos, 6931 South 66th East Ave. #300, Tulsa, OK 74133
Outdoors America, P.O. Box 548, Atomore, AL 36504
Oxbow Outdoor Ent., Inc., 14 McGill St., Box 242, Marmora, Ont. K0K 2M0, Canada

P

Patrick McCanney Traditional, Archery Co., P.O. Box 251, Wyoming, MN 55092
Patriot Broadheads, 42812 Mound Rd., Sterling Heights, MI 48314
Pearson Archery, Ben, P.O. Box 11804, Fort Smith, AR 72917

Penguin Industries, Airport Industrial Mall, Coatesville, PA 19320
Penn's Woods Products, 19 West Pittsburgh St., Delmont, PA 15626
Perfection Turkey Calls, P.O. Box 164, Stephenson, VA 22656
Perkins Stabilizer, Inc., 400 Trillium Ridge, Dawsonville, GA 30534
Pete Rickard, Inc., Rd #1 Box 292, Cobelskill, NY 12043
Phillips Industries, 2601 Davison Rd., Flint, MI 48506
Pick A Spot Targets, 1637 Westhaven Boulevard, Jackson, MS 39209
Piney Woods Natural, 1933 West Point Rd., La Grange, GA 30240
Pocket Call Co., P.O. Box 387, Coldwater, KS 67029
Power Light Sight System, 1843 Hertel Ave., Buffalo, NY 14216
Prairie Winds, 1819 East Mulberry, Fort Collins, CO 80524
Precision Archery Targets, 1826 Maury St., Houston, TX 77026
Precision Designed Products, Rt. 4, Box 214-C, Independence, KS 67301
Precision Products, Inc., 1216 S. 48th St., Baltimore, MD 21222
Precision Shooting Equipment, P.O. Box 5487, Tucson, AZ 85703
Predator Produucts, 4030 Chilton, Muskegon, MI 49441
Preston Pittman Game Calls, P.O. Box 568, Lucedale, MS 39452
Primos Wild Game Calls, Inc., P.O. Box 12785, Jackson, MS 39236-2785
Pro Line Co., 106 Cook Rd., Hastings, MI 49058
Pro Release, Inc., 33551 Giftos, Mt. Clemens, MI 48035
Proformance Mfg., 205-B Wellston Park Rd., Sand Springs, OK 74063
Puckets Bloodtrailer, 7716 Dolly Drive, Lorton, VA 22079
Pure Forest, P.O. Box 273, Keene, NH 03431

Q

QAD, Inc., 109 13th, Lynchburg, VA 24504
Quaker Boy, Inc., 5455 Webster Rd., Orchard Park, NY 14127

R

R&R Enterprises, 9700 Highway 29 North, Molino, FL 32577
R&W Targets, 956 Charlotte Highway, Fairview, NC 28730
Rancho Safari, P.O. Box 691, Ramona, CA 92065
Ranger Footwear, P.O. Box 10, Franklin, TN 37065
Ranger Mfg., P.O. Box 14069, Augusta, GA 30919-0069
Rattlesnake Archery, P.O. Box 936, Peoria, AZ 85380
Realbark Hunting System, Inc., P.O. Box 2078, Henderson, TX 75653
Red Feather, Inc., P.O. Box 560, Cibolo, TX 78108-0560
Redishot Products, 32 Country Ln. Ct., St. Charles, MN 63304
Regal Industries, 124 Hopson Rd, Ashlands, VA 23005
Rightnour Mfg. Co., P.O. Box 107, Mingoville, PA 16856
Rivers Edge Hunting Products, P.O. Box 903, Monticello, MN 55362
Robinhood Videos, 255 SW 96th Ln., Ocala, FL 34476
Robinson Labs, 293 Commercial St., St. Paul, MN 55106
Rocket Broadheads, P.O. Box 6783, Minneapolis, MN 55406
Rod Benson Game Calls, 1050 Mart St., Muskegon, MI 49440
Roger Wyant's Prods., P.O. Box 1325, Harrisburg, VA 22801
Rothhaar Recurve Co., 7707 Gun Lake Rd., Delton, MI 49046
RP Plastics Corp., 40 River St., Leominster, MA 01453
RTO Systems, 571 S. Mirage, Lindsay, CA 93247

S

S&J Enterprises, 1800 Vine St., Denver, CO 80206
Sasi-Stealth Archery, 1991 Rangeline Rd., Eagle River, WI 54521
Saunders Archery, P.O. Box 476, Columbus, NE 68601
Schaeffer Performance, 509 W. 98th St., Bloomington, MN 55420
Schaeffer Shooting Sports, 1923 Grand Ave., Baldwin, NY 11510
Scott Archery Mfg., 587 Adams Ridge Rd., Clay City, KY 40312
Scout Mountain Equipment, 2100 Dana Dr., Pocatello, ID 83201
Scrape Doctor, P.O. Box 35605, Tulsa, OK 74153
Scrape Juice, Inc., Nordic Sports, Inc., 324 S. Main, Wildwood, FL 34785
Seat-A-Tree, Inc., 25450 Ryan Rd., Warren, MI 48091
Send-A-Scent Arrow Co., 4257 Wedgewood Ct., Indianapolis, IN 46254
Shannon Outdoors, Rt. 3 Box 77, Winnsboro, SC 29180
Shehawken Archery, P.O. Box 407, Canandaigua, NY 14424
Sight Master Bowsight, 1093 Hwy. 12 East, Townsend, MT 59644
Silver Linings, 5891 Wood Bridge Dr., Savage, MN 55378
Simmons System, Rt. 2 Box 49, Jasper, AL 35501
Sky Archery Co., 11510 Natural Bridge Rd., Bridgeton, MO 63044
Skyline Camo, 184 Ellicott Rd., West Falls, NY 14170
Sleeping Indian Design, P.O. Box 8517, Jackson Hole, WY 83001
Slings 'n Things, P.O. Drawer 4053, Omaha, NE 68104
Snake Creek, Rt. 3 Box 218, Taylorsville, MS 39168
Southern Archery, P.O. Box 204, Louisville, MS 39339
Southland Callers, 2031 Horns Lake Rd., Talladega, AL 35160
Southland Hunting Products, 3587 Shady Grove Rd., Fultondale, AL 35068
Spartan-Realtree Products, 1390 Box Circle Rd., Columbus, GA 31907
Specialty Archery Products, 800 12th St. NW, Mason City, IA 50401
Spence's Targets, 3056 Lincoln Highway, Lynwood, IL 60411
Spider Oak Outfitters, P.O. Box 551695, Dallas, TX 75355
Spike-It, Inc., 340 Beamer Rd., Calhoun, GA 30701
Sport America, Rd 2 Del Box 52, Elmira, NY 14901
Sport Climbers, Inc., P.O. Box 597, Kenosha, WI 53141
Sportline Mfg. Co., 610 Industrial Park, Antigo, WI 54409
Sports Heat, 15 Hammond, Suite 301, Irvine, CA 92718
Sportshield Mfg., 2220 Clark Rd., Central Lake, MI 49622
Sportsman's Outdoor Products, 541 West 9460 South, Sandy, UT 84070
SSSH Archery Products, 2885C Aiello Dr., San Jose, CA 95111
Stacey Archery Sales, Inc., 6866 Jennifer Ln., Idaho Falls, ID 83401
Staghorn Treestands, 410 W. Lincoln Ave., Goshen, IN 46526
Stalk-Ing Feet, 4262 S. Evansway, Gilbert, AZ 85234
Stand Alone Products, P.O. Box 335, Parker, CO 80134
Stanislawski Archery, 7100 SE 72nd, Portland, OR 97206
Stanley Hips Targets, 17585 Blanco Rd., San Antonio, TX 78232
Stay Warm, Inc., P.O. Box 1098, Wise, VA 24293
Stealth Hunter, Inc., 10650 Glasgow Rd., Smiths Grove, KY 42171

Sterling Machine Co., P.O. Box 12363, Green Bay, WI 54307-2363
Sticks 'n Limbs, Box 63, Pancake, TX 76538
Stoney-Wolf Productions, Inc., Box 459, Lolo, MT 59847
Stratton Outdoor Products, 2896 Neuman, Rhodes, MI 48652
String Swing Mfg., P.O. Box 132, Ontario, WI 54651
Strongbuilt/Moultrie, Highway 568, Waterproof, LA 71375
Sugar Valley Products, P.O. Box 100, Mound City, KS 66056
Summit Specialties, P.O. Box 786, Dactur, AL 35602
Supreme Outdoor Products, 33057 Groesbeck, Fraser, MI 48026
Sure Stop Archery Targets, 20 Vernon St., Somerville, MA 02145
Suzy Smith Outdoor Sportswear, P.O. Box 185, South Fork, CO 81154
Swanmar Co., 1121 Toledo Ave. North, Golden Valley, MN 55422
Swanson True Scent, 18 Howard St., Palo Alto, PA 17901

T

T&M, P.O. Box 3824, Bozeman, MT 59772
Tacstar, Inc., P.O. Box 70, Cottonwood, AZ 86326
Tailormaid Archery, 12731-B Huron River Dr., Romulus, MI 48174
Tallahatche Woodworks, 483 West Clovehurts Ave., Athens, GA 30606
Tepper Innovations, P.O. Box 7, Shady Cove, OR 97539
Texas Triangle Innovations, P.O. Box 560511, Lewisville, TX 75056-0511
The Varminter, P.O. Box 32, Whitlash, MT 59545
Third Hand Archery, 77 W. Southgate, Ft. Thomas, KY 41075
3 D Target-Eeze, Howard Coffey, P.O. Box 185, Buckner, KY 40010
Tiger Tuff, 201 Old Batson Rd., Taylors, SC 29687
Timberline Archery Products, P.O. Box 333, Lewiston, ID 83501
Timberlin Targets, P.O. Box 667, Williston, ND 58802
Timeless Archery Prods., Inc., 3498 N. San Marcos Pl. #2, Chandler, AZ 85224
Tobacco Root Trad. Archery, P.O. Box 272, Whitehall, MT 59759
Total Hunting Technologies, P.O. Box 223, Iron Ridge, WI 53035
Toxonics, 1324 Wilmer Rd., Wentzville, MO 63385
Trackmaster, P.O. Box 950, Latrobe, PA 15650
Trail Timer, P.O. Box 19722, St. Paul, MN 55119
Trailhawk Treestands, 2605 Coulee Ave., La Crosse, WI 54601
Trailpro, 279 Aikane Place, Kailua, HI 96734
Trautman's Outdoor Creations, 2082 S. First, Hamilton, MT 59840
Trax America, P.O. Box 898, Forrest City, AR 72335
Trebark Camouflage, 3434 Buck Mtn. Rd., Roanoke, VA 24014
Tree-Pod, Inc., P.O. Box 7584, Saint Cloud, MN 56302
Trophy Targets, 7813 N. 107 Dr., Glendale, AZ, 85307
Trophy Whitetail Prod., 329 East Shockley Ferry Rd., Anderson, SC 29624
Tru-Fire Corp, 7355 State St., N. Fond Du Lac, WI 54935
Tru-Glo, Inc., P.O. Box 1612, Mckinney, TX 75070
True Flight Arrow Co., P.O. Box 746, Monticello, IN 47960
Trueflight Mfg., P.O. Box 1000, Manitowash Water, WI 54545

U

U-Nique Archery, Rt. 2, Box 267, Hartselle, AL 35640
Ultimate Lures, Rt. 2, 9506 Hwy. Y, Sauk City, WI 53583

V

Vador Corporation, 3100 Adventure Ln., Oxford, MI 48371
Van Dyke's, P.O. Box 278, Woonsocket, SD 57385
Viper Products, 19082 Crystal St., Huntington Beach, CA 92648
Volunteer String Prod., 800 Highway 52 By-Pass East, Lafayette, TN 37083

W

Walker's Game Ear, P.O. Box 1069, Media, PA 19063
Warren & Sweat, P.O. Box 446, Grand Island, FL 32735
Wasp Archery Products, Inc., P.O. Box 303, Plymouth, CT 06782
Weaver's Scent Co., 2006 Snow Hill Rd, W. Harrison, IN 47060
Wellington Outdoors, P.O. Box 244, Madison, GA 30650
Wells Creek Trading Co., 16242 Metcalf, Stillwell, KS 66085
West Coast Archery, 650 A West Omstott Rd., Yuba City, CA 95993
White Buffalo Archery, Rd #4, Box 709, Monroe, NY 10950
Whitetail Institute, Rt. 1, Box 3006, Montgomery, AL 36043
Whitetail Treestands, 855 Chicago Rd., Quincy, MI 49082
Whopper Stopper, Inc., 6171 West 400 North, Suite D, Greenfield, IN 46140
Wilderness Country, Inc., P.O. Box 367, Huntington, TX 75949
Wilderness Tree Stands, 3645 Whitehouse-Spencer Rd, Swanton, OH 43558
Wildlife Research Center, 4345 157th Ave. NW, Anoka, MN 55304
Will-Stop Target Co., 6687 Amah Parkway, Claremore, OK 74017
Winn Archery, 13757 64th, South Haven, MI 49090
Wisconsin Pharmacal Co., P.O. Box 198, Jackson, WI 53037
Wizard Of The Woods, 6045 N Michigan Rd., Box 35, Plymouth, IN 46563
Woods Wise Products, P.O. Box 681552, Franklin, TN 37068
Woodstream Corp., Box 327, Lititz, PA 17543
WRI/Vista, 3505 East 39th Ave., Denver, CO 80205
Wyandotte Leather, Inc., 1811 Sixth St., Wyandotte, MI 48192

X

X-Ring Archery Products, HC 82, Box 163½, Ravenna, KY 40472
Yellow Jacket Ent., 4627 West Elgin St., Chandler, AZ 85226

Y

Yellowstone Archery, P.O. Box 5083, Idaho Falls, ID 83405
York Archery, P.O. Box 11804, Fort Smith, AR 72917

Z

Zephyr Mfg., Inc., P.O. Box 42, Sabetha, KS 66534
Zwickey Archery, 2471 E. 12th Ave., N. St. Paul, MN 55109